Club Grampian, Edmund Chisholm-Batten

The Charters of the Priory of Beauly

with notices of the priories of Pluscardine and Ardchattan and of the family of the

founder, John Byset

Club Grampian, Edmund Chisholm-Batten

The Charters of the Priory of Beauly
with notices of the priories of Pluscardine and Ardchattan and of the family of the founder, John Byset

ISBN/EAN: 9783337262822

Printed in Europe, USA, Canada, Australia, Japan

Cover: Foto ©Lupo / pixelio.de

More available books at **www.hansebooks.com**

In compliance with current copyright law, BookLab, Inc.
produced this replacement volume to replace the
irreparably deteriorated original owned by
Columbia University Libraries 1992. This
photocopy was produced on paper that
meets the ANSI Standard
Z39.48-1984.

Hic jacet Kenitus MKingth dus. de Kintail,
q. obiit vii die Februarii a.d. m.cccc.lxxxxi.

THE CHARTERS

OF THE

PRIORY OF BEAULY

WITH

NOTICES OF THE PRIORIES OF

PLUSCARDINE AND ARDCHATTAN

AND OF

THE FAMILY OF THE FOUNDER

JOHN BYSET

BY

EDMUND CHISHOLM BATTEN

LONDON: PUBLISHED FOR THE GRAMPIAN CLUB
BY HOULSTON & SONS, PATERNOSTER SQUARE

1877

EDINBURGH
PRINTED BY M'FARLANE AND ERSKINE,
ST JAMES SQUARE.

PREFACE.

IN performing the task of editing the Charters of Beauly Priory for the Grampian Club, I have added illustrative notices in order to make these documents connected and intelligible. I am sensible that in trying to do this I have not infrequently explained what is obvious, and supplied information which was already possessed by most of our members. But I have felt, in going through the Chartularies published by the elder clubs, such a desire to have the explanations and illustrations which a Thomson or an Innes could have given, and such gratitude for the light thrown upon those he edited by the notes of Joseph Robertson, that I shall be rewarded for much labour if every one who takes the trouble to read these illustrations gleans at least something from them that is new to him.

The Charters themselves cannot but be interesting; they tell the story for three centuries and a half of a religious community founded by the wise piety of one of those Great Houses which linked Scotland and England by the silken, yet adamantine, band of family connection, which, untwisted and almost broken for three centuries of—for Scotland—ruin and rapine, fire and sword, when again rewoven, brought back to her a restoration of those good old times when the Alexanders reigned over a courageous and therefore respected, an industrious and therefore prosperous, and a religious and therefore happy people.

The monastery of Beauly was small, and the order to which it belonged neither powerful nor popular; but amidst the havoc and slaughter which the annals of Scotland for the period detail, it is refreshing to trace the quiet flow of the Priory's history, uneventful it may be, yet smooth and clear, and undimmed by stain or crime.

Two gentle tastes were cultivated within its walls—the love of gardens and the love of books; none who have nourished these affections but will reverence its ruins. There, was kept up a monastic school which made the house the Lamp of learning to the North; and there, the simple life and frugal habits of its inmates enabled them to let their lands to kindly tenants on such easy terms that a perpetual feu at the rent they received was worth some forty years' purchase.

I have two duties to perform; one to apologise for the defective way in which I have done my work, the other to thank those who have assisted me. Unable to give continuous attention to it, the notes are disjointed and uneven, and would be of little use but for the abundant kindness which has been shown in giving me materials for them.

Among those whom I have to thank, in the text *not specially mentioned*, are Dr Stuart, Mr W. Fraser, Dr Carruthers, Dr Corbet, Mr R. Matheson, Mr A. Ross, and Mr T. Dickson. Besides these, I have met at every turn in my investigations in the Highlands with constant attention and courtesy, owing, I believe, to the respect and regard there felt for her whose descent from the founder of Beauly Priory first suggested the work.

E. C. B.

ATHENÆUM CLUB, *Martinmas* 1876.

CONTENTS.

INTRODUCTION.

Order of Valliscaulians, Grande Chartreuse, Viard, Founder of Order, 2; Bishop Malvoisin, 3; Dominicans, Culdees, 5; Alexander II., 6; Site of Beauly, 7; Rule of Valliscaulians, 9; Transcripts of Beauly Charters, Macfarlane MSS., 13.

CHARTERS OF BEAULY PRIORY.

1. BULL OF POPE GREGORY IX., CONFIRMING ENDOWMENT OF BEAULY PRIORY BY JOHN BYSET, A.D. 1231, ... 14

   Name of Beaulieu, 15; Beauly Charters, quoted in Wardlaw MS., 16; John Byset, Founder, 18; English Bysets, 20; Fraser MSS., 21; Parishes of Dunballoch, Wardlaw, 22; Kiltarlity, 23; Leper House, Rathven, 24; Parish of Fearnua, 26; Possession of Priory, 28; Fishings, 29; Forged Foundation Deed, 30; Forged Charter, 32.

2. CHARTER BY WILLIAM BYSET OF THE CHURCH OF ABERTARFF TO BEAULY PRIORY, A.D. 1231, ... 33

   Seal of Byset, 34; Parish of Abertarff, 35; Thomas de Thirlstan, 36; Scottish Lords of Parliament, 37.

3. CHARTER BY ANDREW, BISHOP OF MORAY, OF THE TITHES OF GRAIN AND SALMON OF THE PARISH OF ABERTARFF, A.D. 1242, 38

   Appropriation, Simple Benefice, 39; Beaufort Castle, 40; Chapter of Elgin Cathedral, 41; Chapter of Wells Cathedral, 42; Murder of Earl of Athol, 43; Banishment and Alleged Forfeiture of Founder, 44; John Byset in Bordeaux, 45; in Ireland, 46; John Byset the younger, 47.

4. CHARTER BY LAURENCE THE KNIGHT, SON OF PATRICK, THE PORTER OF INVERNESS, OF BROMIHALU AND THE ISLAND TO BEAULY PRIORY, A.D. 1255, ... 49

   Portership of King's Castles, 50; Black Isle, Thorney Island, Westminster Abbey, 51; Vicar of Inverness, 52; Church of Conveth,

Origin of the Grants, 53; Three Co-Heiresses of John Byset the younger, Muriel de Graham, Cecilia de Fenton, Elizabeth de Boscho, 55.

5. CHARTER BY MASTER HENRY OF NOTTINGHAM, RECTOR OF TARRA-
DALE, TO BEAULY PRIORY, A.D. 1274, ... 56

Tarradale, 57; Master, 58; Cistercian Privileges, 59.

6. CHARTER BY DAVID OF INNERLUNAN OF THE LAND OF OUTER
TARRADALE TO BEAULY PRIORY, A.D. 1275, . . . 60

Gillicrist Macgilliduffi, Gilchrist a Rosse, Angus Family, 62.

7. CHARTER BY ANDREW DE BOSCHO AND ELIZABETH BYSET OF AN
ANNUITY TO BEAULY PRIORY, A.D. 1278, ... 63

Customary Terms of Payment in Scotland, 64; Value of Money, 65; William, third Earl of Ross, Boiamond's Taxation, 67; Lease of Kilcoy, 67; Sir David de Graham, 68; Excommunication of William de Fenton and Cecilia Byset, 69; Fishings of Kiltarlity Church Lands, 70; Parliament of Brigham, 71.

8. CHARTER BY CECILIA BYSET OF HER THIRD PART OF ALTYRE TO
BEAULY PRIORY, *c.* A.D. 1215, ... 74

Grant of Birds' Nests, 75; Sir Patrick de Graham, Chapel of Beaufort, 76; Parish of Fearnua, 77.

9. CHARTER BY PATRICK DE GRAHAM OF HIS THIRD PART OF
ALTYRE TO BEAULY PRIORY, IN EXCHANGE FOR THE MULTURES
OF LOVAT, ETC., *c.* A.D. 1325, ... 78

The Grants, 80; the Corbets, 81; Buildings of Beauly Priory, 81; Early English Style, 82.

10. CHARTER BY WILLIAM DE FENTON, LORD OF BEAUFORT, OF AN
ANNUITY TO BEAULY PRIORY, A.D. 1328, ... 83

Sir Christian del Ard, 85; the Forbeses, 86.

11. CHARTER OF RELEASE BY THE VICAR OF ABERTARFF TO BEAULY
PRIORY OF THE TITHE OF FISH, A.D. 1340, . . . 87

Rural Dean of Inverness, 88; Homage of William de Fenton, 88; of Hugh Fraser, 89; of Alexander de Chisholm, 90.

12. BULL OF POPE GREGORY XI. TO BEAULY PRIORY, A.D. 1373, . 91

The Wolf of Badenoch, 92; Thomas de Chisholm, 93; Alexander de Insulis, 94; Alexander del Ard, 95; the Stirlings, 95; Marriage of Hugh Fraser with Janet de Fenton, 96; Thomas Fraser of Lovat, 97; Co-Heiresses of Fenton, 98; Heiress of Chisholm, 99; Lovat Peerage, 99; Vicarage of Conveth, 100.

CONTENTS. ix

13. COLLATION BY WILLIAM, BISHOP OF MORAY, OF THE VICARAGE OF
    CONVETH, ON PRESENTATION BY BEAULY PRIORY, A.D. 1480, . 101
    Institution and Collation, 103.

14. PRESENTATION TO THE VICARAGE OF CONVETH BY BEAULY PRIORY,
    A.D. 1493, ... 104
    Sir Kenneth Mackenzie of Kintail, 105.

15. BULL BY POPE ALEXANDER VI., APPOINTING DOUGAL RORIESON,
    CLERK, TO THE PRIORATE OF BEAULY PRIORY, A.D. 1497, . 106
    Admission of a Secular Priest into a Religious Order, 110.

16. FORM OF OATH OF THE PRIOR OF BEAULY PRIORY ON NOMINA-
    TION BY THE SUPREME PONTIFF, A.D. 1497, . . . 111
    Provision against Alienating the Monastic Possessions, 112.

17. PROMULGATION OF THE BULL (No. 15) BY ANDREW, BISHOP OF
    MORAY, A.D. 1501, ... 113
    Prior Dougal, 121; Sits in Parliament, 122; Rebellion of the Isles, 123;
    Pluscardine Priory, 124; Charters of Alexander II., 126; and Bishop
    of Moray, 129, to Pluscardine; Bull of Pope Urban IV., 130; Vallis-
    caulians submit to Diocesan Jurisdiction, 131; Pluscardine and Sir
    Robert de Chisholm, 133; Election of Prior, 134; Urquhart Priory,
    135; United to Pluscardine, 137; Pluscardine made Benedictine, 137.

18. COMMISSION OF VISITATION OF ARDCHATTAN PRIORY, SENT TO
    THE PRIOR OF BEAULY BY THE GENERAL OF THE VALLIS-
    CAULIANS, A.D. 1506, ... 140
    Monastery of Val des Choux, in Burgundy, 142; Viard, 143; Alien
    Priories in England, 144; Concordat of Francis I., 145; French
    Revolution, 146; Ardchattan Priory, 147; Founder, Duncan of Lorn,
    148; Endowment of Ardchattan, 149; Sanctuary, 150; Hereditary
    Incumbents, 151; Tombs of Ardchattan, 152; Priors Duncan and
    Dougal Macdougall, 153; Amenity of Ardchattan, 155.

19. LETTER FROM THE GENERAL OF THE VALLISCAULIANS TO THE
    PRIOR OF BEAULY, A.D. 1506, ... 157
    Travelling Priests, 159; Valliscaulians subject to Diocesan, 162; Fox-
    hunting Antiquaries, 163 *n.*; Trade between Beauly and Bruges, 165.

20. PRESENTATION TO THE VICARAGE OF CONVETH BY THE PRIOR OF
    BEAULY, A.D. 1512, ... 167
    Bishop Forman of Moray, 169; Seals of Beauly, Pluscardine, and Ard-
    chattan Priories, 170; Appropriation of Great Tithes, 171; Heirs of
    Founder of Beauly, 172; the Fentons, 173; the Lindsays of Beaufort,
    174; the Haliburtons of Erchless, 175; the Chisholms of Comer, 176.

b

CONTENTS.

21. PROMULGATION OF BULL OF POPE JULIUS II. IN FAVOUR OF BEAULY PRIORY, A.D. 1514, ... 177

Library of the Priory, 182; Rebellion of Sir Donald of the Isles, 184; Cathedral of Fortrose, 185; Bishopric of Ross, 187; Constitution of Chapter of Ross, 190; Buildings of Cathedral, 191; Dilapidation, Existing Remains, 194; Heraldic Bosses, Bishop Bullock, 195; Eufamia Leslie, Countess of Ross, 197; Endowment of Chapter, 200; List of Bishops of Ross, 201.

22. PRECEPT OF SYLVESTER, THE NUNCIO OF THE APOSTOLIC SEE, TO THE ABBOTS OF KINLOSS AND FEARN, IN FAVOUR OF HUGH, LORD FRASER OF LOVAT, A.D. 1532, ... 205

Thomas, Lord Lovat, 210; Beaufort Castle, 211; Kilmorack and Kiltarlity Church Lands Right of Fishing, 213; Feu of Kilmorack Church Lands, 214; Magnus Waus, 215; Lochslyn, 216; Abbot Donald of Fearn, 217; Bishop Reid, 218; Restores Beauly Priory Church, 219; Ferrarius, 220; Monkish Correspondence, 222; Battle of Blair-na-Leine, 225; Prior Walter Reid, 226; Bishop Reid, Founds University of Edinburgh, 228; Alexander, Lord Lovat, 230; Reformation, 231; Queen Mary, 233; Visits Inverness, 234; Rental of Priory, 235, 236; Conveth, 238; Comar, 239; Abertarff, 240; Stipends of Reformed Clergy, 242; Union of Parishes, 244; Abertarff and Boleskine, 245; Comar, Conveth, and Kiltarlity, 246; Results of Union, 246; Dress and Diet of the Monks, 247; Pension to the Court of Session, 248; Tithe Fish of Wardlaw, 249; Union of Wardlaw and Fearnua, 250; Queen Mary at Fortrose, 251; probably at Beauly, 252.

23. TACK OF SOME OF THE LANDS OF BEWLY BY WALTER, PRIOR OF BEWLY, TO JOHN AND ALEX. CLERK, A.D. 1568, . . . 254

Form of Lease, 258; Alehouse of Beauly, 259; Markets and Fairs, 259 n.; Whisky, 260; Macfarlane's List of the Charters, 261.

CONCLUSION.

Chartulary of Beauly, 263; Hugh, Lord Lovat, and Huntly, 264; Feu-Charter of Barony, 266; Extent of Priory Lands, 269; Charter of Prior's House, 272; Prior John Fraser, 275; Simon, Lord Lovat, 276; Fraser of Strichen, 278; Monastic Schools, 279; Last of the Monks, 280; Priory Buildings, 280; Church, 281; Ardchattan and Pluscardine Churches, 283; the Chapels, 284; Bishop Reid's additions, 285; Kirkwall Cathedral, 286; Dilapidation, 287; Pennant, 288; Cordiner, 289; the Lovat Tombstone, 289; Armour, 290; Ruins in 1815, 291; Litigation in Court of Session, 292; Crown Lease to Lord Lovat, 293.

CONTENTS.

APPENDIX.

		PAGE
1.	Name of Beauly,	294
2.	Lepers' Houses,	294
3.	Castles,	295
4.	List of Bishops of Moray,	296
5.	Extracts from Record Office, London,	298
6.	English Bysets,	299
7.	Scottish Bysets,	300
8.	Irish Bysets,	301
9.	Chapels,	302
10.	Del Ard Family,	303
11.	Marriage-Contract, Fraser and De Fenton, 1416,	303
12.	Marriage-Contract, Thomas Dunbar, Earl of Moray, and Hugh Fraser of Lovat, 1422,	305
13.	Sir Kenneth Mackenzie of Kintail,	306
14.	"*Extra Romanam Curiam*,"	308
15.	Sanctuary of Ardchattan,	308
16.	French Priories of the Order,	309
17.	Surnames,	309
18.	Vicars,	310
19.	Note on Luther,	311
20.	Scottish Kalendar,	311
21.	River Beauly,	312
22.	List of Abbots of Fearn,	313
23.	Church Bells of Scotland,	316
24.	Dress of Beauly Monks,	318
25.	Chapter of Kirkwall,	318
26.	Diary of Queen Mary's Journey north, 1562,	320
27.	Abertarff and Boleskine,	321
28.	Conveth and Kiltarlity,	322
29.	Wardlaw and Fearnua,	322
30.	The Priory Gardens,	323
31.	Contract betwixt Lord Huntly and Lord Lovat, 1570,	323
32.	Scottish Monastic Schools,	324
33.	Lease to Thomas Alexander, Lord Lovat, of the Priory of Beauly, 1847,	325

PRIORS OF BEAULY, ... 329

HISTORICAL NOTICES

OF THE

PRIORY OF BEAULY.

IT is difficult now to conceive of the rapid transmission of opinions and usages, which existed at the time when there was but one Church in Western Christendom. As in the age of the Antonines, a fashion at Rome was soon taken up in distant provinces, so during the pontificate of Innocent III., a novelty in religious practice quickly spread throughout Europe. The imperial roads and post-houses did not more securely send on the orders of the reigning Cæsar to Alexandria or York, than the lines of convents and parsonages passed the fiat of the occupant of St Peter's Chair to the extremity of Scotland or Spain. This is strongly exemplified in the origin of the Priory of Beauly, the religious House whose records are now for the first time collected.

He who would judge best of the rigour of the rules of St Bruno, should climb the mountain of the Grande Chartreuse, where the Saint established his Reformed order with vows of unusual austerity, under the protection of the Virgin Mary, and also of John Baptist, whose severity of life was the pattern. "Ora et labora" was the ruling maxim of the Charterhouse, and the wild and desolate region in which it is built, compelled as well as nerved the toil of the brethren.

But very soon was introduced a distinction between the inmates of even Carthusian houses; and in these monasteries as well as others, the brethren were divided into two classes, the brethren of the choir, and the lay brethren (*conversi*). The first alone received holy orders, and performed the functions of the priesthood. These offices, and study and contemplation, occupied their time; while the bodily labour, both domestic and agricultural, prescribed by the rules, was the duty only of the lay brethren.

Viard, a lay brother of the Charterhouse of Louvigny, in the diocese of Langres, in Burgundy, believing himself called to a life of more severity and greater freedom from temporal cares than his position of lay brother allowed, obtained permission from the superior to retire as a hermit to a cavern in a wood, a few miles off, and there practised the most extraordinary austerities. He was discovered by the inhabitants of the neighbourhood, and his strict observances soon gained him a just reputation. The Duke of Burgundy came often to visit him, and at last vowed that if success should attend the ducal arms in a military expedition then projected, a monastery would be founded on the spot which Viard had made holy, and Viard should be its head.

Viard, like other hermits, and not forgetful of the maxims of St Bruno, worked in his own garden, and supplied his "vegetable store" by his own labours. In this way, probably, the valley in which his cavern was situated acquired the name of Vallis Caulium, or Vallis Olerum, the Valley of Herbs. The duke returning victorious from his expedition, built the promised monastery in the Holy Vale; and Viard, as the first prior, completed the foundation, and, according to an ancient inscription over the church, took up his abode there on the 2d November 1193. Viard framed a set of rules for the governance of the new society, and in the Register of the Bishopric of Moray, we have these regulations set out and approved by Innocent III., in a Bull of protection, dated the 10th of February 1205.

No house of this order was ever established in England, but within twenty-five years from the confirmation of the new rules by Pope Innocent, three houses of the order were founded in Scotland, and that too in the extremities of that kingdom.

This was brought about by William Malvoisin, Bishop of St Andrews. The history of the Alexanders, and of William the Lion, has yet to be written, and when this is done, full justice will be rendered to the character of Malvoisin. Among the band of prelates who surrounded the throne of William the Lion, none stands higher than Bishop Malvoisin, appointed before 1180 one of the Clerici Regis, or King's secretaries. It is impossible to doubt that even before his elevation to the chancellorship, he exercised considerable influence over the king. As the first instance of William insisting on the election of his own nominee as bishop takes place just about the time that Malvoisin first appears as the king's official, it was probably by his encouragement that the king introduced the rule; for it was a principle established by Charlemagne, and strictly adhered to by the Norman kings of England, that the cathedral chapters, if permitted to elect, should choose the nominees of the Crown as their bishops; and Malvoisin was a Norman, and doubtless taught this lesson of Norman tyranny, as Giraldus Cambrensis calls it,* to the Scottish king.

It is probable that the young councillor supported the king in his resistance to the Pope, who ordered the elect of the chapter of St Andrews to be consecrated bishop in opposition to the king's nominee. The king banished the bishop from the kingdom, and the Pope laid Scotland under an interdict, and excommunicated the king. But in the end the Crown prevailed. And even in the days of Victoria, the queen's irresistible recommendation to a bishopric betokens its Nor-

* Giraldus Camb., De Instruct. Princ. ; Robertson's Preface to Stat. Conc. Ecc. Scot., xxxiv., n. 2.

man origin by assuming the form of a *congé d'élire*, with a letter-missive containing the name of the person to be elected.*

In September 1199 Malvoisin was appointed Chancellor of Scotland. When made Chancellor he was only in deacon's orders, and not till his election to the bishopric of Glasgow was he advanced to the dignity of the priesthood. On Saturday the 24th September 1200, he was ordained priest at Lyons by the archbishop of that city; and on Sunday the 25th he was consecrated bishop by the same prelate under the mandate of Pope Innocent III. There is extant a letter addressed by this archbishop to Malvoisin, which shows how anxious the latter was to obtain the fullest information and the best advice as to the duties of the episcopal office he had just undertaken.† The archbishop suggests to Malvoisin that on his proposed stay at Paris he would be able to consult those skilled in canon (divine) and civil (human) law. It is probable that Malvoisin was educated at Paris, and he seems to have kept up his connection with the learned there.

In 1201, Malvoisin was translated from Glasgow to St Andrews, the see which, though not yet an archbishopric, constituted its possessor the Primus, or first in dignity of the Scottish bishops.

Sent as ambassador‡ by his young king to John, sulking in the Isle of Wight after his mortification at Runnymede, Malvoisin proceeded from England to attend the Fourth Lateran Council at Rome in November 1215. This was the best attended Council of the Latin Church. It consisted of nearly five hundred archbishops and bishops, beside a great multitude of abbots and priors and ambassadors from

---

* The Queen *v.* the Archbishop of Canterbury, 11 Queen's Bench Reports, 483.

† The letter is printed in Appendix to Preface to Stat. Conc. Ecc. Scot., xxx.

‡ Malvoisin went to visit his parents in Normandy in 1212, and probably attended the Council at Paris that year. On his return he presided over a Synod of the Scottish clergy at Perth; on William the Lion's death, 4th December 1214, he enthroned the young king, with more than usual ceremony. He was appointed ambassador to England 9th July 1215.

most of the Christian courts in the West and East. Next to
the recovery of the Holy Land, the reformation of the Church
in faith and discipline formed a subject of consultation, and
great complaints were made respecting monastic corruption.
It was urged that new orders of religious men were too
common, and the Council enacted that their foundation
should be discouraged, but this enactment could not apply
to the orders already sanctioned by Pope Innocent, such as
those of St Dominic and the Valliscaulians.

Malvoisin saw the fitness of these two orders for Scotland. The Dominicans, intrepid preachers, to be placed in
the towns and cities of the kingdom; and the Valliscaulians,
men of austere lives, whose little communities might attract
attention and secure respect, in the wildest and most remote
districts. Both orders were in startling contrast to the decayed and effete Culdees of Mucross who still remained at
St Andrews, at the very gates of the Primus's own cathedral;
a small priestly caste who had lost all voice in the election of
a bishop; and though clinging to their hereditary possessions,
had given up their cure of souls and their charge of the hospital for the sick and the poor, the pilgrim and the stranger.*

In 1225 the Scottish clergy were, by an unusual exercise
of the grace and prerogative of the papal see, empowered
to meet in council without the summons or presence of a
papal legate. Malvoisin secured the precedence of his see in
the council: beginning with the Bishop of St Andrews—
the Bishop of the Scots, as Malvoisin proudly styled himself—
each bishop was in turn to preach at the opening of the
council. The Chancellor was upon such friendly terms with
the king, whom he had baptized and invested with the ensigns

---

* Yet these clerics, whose name had already become a bye-word, had rights
which Malvoisin defended against the dignified Augustinian canons of St Andrews.
The hereditary property of the Culdees was possibly attacked, or their right to
mutter divine service after their manner in a corner of the cathedral; at all events,
in February 1221, the papal legate at Perth heard a litigation commenced by the
prior and canons of St Andrews against their bishop and certain clerics of St Andrews, commonly called Culdees—"et quosdam clericos de S. Andrea, qui Keledei
vulgariter appellantur" (Theiner, Mon. Vet. Hib. et Scot., p. 16).

of royalty, that he must have readily attested the writ which sent two doctors of civil law to attend the council as Commissioners on behalf of the Crown.

And now the monarch and Primus were to testify their sense of the Pope's benefits by establishing the new orders in Scotland. At the end of the year 1229 peace was established throughout Scotland; for some years before, the towns and the southern part of the kingdom had been freed from war, and had increased in wealth by trade and commerce. The marriage of the young King of Scotland, in 1221, to the sister of the King of England, and of two princesses of Scotland, sisters of Alexander, to Hugh de Burgh and Roger Bigod, two of the most powerful English nobles, put a stop to all hostilities between the two nations, and introduced a friendly intercourse between their ruling families.

The insurrection of Somerled, Lord of the Isles, in 1221, which led to the expulsion of his family from Argyle by Alexander in 1222, freed the vassals of Somerled from their fealty to him, and they were made vassals of the Crown. North Argyle or Wester Ross was given to the Earl of Ross. Lorn was granted to be held of the king *in capite* by the sons of Dougal. In 1228 the last effort was made by the Gaelic population to place upon the throne the heir of Malcolm Canmore, according to the Celtic laws of descent. Gillespic M'Farlane broke out in open rebellion against the king, killed Thomas of Thirlstane, to whom Malcolm IV. had given the district of Abertarff, and set fire to the town of Inverness. The king went himself against Gillespic, who was overcome and slain; the insurrection was completely extinguished; and the kingdom enjoyed peace.

In the year 1230 four monasteries of the Dominicans and three of the Valliscaulians were founded. The Dominicans, the Preaching Friars, were placed, two by the king himself in Edinburgh and Berwick-upon-Tweed, one at Ayr by the king and William Malvoisin, and one by Allan Durward (*ostiarius*) in Montrose. The Valliscaulians, almost hermits, were placed, one by the king at Pluscardine in Moray, another by Duncan

Macdougal of Lorn at Ardchattan on Loch Etive, in Argyle; and the third by John Byset at Beauly, at the head of the Beauly Firth, in Ross.

This House of Beauly is the foundation whose few charters are printed in the sequel. It was planted in a situation admirably fitted for the object of its institution. Amidst a tract of rich alluvial soil brought down by the river and stretched between the hills and sea-shore, on the great highroad from Inverness to the North, the baron of English descent, who had recently acquired the large possessions of the Aird, built the new monastery. Just where the noble river, after wasting the speed acquired by its rush over the rocks of Kilmorack, in the windings below the founder's new castle of Beaufort, spreads out into the Beauly Firth, and opposite the wooded hills of Balblair, open to the sunny south, surrounded by level land productive of the finest wheat and the most luxuriant grasses, John Byset reared his priory and its church, whose walls six centuries and a half have not been able to pull down. He or his protegés, the monks, gave the spot a new name, Bellus Locus, the Beautiful Place,—a name which the queen's father had given some twenty-six years before to the noble monastery he had erected on the shores of the Solent; and looking at the surrounding scenery, we cannot wonder it should be said that when Queen Mary slept at the Priory of Beauly she, on hearing its name adopted from the language of her beloved France, exclaimed, " C'est un beau lieu."*

The Dominicans were bound to be instant in preaching the Gospel. Their founder was distinguished by a fervid and persuasive eloquence, and feeling the power of this faculty, he

* This is the probable version of the story of the parish minister of Kilmorack. He says: " In the house of the priests who officiated in this priory, Queen Mary, it is said, was entertained for a night; and upon seeing in the morning the beautiful view from its windows, she exclaimed : ' C'est un beau lieu,' and hence the name Beauly was given to the village and river" (Stat. Acct. Inverness-shire, 1842, p. 366). As this minister supposes the name of his parish, Kilmorack, the church of Mary, to be derived from a lady, a descendant of one of the lairds of Chisholm, we must not give him implicit credence. See the amusing criticism on this, Quart. Rev., vol. lxxxii., p. 360.

established a fraternity devoted to its exercise—a society of itinerant preachers. Accordingly their houses were centres in which the brethren were trained to their profession, and from which they went forth into the streets of towns and the lanes of villages to preach to the poor tidings of salvation.

Far different was the rule of the Valliscaulians; their own salvation, and not the rescue of others, was the object of their retreat from the world. They lived in very small cells, that at the times of prayer, of study, and of meditation, they might be withdrawn from other objects, and alone with God. They kept no oxen, sheep, or any lands cultivated by their own labour, surrendering all possessions which might divert their attention from spiritual exercises by the care which such property required to make it valuable. They had marked bounds outside the inclosure of their priories, beyond which none were permitted to wander, save the prior and those he took with him to visit dependent houses. Personally they worked only in their gardens, and never went even to these but at hours allowed for bodily labour. They were content with such incomes as they could receive without giving themselves much anxiety—such incomes as provided them with the necessaries of life, and relieved them from the obligation of quitting the precinct to obtain the means of living. They received into the house no more brethren than its revenues could maintain. They wore the dress of the Cistercians.

Such is the account given by Helyot,[*] on the authority of Cardinal Jacques de Vitri, whom he styles a contemporary writer. We find a more elaborate and authentic statement of the rules of the founder in the Bull of Pope Innocent III., to which we have referred. It is recorded in the Register of Moray probably as the Rule of the House of Pluscardine, in that diocese:

"Innocent the Bishop, servant of the servants of God, to his beloved sons, the Prior and the Brothers of the Valley of Herbs, sends health and the apostolic blessing. The apostolic see is wont to assent to

---

[*] Histoire des Ordres Monastiques, vol. vi., p. 178.

pious wishes, and to extend to the honourable prayers of those seeking it a willing favour. We received from the letters of our very venerable brother G. elect of Rheims, that on his passage through the diocese of Langres, he found that you had in the Valley of Herbs taken upon yourselves the new institution of an order: inquiring diligently as to its merits, he found nothing in it but what was religious and honourable. He found, indeed, as his same letters express, that among you one monk, whom you, my sons the monks, elect, is by right prior, to whom all the monks, of course, and also the lay brothers, the company of whom may not exceed the number twenty, as to their spiritual father, are to take care to show reverence and obedience.

"None of you are to possess any separate property.

"In assembling every day, the mass and the canonical hours* shall be sung. Private masses, whoever wish, may also celebrate.

"You shall hold a chapter every day, making twelve readings at the appointed times.

"You shall work together, and you shall eat together in the refectory, not using flesh or fat (*sagimine*). The prior shall eat with you in the same refectory†—contented with the like food and clothing as the rest. From the feast of the Lord's Resurrection down to the exaltation of the Holy Cross (14th September), you shall eat twice in the day, passing the rest of the time under the abstinence of fasts, being content on Fridays with bread and water and one relish‡ to it. On the day of the Lord's Nativity you shall not fast, nor on Friday in summer when a feast shall happen to fall of twelve readings.

"You shall live on your revenues (*redditibus*).

"You shall observe silence. Women shall not enter the inner bounds, nor shall you pass the outer bounds, except the prior on the

---

* The canonical hours of prayers were seven, after Ps. cxix. 164: (1.) at 2 A.M.—the monks went to bed at 8 P.M.; (2.) Matins, at 6 A.M.; (3.) 9 A.M.; (4.) at high noon; (5.) 3 P.M.; (6.) Vespers, 6 P.M.; (7.) at 7 P.M. See Concordiæ Regularum by St Benedict, in Fuller's Church History, book vi., § 3.

† In abbeys, the abbot only on great solemnities graced the monks with his presence in the dining-hall or refectory.

‡ *Pulmentum*. The ancient Romans lived on the simplest fare, chiefly on pottage (*puls*), or bread and pot-herbs, hence everything eaten with bread, or besides bread, was afterwards named *Pulmentum* or *Pulmentarium* (ὀψώνιον, *opsonium*, called in Scotland, Kitchen).—Hor. Sat. ii., 2, 20; Ep. i., 18, 48. Adam's Roman Antiquities, p. 401.

business of the order. The prior, however, if he shall be occupied or sick, and urgent necessity or evident utility shall require it, shall be able to select any other monk, who may pass the outer bounds.

"You shall wear hair-shirts next your skin: those, however, who cannot endure these are not to be compelled to do so. You are on no account to put on linen or hempen garments, but to clothe yourselves in white dresses of coarse wool and fur (*pelliceas*). You shall all lie down in your tunics, with your girdles on, and shoes on. And besides this, you, my sons the monks, with your cowls on, nowhere and never resting upon mattresses.

"Your novices shall be in probation for a year.

"And you, my sons the monks, from matins to the hour of labour, and from vespers to sunset, shall devote yourselves to reading, prayer, and contemplation, except those whom, at the discretion of the prior, he, for some certain and necessary cause, shall consider ought to be withdrawn from this.

"We, therefore, assenting to your just entreaties, take under the protection of the blessed Peter and ourselves, your persons and the place in which you shall give yourselves up to divine service, with all things that you reasonably possess at present, or which by the grant of pontiffs, the bounty of kings or princes, or the oblations of the faithful, or by any other just means, God favouring you, you shall be able to acquire.

"Specially, however, we, by the apostolic authority, confirm the order itself, constituted by careful deliberation, with the assent of the diocesan, and we fortify it by the defence of this present script.

"It is altogether prohibited, therefore, to any man to violate this page of our protection and confirmation, or to oppose it by any rash doing. If this, however, any one shall presume to attempt, let him know that he will incur the indignation of Almighty God, and of the blessed Apostles Peter and Paul. Dated at Rome, at St Peter's, the 1205th year from the Lord's incarnation, the 4th day before the Ides of February, in the seventh year of our pontificate."

The monks wore a white cassock with a narrow scapulary, and over that a black gown, when they went abroad, and a white one when they went to church.

They were daily employed in dressing the gardens of fruits and herbs, which were within the bounds of the monastery, and improved for the use of it.*

Such regulations were excellently adapted for a religious establishment to be placed in the remote districts of the Highlands of Scotland, and the selection shows the sagacity of the Primus.

I shall now, with a view to throwing as much light as I can on the documents that are printed, illustrate each of them in chronological order by reference to the circumstances under which they were originally produced, and I shall endeavour to give an account of the personages who appear either as parties to the documents, or as witnesses to their execution. Such an account of the history of the Priory of Beauly as is necessary to connect the documents together, I have also thought would not be unacceptable; and that everything which contributes to the history of the sister priories of Pluscardine and Ardchattan would be properly introduced.

The documents are printed from the transcripts of Macfarlane of Macfarlane in the Advocates Library. An excellent account of him is given in the Chartulary of Cambuskenneth.† The transcripts are in the second volume of the MSS. called "Diplomatum Collectio," twenty-three in number, and are the only documents extant of the charters of the Priory.

There is no date to the transcripts, but from their juxtaposition to the Chartulary of Cambuskenneth, transcribed in 1738, it is probable that they were transcribed shortly before that time. In whose possession the documents were at the time of their being transcribed is not stated. Two of them—one, No. XVII., dated the 11th February 1500, and the other, No. XI., dated June 1340—correspond with the titles of two of the documents inventoried in the list of Lovat charters, which now belongs to Captain Dunbar Dunbar, and has been

* Orem's History of Aberdeen. Bibliotheca Top. Brit., 1790, p. 73.
† Preface to the Chartulary of Cambuskenneth, printed for the Grampian Club.

kindly lent by him. This list contains the titles of those writs belonging to the Lovat family, which Alexander, Master of Lovat, and tutor to Hugh, Lord Lovat, gave to Mr Alexander Abernethie, writer in Edinburgh, in 1651, before he set out to fight with King Charles II., at the fatal battle of Worcester, and which were restored to him on the 6th November 1652. The Lovat estates passed on quietly from Hugh, Lord Lovat, to his son of the same name, who died in 1696, leaving issue daughters only; the eldest, Amelia, married, in 1702, Alexander Mackenzie, styled, of Fraserdale.

Although Simon, Lord Lovat, soon raised his father's and his own claims to the succession, yet he did not get the papers of the family. On the 10th May 1716, he writes to Duncan Forbes, afterwards Lord President, then advocate in Edinburgh: "My service to Mr Macfarlan and his lady. I would wish he would search Fraserdale's right to the estate; and what we can do to find the old papers of the family." The papers would naturally be with Hugh, the eldest son of Amelia Fraser; Hugh certainly acted as owner of the estate of Lovat and the superiorities belonging to it. One of the transcribed writs, No. XXII., confirmed on the 26th April 1532, is produced by Hugh, titular Lord Lovat, on 22d July 1729,* in the pleadings of the cause relating to the right to the peerage between him and Simon, Lord Lovat.

John Spottiswoode, advocate, wrote notes on "Hope's Minor Practicks," and an account of religious houses in Scotland. In his account of Beauly, he refers to four of the writs which are transcribed, Nos. I., III., XV., XXIII. He died in 1728, though the account was not published by his son till 1734.† He married the mother of Walter Macfarlane, at whose expense the transcripts were made, and there seems every reason to believe that at the time they were seen by Spottiswoode, they were in the possession of Hugh, the titular Lord.

There was a submission to arbitration between Hugh, Lord

* Printed Memoir for Hugh, Lord Lovat, 22d July 1729, p. 22.
† Hope's Minor Practicks. Edin. 1734.

Lovat, and Simon, Lord Lovat, in March 1733, which was completed by a decreet-arbitral not long before 1738, on the 26th July of which year Simon made up titles to the whole lands of Lovat. At this time it may be supposed that all the writs of 1652 were given up to Simon, Lord Lovat; whether he destroyed any of them is not known. Those which are grants of the Beauly Priory lands after the Reformation such as Nos. XVIII. and XIX. in the Inventory of 1652, being title deeds of the Lovat estate, are now, it seems from Dr Stuart's "Book of Kinloss," in the possession of the present Lord Lovat.

But what, on the forfeiture of Simon, Lord Lovat, became of the transcribed writs which concerned the previous history of the Priory, does not appear. No reference is made to them in the publication of the Hon. Archibald Fraser of Lovat, entitled "Annals of the Frasers," so that it seems doubtful whether they ever came into his possession. We can only hope that by calling public attention to the matter, the original documents may be discovered.*

* There are only three places where they can be, if they were in the custody of Hugh, titular Lord Lovat, in 1729: (1.) In the custody of his personal representatives, or their law agents; (2.) In the custody of the Crown; (3.) In the custody of Mr Fraser of Abertarff. There appears no probability of their being in Lord Lovat's possession.

No. I.

BULLA GREGORII PAPÆ PRIORI DE BELLO LOCO ORDINIS VALLISCAULIUM ROSSENSIS DIOCŒSIS.

Ex Autographo [1231].

"Gregorius episcopus Servus Servorum Dei dilectis Filiis priori Fratribus Monasterii de Bello loco ordinis Vallis Caulium Rossensis Diocœsis Salutem et Apostolicam Benedictionem. Cum a nobis petitur quod justum est et honestum, tam vigor æquitatis quam ordo exigit rationis, ut id per solicitudinem officii nostri ad debitum perducatur effectum. Ea propter, dilecti in Domino filii, vestris justis postulationibus grato concurrentes assensu, personas vestras et Monasterium de Bello loco, in quo divino vacatis obsequio, cum omnibus bonis, quæ impræsentiarum rationabiliter possidet, aut in futurum justis modis possidere vel adipisci poterit præstante Domino, sub Beati Petri et nostri protectione suscipimus; Specialiter autem de Sitheney et de Karcurri possessiones, et de forne piscaria, quas nobilis vir Johannes Biseth ad ipsum spectantes vobis contulit, intuitu pietatis, sicut in litteris inde confectis plenius dicitur contineri, nec non terras, possessiones, et alia bona vestra, sicut ea omnia juste et pacifice possidetis, vobis et eidem Monasterio per vos auctoritate Apostolica confirmamus, et præsentis Scripti patrocinio communimus. Nulli ergo omnino hominum liceat hanc paginam nostræ protectionis et confirmationis, vel ei ausu temerario contraire. Si quis autem hoc attemptare præsumpserit, indignationem omnipotentis Dei, et Beatorum Petri et Pauli Apostolorum ejus, se noverit incursurum. Datum Laterani. . . . Nonas. . . . Pontificatus nostri Anno D. . . ."

" Not.—The tag yellow silk ; no seal."

This document is a Bull of Pope Gregory addressed to the prior and brethren of Beauly. It takes their persons and monastery of Beauly (*de Bello Loco*) under the protection of the blessed Peter and of himself, particularly the possessions of SITHENEY, and of KARCURRI, and the FISHINGS OF FORNE, which a noble man, JOHN BYSET, had given them.

Gregory IX. was Pope from 1227 to 1241. The reference to John Byset shows that the Bull was granted by Gregory IX.

The transcript has only these words of the final part,— ". . . Nonas. . . . Pontificatus nostri Anno D. . . ;" but as Spottiswoode, who must have seen the originals from which these transcripts are made, speaking of John Byset's foundation, says his charter is confirmed by Pope Gregory, "3tio : Non. Julii, pontificatus anno 4to," we may fairly assume that the lacuna after "anno" should be filled up by "quarto," and that the Bull was dated the fourth year of Pope Gregory IX., or 1231.

We here first meet with the name of the House, Bellus Locus, Beau Lieu, the Beautiful Place. This was a not infrequent title for monasteries in France and England. There was in France a monastery of Beaulieu at Langres; while King John distinguished his splendid abbey of Beaulieu in the New Forest by styling it Bellus Locus Regis, or King's Beaulieu.*

A writer who is anxious to vindicate the high claims of the Gaelic language says, the low country etymologists, because they are ignorant of Gaelic, seek in French the derivation of a native name, and grace the Celtic "Beula" with the transmigration of the French "Beau-lieu." He proceeds: "The name, however, is simple Gaelic. 'Béul-àlh,' the *mouth*, of the *ford*, from 'Béul,' a mouth, or deboucheur, and 'àlh,' pronounced 'à,' *a ford*. Like all other native designations, it is expressive of a local distinction ; for the Priory and the town

---

* Beaulieu, in Hampshire, is pronounced as Beauly in Inverness-shire is—the *Beau* like the same syllable in Beauty, and the *lieu*, "ly." Macaulay's trumpet-stirring lines in the Armada (1832):

"O'er Longleat's towers, o'er Cranbourne's oaks, the fiery herald flew :
He roused the shepherds of Stonehenge, the rangers of Beaulieu,"

prove that he had then learned more by reading than by hearing.

are situated upon the *mouth* of the river, and opposite to the most important *ford* upon the lower Glass, and which in old times was the principal passage into Ross."*

A little historical inquiry would have led to a different conclusion, and if the name had a Celtic origin we should expect it to be used now by the Celtic population, but it is not so. " Beauly is not the Celtic name of the place, but ' Manachain ;' you never hear a Highlander asking in Gaelic ' C'ait am bheil Beauly ?' If he is not acquainted with English he does not know what the term refers to. He will ask you in his own language, ' C'ait am ·bheil a Manachain ?' this is the Gaelic for ' Where is Beauly?' 'Manach ' is the Gaelic for monk, and ' manachain ' is the Gaelic for priory or monastery."†

Of course it is possible that the special name of the place may, though Celtic in origin, have been lost in the more generic title taken from the peculiar purpose to which it was dedicated, and, after all, the Bull of Pope Gregory is the best proof that the Priory was on its foundation called in French the Priory of Beaulieu.

Before examining the contents of this Bull, the earliest of the Beauly charters now printed, let us examine the account of the earliest charters given by the Wardlaw MS., which we shall afterwards more particularly describe. This account is as follows:

(1.) John Bisset by vow and promise erecting a priory of monks in Beauly, and granting a donation and mortification by charter and confirmation of the lands of Strathalvy and Achinbady or Beauly, to the monks Ordinis Vallis Caulium there. The limits of their possessions about the precinct, specified to be Onach-Tarridel to the east, and Rivulum de Breckach westward. This charter is by the said Dom. Joan. Bisset, apud Cellam de St Durstan, die 9 mensis Julii anno Xti. 1223.‡

* Provincial Geography, Lays of the Deer Forest, vol. ii., p. 503. Edin. 1848.
† Transactions of Gaelic Society of Inverness, vol. i., Mr A. Mackenzie on Local Topography.
‡ Hutton MS., Add. MSS., B. M., 8144, p. 166; Extracts from Wardlaw MS., by the late Lewis M. Mackenzie of Findon.

(2.) Donation and charter of confirmation of the Half Davoch Lands of Tarridale to the monks Ordinis Vallis Caulium by Gillichrist a Rosse, granted and subscribed in burgo de Inverness, in mense Martis anno Domini 1235.*

(3.) Donation and charter of mortification of the multures of several lands within the parochin of Wardlaw and Kiltarlity, by Joannes Bisset to the monks of Beauly, such as: Loveth, Lusfinan, Finasses, Monchitech ex utraque parte rivuli, Fochines et dimidiæ davach de Beaufort et Duary, Davatus de Muy et de Bruchach et de Kenniath, etc.†

(4.) Confirmation of all these donations by King Alexander II. to the monks of Beauly, A.D. 123 ;‡ as they are set down at large by themselves.

Among the Lovat writs of 1652 we have this entry:

"Confirmation by King Alexander of the miln mutors of the Half Davach Lands of Louich and Milne of Dowatrie, dated 20th Decr and 17th year of his reign."

The seventeenth year of Alexander II. is 1231.

Possibly among "the eight and forty pieces of parchment in old character," mentioned in the Dunbar Dunbar MS. as not of any importance in the eyes of Mr Alexander Abernethie, there may have been these charters from John Byset and Gillechrist a Rosse.

But to return to the Bull of Gregory IX. It introduces us to the founder of the House of Beauly, John Byset.§ The first person of the name recorded in contemporary documents in Scotland is Henry Byset, who is a witness to a charter of William the Lion before 1198.‖

---

* Findon Extracts, Wardlaw MS., 1225.

† Loveth is Lovat; Finasses, Fingask; Monchitech, Moniack Easter and Wester; Fochines, Phoineas; Beaufort et Duary, Beaufort and Downie; Muy, Moy; Bruchach, Bruiach.

‡ Findon Extracts, 1231.

§ The spelling is various, and was afterwards corrupted into Bisset; but we shall adopt this form of Byset, as having been used by the founder of the Priory of Beauly, and by writers of contemporary charters.

‖ Chart. Melrose, vol. i., p. 123.

John Byset first appears as the Lord of the Aird in the deeds of arrangement between him and Bricius, Bishop of Moray, who died in 1221, and which are confirmed by King Alexander II. in 1221. Byset must have been the first of the family who acquired the lands of the Aird, for the king's confirmation expressly mentions that the lands had been granted to John Byset personally. When, in 1226, giving the church of Kiltarlity to the leper house of Rathven, he does so, among other objects, for the soul of William, King of Scotland; so that the grant referred to by King Alexander II. had probably been made to Byset by King William the Lion.

The Scalacronica states that William the Lion, in 1174, on his return from captivity at Falaise and in England, brought back young Englishmen of family to seek their fortunes at the Scottish court. Among these are named the Bysets [Biseys].* At this time Henry Byset may have come into Scotland.

From 1179 to 1187 William the Lion was engaged in putting down the rebellion of Donald Bane,† who, after the Boy of Egremont's defeat, claimed to be the Celtic heir of Malcolm Canmore. William completed with the people of Moray and Ross what his brother Malcolm had begun with the people of Moray, expelling great numbers of the Celtic inhabitants, putting the land under the feudal system, and granting it out in baronies, to be held of the Crown. Among these, in the province of Moray, the barony of the Aird was probably granted to John Byset, to secure his victory over Donald Bane; and about 1187 William the Lion founded two castles in Ross, one of which was called Ethirdover. This,

* Scalacronica, Maitland Club, Edinb. 1836, p. 41.
† It is said that Edmund, a son of Malcolm Canmore and St Margaret, joined in the conspiracy of Donald Bane against the succession of King Edgar, and when that king succeeded, Edmund seems to have adopted a course which saved his own life and preserved the honour of his family. He assumed the cowl at Montacute, the Cluniac priory, in Somersetshire. I note the fact as an illustration of the intimate connection then subsisting between England and Scotland, which is likewise shown in the history of the founder of Beauly.

by the combined light thrown on it by the lease of Kilcoy,* afterwards referred to, and the grant of Andrew de Boscho (Beauly Diplomata, No. VII.), is settled to be the castle of Edirdor, or Redcastle, on the Beauly Firth. In the latter part of his reign, the king probably appointed John Byset hereditary constable of this castle, and attached to it the lands of Edirdor, and at the same time gave him the barony of the Aird and the lands of Kilravoch, for we find all these—the castle and lands of Edirdor, the barony of the Aird, and the lands of Kilravoch—were the hereditary possessions of the granddaughters of John Byset.

The name of John Byset first occurs in contemporary documents in 1204 in the Register of the Abbey of Newbattle, and as a witness to a charter of Henry de Graham.† As we find that the papal Bull for translating the parish church of Kirkhill was obtained in 1210, just about the time that the insurrection of the son of Donald Bane broke out in Ross-shire, and as John Byset's confirmation of this translation seems to imply his having promoted it, we may not err in assuming that this grant was made by King William on the quelling of the rebellion in 1211.

John Byset's mother was alive in 1221, as in the deeds of arrangement he grants a glebe to the parish church of Kirkhill for the soul of his father, who was therefore dead, but not for the soul of his mother, who was therefore living. From the time of these deeds to 1232, we find John Byset witnessing the charters of King Alexander II. with William his brother, and with Walter Byset, who was the lord of Aboyne, in Aberdeenshire.

The Bysets in England were a family of baronial rank; they had the types and insignia of nobility; they held high office about the person of the Plantagenets; they witnessed the confirmation of Magna Charta, endowed abbeys and priories, and left that indubitable mark of their importance by the additional name which some English parishes have derived

* Preface to Orig. Par. Scot., p. xxi.; Book of Kilravock, p. 109.
† Reg. Newbattle, p. 7.

from them. Preston-Byset tells the country folks of Buckinghamshire now, as Combe-Byset informs the men of Wilts, of the days long ago, when a Byset was the lord of Preston and of Combe.* In particular, Manassar Byset, Sewer of the Household to King Henry II., founded a house of lepers at Maiden Bradley, in Wiltshire, and the successive members of his family confirmed and added to the endowment. The pious maid of honour, Margaret Byset, who, passing the night in watching and prayer, saved the life of Henry III. in 1238 at Woodstock from the hands of an assassin, had some time before added to the possessions of Maiden Bradley.

The English Bysets were a united family, each member assisting the other; and we find Manassar Byset giving the manor of East Bridgeford, Nottinghamshire, to his brother William, and this William Byset obtaining the consent of his son William, his brother Manassar, and his nephew Ernulph, to his grant to the priory of Thurgarton for the souls of his father and mother and wife, and of his brothers Henry and Ausold, and his nephew Henry. It seems probable that Henry Byset of 1198, the courtier of King William the Lion, was a member of the family of East Bridgeford.

We may not proceed further without referring to the MSS. which are mentioned by writers on Beauly Priory, while it is impossible to avoid saying that these MSS. are entitled to no real credit. One is a history of the family of Fraser of Lovat, intended for publication, 1749; and the other "a short chronology and genealogy of the Bissets and Frasers of Lovat,"† which, although said to be written by Mr James Fraser, minister of Wardlaw, purports only to be a transcript of the Wardlaw MS. by Robert Fraser, 1725. These two MSS. appear to have been written in the interest of Simon, Lord Lovat, who wished the history of his family coloured to suit

---

* There is no more certain mark of the early importance of a family than the affix of its name to that of an English parish. It is more to be relied on than the family having the same name as the parish; in the origin of surnames many families other than the owners of a village took their names from it; but no village ever took its second name from any family but that of its lords.

† MSS., Advocates Library, Genealogical Collection, 38, 4, 8, 409-417.

his claims against Amelia Fraser, who, in 1702, pretending to be heiress of line of the Byset, obtained a decree of the Court of Session, for the peerage of Fraser of Lovat.

The Wardlaw MS., to which we before referred, was written by James Fraser, minister of Wardlaw from 1661 to 1709. It is probable that he had access to the Lovat Writs of 1652, and so far as he professes to copy actual charters, he may be trusted. We have not seen the MS., but have obtained extracts from it among General Hutton's MSS. in the British Museum, and also extracts made by the late Lewis M. Mackenzie, Esq. of Findon, whose loss northern archæologists have to regret. When the Wardlaw MS. passes from transcribing charters or recording the events which passed before the eyes of the writer, it is hardly to be relied on more than the MSS. of 1725 and 1749; but as the compiler died before Simon, Lord Lovat's contention arose, his story is not twisted to suit the claims of rival parties.

As a specimen of the inventive powers or credulity of the writer of the Wardlaw MS., he states that John Byset, the founder of Beauly Priory, was the son of Byset, a courtier of William the Lion, which Byset married Agnes, daughter of the king. This marriage is a stupid invention of the seventeenth century. The daughters of William the Lion, legitimate and illegitimate,* are perfectly well known, and duly inquired into on the claims to the crown of Scotland in 1296.

John Byset of Lovat, the founder, makes the arrangement we have alluded to with Bricius, Bishop of Moray, respecting the glebe of the parish of Kirkhill, which cannot be later than 1221. The arrangement is confirmed by King Alexander II.,

---

* William the Lion had three legitimate daughters: (1.) Margaret, who married Hubert de Burgh, chief minister to Henry III., and left an only daughter, Magota; (2.) Isabella, married Roger Bigod, Earl of Norfolk, *ob. s. p.*; (3.) Marjory, married Gilbert the Marshal, Earl of Pembroke; she survived her husband, and died at London, 1244, *s. p.* He had four illegitimate daughters: (1.) Isabella, married in 1183 to Robert de Bruce, and in 1191, to Robert de Ross; (2.) Ada, married in 1184 to Patrick, Earl of Dunbar; (3.) Margaret, married in 1192 to Eustace de Vesci; (4.) Aufrida, married to William de Say.

by a deed dated at Elgin on the 15th October 1221,* just at the time when the king had succeeded in repressing the rising of Somerled in South Argyle and North Argyle or Wester Ross. The arrangement relates to the advowsons of the churches of Conveth (Conway) and Dunballoch (Dulbalach). Shaw, in his "Province of Moray," under the head of Kirkhill, writes:† "This church stood formerly at Dunbalach a mile up the river, and was dedicated to St Maurice. I have seen in the hands of Mr Fraser of Dunbalach, a papal Bull, dated anno 1210, for translating the church of Mauritius from Dunbalach to Wardlaw."

The charters, of which there are two copies in the Register of Moray, in the first place mention the lands of John Byset as having been granted to him, and as having before that grant been part of the parishes of Dunballoch and Conway. John Byset releases to Bricius, Bishop of Moray, and his successors, the advowson of the church of Dunballoch, and the bishop releases to John Byset the advowson of the church of Conway. The bishop agrees to have the charter confirmed by the chapter of the church of Spynie; and John Byset agrees to have it confirmed by the Crown. Byset also agrees to give seven acres of ground to the church of Dunballoch, in a competent place, and near to the parish church of Dunballoch, when it shall have been translated to Fingask, to the place which is called Wardelaue (Wardlaw). It appears that the translation, which had been provisionally sanctioned by the papal Bull, had not yet been effected. It was afterwards carried out, and the site of the old church of Wardlaw is now occupied by the ruins of that church and its burying-ground.

In passing, we may remark the distinction observed in the deed between the Saxon-Scottish and the Gaelic-Scottish languages; the Gaelic is called Scots: this was the rule down to the time of the Reformation. The place was called Wardlaw by the Saxons because it was the law or hill from which ward or watch was kept, probably

* Reg. Moray, p. 52.   † Shaw's Moray, p. 361.

against a possible incursion from the Gaelic inhabitants, who called it Balblair, or the town of or overlooking the plain. Shaw states* that the parish was called Wardlaw, because the garrison of Lovat kept ward or watch on this law or hill: we find no mention of Lovat till John Byset acquired it; but being a castle or fort on the plain below, defended by water, it would be convenient for it to have a look-out above, and Byset may have established the watch-tower on the hill to communicate with the fort. As he also had the Red Castle, his positions were strong on the Firth.

Byset had, it appears by the deed, the lands of the two parishes of Dunballoch (now Kirkhill) and Conveth (now united with Kiltarlity). There were nine davochs in Kirkhill: Fyngask (Fingask), Morevayn, Lusnacorn, Monychoc and another Monychok (Easter and Wester Moniack), and three davochs of Ferge or Fere (Fearn, Fearnua). There were eleven davochs in Conveth: Gulsackyn (Guisachan), Buntach (Buntait), Herkele (Erchless), Comber (Comerkirktown), Coneway, two davochs (Easter and Wester Conveth), Bruiach Muy and another Muy, Dunyn (Downie), and Fotheness (Foyness, Phoincas).

The lands of Dunballoch and Conveth had been granted by the Crown to John Byset at a yearly rent of £10. The bishop of the diocese claimed for the churches of Dunballoch and Conveth a tenth of this rent, under the grant of William the Lion, to the church of Moray, that is, claimed it against the Crown. Byset had retained the tenth out of the Crown rent, but had not paid it to the churches.

John Byset next founded the church of Kiltarlity, and gave it a parish out of the parish of Conveth, which before included all that ever belonged to Kiltarlity. The new parish of Kiltarlity included Erchless, a davoch in the earldom of Ross. A davoch was as much arable land as would employ four ploughs, and this in so hilly a country as Strathglass would carry with it probably a large district of pasture. Erchless was an important part of the new parish, and for this reason

* Shaw's Moray, p. 144.

the parish may have come within the jurisdiction of the Bishop of Ross, which was co-extensive with the earldom of Ross.

John Byset, intending to make use of the church of Kiltarlity, first secured the patronage by deed from the Bishop of Ross early in 1226.* The Bishop of Ross, Robert, with the consent of the chapter of Rosemarkie and his other clergy, quit-claims to John Byset and his heirs, for their homage, his right of patronage of the church of Kiltarlity; and John Byset and his heirs quit-claimed to the bishop whatever right they had to the kirkland of the said church; and Byset, beside, for the purpose of settling the controversy, and as an atonement for his own sins, contributed 15 merks of silver to the fabric of the church of St Peter of Rosemarkie, and a stone of wax yearly from himself and his heirs to the light upon the altar of that church; and the bishop and canons gave John and his heirs an interest in the orisons which should be presented in praise of God in the church. A merk was equal to thirteen pence and one-third of a penny sterling. Farquhar, Earl of Ross, Peter Byset, Anselm Byset, and William Byset, are witnesses. John Byset and Peter Byset are witnesses to a charter by Thomas de Galloway, Earl of Atholl.†

John Byset having divided the parish of Conveth into two parishes, those of Kiltarlity and Conveth, next proceeds to appropriate the church of Kiltarlity to the House of Lepers at Rathven, Banffshire.‡ The parish church of Rathven was appropriated to the Bishop of Moray. He and David de Strathbolgy agreed that the minister serving in the church should have a glebe and manse; and Bishop Bricius, between 1203 and 1216, adding eight canons to the chapter, endowed the eighth canon as a prebend, with the churches of Rathven and Dipple on the Spey, and the canon had the tithes of the parish of Rathven. Notwithstanding this, the church of Rathven seems to have had a sufficiently independent exist-

* Reg. Moray, p. 333.
† Reg. Dunfermline, p. 86.
‡ Provisions for the victims of that terrible disease are among the most frequent, as well as the most useful, institutions of that age.

ence to enable John Byset to establish a leper house in connection with it.* Byset, first by one deed grants for the soul of William, King of Scotland, and for the salvation of his lord, Alexander, the noble king, and for the salvation of the souls of his predecessors and successors, the right of patronage of the church of Kiltarlity to the church of St Peter of Rathven, for the maintenance of the lepers serving God there. Besides he had given to the house so much of his means that the members had promised, and by a solemn instrument obliged themselves, to keep a chaplain there, ministering in sacred things, and seven lepers, and one male domestic serving them; and it was provided that if any of the lepers should die or depart from the house, another should be presented by him or his heirs until the number was complete.† Among the witnesses is "W., my brother." This charter seems to have been insufficient to appropriate the church of Kiltarlity to the House of Lepers, and on the 19th of June 1226,‡ John Byset grants to the church of St Peter and the House of Lepers of Rathven, and the brethren serving there, the church of Kiltarlity with its pertinents. Andrew, Bishop of Moray, at the instance of John Byset, and on his presentation, had canonically admitted William, prior of the house, in the name of his brethren, to the church, and had confirmed the said church to the House of Lepers and the brethren there, to be held for their proper use, with all appurtenances in lands, tithes, and oblations.

This benevolent foundation of John Byset survives, not indeed for lepers, but for bedesmen. The Bedehouse is still standing at the village of Rathven, and was lately repaired. Two of the six bedesmen, who are maintained in the establishment, live in the house. The appointment of the bedesmen belongs to the Earl of Fife.§

* See lease of these tithes, by the parson of Dipple, in 1574, Shaw's Moray, App. xlv.
† A similar provision for two almsmen in the hospital of St Leonard is provided by Robert Byset of Upsetlington in his grant to the monastery of Kelso, 1240. Walter Byset and William Byset are witnesses to this deed (Chart. Kalchow, 240).
‡ Reg. Moray, p. 258. § New Statistical Account, Banff, p. 268.

No vicarage of Kiltarlity is mentioned in the Moray Taxatio—the church itself being taxed at 111 merks.* It is joined with Wardlaw in being liable to a procuration fee of 40s., and paid 2s. for synodals. How the religious services of the church were provided for does not appear, but in 1563 the church of Rathven preserved its property in the parish of Kiltarlity, which is entered thus: †

" Item, the kirk of Kintallartie sett for xxiii. lib."

The Bishops of Moray did not neglect making the best use of the release of Dunballoch parish. They divided it into the parishes of Wardlaw and Fearnway; and in 1239,‡ Andrew, Bishop of Moray, grants, with other churches, the church of Fearnway, with all its pertinents, to the common use of the canons of Elgin. The bishops constituted a vicar in Dunballoch, who appears in 1224, 1226, and 1227,§ and after the division, a vicar in Wardlaw. ||

Not only does William Byset, in his grant of Abertaff to Beauly (No. II.), mention " John, my brother," but to a charter of King Alexander II.,¶ John Byset is a witness, "and William, his brother;" so that we may assume that the "W., my brother," is William Byset.

The Bishop of Ross having acquired, by the arrangement with John Byset, the right to the stone of wax from the noted bees of Strathglass, proceeds to settle, in February 1227, a dispute between him and the Bishop of Moray. The Bishop of Ross had surrendered the patronage of Kiltarlity to John Byset, and the Bishop of Moray had assented to its appropriation to the church and leper house of Rathven; so that there was not left any episcopal interest in the church of Kiltarlity, but it was enough to enable the Bishop of Ross,

---

* Reg. Moray, pp. 362, 364, 365.
† Antiquities of Aberdeen and Banff, vol. ii., p. 144. Spalding Club.
‡ Reg. Moray, p. 35. § Ib., pp. 76, 77, 78, 82, 333.
|| The Vicar of Wardlaw is charged 9s. 4d. in 1274 and 1275 (Theiner, Mon. Vet. Hib. et Scot., pp. 111, 116).
¶ Reg. Glasgow, p. 116.

by giving it up, to retain without question his anomalous rights over the church of Ardersier, in the province of Moray.

The controversy* had arisen between Andrew, Bishop of Moray, on one side, and Robert, Bishop of Ross, and his chapter, on the other—the former asserting in the presence of the Pope's delegates, namely, the Abbot of Deer and the Dean and Archdeacon of Aberdeen, the right of diocesan over the churches of Kiltarlity and Ardersier, and having been put in actual possession of the churches a year before *causa rei servandæ*. The controversy was settled by the advice of the delegates, and with consent of the chapters and clergy of both dioceses, in the following manner: That the Bishops of Moray should possess the church of Kiltarlity as in diocesan right, and the Bishops of Ross should have the church of Ardersier, as to all ecclesiastical matters, as their predecessors formerly held it. Moreover, the Bishop of Moray, for himself and his successors, and with the consent of his chapter, renounced all right, if any, which he had, or might have, in the church of Ardersier, and all action and demand, solemnly promising that neither he nor his successors should afterwards claim any right in that church, or in aught belonging to it; the Bishop of Ross, for himself and his successors, and with the consent of his chapter and clergy, making a similar renunciation and promise as to the church of Kiltarlity. The Bishop of Ross, with same consent, gave to the cathedral church of Elgin, a stone of wax, to be held for confraternity and the orisons and other benefits there to be rendered which stone of wax John Byset and his heirs will give to the cathedral church of Ross, as is testified by his charter thereupon executed. It was further settled that if either of the said churches should attempt to contravene the agreement, it should pay £100 sterling to the other, and the agreement should, notwithstanding, remain valid. The deed is dated at Kenedor, near Elgin, the vigil of the Purification (1st February), 1227. The place of date indicates that the house built

* Reg. Moray, p 75.

by Bishop Archibald of Moray at Kenedor in 1280 was a restoration of the episcopal residence there.

In accordance with the papal Bull of 1224, the church of the Holy Trinity at Elgin was appointed the cathedral church of Moray. Andrew, the bishop, commenced the building of a cathedral, in substitution for the church of the Holy Trinity. The continuance of this great work for the next eighteen years provided a resort for architects, and hence within that period the churches of the priories of Beauly and Pluscardine were begun.

The three subjects given by John Byset to the monks are specified to be the possessions of Sitheney, of Karcurri, and the fishings of Forne.

Sitheney.—This word, probably distorted by the papal scribe, it is difficult to recognise. If it were more like Strathalvy it might be taken for that, for in the MS. of 1728,* we read: "Anno dom. 1245. By Bull from Pope Innocent IV. the Priory of Beauly was erected for the Benedictine monks, Ordinis Vallis Caulium, and King Alexander II. mortified and confirmed to the monks all the lands of Strathalvy, the monastery to be erected in Insulâ de Achinbady in Strathalvy, where stood a chappel of St Michael, and John Bisset entrusted with the erection, and to take care of the edifice, which he did accordingly carry on. The Prior Pater Jacomo with six monks came to Lovat then, and the country provided for them, and the monks called that place which was formerly termed in the French *Boulu*, a fair, good place."

In the Inventory of the Lovat writs, 1652,† we get :

"Confirmation be K. Alexr. of ye lands of Sethink, ·daitit 20th August and 15th year of his Reign" [1230].

It may be a name for the island of Achinbady. The final *cy* of Sitheney may mean Island.

Karcurri.—We find this in *Craigscorrie* (Hawkhill), a part

---

* Adv. Lib. MSS., Genealog. Coll., 35, 4, 8, p. 411.
† Dunbar Dunbar MS.

of the barony of Beauly. *The fishings of Forne* or Farrar, now Beauly, were a notable possession of the monks, and of extreme value to them, as by the rules of their order they were to abstain very much from flesh ; and were neither to breed cattle or sheep, or to cultivate arable land.

The foundation charter of the Priory of Beauly, to which both Rose, in his "History of the Family of Kilravock," and Spottiswoode, in his "Religious Houses of Scotland," refer, is probably a forgery. Spottiswoode writes,* "The Priory of Beauly or Ross was founded in the year 1231 by James Bisset, a gentleman of a considerable estate in that shire." After mistaking the name and position of the Byset estates, which, except Erchless and its pertinents, lay in Moray, we cannot expect accuracy. He proceeds: "The terms of its foundation were, Ut pro ipso, dum viverent orarent monachi : post mortem funus corpusque exciperent, atque animam de corpore abeuntem per continua sacrificia et opera pietatis prosequerentur. His charter is confirmed by Pope Gregory 3tio: Non. Julii, pontificatus anno 4to." Rose has the following :† "I have heard it reported of the Right Honourable Sir George Mackenzie of Tarbat, now Lord Register, that in the foundation of the Priorie of Bewlie there is insert as witnesses Urquhart of Cromartie and Rose of Geddes ; which, if so, Kilravock's predecessors have been near a whole centurie of years in this countrie before their getting of Kilravock ; for, by search of historie and records, I conceive that priorie was built by Bisset of Lovat, either in the latter end of the reigne of King William or the beginning of Alexander Second betwixt the years 1200 and 1220. And if he were witnes under that title and designation at that time (though it be more than *ordinarie antiquitatis*), yet he might have so much older standing in the countrie." In connection with Agnes Urquhart, Lady Kilravock, Rose remarks :‡ "As to the familie of Cromartie, whereof she was descended, it was verie ancient : Sir George Mackenzie of Tarbat, now Lord

---
* Spottiswoode's Relig. Houses, Minor Practicks, Edin. 1734.
† Hist. Fam. Kilravock, Spalding Club, p. 26. ‡ *Ib.*, p. 70.

Register, reporting that Urquhart of Cromartie and Rose of Geddes were witnesses in the foundation of the Priorie of Bewlie, which behooved to be betwixt the year 1200 and 1220, as farr as I can gather."

Now anything more certainly a forgery than to put an Urquhart of Cromarty as witness to a charter of 1230, cannot be conceived. William de Montealto was sheriff of Cromarty in 1263. In 1315 King Robert the Bruce granted the sheriffdom and burgh of Cromarty to Hugh, son and heir of William, Earl of Ross; and before 1349 King David II. granted, on the resignation of William, Earl of Ross, son of this Hugh (Hugh having fallen at Halidon Hill, St Margaret's Day, 22d July 1333), the sheriffdom of Cromarty to Adam Urquhart. This was the first grant of Cromarty made to the Urquharts.*

It is perfectly clear that the foundation deed of Beauly seen by Sir George Mackenzie, first Earl of Cromarty, must have been a forgery; just such a fabrication as the grant of Kintail to Colin the Irishman by King Alexander III., the earliest copy of which is said to be in the handwriting of the same Earl of Cromarty.† What was the document seen by Spottiswoode is not so clear, but it is worth while to bestow a little investigation on a matter so interesting as the foundation charter of the priory which it is our object to illustrate.

Walter Macfarlane of Macfarlane, to whose zeal for the preservation of ancient charters we owe the transcripts of the Beauly writs, was son of John Macfarlane of Macfarlane by his wife Helen, daughter of Robert, third Viscount Arbuthnot. After the death of John Macfarlane, Helen, his widow, Walter's mother, married in 1710 John Spottiswoode, advocate, who, having published a valuable work on law and taught a Scottish law class, was likely to have access to the same sources of information as the Lord Justice General, the Earl of Cromarty. John Spottiswoode died in 1728, and his

* Orig. Par. Scot., vol. ii., ".Cromarty."
† *Ib.*, p. 391.

edition of Hope's "Minor Practicks," printed in 1734 by his son, had appended to it his account of the Religious Houses in Scotland. It is probable, we have seen, that the Beauly charters were transcribed between 1734 and 1738, from their position among the Macfarlane transcripts. Now it is remarkable that John Spottiswoode, in his account of Beauly, mentions no document, except this foundation deed, other than those transcribed by his step-son, Macfarlane; and it seems most likely that Macfarlane had access to the so-called deed of foundation, but that he rejected it as a forgery, and would not allow his transcriber to copy it.*

Another forgery in connection with the foundation deed requires only a simple statement to secure its detection. The MS. historian of the Fraser family, in the Advocates Library,† whom we have already quoted as to the date of foundation, adds: " I saw the originall charter given to John Bisset by Macdonald, which begins in these terms: 'Ego Donaldus Insularum Rex, &c., Dono et concesso amico nostro charissimo Johanni Bizet D⁰ de Lovat totum et integras terras de Achterloss Idem Montessen, Eq.;' and the charter closes thus: 'Datum apud castrum nostrum de Dingwall anno a partu Virginis M.CC.XLIII v. Idis Julii anno II. Innocentii iiii. S. D. N. Pontificis optimi maximi coram consanguineis et Consiliariis nostris M'Lean de Lews et M'Leod de Harris.'" Except to show the extent of the possessions of John Byset, what object the historian of the Frasers could have in putting forward this charter, it is difficult to perceive; but Dempster, in his "Apparatus," connects Byset and Auchterless and Beauly thus:‡ "Bewlin in Rossia; ordinis Vallis Caulium qui ingressus Scotiam fertur anno 1230" (Scotichronicon, lib. ix., cap. xlvii.). "Hunc prioratum vero fundavit Joannes Biset, a quo nos Dempsteri habuimus Achterlos, præcipuam

* For the care which Walter Macfarlane took in revising and authenticating his transcripts, see instances in Robertson's Introduction to the Register of Paisley, published by the Maitland Club, p. viii., note.

† Adv. Lib. MSS., Genealog. Coll., 35, 4, 8, p. 411.

‡ Dempster's App. De Religione, cap. 19, lxxx. In fact, the name of Dempster does not appear on record till 1296.

familiæ nostræ hac tempestate patrimoniam." The whole of the forged charter quoted in the MS. is printed in the annals of the Frasers:* "Ego Donaldus Insularum Rex tenore presentium, do dono et concedo amico nostro dignissimo Domino Johanni Bisset. D. de J. totas et integras terras de Achterlos et Mancester, cum omnibus ad eas pertinentibus tam infra quam supra terram hacce in provincia Barniæ jacentes idque sibi et suis successoribus in perpetuum chartamque hanc firmam et stabilem iis teneamur, quam nostro sigillo et chirographo confirmamus et attestamus, apud castrum nostrum de Dingwall coram consanguineis et consiliariis nostris charissimis M'Leod de Lewis et M'Leod de Harise; die decimo nono Idus Jan anno a Christo nato MCCXXV anno pontificatus. S. D. N. Gregorii ix. P. O. N. primo Pontificis optimi maximi. S. M. P."

The nineteenth day before the Ides!—But we have dwelt too long on this rubbish.

* Annals of the Frasers, 1795, p. 24.

No. II.

CARTA WILLIELMI BYSETH DE ECCLESIA DE ABERTERTH FACTA FRATRIBUS DE BELLO LOCO ORDINIS VALLIS CAULIUM.

EX AUTOGRAPHO [1231].

"Omnibus hoc scriptum visuris vel audituris Willielmus Byseth Salutem. Sciant præsentes et futuri me dedisse, et concessisse, et hac Carta mea confirmasse pro salute animæ meæ, et animarum patris et matris meæ, et omnium antecessorum et successorum meorum Ecclesiam de Aberterth Deo et Beatæ Mariæ, et B° Johanni Baptistæ et Domui de Belloloco et Fratribus Vallis caulium in eadem Deo servientibus et servituris in liberam puram et perpetuam Eleemosynam, cum omnibus ad eandem Ecclesiam juste pertinentibus, in terris, decimis, oblationibus, obventionibus et omnimodis Ecclesiasticis rectitudinibus. Testibus Andrea Moraviensi Episcopo, Duncano Decano, Ranulfo Archidiacono Moraviensi, Radulpho Capellano Episcopi prædicti, Johanne Bridin Capellanis, Domino Johanne fratre meo, Bartholomæo Flandrensi, Hugone Corbet, Gillandes Macysac, Hugone Augustini, Godefrido Arbalaster, Henrico Cuch, Yone Venatore et pluribus alijs."

" Not.—The seal white wax, on a shield plain a bend ; no crown, the circumference not legible."

The preceding charter is a grant by William Byset, his brother John and the officials of the church of Moray being witnesses, of the church of Abertarf (Aberterth) to God, and the blessed Mary, and the blessed John Baptist, and the House of Beauly, and the Valliscaulian brethren there serving God, in pure and perpetual frankalmoigne, with all the pertinents of the same church, in lands, tithes, oblations, obventions, and all kind of ecclesiastical rights. Among the witnesses are Bartholomew the Fleming, who witnesses a charter of King Alexander II. in 1235, and the Bishop, Dean, and Archdeacon of Moray; notwithstanding which we get subsequently a confirmation of the grant by the bishop.

The seal has the arms of Byset, "on a shield plain; a bend." The transcriber adds, " no crown;" the opinion then prevailing that the crowns quartered in the Fraser of Lovat coat were the arms of Byset: whereas they are the arms of Grant. This simple ordinary shows the antiquity of the Byset achievement. The same coat is given by Sir David Lyndsay, in 1542, with the tinctures, the field *azure*, and the bend *argent*, as the arms of—

"Lord Bissart of Bewfort of auld."

These coats are identical, the tinctures were not blazoned in engraving till a much later date, and this coat is the arms of the founder of Beauly Priory.*

The parish of Abertarff is first mentioned in the foundation deed of the College of Canons, by Bricius, Bishop of Moray, between 1208 and 1216; to this Gillebride Persona de Abirtarf is a witness.† The next time it is mentioned is in an agreement between Thomas de Thyrlestan and Andreas, Bishop of Moray, in 1225.‡ This agreement mentions the tithes of the royal *Can*, which tithes were wont to be paid before the infeftment of Thomas, out of the land of Abertarff. This reference to the tithes payable out of what was coming to the Crown, is the same we have before observed in the agreements of John Byset with relation to Kirkhill; and it shows that William the Lion had granted to the church a tenth of the rent in kind, which was paid to the Crown by the owners of land in Moray, as well as a tenth of the money rent which was so payable.§

* Sir David Lyndsay's Heraldry, Edin. 1822.   † Reg. Moray, p. 43.
‡ Reg. Moray, p. 20.
§ King William, by a precept in the Register of Moray (p. 2), 1171-84, directs his bailiffs of Moray to pay to the church of Moray and the bishop there the tithes of all his rents in Moray and of his rents in kind, which had not been granted to other churches y himself or his ancestors.

Thomas de Thyrlstan was the proprietor of Thirlstane, in Berwickshire; and it is said, as we have before mentioned,* that Gillespic in 1228 raised an insurrection in Moray, burnt some wooden castles, and surprised and slew a baron called Thomas de Thirlstan, to whom Malcolm IV. had given the district of Abertarff. This must be the same Thomas de Thirlstan. He was succeeded at Thirlstan by Richard Maitland, who is said to have married his daughter, and about 1260 gives lands in the territory of Thirlstane to the monks of Dryburgh, excepting the third part to the Lady Agnes, formerly the wife of Thomas de Thirlstan, for her life.†

This charter of William Byset, from a witness being Duncan, the dean of Moray, is probably of the date 1231, as in 1232 Symon became dean of Moray, and continued dean until he succeeded to the bishopric in 1242; and in 1228 Freskin was dean of Moray.

We find among the suggestive and ill-understood list of the charters in the Treasury at Edinburgh, made up in 1282,‡ the following items relating to this subject, although others intervene:

" Item. Carta de Abirtarf. . . .
" It. Carta Thome de Thirliston.
" It. Littera quiete clamationis Ricardi Mauteland de trā de Abyrtharf.
" It. Carta Walteri Byset de Stratharkik.
" It. Carta de Obeyn."

Walter Byset, Lord of Obeyn (Aboyne), according to the Chronicle of Melrose, was uncle of John Byset, and therefore of William Byset, John's brother; and the charter of Walter Byset of Stratherrick means, according to the usual form of entries in these early lists, not a charter from Walter Byset of the lands of Stratherrick, but a charter belonging to Walter Byset by which he holds the lands of Stratherrick.

---

* Bower's Interpolation to Fordun.

† Thomas de Thirlstan had, by charter without date, granted the tithes of his mill of Thirlstane to the canons of Dryburgh (Reg. de Driburg, p. 87).

‡ Act. Parl. Scot., vol. i. Robertson's Index, preface, p. xxiv.

Whether Stratherrick then included Abertarff or not is uncertain; afterwards Stratherrick was styled a pertinent of the barony of Abertarff;* but the present charter and these entries prove that Walter Byset was about this time the proprietor of Stratherrick, and William Byset patron of the church of Abertarff.

In the grant of the church of Kiltarlity to the Leper House at Rathven, at the end of the list of witnesses, appears " W. Byset gyntallarty ;" † and it is suggested ‡ William Byset was parson of Kiltarlity, the parish created by his brother John, and the grant of which to Rathven he witnesses.

This is improbable, as there is another occasion on which his name appears as an ecclesiastic.§ It was an unusual circumstance then for a churchman to be himself the patron in his lay right of a parish and also the incumbent; and the form of grant of Abertarff clearly shows William Byset to have been the patron. The Bishop of Moray, in confirming his grant, styles him "nobilis vir." He with his brother John is a witness to a charter of King Alexander II. in 1225, while Abertarff was the property of Thomas de Thirlstan, and he and Walter Byset are witnesses in 1225 to another charter of King Alexander II. William is a witness to several royal charters; and the last occasion on which he appears is together with Walter Byset as witness to the grant by Robert Byset, Lord of Upsetlington, with the assent of Christiana, wife of Robert (whose consent implies that Upsetlington was her property) of the Hospital of St Leonard of Upsetlington to the monastery of Kelso.‖ This Robert is expressly called by Walter Byset of Aboyne, in Walter's obligation, to respect the rights of Kelso, "Robert my cousin."¶

We have thus the family of Byset in the year 1240 possessing the estates following: Walter is lord of Aboyne, and resided at Aboyne Castle, Aberdeenshire; his nephew, John, is lord of the Aird, and resided at either Lovat or

* Memoir for Hugh, Lord Lovat, p. 22.   † Reg. Moray, 72.
‡ O. S. P., vol. ii., p. 509.   § Willelmo Bisett persona, R.M., 333.
‖ Reg. de Kelso, p. 195.   ¶ Ib., p. 191.

Beaufort, Inverness-shire; another nephew, William, is patron of the church, and probable owner of the estate of Abertarff, in the same county; and Robert Byset, cousin of Walter Byset, is the lord of Upsetlington, in Berwickshire.

In the witnessing part of the charter John Byset our founder is called " Domino Johanne fratre meo ;" but it does not appear from any record that he was one of the barons of the kingdom. Before the Act 1427 no general rule can be laid down for distinguishing between one holder of a property directly from the Crown and another, and the expressions "nobilis vir" and "dominus," in the charters of subjects, at all events go for nothing in establishing any parliamentary dignity; the premier baron of Scotland claims no higher creation than 1436.

No. III.

CARTA ANDREÆ MORAVIENSIS EPISCOPI DE DECIMIS GARBARUM ET SALMONUM PAROCHIÆ DE ABERTARFF.

" Universis Sanctæ Matris Ecclesiæ filijs hoc scriptum visuris vel audituris, Andreas divinâ permissione Moraviensis Episcopus æternam in Domino Salutem. Noveritis universi, nos de consensu Capituli nostri dedisse, concessisse, et hac cartâ nostrâ confirmasse Deo et Beatæ Mariæ, et Beato Johanni Baptistæ, et Domui Belli loci juxta Beaufort, et fratribus ordinis Vallis Caulium ibidem Deo servientibus et servituris in perpetuum, omnes Decimas Garbarum provenientium infra Parochiam Ecclesiæ de Abertarf cum terrâ pertinente ad eandem Ecclesiam, et cum Decimâ Salmonum de omnibus piscarijs in prædictæ Ecclesiæ parochiâ existentibus, nomine simplicis Beneficii. Quam Ecclesiam nobilis vir Willielmus Byseth eisdem fratribus et sibi successuris dedit, et concessit, et cartâ suâ confirmavit, in puram et perpetuam Eleemosynam. Quare volumus et concedimus, quod prædicta domus de Bello loco, et fratres prædicti dictas decimas omnes Garbarum infra parochiam præfatæ Ecclesiæ provenientes, cum totâ terrâ ad eandem Ecclesiam pertinente, et cum Decima Salmonum de prædictis Piscarijs omnibus, in ipsa Parochia existentibus, habeant et possideant nomine simplicis beneficij, in puram et perpetuam Eleemosynam ad sustentationem eorum adeo libere, quiete, plenarie, et honorifice, sicut aliquod simplex beneficium in Diocœsi nostrâ, ab aliquo liberius, quietius, plenarius, et honorificentius habetur, tenetur, et possidetur. In hujus autem rei firmum et indubitabile testimonium huic Scripto appensum est Sigillum nostrum et Sigillum capituli nostri Subscriptionibus Canonicorum. Testibus Symone Decano Majore Magistro Ricardo Præcentore, Magistro Henrico Cancellario, Roberto Thesaurario, Magistris Willielmo et Andrea Canonicis Ecclesiæ Moraviensis Radulpho et Symone Capellanis Moraviensibus et alijs multis.

OF THE PRIORY OF BEAULY. 39

✠ Ego, ANDREAS, Episcopus Moraviensis, Com. de Fotherum, Subscribo.
✠ Ego, ARCHEBALDUS, Canonicus de Crom., Subscribo.
✠ Ego, RAN., Archidiaconus Moraviensis, Subscribo.
✠ Ego, PETRUS, Canonicus Moraviensis, Subscribo.
✠ Ego, RAD. HAY, Canonicus de . . . Subscribo.
✠ Ego, WILLIELMUS, Canonicus de Pett, Subscribo.
✠ Ego, SYMON, Decanus Moraviensis Ecclesiæ, Subscribo.
✠ Ego, RICARD., Præcento Ecclesiæ Moraviensis, Subscribo.
✠ Ego, HENRICUS, Cancellarius Moraviensis, Subscribo.
✠ Ego, ROBERTUS, Thesaurarius Moraviensis, Subscribo.
✠ Ego, ROBERTUS, Canonicus de Duppel, Subscribo.
✠ Ego, ANDREAS, Canonicus de Simm., Subscribo.
✠ Ego, WILLIELMUS, Canonicus de Dunbanne, Subscribo.
✠ Ego, LAMBERTUS, Moraviensis Ecclesiæ Subcentor, Subscribo.
✠ Ego, EDWARDUS, Canonicus de Muy, Subscribo."

This instrument is the confirmation in 1242 by Andrew, Bishop of Moray (within whose diocese or province the parish of Abertarff lay), of the grant of it by William Byset.

This confirmation had the effect of wholly appropriating the church of Abertarff and its possessions to the use of the priory; making the convent the perpetual rector, and not merely the patron, as if the grant of the church had been to a layman; such a grant required the confirmation of the Ordinary, the Crown, and the Pope, though in these early times the confirmation of the Ordinary assumed or inferred the other two.

The expressions by which the appropriation is effected are not the usual ones, that the convent should hold the church "ad proprios usus," but "ad sustentationem eorum." The same expression occurs in other charters of the period;[*] the bishop grants the church to be held "as a simple benefice," that is, free from the cure of souls and under no obligation beyond that expressed in the grant.[†]

[*] Chart. Dunfermline, fol. 23.
[†] "The canonists divided benefices into simple and mixed. The first sort lays no obligation but to read prayers, sing, etc.; such kind of beneficiaries are canons,

In this charter we have the first mention of Beaufort, and it is probable that John Byset, after he endowed the parish of Kiltarlity and introduced the foreign appellation of Beaulieu as the name of the priory which he founded, built the castle of Beaufort, and gave it a foreign name. Sir David Lyndsay speaks of the Bissarts of Beaufort, and we may assume that John Byset made this a place of residence instead of Lovat, while it evidently became of great consequence when it was inhabited by his descendants the Fentons of Beaufort. It must not, however, be thought that the castles of the time of Alexander II. in Scotland, or Henry III. in England, were anything in size, strength, or importance, like the Edwardian castles of Henry's son. In Henry III.'s time, in England there were 1153 castles,* and many of these had nothing but the great hall† built of stone; all the other buildings were of wood, surrounded by a wall, which would be quite a sufficient defence against all attacks except by a military force.

The confirmation expressly includes the tithes of grain (*Garbarum*, sheaves) grown in the parish of Abertarff, showing that the principle of tithes belonging to the parish priest was completely established; and also the tithes of salmon in all the fishings within the parish, showing that salmon were then frequent in the waters of Abertarff parish; that must have been, as Abertarff is at the upper end of Loch Ness, mostly in Loch Ness itself. The Statistical Account of 1842 says that some years before salmon was plentiful in Loch Ness, but that since the Caledonian Canal has been opened, they have very much decreased.

The practice seems not yet to have got into use of giving the tithe of fish to the vicar, or if this tithe was usually assigned to the vicar, the priory seems to have determined to reserve the tithe of salmon to themselves, as they get the bishop to specify

---

chaplains, chanters. The second is charged with the cure of souls, the guidance and direction of consciences, etc., such as rectories, vicarages, etc." (Hook's Church Dictionary, art. "Benefices").

* Coke, Second Institute, cap. 17.
† Hudson Turner, Domestic Architecture of England, vol. i., p. 59.

this as well as the great tithe or tithes of corn. When the vicar of Abertarff was first established is not clear; the provision for a toft and croft, secured by the bishop in 1225 from Thomas de Thirlstane,* was for the rector.

This act of confirmation by the bishop of the diocese was a very important step, as it deprived the minister of the parish of the tithes of the parish, and was derogatory of the rights of the parishioners; and the solemnities which accompany it are remarkable, and show that the bishop acted with the consent of his proper council, the chapter of the cathedral, although no property or rights of the cathedral were affected. Neither bishop nor chapter had any rights of property in the tithes and lands then belonging to the church of Abertarff. The confirmation is first said to be made with the consent of the chapter, and the seal of the chapter, as well as of the bishop, is annexed to it, with the signatures of the canons.

The chapter had been fully organised by Bishop Bricius. It had its five dignitaries: the dean, who in the bishop's absence presided over the chapter, and was the general president of the whole institution; the archdeacon, who was the *alter Episcopi oculus*, visited the diocese, and examined and presented to the bishop for approval the candidates for orders; the precentor, who had control of the cathedral services, and especially of those choral services which make up the full pomp and swell of the liturgies of a cathedral church; the chancellor, who probably acted as the chancellor of the diocese, the proper judge of the bishop's court, but was, as a member of the chapter, chancellor of the cathedral, whose office was to instruct the younger canons, and who was the secretary of the chapter, and the keeper of the chapter seal; and the treasurer, who had the special charge of the ornaments of the church. These dignitaries all consent. The bishop himself consents in his double capacity as canon of Fotheross, which, although assigned by Bricius to the chancellor, the bishop now held. The sub-chanter also joins, whose office it was to fill the important place of the precentor

* Reg. Moray, p. 20.

in his absence, so that the daily service of the choir might not be neglected. Besides the dignitaries, eight of the ordinary canons sign, some with the special addition of the parish, which had been appropriated as the prebend of their canonry, and some with the mere addition of canon of Moray.

Many of the instruments of Bishop Andrew, in the Register of Moray, are subscribed by the members of the chapter, and from a careful examination I am inclined to fix the date of this deed as 1242. Two chaplains of Moray (" Capellani Moravienses") are witnesses, but they do not subscribe as members of the chapter, and answer, I suspect, to the position of minor canons in our English cathedrals.

He who wishes to understand the constitution of the chapter of Elgin has only to pass from the ruins of its cathedral, with its ancient register in hand, to the cathedral city of Wells, to find the institutions of a chapter organised at the same time as that of Elgin, still kept up, with the exception that in the diocese of Wells, as afterwards in the province of Moray, the bishop has emancipated himself from the wholesome control of his capitular council.*

Symon, dean of the cathedral church, styles himself "Decanus Major," the greater dean, to distinguish himself from the deans of the four deaneries into which the diocese was divided, being the deanery of Elgin, the deanery of Inverness, the deanery of Strathbogy, and the deanery of Strathspey. These deans were called "Decani Christianitatis," or Deans Christian, and ecclesiastical courts were commonly called, and indeed are now in England called, Courts Christian. These Deans Christian were so called, says Bishop Kennet,† "because their chapters were courts of Christianity or ecclesiastical judicature, wherein they censured their offending brethren, and maintained the discipline of the Church within their own precincts." They afterwards were called rural deans,‡

---

* Freeman's Lectures on Wells, and Proceedings of Somerset Archæolog. Soc. 1873.
† Kennet's Parochial Antiquities, 234.
‡ " Decanus ruralis " is the title of Adam Gobinot in the Inquisition touching the chapel of Kilravock, A.D. 1343 (Family of Kilravock, p. 117).

but it is likely that at first the dean of the cathedral of Elgin was also the dean of the rural deanery of Elgin.

Before the date of our next charter, an important event occurred, which has strangely coloured the history of the family of Byset. It is the banishment of John Byset, the founder of Beauly Priory, with his uncle Walter, Lord of Aboyne. In 1242, Patrick, Earl of Athol, son of Thomas de Galloway, and nephew of Walter Byset's wife, was burnt after a tournament at Haddington.

Matthew Paris, writing about 1250, states that in 1242 Walter Byset at the tournament was worsted by the young Earl of Athol, and that Walter Byset contrived to burn the house in which the earl slept, and the earl with it. When this came, he adds, to the knowledge of Earl Patrick and other nobles, they attacked Walter, who fled for protection to the king. The king promised the nobles that Walter should be disinherited, and should abjure Scotland. Walter swore to proceed to the Holy Land, but went instead to the King of England, and, complaining that he had been unjustly deprived of his inheritance, urged that the King of Scotland, being the liege vassal of the King of England, could not, without his consent, disinherit or banish a nobleman from his country for ever, especially if he was not convicted of a crime. The King of England was incensed, but reserved his anger till a more suitable opportunity.

The Chronicle of Melrose, written not later than 1270, states that in 1242, John Byset, with Walter Byset and other accomplices, was outlawed, because report asserted that the said John, with the advice of the said Walter,* had delivered Patrick of Athol to death. It also records that in 1244, the most wicked traitor,† Walter Byset, with his accomplices, de-

* Mr Stevenson, in his edition of the Chronicle for the Bannatyne Club, inserts *dicti Willielmi;* but I have been informed since writing the text, that in the MS. from which the Bannatyne edition is printed it is " W.," that is, Walteri.

† This expression, "nefandissimus proditor," is used by John of Peterborough, and the use of it serves to show that John wrote after the Chronicle of Melrose was compiled, and clears up the question as to whether this John was John de Calceto, who was abbot 1250-62, or John Deeping, who was abbot in 1410-39

sisted not from pouring the poison of discord into the ears of Henry, King of England, until he advanced to Newcastle with an army against the King of Scotland, when the treaty of Ponteland was made, 24th August 1244.

Now, upon this subject, Fordun is often quoted, but Fordun's Scotichronicon contains nothing about it. Fordun mentions the treaty made at Ponteland, and the account that is quoted as Fordun's is that of his commentator, Bower, who did not write till 1441. About that time Wynton compiled his Chronicle. He states that William Byset was Lord of Aboyne, and that John Byset and Walter Byset were his brothers; whereas William Byset does not appear in contemporary documents after 1240, and we know that Walter Byset was the Lord of Aboyne.

Matthew Paris, in his English History, which is a repetition of the Chronicle in which this story of Walter Byset appears, does not repeat it; but still there it is, apparently in his original manuscript, written within six or seven years of the event.

The histories of Bower and Wynton allege that the estates of the Bysets were all forfeited, and the whole family banished the kingdom, and this has been improved upon by later Scottish historians, till Mr Burton disposes of the matter thus: " A strong feeling set against the Bysets. Their estates had to be forfeited, and the head of the house escaped alive with great difficulty. The family afterwards pushed their fortunes, with the other Norman houses in Ireland, and their Highland estates went to the Frizelles or Frasers, who founded an influence which became troublesome to the Government five hundred years afterwards."* Seeing that the Frasers did not get possession of any portion of the Bysets' Highland estates till 125 years after 1242, and then only of a third of those estates, two-thirds of which were acquired by the Fentons and

—"a mystery," Sir Thomas Hardy writes, " I am not able to solve" (Catalogue of MSS. for Early English History, vol. iii., p. 216); for the Chronicle was no closed till 1270, when John de Caleto was dead.
* Burton's History of Scotland, vol. ii., p. 89.

the Chisholms, the former by the peaceful act of marrying a Byset lady, this is strongly expressed. The only fact certain in relation to this matter is that Patrick, Earl of Athol, was burnt in 1242, and that King Alexander II. assisted Walter and John Byset in leaving Scotland, where a strong party accused them of the murder.

Matthew Paris mentions among the anti-Byset party Patrick, Earl of Dunbar; and Bower names David de Hastings, who became Earl of Athol in right of his wife on the death of Patrick of Athol.

It is difficult to see any motive for the commission by Walter Byset of so horrible a crime. His wife was aunt of the young earl, but he was not in any way in the line of succession, while the young earl had two sisters married; nor does it appear that Walter Byset had any children by his wife: his nephew, we shall see was his heir. But it is not improbable that Walter was likely to make himself disagreeable to David de Hastings on his succession to the earldom.

Bower says that after the Provincial Council held at Perth in 1242, the king, retiring with his barons, and separating himself and them from the clergy, all the earls complained to him of the burning of the Earl of Athol.*

We get more light on the exile of John and Walter Byset from the English records. Henry III. became King of England in 1216, when he was nine years of age. His sister Joan married Alexander II. in 1221. He, in January 1236, married the daughter of the Count of Provence, and mixed himself much in French affairs. Claiming the recovery of Normandy, he declared war against Louis IX. in 1242, and that year went to France and passed the winter at Bordeaux. There, in December 1242, he was in want of soldiers, and must have heard with pleasure of the banishment from Scotland of John and Walter Byset. With his queen was Margaret Byset, now advanced in years, and who had lost this year her cousin, John Byset of Wiltshire, Chief Forester of England.

* Ford. Scotichron., ed. Goodall, lib. ix., cap. 59.

In 1224 and 1226, after the connection between the Scottish and English courts was established, and while Hubert de Burgh, brother-in-law of Alexander II., was still the supreme minister of Henry, the Close Rolls tell us that gifts were made from the Royal Treasury to Walter Byset, so that Walter was well known to the English king.

John Byset went, in 1242, from Scotland to Ireland, and there met with Sir James de Savill, a knight in the service of the Justiciary of Ireland, who suggested to John that he should serve the King of England in his wars in Guienne, upon the terms that he should obtain the grant of a knight's fee in Ireland. To this Byset agreed, and the king, on 17th December 1242, at Bordeaux, confirmed it by directing a writ* to the Justiciary of Ireland, ordering him to give a knight's fee to Byset if he would go to parts beyond the sea in the royal service.

This was done, and we have the extent of the knight's fee, shown by a verdict of a jury in the following reign. It included the island of Rachrin or Rathlin, on the coast of Antrim, destined afterwards to become famous as the retreat of Robert the Bruce, and from being illustrated by the poetry of Scott. I suppose John went to Bordeaux, where Margaret Byset died that winter, and where the king remained.

In August 1243,† King Henry granted to Walter Byset the manor of Lowdham, in Nottinghamshire, adjoining the manor of East Bridgeford, the property of the English Bysets. The object of the grant was to maintain Walter in the service of the king as long as the king pleased. In the following year, Henry, having returned from France, declared war against Scotland, and advanced in the summer with an army to Newcastle. The Chronicle of Melrose informs us this was at the instigation of Walter Byset, who, probably, as well as John, accompanied the king.

The leading families of the two nations were so connected by marriage and blood, that it was not difficult for those who loved peace to arrange the treaty which was made at

* Pat. and Chart., 27 Hen. III., p. 739.   † Ib., m. 4.

Ponteland in 1244; and not only was it confirmed by the King of Scotland's charter (which is printed in Rymer), but also by the Pope's Bull, obtained on a letter from the earls and barons of Scotland.* This letter is given by Matthew Paris (1244); it has, after the great earls of Scotland, the names of Duncan of Argyle, the founder of Ardchattan, and of John Byset the younger.

It would seem, therefore, that John Byset, founder of Beauly Priory, on his being compelled to foreign exile, made over his barony of the Aird, with his other estates adjoining, to his son, John Byset the younger; and the John Byset whom we shall find acting as Lord of Lovat in 1258 was this John Byset the younger. John Byset the elder, with Walter, returned to Ireland, and came from Ireland in October 1244, to the king in Wales; and afterwards Walter Byset received two of the king's shields from Windsor Castle armoury, to go into the king's service in Ireland.

It is said by Bower,† that Alan, illegitimate son of Thomas of Galloway, and the natural half-brother of Patrick, the earl who was burnt, landed and burnt a certain small house belonging to John Byset, called Viteris, to revenge his brother's death. It is certain that in 1252, this Alan obtained pardon from King Henry of his offence in having killed a follower of John Byset in Ireland, in a conflict which took place between him and John Byset.‡

Walter Byset obtained, in December 1246, a grant § from Henry III. of Lowdham, to himself and his heirs, until Walter or his heirs should recover his lands in Scotland. The adjoining manor of East Bridgeford seems at this time to have been held by William Le Grant, who had married Alfreda Byset, one of the heiresses of Henry Byset.|| Walter Byset returned to Scotland, and witnesses a grant of King Alexander II. in 1248,¶ and a deed by Gregory de Melville in 1251;** in 1252

---

* Fœdera, vol. i., p. 428.   † Bower, Continuation of Fordun, b. ix., c. 62.
‡ Patent Rolls, 36 Hen. III., m. 12.   § Chart. 31 Hen. III., m. 13.
|| Thoroton's Nottinghamshire, ed. 1677, p. 149.
¶ Chart. Dunfermline, p. 44.   ** *Ib.*, p. 93.

he died in the island of Arran,* leaving Thomas, his nephew, his heir,† who was, in 1256, a knight,‡ and may have been the son of William Byset.

We shall see that practically no forfeiture of any of the Byset estates took place—Aboyne was restored, of the Aird and Upsetlington they had never been deprived, and though the remarkable family group of Bysets which surrounded Alexander II. does not seem to have reappeared, yet we shall see that the truth lies with Mr Chalmers, in his " Caledonia,"§ who says that, notwithstanding the check occasioned by the accusation against John and Walter, the Bysets still continued a family of importance.

* The Inquisition says Arran in Scotland, but, in fact, until 1266, Arran belonged to the King of Norway, and was held under him, in 1250, by Reginald, son of Somerled, which Reginald then called himself King of the Isles.

† Coll. Genealog. Inq. post mort, 36 Hen. III.

‡ Reg. Arb., p. 228. § Vol. ii., p. 548.

No. IV.

CARTA LAURENTII MILITIS, FILIJ PATRICIJ JANITORIS DE INNERNES PRIORI DE BELLO LOCO.

Ex Autographo [1255].

"Omnibus has litteras visuris vel audituris Laurentius miles filius Patricij Janitoris de Innernes, salutem. Noveritis me quietum clamasse de me et heretibus meis in perpetuum pro salute animæ meæ et antecessorum meorum totvm jus quod habui vel habere potui in Bromihalu, et in Insula, Deo et Beatæ Mariæ et Sancto Johanni Baptistæ de Bello loco, et Priori et Monachis ibidem Deo servientibus et servituris. Ita quod de cætero nec ego nec hæredes mei aliquod jus vel clamium in dictis terris vindicare possimus. In cujus rei testimonium huic scripto Sigillum meum apposui his testibus, Magistro R. de Eginton Præcentore Rossensi, Domino R. Cancellario Rossensi, Domino Johanne Vicario de Innernis, Domino Willielmo Roher, David de Giulan, Gilberto Senescallo, et alijs. Datum apud Rosmari die Jovis proxima post festum Exaltationis Sanctæ Crucis—Anno Gratiæ millesimo ducentesimo quinquagesimo quinto."

By this charter, Laurentius, knight, son of Patrick, the Porter of Inverness, in the year 1255, releases all right he had in Bromihalu and the island to God and the Blessed Mary, and the Blessed John Baptist of Beauly, and to the prior and monks serving and to serve God there.

Inverness was at this time a king's castle, and the Porter of the Castle, the Portman or Durward, was one of its most important officials. He had attached to his office, lands and privileges; and it was, in the case of a royal castle, an hereditary office, which might be possessed by females. The portership of the castle of Montrose was hereditary.

To the charter of John Byset to the Bishop of Ross, 1225, Patrick the porter is a witness.

What Bromihalu means I am unable to say; but the suggestion of the editor of the "Origines Parochiales Scotiæ," that "Insula" means the island of Aigas in Strathglass, is inadmissible. Strathglass and Skye were given to Hugh, son and heir of William, Earl of Ross, by King Robert the Bruce.* Hugh de Ross married Mauld, the king's sister, between 1308 and 1309, and succeeded his father, William, Earl of Ross, in 1323; William dying at Delny that year. This Hugh, Earl of Ross, was killed at Halidon Hill on St Magdalene's Day, 1333, having apparently that same year granted to his second son, Hugh Ross, the lands of Philorth, in Aberdeenshire, and the lands of Balnagoun, in Kilmuir, Ross-shire.† Between 1362 and 1372, Hugh, Lord of Philorth and Balnagoun, acquired, by exchange for lands in Buchan with his brother William, Earl of Ross, the lands of Ergyle, which means of North Argyle or Wester Ross and Strathglass, with the castle of Ellandonan.‡ This Hugh of Ross died without issue, and William, Earl of Ross, his brother, reacquired his lands; on William's death, Philorth and Strathglass went with his second daughter, Johanna, to a Fraser, who became Lord of Philorth. When, in 1423, William Forbes of Kinaldie married Agnes, daughter of Fraser of Philorth, the barony of Pitsligo was granted to Agnes and her heirs, and with this was granted Strathglass. In 1455 the barony of Pitsligo included Strathglass; of Strathglass Isobell Wemyss, Lady of Pitsligo, released her terce to her son, John Forbes of Pitsligo, in 1524; and he, in 1536, sold the lands of Easter and Wester Aigas, with the island of Aigas, to Hugh Fraser, Lord Lovat, so that Aigas was never a part of the possessions of the Priory of Beauly.

The *Island* is doubtless that island of Achinbady, spoken of by the writer in the MS. of 1728, which we have already quoted as stating that the monastery was erected in the

* Rob. Index, p. 2, Nos. 56, 60; p. 16, No. 7.   Reg. Moray, p. 342.
† O. S. P. Ross, vol. ii., p. 461.   ‡ *Ib.*, p. 391.

island of Achinbady. There is not now, and there does not seem ever to have been, an island, in the modern sense of the term, at Beauly. But the word island is often in early times used to denote what we now call a peninsula—a tract of land almost surrounded by water; thus the Isle of Ely and Isle of Thanet, in the east of England, are not, and never were, islands; nor is the Black Isle in Ross-shire—they are all peninsulas. The fourth side of these islands, which fourth side is now firm land, may have been in early times a marsh, thus giving the peninsula in effect the character of an island.

At the time of building Beauly Priory, the land on which it stands had the river on its south side, two small streams on the east and west, and land which was probably bog or marsh on the north. It may be traced by a careful examination of the environs of the priory; the surrounding water made the island a place capable of being easily strengthened against a raid of the neighbours. The castle of Lovat was built in a low situation, where a moat could easily be made; and in selecting this island-spot for his priory, John Byset and his advisers followed the example of earlier founders of monasteries. Westminster Abbey—the most glorious foundation in England—was placed by Edward the Confessor on Thorney Island, a peninsula formed by small streams flowing into the Thames and marshes communicating with that river.

The charter of Laurence the Knight is dated at Rosemarkie, and is witnessed, first, by the precentor of Ross, and next by the chancellor of Ross. In 1255 the Pope* confirmed the arrangement of the Bishop of Ross, by which all the tithes of corn of the parishes of Kinnettes and Suddy were given to the precentor or chancellor of Ross; but at the dissolution† we find these two churches belonging to the chancellor, and not the precentor of Ross. No gift of any church to the chancellor is contained in the same Bull. At the dissolution the churches of Kilchrist or Tarradale and of Kilmorack be-

---

* Theiner. Mon. Hib. et Scot., p. 69.
† House of Lords Appeal Cases, vol. x., p. 637 (1814).

longed to the precentor of Ross; and I suspect that before 1255, the year of this charter and Bull, the church of Kilmorack, within which parish the Priory of Beauly stands, had been appropriated to the chancellor, and was exchanged by him with the precentor of Ross.

The vicar of Inverness is also a witness to the charter of Laurence. The vicarage had been ordained only seven years before. William the Lion, making Inverness a royal burgh, assumed to be entitled to the proprietorship of the church; and about 1189 granted it, with its chapels, lands, and tithes to the monastery of St Thomas à Becket, at Arbroath. Ratified by two bishops and the chapter of Moray and the Pope,* the liberty given to Arbroath to appoint chaplains for Inverness seems not to have been exercised so as fully to provide for the town; and in 1248† a vicar was appointed, who was to have a house near the church where he might fitly entertain the bishop and the abbot of Arbroath when they should visit Inverness, and this vicar was to cause the church of Inverness and its chapels to be properly served. The endowment was small for so considerable a charge, but the altarages and other fees received at the chapels for the many offices of the pre-Reformation Church rendered a small endowment sufficient for the chaplains.

Before passing to the next charter, we had better refer to a transaction in 1258 of John Byset, son of the founder —John Byset the younger of 1244. He appears to have been remiss in providing that stone of wax for the cathedral of Elgin which his father had originally agreed to give the cathedral of Ross, and which had been handed over, somewhat without reference to the giver, by the Bishop of Ross to the Bishop of Moray. The bishop also appears to have claimed not only the tithe of the can of the lands of the Aird held by John Byset—the tithe of the can of all the king's lands in Moray having been granted by William the Lion to the church of the bishop in 1171-84—but also the can itself.‡

* Registrum de Aberbrothock, pp. 24, 140, 141.
† Ib., p. 190.   ‡ Reg. Moray, pp. 133, 134.

The bishop also claimed a davoch of the church land of Conveth, and a davoch in Ross, called Erchless, which John Byset claimed as belonging to his fee of the Aird by hereditary right. The controversy was settled by the bishop surrendering his claims, which seem after the transactions that had taken place to have been unfounded, except the claim to the stone of wax; and taking in lieu of them a rent charge of 60 shillings, or three pounds' weight of silver, payable out of the lands of Wester Moniack.

It would seem from no mention being made of the connection of the church of Conveth with the Priory of Beauly that it had not yet been appropriated to the priory. We shall see hereafter that it was part of their possessions, and it is probable that the deed of arrangement of 1258 was made to enable John Byset the younger to give it to the priory. By 1275 it must have been appropriated, as it then had a vicar,[*] the tenth of whose stipend was 9s. 4d., so that between these intervals the rectory was granted to some religious body, and probably to Beauly Priory, whose possession it afterwards was. John Byset is in this instrument of 1258 no longer called the younger as in 1244, and holds his property by descent and not, as John Byset the founder did, by grant from the Crown. John, founder of Beauly, had died in Ireland, leaving Agatha, his widow, by whom he seems to have had a second family, who formed the clan Eoin, or Bysets of the Glens of Antrim.

Among the witnesses to the instrument are Dominus Laurentius et Robertus dicti Grant; and looking at the fact that William le Grant not long before had the Byset manor of East Bridgeford by marriage with the heiress, and that this is the first mention of the name in any Scottish record or document, we may suppose that the Grants were brought to Scotland from England by John and Walter Byset on their return from the exile of 1242. Another witness is Robert Byset, probably the lord of Upsetlington.

The time of the death of John Byset the son, is accurately fixed by the inquisition of a jury in Ireland in 6 Edward I.

[*] Theiner. Mon. Hib. et Scot., p. 111.

(1278), who find that he died nineteen years before that date, or in 1259, and that he had before his death given dower to the Lady Agatha, his stepmother, and left three daughters his co-heiresses,—Cecilia, the wife of William de Fenton; Elizabeth, the wife of Andrew de Boscho; and Muriel, the wife of David de Graham. They must have been all married before 1268. Being heiresses, they probably married young. Their history is detailed in the charters.

In the Chamberlain Accounts, vol. i., p. 31, which range from 1263 to 1266, the Chamberlain accounts for four merks as the tenth of the Bishop of Moray of the fine imposed on the wife of John Byset. She was probably widow of John Byset the younger.

Among the records of Scotland delivered by King Edward I. to John Baliol in 1292 was a letter of William de Fenton, Andrew de Boscho, and David de Graham, acknowledging that they had received from William Wyseard, Archdeacon of St Andrews, chancellor of the king, those charters which the late John Byset [filius* h . . militis junioris] had deposited in the Abbey of Jedburgh. As William Wyseard or Wishart ceased to be Archdeacon of St Andrews in 1268,† this transaction must have taken place before that year. The blank here preceding the words "militis junioris," when taken in connection with the epithet John Byset the younger, in the letter of confirmation of the Treaty of Ponteland in 1244, must be filled by the words "John Byset;" and the entry seems to establish that the deeds were deposited by John Byset, a son of John Byset the younger; that on his death in 1259 John Byset the younger must have left a son and three daughters, and that the son died without issue, leaving the daughters co-heiresses of his father and himself; so that there were three John Bysets.

If Forsyth's‡ account of the earliest writ to the family of Grant is correct, the third John Byset was witness to this writ,

---

* Act. Parl. Scot., vol. i., App. 18, pref., p. 17. There is no *h* now in the original which is zincographed by H. M. Treasury.

† Crawford's Officers of State, p. 15. ‡ Forsyth's Moray, p. 20.

which was a grant to Robert le Grant about 1268 from John Prat, knight. If Chalmers * is correct, that Gregory le Grant married Mary, daughter of Byset of Lovat, she must have been the daughter of the first John Byset, founder of Beauly Priory.

Gregory le Grant was sheriff of Inverness in 1263,† and the Grants certainly appear about 1345 to be in possession of Stratherrick, when they succeeded the Bysets; and looking at the circumstances of their introduction into the North, it is probable they obtained the lands of Stratherrick in marriage with a Byset.

* Caledonia, vol. i., p. 596. † Chamberlain Accounts, vol. i., p. 21.

No. V.

CARTA MAGISTRI HENRICI DE TOTTYNGHAM PRIORI DE BELLO LOCO.

Ex Autographo 1274.

Magister Henricus de Tottyngham erat Rector Ecclesiæ de Taruodal.

" Sciant præsentes et futuri hoc scriptum visuri vel audituri, quod cum mota esset controversia inter Priorem et Conventum Monasterii de Bello loco ex una parte, et Magistrum Henricum de Tottyngham Rectorem Ecclesiæ de Taruedal ex altera, sub omnibus querelis, petitionibus, controversijs, injurijs, et dampnis inter eos datis et habitis; tandem de consensu partium concorditer compromiserunt in venerabilem virum Archibaldum Archidiaconum Moraviensem Dei gratia tunc electum Kattanensem et Magistrum Radulphum dictum Reny Subdecanum Moraviensem, et Magistrum Thomam de Boch Canonicum ejusdem Ecclesiæ et fideliter consenserunt in eosdem fide data, in manibus prædicti Domini tunc electi, quod dictorum compromissariorum arbitrio starent de præmissis omnibus et singulis sub pœna centum Marcarum solvendarum parti nolenti a prædictorum arbitrio resilire. Ad quam pœnam si fuerint, quod absit, commissa, solvendam obligaverunt seipsos hinc inde, et omnia bona sua, mundana et Ecclesiastica, mobilia et immobilia, subjicientes se jurisdictioni Domini Archibaldi Archidiaconi Moraviensis Dei gratia tunc electi Kattanensis, quo de plano et sine strepitu judiciali per sententiam excommunicationis posset partem volentem resilire a prædicto arbitrio, compellere, sicut prædictum est, ad pœnam supradictam solvendam. Renunciaverunt in super hinc inde litibus, processibus habitis et habendis, appellationibus interpositis et interponendis, coram quibuscunque Judicibus, nec non et litteris impetratis et impetrandis, super præmissis omnibus et singulis ab ordinario, seu delegatis Judicibus, seu ad ordinarios vel delegatos Judices. Renunciaverunt et privilegio cruce signatorum, et regiæ prohibitioni et constitutioni de duabus dictis, et omni Juris remedio tam Civilis quam Canonici. Tandem partibus præsentibus die Jovis infra octav. Epiphaniæ anno gratiæ Millesimo ducentesimo septuagesimo quarto in Ecclesia Cathedrali de Elgyn, habito prudentium virorum consilio, quorum nomina inferius sunt expressa, dicti Arbitri in hunc modum sunt Arbitrati, viz., quod partes prænominatæ, omnibus querelis, petitionibus, controversiis, injurijs et dampnis omnibus et singulis renunciaverunt et dicti Prior et Conventus haberent libere omnes decimas totius terræ suæ pertinentes ad ecclesiam de Taruedal, usque ad terminum octo annorum plenarie completorum : termino incipienti ad Pentecosten anno gratiæ milesimo ducentesimo septuagesimo quinto : Et quod dicti Prior et Conventus recipiant annuatim suis proprijs costis et expensis infra dictos octo annos, in quolibet anno, per dimidium annum dictum Magistrum Henricum cum duobus equis et duobus garcionibus, et quod dictus Magister Henricus fidele patrocinium cum expensis eorundem præstaret et similiter serviet fideliter eisdem Priori et conventui quotiescunque servitio ipsius indiguerint, usque ad terminum octo annorum plenarie completorum. In cujus rei firmum testimonium huic scripto sigilla dictorum arbitrorum sunt apposita hijs testibus Domino Willielmo Decano Moraviensi, Domino Waltero Sureys Officiali Moraviensi, Domino Roberto vicario de Duffhus, Domino Willielmo Priore de Pluscardyn, et Domino Roberto de Bosyll commonacho suo et multis alijs."

Not.—There are three Tags appended to the charter; to the middle one only is affixed a seal.

This charter explains and illustrates the note already printed from the transcript of the Wardlaw MS.

The MS. stated that in 1235 Gillichrist a Rosse gave and confirmed the Half Davoch Lands of Tarradale to the monks of Beauly. The monks retained the lands of Tarradale, at least that portion which is now called Kilchrist, to the dissolution; this was in the parish of Tarradale, of which there seems to have been a chaplain rector in 1240.[*]

It appears that a controversy had arisen between the Prior of Beauly and Master Henry of Tottingham or Nottingham,

[*] Reg. Moray, p. 275.

rector of the church of Tarradale, respecting the lands of the priory in Tarradale, which, by the judgment of Archibald, Archdeacon of Moray, and then bishop-elect of Caithness, and others, was settled in the cathedral church of Elgin on Thursday within the octave of the Feast of the Epiphany 1274, as follows: that the prior and convent should have free of rent the tithes which belonged to the church of Tarradale, and which arose from their lands, and this for eight years from Whitsunday 1275; that during that time the prior would entertain at his own cost the said Master Henry, with two horses and two grooms, for the half of each year; and that during the same period Master Henry should protect and faithfully serve the prior and convent as often as required.

I suspect the name was Nottingham, and that this Henry was the Henry de Nottingham who was a canon of Caithness in 1272.* If so, he was bound to reside at Dornoch for three months in the year at least by the constitution of that cathedral ;† he was also, by the ordinary law, obliged to reside six months in his parish. Probably there was no house of residence at Tarradale, so that his six months' residence on his living was arranged by his residing within the limits of the priory, by this time a commodious edifice.

The charter is witnessed by Dominus William, Dean of Moray; Dominus Walter Sureys, the official of Moray; Dominus Robert, vicar of Duffus; Dominus William, Prior of Pluscardine; and Robert of Bosyll, his fellow monk.

Magister [Master] signifies that the ecclesiastic who bore this prefix was a Master of Arts of a university; Dominus was used to signify an ecclesiastic who was either not a graduate, or only a Bachelor of Arts, and it was afterwards commonly translated into Sir.‡ Sir Hugh Evans, in Shakespeare's "Merry Wives of Windsor," was a priest. The host says, "Shall I lose my parson—my priest—my Sir Hugh?"

The release entered into is from all claims, suits, actions, and

* Liber Eccles. de Scon., p. 85.   † O. S. P. Dornoch, p. 602.
‡ Fuller's Church History; Nash, Worcestershire, vol. ii., p. 23 (N.); Kennett's Parochial Antiquities, p. 684.

OF THE PRIORY OF BEAULY.

appeals; and renounces for each party, among other things, the privilege of crusaders—" cruce signatorum"—who were allowed special exemptions from prosecutions and suits.*

The rector of Tarradale was entitled to tithes from the Priory lands, for there is no privilege of exemption from tithes mentioned in the Bull of the Pope to Beauly. Even if the Valliscaulian order were entitled to the privileges of the Cistercian order as to tithes, without the exemption being mentioned in the Pope's Bull, the Priory of Beauly would not be free. The Cistercian order was exempted from paying tithes of lands which were cultivated by the hands of the monks, or at their expense.† But by the Lateran Council, at which William Malvoisin assisted, in 1215, it was provided the exemption should extend only to the lands then in possession of the order. Of course, as the Beauly lands were acquired, and the priory founded, after 1215, the ordinary exemption could not apply. It would not, however, be necessary to mention an exemption for lands called *novalia*, those which should, after they had been acquired by the monks, be brought into cultivation by the monks, and cultivated by them, and at their expense.

* See Robertson's History of Charles V., note xiii.
† Connell on Tithes, vol. ii., p. 333.

No. VI.

CARTA DAVID DE INNERLUNAN DE TERRA DE AUCHTERWADDALLE SEU ONACHTERWADALE EX DONO GILLECHRIST MACGILLEDUFFI FRATRIBUS DE BELLO LOCO.

Ex Autographo [c. 1275].

"Omnibus hoc scriptum visuris vel audituris David de Innerlunan æternam in Domino Salutem. Sciant præsentes et futuri me ex consensu et voluntate Gillicrist Macgilliduffi concessisse et quietum clamasse Deo et Beatæ Mariæ et B. Johanni Baptistæ et Fratribus Belli loci ordinis Vallis Caulium ibidem Deo servientibus et in perpetuum servituris, totam terram meam de Ouchterwaddale quæ est dimidia Davata terræ, quam scilicet terram habui et tenui ad Feodifirmam de prædicto Gillicrist. Tenendam et habendam dictis fratribus et eorum successoribus cum omnibus pertinentijs et aysiamentis ad dictam terram spectantibus. Quare volo et concedo et quietum clamo dictam terram de Onachterwaddale de me et hæredibus meis dictis fratribus et eorum successoribus ut ipsi dictam terram habeant teneant et pacifice possideant adeo libere quiete, plenarie et honorifice sicut illam terram habent ex dono prædicti Gillicrist, prout Carta ejusdem eis inde confecta plenius testatur. Volo insuper et concedo, quod si aliqua Scripta vel instrumenta de prædicta terra de Onachterwedalle confecta a me, vel quocunque hæredum meorum sive assignatorum aliquo tempore fuerint reperta, quæ prædictæ quietæ Clamationi meæ in aliquo poterint eludere, vel prædictis fratribus in prædicta terra in aliquo nocere, irrita sint et quassata, mihi et hæredibus meis sive assignatis nullo tempore valitura: Et ut hæc mea Concessio et quieta clamatio rata sit et stabilis, præsenti scripto, una cum sigillo meo non satis cognito, appensum est sigillum nobilis viri Domini Walteri de Moravia.

Testibus Domino Andrea de Moravia, Willielmo Comite Sutirland, Alano fratre dicti Domini Andreæ, Isaac Macgillendres, Johanne filio Cristini, Duncano Duff, Bochly Beg, et alijs."

It is not improbable that the good offices of Henry de Nottingham procured for the monks this charter. It is by David de Innerlunan, who, because his seal is not sufficiently known, uses the seal of Walter de Moray. Andrew de Moray, William, Earl of Sutherland, and Alan, the brother of the said Andrew de Moray, are witnesses.

William, Earl of Sutherland, in 1275, by the advice of certain prelates and noblemen, grants* to Archibald, Bishop of Caithness (the bishop-elect of the last charter), the Castle of Skibo; and to this grant the seals of the earl, William de Monte Alto, Sir Andrew of Moray, Sir Alexander of Moray, and Sir David of Innerlunan, were appended. Innerlunan was a barony in the sheriffdom of Forfar. The witnesses seem to fix the date of the one charter of David de Innerlunan at the same period as this charter of William, Earl of Sutherland, William de Monte Alto, Andrew de Moray, and David de Innerlunan, being parties to both deeds. David de Innerlunan, by this charter, declares that by the consent and will of Gillicrist Macgilliduffi, he granted and confirmed to God and the Blessed Mary and the Blessed John Baptist, and the brethren of Beauly of the Valliscaulian order, then serving and for ever to serve God there, all his land of Ouchter-Tarradale, which is a half davoch of land which he holds at fee-farm of the said Gillicrist, and which they are to hold, as they have that land from the gift of the said Gillicrist, as by Gillicrist's charter made to them thereon is more fully testified; and David declares that if any charter should be found by him or his heirs contrary to this quitclaim, it should be void and of none effect.

Who was this Gillicrist? Although the grant is said *to be by his consent*, this expression is explained afterwards, I think, by reference to the charter of Gillicrist. That charter may

* Bannalyne Miscellany, vol. iii., p. 24.

be the one referred to by the Wardlaw MS., as granted of the Half Davoch Lands of Tarradale by Gillicrist a Rosse in 1235; but whether the name or date is accurate as given by the Wardlaw MS. is doubtful.

David de Innerlunan was, as we have said, of Lunan or Innerlunan in Forfar, and held his barony there of the earldom of Angus. Gilchrist, the son of Gillibride, was Earl of Angus in 1207.* This small outlying portion of land in Tarradale, on the break up of the old holders of Ross-shire lands by William the Lion, may have been granted to the Earls of Angus, and feued out by them with the lands of Innerlunan, to David de Innerlunan; and the Gilchrist Macgilliduffi of this charter belonged perhaps to the Angus family.

* Lib. de Aberbrothock, p. 33.

No. VII.

CARTA ANDREÆ DE BOSCHO DOMINI DE EDIRDOR FACTA FRATRIBUS DE BELLO LOCO ORDINIS VALLIS CAULIUM ANNO 1278.

Ex Autographo.

"Omnibus Christi fidelibus hoc scriptum visuris vel audituris Andreas de Boscho et Elizabetha sponsa sua salutem. Sciant præsentes et futuri nos pro salute animarum nostrarum, et pro salute animarum Antecessorum et Successorum nostrorum, dedisse, concessisse, et hac præsenti carta nostra confirmasse, Deo et Beatæ Mariæ et B. Johanni Baptistæ et Domui Belli loci et fratribus ordinis Vallis Caulium ibidem Deo servientibus et servituris in perpetuum, in liberam puram et perpetuam Eleemosynam, duas Marcas Annuas recipiendas, singulis annis, apud Castrum Nostrum de Eddyrdor a nobis et ab hæredibus nostris, vel a Ballivis nostris, quicunque ibidem fuerunt pro tempore, vel in tenemento nostro de Eddir-dor, ad duos terminos anni, medietatem scilicet ad Pentecosten, et aliam medietatem ad festum sancti Martini in Hyeme, Tenendas et habendas dictæ domui et dictis fratribus a nobis et hæredibus nostris, libere, quiete, plenarie et honorifice in perpetuum, in liberam, puram et perpetuam Eleemosynam. Renunciamus etiam pro nobis et omnibus hæredibus nostris, omnibus litteris impetratis et impetrandis tam Papalibus quam Regalibus, et Regiæ prohibitioni et Constitutioni de duabus Diætis et omni etiam juris remedio tam Civilis quam Canonici quæ huic donationi in aliquo possint obviare vel resistere, aut dictæ domui vel dictis fratribus Super dicta Donatione nostra in aliquo valeant nocere; nos vero dictus Andreas et Elizabeth sponsa mea et hæredes nostri Dictas duas marcas annuas prædictæ domui et prædictis fratribus in perpetuum contra omnes homines et fæminas warrantisabimus, acquietabimus et defendemus—In cujus rei testimonium præsenti Scripto sigilla nostra fecimus apponi hijs testibus

Domino Roberto Dei Gratia Episcopo Rossensi, Domino Johanne Decano Rossensi,. Domino Duncano Cancellario Rossensi, Domino Willielmo Succentore Rossensi, Willielmo Comite de Ross, Domino Willielmo de Haya, Willielmo Vicario de Eddyr-dor, Johanne filio Christini MacGillo, Isaac Mac-gillendris, Stephano filio Galfridi Molenctinarij, Colino Gove tunc Constabulario de Taruedal, Roberto de Rolloc, et multis alijs. Datum apud Eddyrdor die Veneris proxima post festum Exaltationis Sanctæ Crucis Anno Gratiæ Millesimo ducentesimo septuagesimo octavo."

Not.—A tag parchment; no seal.

This charter is by Andrew de Bosco and Elizabeth his wife, which Elizabeth was the grand-daughter of the founder of the priory. They dwelt at Redcastle—the Castle of Eddy-r-dor, one, as we have seen, of the two castles built by William the Lion in 1179 to overpower the district of Ross proper.

And as Elizabeth joins her husband in the grant payable by them and their heirs at their castle of Eddy-r-dor, this castle must have formed part of the possessions of John Byset, her father, to which she and her sisters, Muriel de Graham and Cecilia de Fenton, succeeded in 1259.

By this charter, which is dated the Friday after the Exaltation of the Cross [14th December] 1278, two marks a year, payable one half at Whitsunday and the other half at the feast of St Martin in winter, are granted to the monks of Beauly.

Thus early in Scotland was established the custom of making the terms of half-yearly payments at Whitsunday and Martinmas, a custom which prevailed throughout the counties of Northumberland and Cumberland, but did not extend to the southern parts of England, where the terms were Lady Day and Michaelmas Day. The origin of the difference was doubtless the later period of harvest in the north of the island, which made the periods of payment of agricultural rents later, and these later periods were adopted for other annual payments.

Two marks were two-thirds of a pound, the pound then

being a pound of silver; two-thirds were eight ounces of silver.

In 1458 the chamberlain of the king on the north of the water of Spey, in his account of the preceding year, beginning with 1456, claims as paid by him to the Prior of Beauly the sum of £4, which was yearly due to the prior from the fermes of the baronies of Avach (Avoch) and Eddiordule (Eddirdor) by ancient infeftment; and also the sum of 3s. 4d. paid to the prior as the price of one pound of pepper due to him yearly from the same baronies by the same ancient infeftment.[*] The present charter must be the grant on account of which the sum of £4 was paid, but the origin of the pound of pepper does not appear.

James II. of Scotland, in 1456, increased the amount of money coined out of a pound of silver to £3, 4s., which made the ounce of silver worth about 5s.; eight ounces would be £2. The standard before the depreciation of James II. was the same in England as in Scotland, but it was not till the time of Henry VIII. that any depreciation was attempted in England; in his reign, and under the feeble rule of his son, the standard fell to the same level as the Scottish standard of 1456. Hume passes over these depreciations by Henry VIII. and his son in silence, though he points out the impolicy of Elizabeth's tampering with the coin by dividing the pound of silver into 62s. instead of 60s.[†] In Scotland, the year 1456 commenced a fearful system of degradation; the king may have applied to himself the trite quotation from Horace if he had foreseen his "progenies vitiosior," James VI., coining £36 out of a pound of silver, or, in other words, bringing down the Scottish shilling to the value of an English penny.

Great care is taken in framing this charter of Andrew de Boscho to make it effectual; the grantors guard against every attempt that might thereafter be made to weaken it by papal or regal exemptions;[‡] and in this way probably, though not

---

[*] Exchequer Rolls, No. 227, quoted in O. S. P., vol. ii., p. 840.
[†] Hume's History of England, vol. v., p. 477, ed. 1778.
[‡] The renunciation of the constitution of two diets refers to the practice which

expressed to be marks of silver, in after-times the payment was made as if so granted.

The charter is witnessed by some notable persons,—the bishop and other officials of the cathedral of Ross; William, Earl of Ross;* William de Hay;† the vicar of Eddyrdor, and the Constable of Tarradale. The church of Eddyrdor was part of the prebend of the Archdeacon of Ross. The name of the Constable of Tarradale shows that a castle existed there at this time.

In 1274 the Council of Lyons granted a tax of a tenth part of all church revenues during the six following years for an expedition for the relief of the Holy Land. Boiamond of Vicci was appointed collector of this tax in Scotland, on the 20th September 1274.‡ His taxation is commonly called *Bagimont's Roll.* In this roll the entry of Beauly among the abbeys and priories is, "The Priory of Beauly, £200;" Ardchattan is also £200; Pluscardine is valued at £533. This is for the three years following Midsummer Day, 1274.

---

prevailed in those times and down to the establishment of the Court of Session, of having two summonses served instead of one (Bankton's Institutes, book i.).

* This William is usually called the third Earl of Ross. He succeeded William, the second Earl of Ross, who, according to the "Chronicle of the Earls of Ross," died in 1274. In this charter the third earl, for the first time, appears on record. He afterwards was compelled by Archibald, Bishop of Moray (Reg. Moray, 281), to grant Cadboll to the Friars Minorites, or Franciscans, at Elgin, as compensation for injuries done by him to the churches of Petty and Buachaly. In 1291 he swore fealty to Edward I., but fought against him at Dunbar in 1296, and was taken prisoner and sent to the Tower; and in August 1297 was allowed to send for his son, Hugh, to visit him there. He was soon released from prison. In the winter of 1306 he took the wife and daughter of King Robert the Bruce out of the sanctuary of St Duthac at Tain, and gave them up to Edward I.; and his son, Hugh, is one of the knights accompanying that king on his last expedition to Scotland in 1307, Hugh asking in May before they set out for a grant of the lands they hoped would be forfeited. After the death, in 1307, of Edward I., the young king, in 1308, wrote to Earl William and his son as allies asking their aid, but Bruce secured the friendship of the earl; and at Auldearn, 31st October 1308, restored to him all his lands. In 1309 his son Hugh had already married Matilda Bruce, the king's sister. The earl died in 1323.

† This is probably William de la Haye, who, when Earl William was prisoner, is styled by Edward I. (Rotuli Scotiæ, i., p. 32), Warden of the Earldom of Ross.

‡ Theiner, Vet. Mon. Hib. et Scot., p. 116.

The Prior of Beauly was also taxed separately in the bishopric of Moray, which must have been for the appropriated parishes in that diocese, the rectories of Abertarff and Conway. The amount was 38s. 8d.

Andrew de Boscho died before 1291. His name does not occur in the "Ragman Roll;" and his wife's charter, we next mention, must have been about that date. He had a son and heir, John de Bosco. Grace's "Annals of Ireland" mention John de Bosco and John Byset as coming with the Scots to Ulster in Edward Bruce's time. In 1327, at Inverness, Elizabeth, the wife of Alexander de Strevelyn, a daughter of Sir John de Bosco, releases any claim she had on the lands of Kilravock to the Roses. Between 1323 and 1333, Nelo de Karrick and Johanna, his wife, release any claim they had to Kilravock; and in 1349, at Dunachton, Joneta, a widow, the daughter and one of the heirs of the late Sir John de Bosco, knight, executes a similar release. We shall see, hereafter, the third of the barony of the Aird, which must have belonged to Elizabeth de Bosco, belonging to the family Del Ard. Elizabeth Byset, widow of Andrew de Bosco, grants a charter,* in which she describes herself as Elizabeth Byset, daughter of a nobleman, the late John Byset, lady of Kilravock, spouse of the late Andrew de Bosco; this deed grants Kilravock to Hugh de Rose, and Maria, his wife, her daughter, and the heirs of their bodies. She also resigned the same into the hands of John Baliol (1292-96). This grant of land by Elizabeth Byset to her daughter was the common mode of providing fortunes in marriage in those days, when there was no money, and does not imply that the daughter was an heiress.

In 1294, at Lovat, in the Aird, Hugh de Rose,† and Maria, his wife, granted to Sir David de Graham, knight, a lease of the davoch of Kilcoy (Culcolly), in the tenement of Redcastle (Eddyrdor), for eight years. The first four years' rent was paid down, and for the last four it was to be eight marks. Kilcoy must have been included in the grant of

* Family of Kilravock, p. 28.   † *Ib.*, p. 109.

Kilravock. The lease is curious. There is a clause, that if the land was wasted by civil war, it should remain in the hands of the lessee until he should receive the fruits which he had lost by war—a wise provision in the very year which saw Edward I. summoning King John Baliol as his vassal to attend the English Parliament.* This Sir David de Graham, husband of Muriel Byset, was one of the nominees of Baliol in his competition for the crown of Scotland, 5th June 1292. He swore fealty to Edward in that year; but his anticipation of war was correct; and he was taken prisoner at Dunbar, in 1296, by Edward, with his nephew, Sir David de Graham, when his brother, Sir Patrick de Graham, was killed. They were released on the 30th July 1297, on condition of serving Edward in his wars against France. Meanwhile, his co-heir, William de Fenton, had not been idle, and had so sharply held his portion of the Byset property against the Church, as to call down the most signal punishment. John Byset, the founder, appears, as we have seen, to have first erected the castle of Beaufort; and William de Fenton and his wife, Cecilia Byset, dwelt sometimes at the castle of Beaufort, as well as at their house of Fenton in Lothian, and their castle of Baky in Aberdeenshire.

In 1280, William de Fenton, as Lord of Beaufort in the Aird, in right of Cecilia Byset, his wife, had taken possession of a half-davoch of church land in Kiltarlity, which the Bishop of Moray claimed. In 1226 the church, and everything belonging to it, had been given to the Leper House at Rathven, by John Byset, with the Bishop of Moray's consent. But the church of Rathven was part of the prebend of the eighth canon of the cathedral of Elgin, and, in this way, the bishop may have claimed Kiltarlity. However, the claims were made, the conflict was severe, and the cause was at issue before the Pope himself. Pope Nicholas III. remitted it to the Abbot

* The seal of Sir David de Graham is yet preserved attached to the lease. It is "semée of crosses fitchée, three escallop shells," with the legend, "S. David de Graham;" and precisely the same seal seems attached to the declaration of allegiance of David de Graham to Edward I. in 1292, now in the Record Office, London.

of Deer. Archibald, Bishop of Moray, was the plaintiff; and William de Fenton, Lord of Beaufort in the Aird, and Cecilia, his wife, defendants. The abbot deputed the Bishop of Ross, the Dean of Ross, and the Prior of Beauly, to act for him; and these three churchmen, on Wednesday, the 26th September 1279, met at the church of Kiltarlity, and there inducted the Bishop of Moray, in the name of his cathedral church, into the corporal possession of this half-davoch of land, as belonging of right to the church of Kiltarlity, and adjudged by the second and final decree of the Abbot of Deer to belong to the Bishop of Moray. They also, by the authority of the Apostolic See, publicly warned William de Fenton that he should in no wise hinder the bishop from dealing with the land as he liked. The baron heeded not, as the delegates met at Kinloss on the 26th March 1280, and directed three monitions to be served upon him and his wife at the castle of Beaufort, warning them that if they resisted till the 21st of April, they would be suspended from entering the church, which suspension was to be denounced through the Rural Deanery and Provinces; and if, by the 2d of June, the recusants had not obeyed the monition, from thence they were to be excommunicated, throughout the district, on all Sundays and festivals, with pealed bells and lighted candles; and if they did not return to the bosom of Mother Church before the Feast of St Peter *ad vincula* (30th June), then the sentence of interdict was to be announced against them. This was done; and the Bishop of Moray, on the Sunday after the Feast of the Assumption, addressed a letter to the Provincial Council at Perth, which assembled in the church of the Dominicans on Monday, 19th August 1280, setting forth the facts, and calling upon the bishops to denounce the offenders in all the churches of their dioceses, under the ban of the Church, to be shunned by all faithful Christians.*

The real value of this half-davoch of Kiltarlity church land was its carrying with it and the general pertinents conveyed that of "fishing" (*piscaria*)—a right of salmon fishing in the

* Reg. Moray, 140-142.

river Beauly. This flowed past the castle of Beaufort, in which William of Fenton and his wife, Cecilia Byset, lived; and her grandfather having given some share of the fishing in it to the monks of Beauly, it was hard to be deprived of the rest by a distant prelate.

The limits of the monks' right of fishing probably are correctly stated in the Wardlaw MS.,* which says there were cruives of wood and stone above the ford of Dunballoch, as a division between the monks of Beauly and the upper proprietors, and that all the part of the river which was below the cruives to the sea-side was termed vulgarly Avin-na-mannich, or the monks' water. The minister adds elsewhere this statement:† "The monks of Beauly were very strict keepers of their own part of ye river below the cruives at Dunballoch; nay, so churlish and near that they would not permit any to angle with hooks and lines on either side." The monks' right seems to have extended on both sides the river from the Firth up to the boundary between the parishes of Wardlaw (Kirkhill) and Kiltarlity; and the fishing of the Beauly in Kiltarlity, Kilmorack, and Kirkhill has always been rated as belonging only to the three parishes.

Above the Kirkhill boundary the fishing would naturally belong, as the water does, half to the Kilmorack parish, and half to Kiltarlity, and the church land of Kiltarlity appears to have carried with it the fishing of the Esse in the river, which I understand to be the fishing of the pools below the falls upon the river Beauly, well known as the Falls of Kilmorack.

Eventually, the bishop seems to have been too powerful for the Lord of Beaufort, as he was for William, Earl of Ross, and he appears to have recovered his land and fishing from William de Fenton, and then by a deed to arrange with Sir David de Graham, knight, the Lord of Lovat, a dispute respecting the fishing of the Esse in the river of Farrar, and settles with him that he is to take a fee-farm lease of the land of Kiltarlity with the whole fishing, as well his own which he gives to the Church, as also that which the bishop had

* Add. MSS. 8144, B. M., p. 3.   † Ib., p. 116.

recovered from William de Fenton, at the rent of £5 a year.*

This deed has no date, but as it speaks of the land recovered from William de Fenton, it must have been after the excommunication of 1280, and before Sir David's capture in 1296.

Beauly Priory was one which had its prior included among those summoned to the Parliament of Brigham, on the 17th of March 1290, whilst Margaret the Maiden of Norway was still living.

The priors assembled are those of Coldingham (£1333), Lesmahagow (dependent on the Abbey of Kelso), Pluscardine (£533), Beauly (£200), Urquhart (dependent on Dunfermline), Whithern (£2000), Rostynot (£523), May (Isle of May, Pittenweem) (£400), Canonby (Domus de Liddel, £40), and Blantyre (£40).

I give the values as in Boiamond's Taxation; Lesmahagow and Urquhart are, I suppose, included in the valuation of Kelso (£2666) and Dunfermline (£3333), but it is clear that it was not the importance of the benefices which caused the holders to be summoned. It is rather to be inferred that every prior in Scotland was summoned, and that those only attended who were favourable to the English alliance, for it was the object of promoting that alliance which convoked the Parliament.

Sir David de Graham was released in July 1297, and undertook to help the English king in Flanders against France; and it is probable that it is this David de Graham who is mentioned as lately dead on the 17th May 1298. On this day Edward I. grants to Robert de Felton, the marriage of Patrick de Graham, son and heir of the deceased David de Graham. The grant is dated at Canterbury.† If the marriage belonged to the king, as the chief lord of David de Graham's lands, Patrick de Graham must have been under twenty-one at least at the time of his father's death; and as the grant is to be without disparagement, that is, the heir was to be married to an equal to him in quality, the king must

* Reg. Moray, 123. † Stevenson, vol. ii., p. 271.

have conceived Patrick to be then under age. His mother was alive in 1278, at the time of the inquisition into the property of John Byset, and he should have actually been twenty-one at the time of his arrangement with the Bishop of Moray. David de Graham must have died in Flanders, as we have an agreement between Archibald, who ceased to be Bishop of Moray in December 1298, with Patrick de Graham, the son and heir of David de Graham.* If this is the same Patrick with the other whose marriage was granted on the 17th May 1298, we cannot be misled as to his age.

By this agreement, which recites the strife which had arisen respecting the land of Kiltarlity, and the fishing of the river of Farrar, between Sir William de Fenton and Sir David de Graham, and Patrick, the heir of Sir David, which land and fishing the bishop had let to Sir David, in fee-farm, for 100s. a year—Patrick surrendering the fee-farm, which had become burdensome—the bishop grants the whole land of the church of Kiltarlity, with its pertinents, and with the whole fishing of Esse of the river of Farrar, pertaining to the said land, to the said William de Fenton and Patrick de Graham; they and their heirs or assignees for ever paying six marks sterling of annual rent—that is, six two-thirds of a pound of silver—at two terms in the year, two annual sums of 20s. by William de Fenton, and two annual sums of 20s. by Patrick de Graham, and their respective heirs or assignees, whether the land was worth as much or not; and the said William de Fenton and Patrick de Graham made homage and fealty with an oath, and promised to continue to do so.

There is no date, but, as we have said, it cannot be of later date than 1298, as Bishop Archibald died 5th December 1298.

This William de Fenton was the son of John de Fenton,† who gave before the second year of King John Baliol two tofts and two acres of land, with the fishing of one net in the water of Tay, to Nicholas of Hay, Lord of Errol, by a charter to which Patrick de Graham, knight, is a witness.

* Reg. Moray, 124. † Spalding Club Misc., vol. ii., p. 311.

This William de Fenton, who, before 1268, gave, with his co-owners, the receipt for John Byset the son's charters, was survived by his wife, John Byset the son's co-heiress, Cecilia ; the next charter is granted by her.

Amidst the storm of the English war with Bruce, the priory had stood firm, and none of the confiscations and destructions of families which took place under Bruce, seem to have affected the family of her founder.

No. VIII.

CARTA DOMINÆ CECILIÆ BYSETH FRATRIBUS VALLISCAULIUM DE BELLO LOCO DE TERTIA PARTE TERRÆ SUÆ DE ALTIR.

Ex Autographo.

"Omnibus hanc Cartam visuris vel audituris Cecilia Bysath Sponsa quondam Domini Willielmi de Fentoun æternam in Domino salutem. Noverit universitas vestra me in legitima mea viduitate et plenaria potestate pro salute animæ meæ et animarum antecessorum et Successorum meorum, dedisse, concessisse, et hac præsenti Carta mea confirmasse Deo et Beatæ Mariæ et Beato Johanni Baptistæ, et fratribus Valliscaulium in domo Belli loci Deo servientibus et servituris in perpetuum, totam tertiam partem terræ de Altyr, quæ me jure hæreditario contingit. Tenendam et habendam eisdem fratribus de me et hæredibus meis in perpetuum, in liberam puram et perpetuam Eleemosynam, cum omnibus pertinentijs suis et rectis divisis in bosco et plano, in pratis et pascuis, in moris et maresijs, Sylvis, aquis, venationibus, et nidis avium, et cum omnibus alijs ad eandem terram spectantibus, vel in aliquo tempore de Jure spectare valentibus tam non nominatis quam nominatis, ita libere quiete plenarie et honorifice, sicut aliqua terra Eleemosynaria in regno Scotiæ ab aliquo liberius, quietius, plenarius, et honorificentius tenetur et possidetur. Ego vero et hæredes mei prædictam tertiam partem terræ de Altyr cum pertinentijs suis prædictis fratribus in liberam puram et perpetuam Eleemosynam Warrantisabimus, acquietabimus et in perpetuum defendemus. In cujus rei testimonium præsenti Cartæ Sigillum meum apposui hijs testibus Domino Patricio de Grahame Milite, Domino Henrico Capellano de Beaufort, Domino Petro Capellano Parochiali de Ferneway, Haraldo filio Dofnaldi del Ard, Roberto clerico et multis alijs."

Not.—The tag parchment ; no seal.

By this charter, Cecilia Byset, widow of William de Fenton, grants, in her widowhood, for the salvation of her soul and the souls of her ancestors and her successors, to God and the Blessed Mary, and the Blessed John Baptist, and the brethren of the Valliscaulians serving and to serve God in the House of Beauly, all the third part of the land of Altyr, which belonged to her by hereditary right.

' Altyre is now a farm lying above Beauly Bridge, but probably then meant a more extensive tract, which either included the land to the west as far as the stream of Breakachy, which afterwards belonged to the priory; or, if these limits were fixed by the founder's charter, then Altyre comprised the land lying between the Precinct and these lands, for the grant of Altyre is, with all its pertinents, in wood and plain, and rights of hunting. It also has an express mention of "birds' nests" (*nidis avium*), which it is unusual to express in a grant of land, and seems to show that the grant extended to the cliffs overhanging the Falls of Kilmorack, which would in those days be the haunt of innumerable hawks.*

Cecilia Byset affixes her seal, doubtless as proud an escutcheon as that borne by her sister, Elizabeth Byset, still preserved in the muniment room at Kilravock Castle;† with the simple ordinary, *a bend*, the only bearing on the shield, but this shield repeated four times, and with the legend "Sigillum secretum Elizabeth Buset."

The first witness is Sir Patrick de Grahame, knight. Patrick de Graham, David's son, was not a knight when he made his bargain with Bishop Archibald in 1298; but we have, in 1304,‡ Patrick de Graham first sent to London as a prisoner to the Constable of the Tower, and his destination changed, for we have Patrick de Graham, a Scottish knight (*chevalier d'Escoce*), sent to the Bishop of Chester to be confined in a castle in England. It seems probable that this was our Sir Patrick, as his uncle Patrick died fighting at Dunbar in 1296, and our Patrick had probably been made a knight by some

---

* Hawks' nests are occasionally reserved (Lib. de Melrose, i. 39).
† Family of Kilravock, p. 111. ‡ Palgrave Documents, p. 353.

of his Scottish brethren in arms. He must have been still a
prisoner in 1307 ; as, on the 12th August 1307, on Edward I.'s
last progress to Scotland, at Ebchester, in Durham, we have
Loughlan M'Lochery of the Isles requesting a grant of the
lands of Patrick de Graham.

Patrick probably remained in an English castle as prisoner,
at least as long as did the wife, sister, and daughter of Robert
Bruce, who were confined also in English castles, for doubtless these would have been the first objects of any exchange ;
and as it was not until after the battle of Bannockburn, in
1315, that the queen and the princesses, with the Bishop of
Glasgow and the Earl of Mar, were exchanged for the Earl of
Hereford, it seems likely that Patrick would be exchanged
about the same time.

Accordingly, we cannot fix the date of this charter of
Cecilia Byset earlier than 1315.

Henry, chaplain of Beaufort, is a witness. This must have
been a chapel for the castle of Beaufort, established after
1280, as there is no mention in the interdict of this chaplain.
It seems to have been a private chapel, without endowment
or parochial jurisdiction ; such chapels were rare in the north
of Scotland, but instances are to be found.* The chapel of
Baky, which William de Fenton, her son, endowed in 1329,
was not in the castle, but stood at some distance from it.†

Sharply contrasted in title with the chaplain of Beaufort,
is the next witness, Sir Peter, the parochial chaplain of
Fearnua.

The three davochs of Fearnua constituted, in 1221, part of
the parish of Dunballoch, but subsequently, and before 1239,
these three davochs must have been erected into a separate
parish, which erection, as John Byset had given up the patronage of Dunballoch to the bishopric of Moray, was in the
power of the bishop, patron as well as ordinary, to effect. In
1239 Bishop Andrew granted to the cathedral church of the
Holy Trinity of Elgin, for the common use of the canons, the
church of Fearnua with its pertinents, except one-half of a

* Appendix, No. IX.　　　† Jervise's Lindsays, ed. 1853, p. 253.

davoch pertaining to the table—that is, for the personal maintenance of the bishop. But notwithstanding the injunction of popes and councils that religious bodies, who had parish churches appropriated to their use, should endow vicars of the parishes and provide them competently, no vicar was endowed at Fearnua, and his place was supplied by a parochial chaplain—often an unendowed minister of the parish, who had nothing to depend on but the fees for the offices of marriage and burial, which could only be canonically performed in a parish church.

Harold, the son of Donald del Ard, is also a witness. This family, Del Ard, is one probably deriving their name, just about this period, from their share in the barony of the Aird, belonging to the founder of the priory; but we may reserve details respecting them till we come to Sir Christian del Ard, in the following charter.

No. IX.

CARTA PATRICIJ DE GRAHAME DE PARTE SUA DE ALTYR FACTA FRATRIBUS DE BELLO LOCO IN EXCAMBIO PRO MULTURIS DE LOUETH, ETC.

Ex Autographo.

"Omnibus hoc scriptum visuris vel audituris Patricius de Graham Salutem in Domino. Noveritis universi me dedisse, concessisse et hac presenti cartâ meâ confirmasse Deo et Beatæ Mariæ et Beatæ Johanni Baptiste et Domui Belli Loci et fratribus ordinis Vallis Caulium ibidem Deo servientibus et servituris in perpetuum tertiam partem meam terræ de Altre, cum omnibus pertinentijs suis et rectis divisis in escambio pro multuris terrarum infra scriptarum, videlicet de Loueth Fingask   et Dofnaldistun. Et etiam in compensationem quadraginta Marcarum in quibus eisdem fratribus teneor pro tertia parte sexies viginti mercarum, in quibus nobilis memoriæ Dominus Johannes Byseth, se et hæredes suos ad Fabricam Belli Loci obligaverat. Necnon in compensationem viginti quinque Marcarum in quibus eisdem teneor occasione injustæ detentionis multuræ terrarum prædictarum. Et etiam in compensationem septemdecem Marcarum in quibus eisdem teneor, de debito Domini David patris mei, in quibus quidem septemdecem Marcis idem Dominus pater meus eisdem fratribus tenebatur obligatus. Tenendam et habendam prædictam partem meam Terræ de Altre eisdem fratribus et suis successoribus in perpetuum, in liberam puram et perpetuam Eleemosynam, cum omnibus pertinentijs suis et asyamentis, libere, quiete, plenarie et honorifice in bosco et pluvio, in pratis et pascuis, in moris et Maresijs, stagnis, aquis, molendinis, piscariis et cum omnibus aliis libertatibus et aysiamentis tam non nominatis quam nominatis ad eandem terram pertinentibus, vel in aliquo tempore de jure pertinere valentibus. Ego vero et hæredes mei prædictam tertiam partem terræ de Altre prædictis fratribus in liberam Eleemosynam in perpetuum contra omnes homines et fœminas warrantisabimus, acquietabimus et in perpetuum defendamus. Et si contingat me vel aliquem hæredum meorum præsentem concessionem et Donationem meam futuris temporibus revocare, quod absit, volo et concedo quod multuræ terrarum prænominatarum ad eosdem Fratres sine aliqua contradictione plene et integraliter revertantur, et in eorundem possessionem, nullius requisito consensu, pacifice ingrediantur. Et nihilominus liceat eisdem fratribus, me et hæredes meos ad solutionem supradictarum quadraginta, viginti quinque et septemdecem Marcarum eis plenarie faciendam per omnimodam Juris civilis seu canonici censuram distringere, compellere et coercere. In cujus rei testimonium præsentibus sigillum meum una cum Sigillo Johannis Le Grant est appensum, hiis testibus venerabili Patre Domino Thoma Rossensi Episcopo, Domino Willielmo de Fentone, Domino Johanne de Fentone filio suo, Johanne filio Cristini de le Ard, Haroldo filio Dofnaldi, Andrew le Graunt, Alexandro Corbuyt, Alano de Lasculis et Multis alijs."

Not.—No tag nor seal.

This charter is by Patrick de Graham. It conveys his third part of Altyre to the House of Beauly, but in exchange for the multures of Lovat, Fingask, and Donaldston, and also as a satisfaction for 40 marks, in which Sir Patrick was held (bound) for the third part of 120 marks, in which John Byset, of noble memory, had bound himself and his heirs to the fabric of Beauly, and also of 25 marks for arrears of multures, and also in satisfaction of 17 marks, in which he was held bound for the debt of his father David, in which 17 marks the same David, his father, was held bound to the monks ; and if the grant of the third part of the land was disputed, these claims were to revive again.

This charter confirms the note of the Wardlaw MS., as to the grant of multures by John Byset to the priory, which include the multures of Lovat and Finasses (Fingask).*

Lovat, Fingask, and Donaldston are described as parts of the barony of Lovat, in General Fraser of Lovat's entail of

* *Supra*, p. 17.

1774,* and not as parts of the barony of Beauly; and therefore were not part of the possession of the priory, but only subject to be astricted to the priory mills.

The charter is evidently of later date than that of Cecilia Byset; it is in different form, although a conveyance of a third part of the same land; but it cannot be later than 1325, when Thomas, Bishop of Ross, died.

The names of the witnesses are interesting and suggestive. Sir Patrick attaches with his own seal, the seal of John le Graunt; and the witnesses are Thomas, Bishop of Ross; William de Fenton, and John de Fenton, his son; John, the son of Christian de le Ard; Harold, the son of Donald; Andrew le Graunt, Alexander Corbet, Alan de Lascelles, and many others.

Thomas, Bishop of Ross, ceased to be bishop of Ross in 1325; he was Thomas de Dono Dei, or of Dundee. He was appointed by the Pope,† and obtained his temporalities in 1297.·

The Grants are first named as witnesses, "Laurentius et Robertus Grant," in the deed of John Byset, the son, in 1258.‡ John de Graunt and Rodolph de Graunt are discharged from prison on the 30th of July 1297, by King Edward I., on condition that they serve against France; they are said to be dependent on John Comyn, Lord of Badenoch; and David de Graham also, as we have seen, was released at the same time.

Their connection with the Bysets seems intimate, and Patrick le Graunt appears about 1357 as Lord of Stratherrick § (Stratharthock), a lordship which, we have seen, was granted to a Walter Byset before 1282.

The Corbets are named by the minister of Wardlaw, and the story is repeated by Anderson in his history of the Frasers, ‖ among the petty vassals, who, from holding lands of the Byset,

---

* 7 and 8 Vict., cap. 26—Private and Personal Acts.
† Theiner's Vet. Mon. Hib. et Scot., p. 159; Stevenson, vol. ii., p. 196.
‡ *Supra*, p. 52. § Forsyth's Moray, p. 28.
‖ Family of Fraser, ed. 1835, p. 19.

were vulgarly called the Byset's Barons, and he specifies Corbet as Baron of Drumchardny; but he includes among these, Baron Haliburton as Baron of Culbirnie, although no Haliburton was in the Aird till one married the heiress of a third of the barony about 1425, and also Fenton as Baron of Eskadale, although the Fentons, being Lords of Fenton in the south, acquired their share of the Aird after the Bysets, and by marriage with one of the heiresses of the second John Byset. The Corbets seem to have accompanied John Byset to the north, for we have Sir Archibald and Sir Hugh Corbet, knights, witnesses to the deed of arrangement between Bishop Brice and John Byset, the founder.

Alan de Lascelles was taken fighting at Dunbar, and side by side with Patrick de Graham's father, and Christian del Ard, in 1296, and was sent a prisoner to Leeds Castle, in Kent. The other witnesses we shall refer to when dealing with the next charter of William de Fenton. But the most interesting fact brought out by this charter is as to the fabric of Beauly. A grant of 120 marks was made to it by John Byset, of noble memory. This was probably Patrick de Graham's grandfather, son of the founder. This second John Byset died in 1259, and a grant by him of 120 marks, or £240 of our money, when the annual value of the priory in 1274 was £600 of our money, implies that the fabric had been completed, or nearly so, at the time of the grant by John Byset.

The fabric of Beauly probably means the whole priory building and not the church of the priory. But as to the church, which alone remains, the character of the architecture is rather that of a building begun soon after 1230 than at a later period, the semi-detached pillars of the side windows, their lancet-shape and character, the mouldings, the ornaments, the interesting round arches, and the piscina and triangular windows above the cloisters, all indicate work of the Early English or First Pointed period, which would be finished before 1272; and this accords with the impression that the grant by Andrew de Boscho in 1278 would produce, for he

F

would hardly have given a money endowment of £4 a year to the priory if it had not then been finished.

Before the war of independence there is to be found a great synchronism of style in architecture between England and Scotland, and the sister priories of Pluscardine and Ardchattan have unmistakable Early English work in them; the toothed ornament in particular is to be seen in the piscina at Ardchattan, and there are other specimens in the neighbourhood. No more exquisite specimens of an Early English gable, with its triple lancet east window, can be found than in the old chapel of Allangrange; and the chapter-house of Fort Rose has a crypt of Early English work. The brotherhood of architects was broken up by the wars of Bruce and Baliol, and probably no addition was made to the priory from the thirteenth to the fifteenth century.

Mr Mure remarks * that the church has features like First Pointed, but that generally the work is Second Pointed, though mostly of Early character, and may date from about the first decade of the fourteenth century. From 1300 to 1310 is a most unlikely period for a building like this to be erected, when the fiercest conflict proceeded between Bruce and the English, and when the division of the property of the founder had made united action difficult on the part of his descendants. The east window is a later insertion, and the north chapel and the prolongation of the nave are later works, but the bulk of the church as it now stands was certainly erected before the end of the reign of Alexander III.

The arrears of multures which Patrick de Graham had contracted may refer to what had taken place during his captivity in England, and the readiness of the priory to take land in lieu of money, marks that the building operations had ceased; and therefore this transaction with Patrick de Graham seems to show the date fixed by Mr Mure to be incorrect, as it is to this period he would assign the erection of the existing church.

* Characteristics of Church Architecture, Edin. 1861.

No. X.

CARTA WILLIELMI DE FENTON DOMINI DE BEUFORD DE DUABUS MARCIS SINGULIS ANNIS PERCIPIENDIS DE MOLENDINO DE BEUFORD FRATRIBUS DE BELLO LOCO.

EX AUTOGRAPHO ANN. CHR. 1328.

"Omnibus hoc scriptum visuris et Audituris Willielmus de Fenton Dominus de Beuford salutem in Domino sempiternam. Noverit universitas vestra, me, pro salute animæ meæ, et pro salute animarum antecessorum et Successorum meorum, dedisse, concessisse, et hac presenti carta mea confirmasse Deo et Beatæ Mariæ et Beato Johanni Baptistæ et Domui Belli Loci, et Fratribus ordinis vallis caulium ibidem Deo servientibus et servituris, in perpetuum, duas marcas annuas, percipiendas singulis annis de Molendino de Beuford, per Ballivos meos de Beuford et hæredum meorum, seu per firmarios dicti Molendini, qui pro tempore fuerint, in liberam puram et perpetuam Eleemosynam; ad duos anni terminos, medietatem scilicet ad Pentecosten, et alteram medietatem ad festum sancti Martini in yeme. Tenendas et habendas dictæ domui et prædictis Fratribus de me et hæredibus meis, libere, quiete, plenarie, et honorifice, Renunciando in hac parte, pro me et hæredibus meis, omnibus Litteris, Impetratis, et Impetrandis, et omni Juris remedio tam civilis quam canonici, quæ huic donationi meæ in aliquo possint obviare vel resistere, aut dictæ domui vel prædictis fratribus in aliquo valeant nocere. Ego vero et hæredes mei prædictas duas marcas annuas prædictæ domui et prædictis fratribus in puram et perpetuam Eleemosynam contra omnes mortales warrantisabimus acquietabimus, et in perpetuum defendemus. In cujus rei Testimonium præsentibus sigillum meum apposui. Datum apud Beuford die Sancti Valentini Martiris Anno Gratiæ Millesimo trecentesimo vicesimo octavo hijs testibus Domino

Cristino del Ard milite, Alexandro Pylche Vicecomite de Innernyss,
Haraldo filio Dofnaldi, Domino Petro Cappellano de Ferneway,
Waltero dicto cancellar., Laurentio Corbeyt et Multis alijs."

 Not.—The seal white wax, on a tag parchment, nothing discernible in the escutcheon nor in the circumference.

 William de Fenton, successor of that William who married Cecilia Byset, grants this charter, which is dated 1328. By it the Lord of Beaufort grants to the priory two marks a year (£4), to be received from the mill of Beaufort, by his bailiffs of Beaufort, or by the farmers (tenants) of the mill of Beaufort for the time being, to be paid half-yearly at Whitsunday, and the feast of St Martin in winter. It is dated at Beaufort on St Valentine's Day, 1328, and the witnesses are Sir Christian del Ard, knight; Alexander Pylche, Sheriff of Inverness; Harold, the son of Donald; Sir Peter, chaplain of Ferneway; Walter, called Chancellor; Lawrence Corbet, and others.

 The name of Christian del Ard, whose son John witnessed Patrick Graham's charter, and whose name was borne by Donald, whose son Harold witnesses the charter, and also Cecilia Byset's, introduces us to a puzzle in the history of the north of Scotland.

 The name " del Ard " first occurs in the " Ragman Roll." In 1296, William Fitzstephen de Ard, of the county of Inverness, swears fealty to King Edward I. The same year Christian del Ard, then a simple esquire, is taken fighting against that king at the disastrous battle of Dunbar, and sent with others, knights and esquires, a prisoner to Corfe Castle, in Dorsetshire, on the 5th June, where he was allowed 3d. a day by the Sheriff of Somerset and Dorset for his maintenance.

 The spectacle of the blue waters of the English Channel in the summer time must have chafed the spirit of the fighting Scottish esquire; and on Hugh, son of Earl William of Ross, coming into England in 1297, Christian not improbably got free with Earl William, and served Edward I. At all events, on Edward I.'s march to Scotland, Christian del Ard and his companion, Hugh de Ross, ask of the king a grant of the lands, which they hope the king would take from his rebellious subjects; and it is strange, as we find Christian del Ard and Alexander Pylche together as witnesses to this charter of William de Fenton, that Christian should, in 1306, have fixed upon not only the lands of Laurence de Strathbogie, but also those of "Alexander Pylche, burgess of Inverness," as his chosen possessions. Whether at this time Christian had any land in Inverness, near that belonging to Alexander Pylche, does not appear; but in 1361, a perch of land is given to a chapel in a charter in the "Register of Moray,"* as lying between the land which John, the son of Hugh, held of Christian de Ard on the south on the one side, and the land of William Pylche to the north on the other.

In 1322,† the Abbot of Arbroath granted to Sir Christian de Ard, knight, the lands of Bught, within the parish of Inverness, at a rent of four marks of silver, and under the obligation to build houses sufficient to enable the abbot to find in them a hall chamber and kitchen for his use when he visited Inverness. A counterpart of the charter is said to be left with the monks, with the seal of the said Sir Christian, which he then used, and with the new seal of his arms.

But he afterwards appears under another name. In Robertson's "Index," among charters of 16 Rob. I. (1322), the charter of Deskford is to Christian de Ard, knight; but the actual charter, which is printed in the "Collections Relating to the Shire of Banff," is granted in 1325 to Sir Christian de Forbes, knight. In 1329 the "Register of Arbroath" mentions him as Christian del Ard, knight.‡ It does not appear what became of his son John, who was a witness to Patrick de Graham's deed. John de Forbes is first of the name mentioned in contemporary documents; this is in 1307. There is no authority for the earlier Forbes of the peerage books.§ Fergus de Fothes is not an ancestor: Fothes and Forbes are two different places. The story of Alexander de Bois defending Urquhart Castle against Edward I., and being killed,

* Reg. Moray, 305. † Reg. de Aberbrothock, vol. i., p. 305.
‡ Appendix, No. X. § Douglas Peerage, "Lord Forbes."

and his son being saved, and becoming the first Forbes, suggests the family originating from the De Bois or De Bosco family, and this identity of Christian del Ard and Christian de Forbes, when connected with the fact that Margaret del Ard afterwards possessed the third of the Byset property, which had belonged to Elizabeth Byset, the wife of Andrew de Bosco, may lead to the discovery of the real origin of the family of Forbes.

No. XI.

CARTA JOHANNIS DE URCHARD VICARIJ DE ABBERTHERFF PRIORI DE BELLO LOCO DE QUIETA CLAMATIONE DECIMARUM SALMONUM DE ABBERTHERFF.

Ex Autographo 1340.

"Omnibus hac litteras visuris vel audituris Johannes dictus de Urchard perpetuus vicarius de Abbertherff Salutem in Domino. Noveritis me quietum clamasse Priori, Domui et Conventui de Bello loco, totum Jus meum si quod habui in Decimis Piscariæ de Abbertherff, aut si de futuro in eisdem habere sperarem vel potuero, quia per vim et inspectionem litterarum quas dicti Monachi habent in dicta piscaria ex concessione venerabilis Patris Domini Andreæ bonæ memoriæ quondam Episcopi Moraviensis, et capituli, satis intellexi, quod nullum Jus in dicta Piscaria habeo nec prædecessores mei habuerunt. Quapropter nullum Errorem contra dictos monachos in suo Jure præsumo sustinere. In cujus rei testimonium Sigillum meum una cum Sigillo Domini Matthæi Reny Decani Christianicensis de Innernyss tunc temporis est annexum. Datum apud Bellum locum die dominica proxima ante festum Sancti Petri, quod dicitur ad vincula Anno Gratiæ Millesimo trecentesimo quadragesimo."

Not.—The tag cut in two: no seal.

This charter deals with that fertile subject of conflict for the House of Beauly, salmon.

Abertarff had a vicar appointed to it, and duly endowed. He is first mentioned in 1274 as taxed at 21s. 4d.[*] He must have had his endowment from the monks, to whom the church

[*] Theiner, 110, Boiamond's Taxation.

was appropriated by William Byset and the Bishop of Moray. However, a claim seems to have been made by the vicar to have the tithe of the fishings of Abertarff; and the monks under Robert,* who was, it appears, then prior, got the vicar to come to Beauly, and probably by showing him the charter of Andrew, Bishop of Moray (*supra*, No. III.), satisfied the vicar that he had no claim. Accordingly by this charter, which is dated in 1340, the Sunday next before the Feast of St Peter *ad vincula*, the vicar of Abertarff quitclaims to the monks all right which he had in the tithe of the fishing of Abertarff, to which he is satisfied he had no claim, from his inspection of the bishop's charter.

The vicar's seal is annexed with the seal of Matthew Reny, " Decani Christianicensis de Inverness." This is another form of the title, *Decani Christianitatis*. The transcriber in his description of the charter calls it the release of the tithes of salmon, but the charter itself does not name the noble fish. The Priory of Beauly itself was situated in the parish of Kilmorack, and as we have seen, the lands of the priory paid tithes to the rector of the church of Kilmorack, which was appropriated to the cathedral church of Ross.

Nineteen years after the date of this charter, we have the first of the Acts of Homage, which are successively recorded in the " Register of Moray," in respect of that church land of Kiltarlity which cost the Church so much ecclesiastical thunder to preserve, but which had connected with it the salmon fishing so valuable to ecclesiastics in those times. These Acts of Homage were three, by the three co-portioners, who, a hundred years later than the time when John Byset in 1259 left his three daughters his co-heiresses, seem to represent them. The co-portioners are William de Fenton, Hugh Fraser, and Alexander de Chesolme.

In 1359,† William de Fenton, Lord of Beaufort, portioner of the Ard, in the chapter of the cathedral church of Moray, did homage to John Pilmore, the bishop, for his part of the

* Balnagown Charters, O. P. S., ii. 2, 509.
† Reg. Moray, p. 285.

half of the davoch land of the Esse and Kiltarlity, which he held of the church of Moray.

In 1367,* Hugh Fraser, Lord of Lovat, portioner of the lands of the Ard, in the chapter of the church of Moray, does homage to Alexander, the bishop, for his part of the half of the davoch land of Kiltarlity and Esse, and for the fishing of Farrar.

How Hugh Fraser came to succeed Patrick Graham as Lord of Lovat is not known. Tradition asserts that he was the son of Simon Fraser, the Lords of Lovat being always in Gaelic called Mac Shimei. In Robertson's "Index," 29, 24, there is entered a complaint of Simon Fraser and Margaret Fraser, his wife, one of the heirs of the Earl of Caithness, respecting the earldom of Caithness, at Kinross, 4th December 1330. On the opposite page is their complaint before the Sheriff of Inverness. The lady is asserted by Mr Skene† to have been daughter of John, Earl of Orkney and Caithness, by the daughter and heiress of Graham of Lovat. That would make Margaret Fraser grand-daughter of Patrick Graham of Lovat. There seems no foundation for this assertion. Hugh, Earl of Ross, in 1329,‡ obtained a dispensation from the Pope for marrying Margaret de Graham, of the diocese of St Andrews; but there is nothing to lead to the belief that she was daughter of Patrick Graham of Lovat, who was within the diocese of Moray, and she was probably of the family of Graham of Montrose. She married again, in 1341, John de Barclay, and had in 1351 § a brother, Peter Graham, living, so that it could not have been through her heirship that the Lovat property came to Simon Fraser.

In 1368,‖ on the Feast of the Blessed Trinity, in the chamber of Alexander, Bishop of Moray, at Spiny, in the presence of the whole multitude of canons and chaplains, and others invited thither to dinner, Alexander of Chisholme (so runs

---

* Reg. Moray, p. 263.   † Skene's High., vol. ii., p. 312.
‡ Theiner, Mon. Vet. Hib. et Scot., p. 247.
§ Collections on the Shires of Aberdeen and Banff, iv. 760.
‖ Reg. Moray, p. 369.

the register following the entries of the homage done by William of Fenton and Hugh of Lovat), "co-portioner of the said William of Fenton," did homage to the bishop for the same lands of the Esse and of Kiltarlity.

Ten years before, in 1358,* the justices of the king, of whom Robert de Chisholm, Lord of Chisholm, in Roxburghshire, and Constable of the Castle of Urquhart, on Loch Ness, was one, remitted a fine to Alexander de Chisholm. His acquisition, seeing that Margaret del Ard and Thomas de Chisholm, her son and heir in 1403, agree with William of Fenton as to the lands of the Aird, must have been from the Del Ard family; and thus Alexander de Chisholm, by marriage with Margaret del Ard, acquired the Erchless branch of the Byset property.

In the meantime, we have a notice of Dompnus Maurice de Bello Loco, a monk, as witness to a charter by William, Earl of Ross, with Mark, Abbot of Fearn, and William, Thane of Cawdor.† This must have been about 1360, and in 1362 we have Simon, Prior of Beauly,‡ as witness to a charter from William, Earl of Ross, dated at Delny, and another witness in the Abbot of Fearn.

In the entries from the "Kalendar of Fearn," printed in the second "Report of the Commissioners on Historical Manuscripts,"§ is an entry of the obit of Alexander Fraser (Frisell), Prior of Beauly, who died there on the 8th August 1371.

* Chamberlain Accounts, vol. i., p. 381.
† Spalding Club Miscellany, vol. iv., p. 126.
‡ Collections on the Shires of Aberdeen and Banff, ii. 384.
§ 2d Report, app., p. 179.

No. XII.

BULLA GREGORIJ XI. PAPÆ PRIORI ET CONVENTUI BELLI LOCI ORDINIS VALLIS CAULIUM.

"Gregorius Episcopus Servus Servorum Dei dilectis filijs Priori et Conventui Monasterij Belli loci ordinis Vallis caulium ad Romanam Ecclesiam nullo medio pertinentis, Rossensis Diocœsis, Salutem et Apostolicam Benedictionem. Justis petentium desiderijs dignum est nos facilem præbere consensum, et vota quæ a rationis tramite non discordant, Effectu prosequente complere. Ea propter dilecti in Domino filij, vestris justis postulationibus grato concurrentes assensu, omnes libertates et immunitates per privilegia et alias indulgentias Romanorum Pontificum Prædecessorum nostrorum monasterio vestro concessas, nec non Libertates et Exemptiones secularium Exactionum a Regibus et Principibus, et alijs Christi fidelibus, rationabiliter vobis indultas, sicut eas juste ac pacifice obtinetis, vobis, et per vos, eidem Monasterio auctoritate Apostolica confirmamus, et præsentis scripti patrocinio communimus; Nulli ergo omnino hominum liceat hanc paginam nostræ Confirmationis infringere, vel ei ausu temerario contraire; Si quis autem hoc attemptare præsumserit, indignationem Omnipotentis Dei, et beatorum Petri et Pauli Apostolorum ejus se noverit incursurum Datum Lugduni Idibus Martii Pontificatus nostri anno tertio."

Not.—No seal nor tag.

William, Earl of Ross, died without male issue at Delny, in Ross-shire, in 1372, and disputes arose as to his succession. Fearing probably that amidst the conflict for this great earldom and its superiorities and rights, the little priory of Beauly might lose some of its possessions, the monks procured from the supreme pontiff, in 1373, the preceding charter. It is a Bull from Gregory XI., dated at Lyons on the ides of March, the third year of his pontificate, simply and in the most general terms confirming all the liberties and immunities which had been conceded to the monastery by the Roman pontiffs, his predecessors. There is a description added to the allusion to the Valliscaulian order which is remarkable: " Ad Romanam Ecclesiam nullo medio pertinentis." This asserts that the order held directly under the authority of the Church at Rome, without the intervention of any intermediate superior; but such a statement seems far from accurate, as we shall see hereafter that the houses of the order were liable to the jurisdiction and visitation of the bishop of the diocese in which they were placed.

Hugh Fraser, Lord of Lovat, appears to have been remiss in his payments of the various rents under which he held from the Bishop of Moray the church lands possessed by John Byset, and in 1304 he agrees, without any further allegation of danger, or war, or other cause, to pay £20 sterling by two instalments, and fifty shillings more, and thereupon to be remitted all back dues, either for the annual rents of Kiltarlity, the Esse, or Moniack, or the grain tithes of the parish of Wardlaw; and he promises to support the bishop in his holdings, particularly in that of the two towns of Kilmylies, and agrees to help the bishop to recover that part of the annual rent of Kiltarlity and of the Esse which affects the portion of a noble man, William of Fenton, in the said lands of Kiltarlity.*

By 1389, Alexander of Chisholm seems to have died, and Thomas de Chisholm† is surety for the performance of the sentence of Bishop Alexander of Moray and Alexander of Ross, against Alexander Stewart, Earl of Buchan, in relation to his wife, Euphemia, Countess of Ross, the co-sureties being Robert, Earl of Sutherland, and Alexander de Moravia, Lord of Coulbin.

This Alexander Stewart was the famous "Wolf of Badenoch," who, getting up a quarrel with the Bishop of Moray, who had decided against him, burned, in June of the following year

* Reg. Moray, p. 195. † Ib., p. 354.

(1390), the town of Elgin, and the noble and beautiful cathedral church of Moray, the glass of the country, and the glory of the kingdom. He died on the 24th July 1394, and his effigy rests upon his monument in full armour in the cathedral of Dunkeld.

On the 10th of May previously, 1394, Alexander of the Isles, Lord of Lochaber, agreed to take custody of all the lands of Moray for Thomas of Dunbar, Earl of Moray, excepting the lands of Hugh Fraser, Thomas of Cheseholme, and Sir William of Fodringham, among whom was a certain agreement concerning their lands, probably a bond of manrent, needful enough in those times.

Thomas de Chisholm was Constable of the Castle of Urquhart in 1391-92, succeeding Robert de Chisholm of Chisholm in Roxburghshire, who acquired from John Randolph, Earl of Moray, in 1345, the lands of Lochletter in Glenurquhart, and was keeper of the castle of Urquhart in 1364, when his daughter married Hugh Rose of Kilravock.* This Alexander de Insulis, Lord of Lochaber, seems to have been a troublesome neighbour to the Bishop of Moray, though a friend to the family of Del Ard. On the 20th November 1398, William, Bishop of Moray, issues a monition to Donald, Dean of Christianity de Inverness, and chaplain of the parish church of Inverness, stating that since Alexander de Insulis, Lord of Lochaber, had granted three portions of the land of Kilmylies to three persons, the dean was to warn these persons not to enter upon these lands.†

Hugh Fraser, first of Lovat, is said to have died in 1398, and to have been succeeded by his son Alexander, who is said to have been served heir to his father in that year.‡ Alexander Fraser of Lovat was a great benefactor to the Priory of Beauly, having built a beautiful steeple of carved oak, which stood upon the western gable, and put a curious bell therein.

In the paucity of charters and records concerning the priory,

---
* Chamberlain Accounts, vol. ii., p. 159; Family of Kilravock, p. 36.
† Reg. Moray, p. 211. ‡ Anderson's Family of Fraser, p. 51.

we may carry on the history of the founder's family and of the barony of the Aird.

Margaret del Ard, mother of Thomas de Chisholm, acts as proprietrix of her portion of the Byset lands in 1401. On 8th January of that year she, styling herself Margaret of the Ard, lady of that ilk, by an indenture dated at Dunballoch, gives Angus, the son of Godfrey of Isles, on his marriage with her daughter Margaret, and their heirs, the davoch of Croychel and half davoch of Conyr Kynbady. Croychel, Crochails, though on the south side of the river Glass, are in the parish of Kilmorack, and were doubtless in the earldom of Ross; Conyr was in the parish of Conveth, and afterwards became a separate parish by the bounty of the Priory of Beauly.*

Godfrey de Insula, Lord of Uist, as he styles himself in a charter to the monastery of Inchaffray, dated 7th July 1389, was eldest son of John, Lord of the Isles, by the wife who was divorced in order to marry the daughter of Robert II.; the descendants of Godfrey were called the Siol Gorrie, or race of Godfrey.

Alexander de Insulis, who undertook the guardianship of the Moray lands in 1394, was son of Godfrey, and brother of Angus, who married Thomas de Chisholm's sister; Mr Skene states that he was that Alexander Macreuvy de Garmoran † who was summoned to the Parliament held at Inverness by James I. in 1427, and there beheaded.

No historian of the Highlands seems to have noticed this Angus, son of Godfrey; and the deed was first published among the Inchaffray charters; it provides, in default of heirs of the marriage, for the return of the lands to Margaret and her sons; and as the Croychels are subsequently found in possession of Haliburton, who married the heiress of Margaret del Ard, I suppose that Angus died without issue. The whole contract is an instance of the way in which alliances were made with persons who had command of armed men.

Alexander del Ard had been induced in 1376 to resign to

---

* Lib. Insulæ Miss., pref. l., li.   † He burned Elgin, 1402.

the king the davoch of Garthyes in Sutherland, part of the earldom of Strathern, which he inherited as the son of Matilda de Strathern. Afterwards he was appointed custodier of the earldom of Orkney by the King of Denmark in a deed given by Torfæus,* and died without issue. Margaret del Ard, probably his sister, was anxious to recover these lands ; and she, by this contract with Angus of the Isles, who had the command, very likely, of some of the two thousand cateranes who were at his brother Alexander's disposal, agreed that if she, with his help, should recover these lands of Garthyes, he and her daughter should have one-fourth of them, leaving the three-fourths to her sons, her other children. She and her eldest son and heir, Thomas de Chisholm, in 1403, by an indenture dated at Kinrossy, between them and William of Fentoun of Baky, divide the lands of which they were heir-portioners, and which lay in the sheriffdoms of Perth, Forfar, Lanark, Aberdeen, and Inverness, and agreed that the lands of the Aird should be participated as they were divided of old. She is styled in this deed Margaret of the Ard, Lady of Erchless.†

In 1407 Hugh Fraser was Lord of Lovat, so Alexander Fraser must have died before that year.‡ On the 31st March Hugo Fraser, Lord of Lovat and of Kinnell, in the sheriffdom of Forfar, grants the lands of Easter Braky, within the barony of Kinnell, to his beloved cousin, Peter de Strivelyn, and John de Stirling, son of the said Peter. The cousinship of Hugh Fraser of Lovat to the Stirlings is to be traced probably on the Byset side.§ Elizabeth Byset, widow of Andrew de Bosco, gave the lands of Kilravock to her daughter Mariot and her husband, Hugh de Rose. And in 1327 Alexander de Stirling and Elizabeth, his wife, daughter of Sir John de Bosco, knight, release to William de Rose all claim to the lands of Kilravock, under the sanction of a fine of £40, to be paid to the fabric of the cathedral church of Elgin. This Peter de Stirling may have been a descendant of Elizabeth de Bosco.

* Torfæus' Hist. Orc.   † Reg. Mag. Sig., lib. xviii., No. 138.
‡ Reg. Mag. Sig., 243, 2.   § Family of Kilravock, p. 114.

The next transaction respecting the Aird property has been so erroneously represented that it must be stated accurately. According to Shaw, Hugh married Margaret, daughter and heiress of William Fenton of Beaufort, and thereby got the lands; the truth being that in 1416, Hugh Fraser married Janet, sister of William de Fenton; and by a deed which we print in the Appendix,* dated 3d March 1415, the Lord of Beaufort, William of Fenton, granted to them and their heirs, Guisachan, Comarkirkton, Mauld, and Wester Eskadale, lying in Strathglass, within the barony of the Aird, and, until the lands of Uchterach were recovered, the two Buntaits in pledge; and for dowry Hugh Fraser was to give £20 lands of the lordship of Golford, in the sheriffdom of Nairn, and if any deficiency, it was to be made up by Hugh Fraser out of the lands of Dalcross. The contract was executed at Baky, the principal seat of the Fentons, where, as at Beaufort, they had erected a chapel, and where, as it appears they did not do at Beaufort, they endowed a chaplain.

Seven years afterwards, on 9th August 1422,† Hugh Fraser enters into a contract for his son and heir, who must have been an infant, marrying a daughter of Thomas of Dunbar, Earl of Moray; and on his part the Earl of Moray conveys the barony of Abertarff and the ward and relief of the late William of Fenton, Lord of the Baky, and of Alexander of Chisholm, Lord of Kinrossy, pertaining to the Earl William, in the Aird and Strathglass. Thomas de Chisholm had been succeeded by Alexander de Chisholm.

Hugh Fraser, in the division of the Byset lands, obtained with the Lovat lands those not granted to the Roses in the sheriffdom of Nairn, such as Golford, in the parish of Cawdor, and Dalcross, in the parish of that name. He made up titles to these in 1431, and in the same year he is Sheriff of Inverness.‡ In 1436 he grants the third of the lands of Glenelg to Alexander of the Isles, Earl of Ross. Among the witnesses are John, vicar of Kilmorack, showing that the parish in which

* Appendix, No. XI.   † Appendix, No. XII.
‡ Reg. Mag. Sig., iii., Nos. 74-79; Family of Kilravock, p. 119.

Beauly Priory lay had now by the favour of the cathedral authorities of Ross obtained a resident minister.

The historian of the family of Lovat remarks of this Hugh Fraser:* His piety afforded the means of building the north work of the church of Beauly and the Chapel of the Holy Cross, and he got the privilege of a fair there on the 3d of May annually, called Cross Fair, which the historian speaks of as continuing in his time. He likewise erected a famous cross at Wellhouse, which was afterwards brought to Beauly. There, we may add, the pedestal still remains just outside the gate to the priory, and around which, on market and fair days, may be seen buyers and sellers, who perhaps think their bargain incomplete unless made near the cross. His seal still remains † attached to an inquisition of 1431. "Lovat's shield is quarterly, one and four, three fraises; two and three, three figures, which may be crowns." He is said to have died in 1440, and to have been buried at Beauly.

On the 20th July 1440, the Lord of Lovat is Thomas Fraser; he is witness to a charter of Alexander de Ile, Earl of Ross, which, by its being contemporary with another to the same effect, dated at Kylmile, seems to show that this considerable estate of Kilmylies had, notwithstanding the Bishop of Moray's monition of 1398, passed from Alexander of Lochaber to his nephew, Alexander, Earl of Ross; and as among the witnesses is one called in one copy "John, son of William de Arde," and in another "John, son of William of Phoineas [Fothnes]," we may conclude that the intimate connection between the heirs of the Byset family and that of the Isles was still kept up. ‡

The historian states that Hugh Fraser, who died in 1440, had issue one son, Thomas, who died young and was Prior of Beauly *ad commendam*.§

Thomas Fraser, Lord of Lovat, probably eldest son of the marriage of 1416, died before 1456, ‖ for the chamberlain

* Family of Fraser, p. 58.   † Family of Innes, p. 129.
‡ Family of Kilravock, pp. 131, 132.   § Family of Lovat, p. 63.
‖ Book of Cawdor, p. 24.

preceding William of Cawdor, in 1456 charges himself with
£143 of rents of the lands of the Aird, Strathglass, Abertarff,
and Stratherrick (Strathardok), then being in the hands of
the lord the king, by the death of the late Thomas Fraser
of the Lovat, in the ward of the earldom of Moray, from the
same term with its tenandries ; and the bargain with the Earl
of Moray for a marriage of Hugh Fraser of Lovat's son with
Lord Moray's daughter, seems to have been carried out with
a second Hugh Fraser, probably a younger brother of
Thomas, who succeeded him, who is mentioned on the 20th
May 1455, as Huchone Fraser of the Lovate, as if married to
Janet, daughter of Elizabeth, Countess of Moray.*

Meanwhile the Beaufort part of the Byset lands had descended by the death of Walter of Fenton,† without male issue, to his four daughters. Margaret de Fenton, of Beaufort, the eldest daughter, married David Lindesay of Lethnot,‡ after marrying Walter de Ogilvy.§ Another fourth went to James of Douglas, knight, who had married Janet de Fenton, another daughter, with whom he had a fourth of the lands of Aird and Strathglass, and whose son was Henry Douglas, styled of Culbirnie in 1509.‖ In 1459 this fourth seems to have been given to Mariota, wife of Sir David Stewart of Rossyth, knight.

The Erchless part of the Byset lands shared the same fate. Alexander de Chisholm, whose ward and relief are granted by the contract of 1422, is said to have died without male issue, leaving a daughter and heir or co-heiress, who married Walter Halyburton, second son of the first Lord Halyburton of Dirleton; and this Walter, by this marriage, obtained, it is said, the barony of Pitcur, in the parish of Kettins, in the county of Forfar, of which he had a charter in

---

* Spalding Club Misc., 4, 218.

† In the Chamberlain's Accounts for 1438, there is a charge for the rent of the third part of the barony of Drumblate, belonging to the heirs of this Walter de Fenton.

‡ Collections on Shires of Aberdeen and Banff, vol. iv., pp. 66-68.   § Ib.

‖ Laing's Scottish Seals, date, 15th September 1509 ; Collections on the Shires of Aberdeen and Banff, vol. i., p. 478.

1432, and so founded the family of Halyburton of Pitcur, an estate still possessed by his descendants.

In 1462, John Halyburton, styled of Kinrossie, which was the designation of Alexander de Chisholm, is proceeded against by the Abbot of Arbroath* for alienating the lands of Bucht, in the parish of Inverness, which had been granted to Christian del Ard in 1322, upon the express condition that he was not to alienate them.

About this time, Hugh Fraser—that is, the Huchone Fraser of the Lovat of 1455—was made a peer of Parliament. His property in Forfarshire, also near Nairn, was considerable; and the first document which styles him a peer, is a contract with the burgh of Nairn in 1472, which shows his strong position there. His fortune was so much increased by his marriage with the daughter of the Earl of Moray as to enable him to secure the peerage. There is a charter under the Great Seal, dated 28th February 1480, where Hugh is styled by the king, "Hugo dominus Fraser de Lovat ac Baro Baroniæ de Kinnell."†

Among the Lovat deeds of 1651,‡ we have one proof that the Priory of Beauly had done its duty in endowing the vicar of the parish of Conveth, which had been appropriated to them, and which vicarage had been endowed and constituted before Boiamond's Taxation (1274), two hundred years before, by the entry:

"72. Presentation of the vicarage of Conveth to Sir David Walker, dated the 7th day of June 1474."

The advowson and right of presentation to a vicarage followed from the endowment of it by the ecclesiastical corporation to whom the rectory was appropriated; and the priory

* Lib. de Aberbrothock, vol. ii., pp. 138-140.
† We hope that our readers will excuse these details, but as Dean Howson says in the Transactions of the Cambridge Camden Society, "The antiquities of Paisley Abbey might not be studied without attention to the history of the Stewart family; nor the antiquities of Beauly Abbey without attention to that of the Lovat family" (vol. 1845, p. 77).
‡ Dunbar Dunbar MS.

having the right of presentation to the vicarage of Conway, shows that they had founded and endowed it. The name of this parish is singular, as it is the same word "Conveth" which so often occurs as a right belonging to superiors of lands, especially ecclesiastical superiors. Mr Innes* seems to think it means the right of having supplies of food, and perhaps other aids, to a journey given to the head of the house, which was the superior of the land, on his progress to inspect the monastic or capitular estates, deriving the word from *Convoi*. In the case of this parish, which is a long valley, terminating in a gorge, running from the highlands above Beauly to the valley of Glenurquhart, the word seems to mean the passage from the valley of the Beauly to the valley of the Ness. The word is evidently the same as "Conway," in Wales, which is a pass. David Walker is called Donald Galle in the next charter.

* Scottish Leg. Ant., 205.

No. XIII.

COLLATIO ECCLESIÆ PAROCHIALIS DE CONUETH AD CONVENTUM DE BELLO LOCO SPECTANT: PER WILLIELMUM EPISCOPUM MORAVIENSEM ANNO 1480.

Ex Autographo.

" Willielmus Dei et Apostolicæ Sedis Gratia Episcopus Moraviensis discreto viro Domino Fynlaio parochialis Ecclesiæ de Wardlaw Nostræ Diocesis vicario Salutem cum Benedictione divina quia vicariam perpetuam Ecclesiæ Parochialis de Conueth, de jure et de facto vacantem per mortem quondam Domini Donaldi Galle, ultimi vicarij et possessoris ejusdem ad Venerabilium ac discretorum virorum Dominorum Prioris et conventus Monasterij de Bewly præsentationem, nostramque Collationem de jure spectantem discreto viro Willielmo Jaksone procuratori, et eo nomine discreti viri Domini Alexandri Fauy nostræ Diocœsis prædictæ Presbyteri, de cujus procurationis mandato nobis constitit sufficienter, caritatis intruitu contulimus et conferimus per præsentes, ipsumque per annuli nostri traditionem induximus et investivimus præsentialiter de eadem. Curam et Administrationem ejusdem in spiritualibus et Temporalibus sibi specialiter committendo. Vobis in virtute santæ obedientiæ tenore præsentium committimus et mandamus, quatenus præfatum Alexandrum Fauy Presbyterum vel suum procuratorem ejus nomine, in et ad realem actualem et corporalem possessionem dictæ Vicariæ Ecclesiæ de Conueth, juriumque et pertinentium omnium ejusdem inducatis et instituatis, inductum et institutum Canonice defendatis, facient, sibi vel dicto Procuratori suo de Fructibus, Redditibus, Proventibus, Juribus et Obventionibus universis ejusdem integre responderi. Contradictores et rebelles, si qui forte fuerint, per Censuram Ecclesiasticam arctius compescendo. In signum vero hujus Institutionis vestræ traditæ, et eidem per vos possessionis, Sigillum vestrum in secunda cauda post nostrum præsentibus appendatis penes prædictum Institutum perpetue remansuris. Datum sub nostro Sigillo rotundo apud nostrum Palatium de Spineto, septimo die mensis Septembris Anno Domini Millesimo quadringentesimo octuagesimo Indictione decimæ tertiæ Pontificatus Sanctissimi in Christo patris et Domini nostri, Domini Sixti divina disponente Clementia, Papæ quarti anno nono præsentibus discretis viris Waltero Weya, Johanne Guthrye et Thoma Tulloch Armigeris cum diversis alijs testibus ad præmissa vocatis specialiter et rogatis.

> " Et ego Thomas Grame Presbiter Moraviensis publicus auctoritate Imperiali Notarius, quia prædictæ Collationi, cæterisque omnibus alijs et singulis, dum sic ut præmittitur, agerentur, dicerentur et fierent una cum prænominatis testibus præsens interfui, eaque omnia et singula sic fieri vidi, scivi et audivi, et de eis notam recepi. Ideoque hoc præsens Publicum Instrumentum manu alterius fideliter scriptum exinde confeci signoque, nomine et subscriptione meis solitis et consuetis, signavi et roboravi, rogatus et requisitus in fidem et testimonium omnium et singulorum præmissorum.
>
> " Et ego Dominus Finlaius feci Executionem istarum litterarum secundum tenorem præsentium, et quia non habui proprium Sigillum, Sigillum venerabilis viri Domini Johannis Fynla Prioris Belli loci feci appendi, coram hijs Domino Patricio Morra et Domino Johanne Duncan, Monachis Monasterij Belli loci, David clerico, Jacobo Alexandri, cum multis alijs ibidem præsentibus."

> Not.—At the side Thomas Grame with his cypher. To the charter are appended two tags of parchment. On the first is a seal of red wax upon white. On the seal, which is oval, is represented a Virgin crowned, holding in her two hands by the extremities a cross, whereupon her Son is crucified and nailed. She is in a handsome niche or portiche of the Church. Under the crucifix is the bishop's escutcheon and arms, viz., a fess charged with three stars betwixt three crosses, and on the circumference "S. Willielmi Dei gratia Episcopi Moraviensis." At the other tag there is no seal.

The instrument is dated in 1480, and called the collation of the parish church of Conveth by the Bishop of Moray.

Its form is: "William to Sir Finlay, vicar of Wardlaw (Kirkhill).—Since we have conferred, and do confer, the perpetual vicarage of the parish church of Conveth, vacant by the death of the late Sir Donald Galle, the last vicar and possessor thereof, appertaining as to presentation to the prior and convent of the monastery of Beauly, and as to collation to us, upon Alexander Fauy, a presbyter of our diocese; and him we have inducted and invested by the delivery of our ring: we direct that you shall induct and institute the said Alexander Fauy into corporal possession of the said vicarage, with all its rights; and in token of this, your institution, you shall attach your seal in the second tag after ours to these presents. Given under our Round seal at our Palace of Spiny." Thomas Grame, a priest of Moray and a notary, signs it; and Sir Finlay, because he has no proper seal, causes to be appended the seal of the venerable Sir John Fynla, Prior of Beauly, before Sir Patrick Morra and Sir John Duncan, monks of the monastery of Beauly. Unfortunately, there is no description of the seal of the prior, which was gone at the time of transcription. This instrument, in 1480 called a collation, had formerly in the Scottish Church been called, as it always was and is in the English Church, an institution, as may be seen in the "Chartulary of Cambuskenneth," 1282 (p. 4), 1295 (p. 143), 1328 (p. 203).

Collation is in England that instrument by which a bishop, who has himself the patronage of a parish church, directs the induction of the presentee into the actual possession of the church, and this instrument, when the presentation belongs to another than the bishop himself, is called an institution.

Now, collation in Scotland is the term used of the act of induction, to the total confusion of the English ecclesiastical lawyer, who is accustomed to see the three essentials of presentation, institution, and induction always proved before a parish incumbent can be entitled to the temporalities of his living.

Doubtless the presentation by the priory followed the form of the following instrument.

No. XIV.

PRÆSENTATIO AD ECCLESIAM DE CONUAY PER PRIOREM ET CONVENTUM DE BELLO LOCO ANNO 1493.

Ex Autographo.

"Reverendo in Christo patri ac Domino, Domino Andreæ, Dei et Apostolicæ sedis gratia Episcopo Moraviensi, sui humiles ac devoti oratores, Prior Belli loci et ejusdem Conventus, Reverentias debitas cum honore—Ad perpetuam Vicariam Ecclesiæ parochialis de Conuay vestræ Moraviensis Diocœsis nunc vacantem, per mortem quondam Domini Alexandri Fauy, ultimi vicarij et possessoris ejusdem, ad nostram præsentationem vestramque Collationem de Jure spectantem discretum virum Dominum Donaldum Walteri, vestræ Diocœsis Presbyterum, animo non variandi, vestræ Reverendæ Paternitati tenore præsentium præsentamus, rogantes quatenus dictum nostrum Præsentatum ad dictam Vicariam admittatis, eandemque sibi vel Procuratoribus suis pluribus aut uni conferatis, ac ipsum in et ad realem, actualem et corporalem dictæ vicariæ possessionem ejusdem inducatis et instituatis, inductum et institutum canonice defendatis, et sibi et procuratoribus suis de universis et singulis Jurium . . . et pertinentium omnium ejusdem fructibus, Juribus, Redditibus, Proficuis, Emolumentis, pertinentijs quibuscunque dictæ vicariæ, et sibi aut procuratoribus suis pluribus aut uni spectant^t integre facien^t responderi. Contradictores, si qui forte fuerint, per censuram Ecclesiasticam ex vestro officio pastorali arctius compescen^t. Cæteraque facient quæ vobis in præmissis incumbunt peragenda In cujus rei testimonium Sigillum nostrum commune præsentibus est appensum apud nostrum Monasterium prædicti Belli loci vicesimo septimo die Mensis instantis Decembris Anno Domini Millesimo quadringentesimo nonagesimo tertio."

Not.—Seal as above, blazoned oval on a tag parchment.

This is dated in 1493, and is the presentation, by the Prior of Beauly and the convent of the same, to Andrew, Bishop of Moray, of Sir Donald Walters, a presbyter of the diocese, to the perpetual vicarage of the parish church of Convay, vacant by the death of the late Alexander Fauy, belonging to their presentation and the bishop's collation.

In the meantime we are told that about this period the Priory of Beauly * was repaired at the expense of the superior, a natural son of Alexander of Kintail, who is there buried, A.D. 1479.

His tomb is opposite the tomb of his brother Sir Kenneth Mackenzie of Kintail, which has on it the date 1491, and which is depicted in the frontispiece plate. Sir Kenneth was the first of his family who was buried at Beauly, all his predecessors having been, it is said, buried at Iona.† The reason is that he had married the daughter of Lord Lovat.

George, Earl of Huntly, holding, under Margaret of Denmark, queen of King James III., the governorship and custody of the Red Castle and lands of the Ardmarnoch, granted this, in 1482, to Hugh Rose of Kilravock. This was closed by Kenneth Mackenzie taking the Red Castle from Hugh Rose; and the way in which this doughty warrior, on the one hand, routed the Macdonalds of the Isles at Blairnaparc, and, on the other, expelled Hugh Rose and his allies, the Clan Chattan, from the Black Isle, shows his physical and mental qualities.‡ The alliance of the Roses and the Clan Chattan is shown by a bond of manrent.

The condition of the earldom of Ross, claimed by John, Lord of the Isles, and forfeited, and again granted to him, must have been very tempting to neighbouring barons, and, I believe, that from the struggle the Mackenzies emerged triumphant, and established a preponderating influence in Ross-shire, which has ever since been the land of the Mackenzies.§

---

* Family of Fraser, p. 61.
† I can find no trace of the tombs of the prior Lairds of Kintail among the descriptions of Iona.
‡ Family of Kilravock, p. 153.   § Appendix, No. XIII.

No. XV.

BULLA ALEXANDRI PAPÆ SEXTI PRO DOUGALLO RODERICI CLERICO ROSSENSIS DIOCŒSIS DE PRIORITATE DE BEAULIEU ORDINIS VALLISCAULIUM ANNO 1497.

Ex Autographo.

"Alexander Episcopus, Servus servorum Dei Venerabilibus Fratribus Aberdonensi et Moraviensi Episcopis ac dilecto filio Officiali Rossensi, Salutem et Apostolicam Benedictionem. Apostolicæ Sedis circumspecta Benignitas Regularem vitam ducere cupientibus, ut eorum pium propositum valeat ad laudem divini nominis, adimplere, Apostolico adesse præsidio et ad eos dexteram suæ liberalitatis extendere consuevit, quos ad id propria virtutum merita multipliciter recommendant. Dudum siquidem omnes Prioratus conventuales ordinum quorumcunque tunc vacantes, et in antea vacaturos Collationi et Dispositioni nostræ reservavimus, decernentes, ex tunc irritum et inane si secus super hijs a quoquam quavis auctoritate scienter vel ignoranter contigerit attemptari, cum itaque postmodum Prioratus de Bello loco, alias Beaulie, Cisterciensis ordinis, Rossensis Diocœsis, qui conventualis est, et quem quondam Hugo Frezel dicti Prioratis Prior, dum viveret, obtinebat, per obitum dicti Hugonis qui extra Romanam Curiam diem clausit extremum, vacaverit et vacet ad præsens, nullusque de illo præter nos hac vice disponere potuerit, sive possit, reservatione et Decreto obsistentibus supra dictis. Et sicut, accepimus dilectus filius Dougaldus Roderici Clericus dictæ Diocœsis cupiat ob melioris vitæ frugem in Monasterio Vallis caulium ordinis et Diocœsis prædictorum, a quo dictus Prioratus dependere dinoscitur, una cum dilectis filijs, Abbate et Conventu, sub regulari habitu virtutum, Domino famulari. Nos cupientes eundem Dougaldum in hujus modi suo laudabili proposito confovere, ac sibi apud nos de religionis zelo, vitæ ac morum honestate, alijsque laudabilibus probitatis et virtutum meritis multipliciter commendato; horum intuitu specialem gratiam facere valentes ipsumque Dougaldum a quibuscunque Excommunicationis, Suspensionis et Interdicti, alijsque

Ecclesiasticis Sententiis Censuris et Pœnis, a Jure vel ab homine quavis occasione, vel causa latis, si quibus quomodolibet innodatus existit, ad effectum præsentium duntaxat consequendum, harum serie absolventes, et absolutum fore censentes, discretioni vestræ per Apostolica Scripta mandamus. Quatenus vos, vel duo, vel unus vestrum per vos vel alium, seu alios, eundem Dougaldum, si sit ydoneus, et aliud Canonicum nonobsistat, in dicto Monasterio in Monachum recipiatis, et in fratrem, sibique regularem habitum, juxta ipsius Monasterij consuetudinem exhibeatis, facientes ipsum ibidem sincera in Domino caritate tractari, nec non professionem per Monachos Dicti Monasterij emitti solitam, si illam in manibus vestris sponte emittere voluerit, eadem auctoritate recipiatis, et admittatis; eaque per vos recepta et admissa, Prioratum prædictum, cujus Fructus Redditus et Proventus, quadraginta librarum Sterlingorum, secundum communem estimationem, valorem annuum, ut Dictus Dougaldus asserit, non excedunt, sive præmisso seu alio quovis modo, aut ex alterius cujuscunque persona, seu per liberam resignationem dicti Hugonis, vel cujusvis alterius de illo in dicta Curia, vel extra eam, etiam coram Notario publico et testibus, sponte factam aut constitutionem felicis recordationis Johannis Papæ XXII. Prædecessoris nostri, quæ incipit, ' Execrabilis,' vel Assecutionem cujuslibet alterius Beneficij ecclesiastici, quavis auctoritate collati, vacat, etiamsi tanto tempore vacaverit, quod ejus collatio, juxta Lateranensis statuta consilij, ad sedem prædictam legittime devoluta, ipseque Prioratus dispositioni Apostolicæ specialiter, vel alias generaliter existat: Et ad illum consueverit quis per Electionem assumi, eique cura immineat animarum, super eo quoque inter aliquos Lis, cujus statum præsentibus volumus haberi pro expresso, pendeat indecisa, cum omnibus juribus et pertinentijs suis, eidem Dougaldo, eadem auctoritate nostra, conferre et Assignare Curetis, inducentes eundem Dougaldum, recepto prorsus ab eo, nostro et Ecclesiæ Romanæ nomine, fidelitatis debitæ solito juramento, juxta formam quam sub Bulla nostra mittimus introclusam, vel Procuratorem suum ejus nomine, in corporalem possessionem Prioratus, juriumque et Pertinentium prædictorum, et defendentes inductum, amoto exinde quolibet illicito detentore, ac facientes Dougaldum vel pro eo Procuratorem prædictum ad Prioratum prædictum, ut moris est, admitti, sibique de illius fructibus, redditibus, proventibus, Juribus, et obventionibus universis integre responderi, Contradictores auctoritate nostra, appellatione posposita compescendos, non obstantibus piæ memoriæ Bonifacij Papæ 8ᵛⁱ etiam prædecessoris nostri, et alijs Apostolicis constitutionibus, ac Monasterii, Prioratus et ordinis prædictorum, juramento, Confirmatione Apostolica vel quavis firmitate alia roboratis, Statutis, et Consuetudinibus, privilegijs quoque, Indultis, et Litteris dicto ordini per sedem prædictam concessis, innovatis et confirmatis; illis præsertim quibus inter alia caveri dicitur expresse, quod nullus Prioratus, vel alia Beneficia Ecclesiastica dicti ordinis retinere, aut illo sibi conferri possint, nisi professionem per Monachos dicti ordinis emitti solitam, expresse emiserit regularem, et saltem per annum integrum in dicto ordine probatus fuerit; et alias de illis etiam per dictam sedem factæ provisiones nullius sint roboris, vel momenti, Monasteriorumque dicti ordinis, abbatas, Conventus et Personæ illos, quibus alios de Beneficijs hujus modi provideri contingeret, etiam cujuscunque dignitatis, status, gradus, ordinis, vel conditionis forent, vel alias litteris Apostolicis desuper concessis obedire nullatenus tenerentur, et ad id compelli; aut propterea interdici, suspendi, vel excommunicari non possint, et sententiæ quas contra inobedientes, proferri contigerit, vigore literarum provisionum hujus modi nullius sint roboris, vel momenti, etiamsi in eisdem litteris de dictis privilegijs et Indultis, et litteris eorumque toto tenore, specialis specifica et expressæ, aut per illam importantes clausulas, mentio fieret, et illis etiam cum motus proprij et certæ Scientiæ, ac de potestatis plenitudine vel alias derogaretur, nisi id fieret de fratrum consilio, ac Abbatis Monasterij Cistertiensis Cabilonensis Diocœsis pro tempore existentis, ac dilectorum filiorum Conventus illius consensu, quæ quidem Derogatio postmodum eidem Abbati et Cofratribus Capituli generalis ejusdem ordinis, per diversas litteras etiam sub diversis datis, cum certo dierum intervallo expeditas, intimari debeat, quibus etiamsi de ijs, eorumque totis tenoribus, pro eorum sufficienti derogatione, specialis, specifica, individua, et expressa, ac de verbo ad verbum, non autem per generales clausulas idem importantes mentio, seu quavis alio expressio habenda foret, tenores hujusmodi, ac si de verbo ad verbum inserti forent, præsentibus pro expressis habentes, hac vice duntaxat, illis alias in suo robore permansuris, specialiter et expresse derogamus, contrarijs quibuscunque. Aut si pro alijs in dicto Monasterio Vallis caulium scripta Apostolica forsan sint directa, seu si aliqui super provisionibus sibi ferendis de Prioratibus hujusmodi speciales, vel alijs Beneficijs Ecclesiasticis in illis partibus, generales dictæ sedis, vel Legatorum ejus litteras importarint, etiamsi per eos ad inhibitionem reservationem, et decretum, vel alias quomodolibet sit processum, quibus omnibus præfatum Dougallum in Assecutioni dicti Prioratus, volumus anteferri, sed nullum per hoc eis, quoad Assecutionem Prioratuum, vel Beneficiorum aliorum præjudicium generari; Seu si Venerabili Fratri nostro Episcopo Rossensi, ac Abbati Monasterij Vallis caulium, et illius, ac Prioratus prædictorum Conventibus, vel quibuscunque allijs, communiter vel divisim ab eadem sede sit indultum, quod ad receptionem vel provisionem alicujus minime teneantur, et ad id compelli, aut quod interdici, suspendi vel excommunicari non possint, quodque de Prioratibus hujusmodi, vel alijs Beneficijs Ecclesiasticis ad eorum collationem, provisionem, præsentationem, electionem, seu quamvis aliam Dispositionem conjunctim vel separatim spectantibus nulli valeat provideri, per litteras Apostolicas, non facientes plenam et expressam, ac de verbo ad verbum de Indulto hujusmodi mentionem, et qualibet alia dictæ Sedis Indulgentia speciali vel generali, cujuscunque tenores existat, per quam præsentibus non expressam vel totaliter non insertam effectus hujusmodi gratiæ impediri valeat quomodolibet vel differi. Et de qua cujusque toto tenore habenda esset in nostris litteris mentio specialis, nos enim, prout est, irritum decernimus et inane. Si secus super hijs a quoquam, quavis auctoritate, scienter vel ignoranter attemptatum forsan est hactenus, vel in posterum contigerit attemptari. Datum Romæ apud sanctum Petrum anno Incarnationis Dominicæ Millesimo quadringentesimo nonagesimo septimo, Septimo Calendas Martij, Pontificatus nostri anno sexto."

> Not.—Below is, "Expedita octavo Idus Julij Anno octavo P. Tuba:" and under the replay on the left hand four names, in the middle three, and on the right hand "Sollicitavit C. Balbus," and other two lines; on the replay in flourished letters, "C. Berotius." On the seal lead hinging to a piece of packthreed, on one side St Peter's head, on the other St Paul's, separate by a cross. On the reverse, Alexander Papa VI., and above the packthreed, on the back of the Bull is " Js. Ortere."

Our next instrument is a Bull from Alexander Borgia, asserting a right to nominate the Prior of Beauly, and exercising the right. It is dated 1497, and addressed to the Bishops of Aberdeen and Moray, and the Official of Ross. The Pope arrogates to himself the collation and disposition to all conventual priories whenever vacant, of whatever order—a most unwarrantable usurpation, and in the teeth of the Bull approving the rules of the Valliscaulian order, whose convents were to elect their own prior.

His Holiness then recites that the Priory of Bello Loco or Beaulie, of the Cistercian order, a conventual priory, was vacant by the death of Hugo Frezel, who finished his days without the Roman court,* and that none but the supreme pontiff could dispose of the office.

The Pope who "drew a line along the map from the north to the south, and gave away, by a stroke of his pen, half the habitable world," † was not likely to hesitate when a petty priory, in the farthest north of Britain, was to be disposed of; and if the Cistercian order had acknowledged his right to so nominate their abbots, then the petty priory must follow the Cistercian order.

The Pope understands that Dougal, the son of Roderic, a clerk of the diocese of Ross, desires for the hope of a better life, in the monastery of the Valliscaulian order, to whom the priory belongs, to serve God, under the habit of a regular; and therefore the Pope directs the Bishops of Aberdeen and Moray, and the Official of Ross, to receive the said Dougal into the state of a monk and a brother and a regular habit, according to the custom of the monastery; and, this being done, they were to confer on him the priory—the annual income of which did not exceed, according to the allegation of Dougal, £40 sterling.

"Forty pounds sterling!" How is the gold become dim! How is the most pure gold changed since the days of the taxation of Boiamond! then £200—and a pound then meant a pound of silver, whereas in 1500 a pound of silver was coined into £7 sterling, so much had Scotland suffered under the rule of the descendants of Robert the Steward.

Dougal was, before admission to the priorate, to take the oath of fidelity to the Pope, which is sent with the Bull, and forms the next instrument that we print.

* Appendix, No. XIV. † Dean Waddington's History of the Church, p. 652.

No. XVI.

FORMA JURAMENTI PRIORIS B. JOHANNIS BAPTISTÆ
DE BELLO LOCO CISTERTIENSIS ORDINIS ROSSEN-
SIS DIOCŒSIS SUB REGULA VALLISCAULIUM A
SUMMO PONTIFICE NOMINATI.

" Ego Dougallus Roderici Prior Prioratus conventualis B. Johannis Baptistæ de Bello loco, ordinis Cisterciensis sub regula Valliscaulium, Rossensis Diocœsis, ab hac hora in Antea fidelis et obediens ero B. Petro, sanctæque Apostolicæ Romanæ Ecclesiæ, ac Domino nostro, Domino Alexandro Papæ sexto, ejusque Successoribus Canonice intrantibus. Non ero in Consilio, Consensu, Tractatu vel facto ut vitam vel membrum perdant, seu quando contra alicujus eorum personam, vel in ipsorum aut Ecclesiæ ejusdem, sevi Sedis Apostolicæ, et auctoritatis, Honoris, Privilegiorum, Jurium vel Apostolicorum Statutorum, Ordinationum Reservationum, Dispositionum sive mandatorum derogationem vel præjudicium, machinationis aut conspirationis fiant, Et si ac quotiens aliquid tractari scivero, id pro posse ne fiat, Impediam, et quanto citius commode potero, eidem Domino nostro, vel alteri, per quem ad ipsius notitiam pervenire possit, significabo. Consilium vero quod mihi per se, aut nuntios, seu Litteras credituri sunt, ad eorum damnum, mesciente, nemini pandam. Ad retinendum et defendendum Papatum Romanum, et Regalia Sancti Petri, contra omnem hominem adjutor eis ero, Authoritatem, Honorem, Privilegia, ac Jura quantum in me fuerit, potius augere et promovere, Statuta, Ordinationes, Reservationes, Dispositiones, et Mandata hujusmodi observare, ac eis intendere Curabo. Legatos Sedis ejusdem honorifice tractabo, et in suis necessitatibus adjuvabo. Hæreticos, Schismaticos, et qui alicui de Domino nostro, Successor. Pontif. rebelles fuerint, pro viribus persequar, et impugnabo. Possessiones vero ad Prioratum meum pertinentes non vendam, neque donabo, neque Impignorabo, neque de novo Infeodabo, vel aliquo modo alienabo, Etiam cum consensu Conventus dicti Prioratus, in consulto Romano Pontifice. Sic me Deus adjuvet, et per hæc Santa Dei Evangelia."

This is the form of oath to be taken by the new prior.

It is entitled "The form of oath of the Prior of Saint John Baptist of Beauly of the Cistercian order, the diocese of Ross, under the rule of the Valliscaulians, named by the supreme pontiff."

By it the prior declares that he will be faithful and obedient to St Peter, the Holy Apostolic Roman Church, and to our Lord, Lord Alexander the Pope the Sixth, and to his successors canonically succeeding.

This provision as to canonical successors was inserted to prevent obedience to a pope *de facto*, though by usurpation.

The prior declares that he will not be party to any counsel or act against them, or to their injury in life or member, power or authority, and will reveal any such counsel coming to his knowledge to them; that he will never reveal, to their injury, the advice which he receives from the holders of the Holy See, either by nuncios or letters; that he will defend the Roman papacy and the regalia of St Peter against every man; and he will, as much as in him lies, increase its authority and obey its commands. He will treat the legates of the see, as delighting to honour them, and keep them if in need, and with all his might prosecute and fight against heretics, schismatics, and all those who shall be rebels against the supreme pontiff.

Finally, he declares he will not sell the possessions belonging to his priory, nor give them away, nor impignorate them, nor grant new infeftments of them, nor in any other manner alienate them, even with the consent of the convent of the said priory, without consulting the Roman pontiff.

No. XVII.

BULLA ALEXANDRI PAPÆ 6ᵀᴵ ANDREA MORAVIENSE EPISCOPO DE PRIORATU DE BEAULIEU IN FAVOREM DOUGALLI RODERICI CLERICI AD ANNUM 1500 XIᴹᴼ DIE FEBRUARIJ.

Ex Autographo.

"Reverendis in Christo patribus et Dominis, Dominis Dei et Apostolicæ Sedis gratia, Aberdonensi et Rossensi Episcopis ac Officiali Rossensi eorumque in Spiritualibus et Temporalibus Vicariis et Officialibus generalibus, nec non Abbati et conventui Valliscaulium, ac etiam venerabilibus et religiosis viris Dominis Suppriori et Conventui de Bello loco, alias Beulie Cistertiensis ordinis, Rossensis Diocœsis, ac illi vel illis ad quem vel ad quos Prioratus de Bello loco alias Beulie prædict. Collatio, provisio, Præsentatio, seu quævis alia Dispositio communiter vel divisim pertinet omnibusque alijs et singulis quorum interest, intererit, et quos infra scriptum negotium tangit seu tangere poterit in futurum, quibuscunque naminibus censeantur, et quavis præfulgeant dignitate, Andreas miseratione divina Episcopus Moraviensis Judex et Executor ad infra scripta una cum quibusdam alijs infra scriptis nostris in hac parte Collegis cum illa Clausula Quatenus vos vel duo, vel unus vestrum a sede Apostolica specialiter deputat. Salutem in Domino et nostris immovero Apostolicis firmiter obedere mandatis Litteras Sanctissimi in Christo Patris et Domini nostri, Domini Alexandri, divina disponente Clementia, Papæ sexti in pergameno scriptas, Ejus vero plumbea cum Cordula Cannabis more Romanæ Ecclesiæ impendent bullatas, sanas et integras non vitiatas, non cancellatas, nei in aliqua suarum parte suspectas, sed omnibus prorsus vitio et suspicione carentes, ut prima facie apparebat nobis, per circumspectum virum Dominum Dougallum Roderici Clericum Rossensis Diocœsis prædict. In præfatis Litteris Apostolicis principaliter nominatum, coram Notario Publico et testibus infra scriptis præsentatas et exhibitas nos cum eaque decint Reverentia noveritis recepisse et per legi fecisse, tenorem qui sequitur continentes ' Alexander Episcopus, &c. Datum Romæ apud sanctum Petrum Anno Incarnationis Dominice Millesimo quadringentesimo nonagesimo septimo Septimo Kalendas Martii, Pontificatus nostri anno sexto.' Post quarum quidem Litterarum Apostolicarum hujus modi præsentationem receptionem, et lecturam nobis et per nos sicut præmittitur, factas, fuimus per dictum Dominum Dougallum in dictis litteris Apostolicis principalem personaliter nominatum debita cum instantia requisiti, quatenus ad executionem dictarum litterarum Apostolicarum, et contentorum in eisdem, juxta traditam seu directam nobis in ipsis formam, procedere curaremus. Nos vero Andreas Episcopus Judex et Executor præfatus attendens requisitionem hujus modi justam fore, et ratione consonam, volensque mandatum Apostolicum nobis in hac parte directum reverenter exequi ut tenemur ac de meritis et idoneitate dicti Domini Dougalli principalis coram nobis personaliter constituti, et alijs in dictis litteris Apostolicis expressis et contentis inquisivimus, et nos super hijs informavimus diligenter, et quia per hujus modi inquisitionem et informationem comperimus præfatum Dominum Dougallum ad hoc utilem et ydoneum &c. et cetera in dictis litteris Apostolicis contenta ita fore, et veritate fulceri. Idcirco Auctoritate Apostolica in hac parte nobis commissa, et qua fungimur, dictum Dominum Dougallum principalem, servatis ad hoc servandis, in Monachum dicti Monasterii de Bello loco, alias Beulie, et fratrem recepimus, et sibi habitum Regularem juxta ipsius Monasterii consuetudinem exhibuimus, faciensque ipsum ibidem sincera in Domino caritate tractari, nec non professionem per Monachos dicti Monasterii emitti solitam, ipso in nostris manibus illam sponte et libere emittente, prout emissit, eadem Auctoritate recepimus et admissimus, eaque per nos recepta et admissa dictum Prioratum de Bello loco, alias Beulie, cum omnibus juribus et pertinentiis suis eidem Dougallo dicta Apostolica auctoritate contulimus et assignavimus, conferimus et Assignamus per præsentes ipsumque, Dominum Dougallum præfatum per annuli nostri in ipsius digito impositionem induximus et investivimus præsentialiter de eodem Curam, Regimen et Administrationem ejusdem in spiritualibus et temporalibus sibi specialiter committendo Recepto prius ab eodem Domino Dougallo, dicti Sanctissimi Domini nostri

Papæ et Ecclesiæ Romanæ nomine, fidelitatis debitæ solito juramento, juxta formam Bullæ nobis de super directæ, ac eundem Dougallum tunc præsentem, in corporalem possessionem Prioratus, Jurium et pertinentium prædictorum per traditionem dictarum litterarum Apostolicarum prout melius potuimus et debuimus, posuimus et induximus ponimus et inducimus ac eundem in eisdem investivimus per præsentes, amoto exinde quolibet illicito detentore. Quæ Omnia et Singula, nec non litteras Apostolicas huncque nostrum processum vobis omnibus et singulis supra dictis et vestrum cuilibet intimamus, insinuamus, et notificamus, ac ad vestram et vestrum cujuslibet notitiam deducimus, et deduci volumus per præsentes, vos nihilominus et vestrum quilibet in solidum, eisdem auctoritate et tenore requiremus et monemus, Primo, Secundo, Tertio, et peremptorie communiter, et divisim, ac vobis et vestrum cuilibet in virtute sanctæ obedientiæ, et sub infra scriptis Sentenciarum pœnis districte præcipientes. Quatenus infra sex dies post præsentationem seu notificationem prædictarum litterarum apostolicarum, et præsentis nostri processus, vobis seu alteri vestrum factas, et postquam per dictum Dominum Dougallum, seu ex parte ipsius, vigore præsentium fueritis requisiti, immediate sequen : Quorum sex dierum duos pro primo, duos pro Secundo, et reliquos duos dies pro tertio et peremptorio termino, ac monitione Canonica Assignamus, eundem Dominum Dougallum principalem vel procuratorem ejus ipsius nomine, in corporalem realem et actualem possessionem, seu quasi dicti Prioratus de Bello loco, alias Beulie, juriumque et pertinentium omnium ejusdem, nostra ymo verius apostolica auctoritate præfata inducatis et instituatis, ac ab alijs, quantum ad vos, et vestrum quemlibet, pertinet, induci et institui faciatis, ac inductum et institutum defendatis, amoto exinde quolibet illicito detentore, quem nos, quantum possumus amovemus et denunciamus amotum, ac ipsum in Priorem ac fratrem dicti Prioratus recipiatis et recepi faciatis, sibique, vel procuratori suo prædicto ipsius nomine, de fructibus, redditibus, proventibus, juribus, emolumentis et pertinentis universis dicti Prioratus faciatis integre responderi, ac inibi sincera in Domino caritate tractari. Quod si forte præmissa omnia et singula non adimpleveritis mandatisque et monitionibus nostris hijs supra scriptis ymo vero Apostolicis non perseveraveritis cum affectu, nos in vos et singulos suprascriptos qui in præmissis culpabiles fueritis, et generaliter in quoslibet contradictores et rebelles, et impedientes ipsum Dominum Dougallum aut Procuratorem suum ejus nomine super præmissis, nec non ipsum impedien*t* auxilium, consilium vel favorem publice vel occulte, directe vel indirecte, quoviscunque sub colore, ex nunc prout extunc, et extunc prout exnunc, singulariter in singulos canonica monitione præmissa, excomunicamus. In capitula vero quæcunque quarumcunque Ecclesiarum, Monasteriorum, Collegiorum, et Conventus in hijs delinquentes et delinquentia, suspensionis a divinis in ipsorum delinquent: Ecclesias et Monasteria interdicti ecclesiastici sententias ferimus in hijs scriptis. Et etiam promulgamus, vobis igitur Reverendis in Christo patribus et Dominis, Dominis Aberdonensi et Rossensi Episcopis prædictis duntaxat exceptis, quibus ob Reverentiam vestræ Pontificalis dignitatis deferimus in hac parte, si contra præmissa, vel ipsorum aliquid feceritis, seu fieri mandaveritis, per vos vel submissas personas, publice vel occulte, directe vel indirecte, quovis quæsito colore, extunc prout exnunc, et exnunc prout extunc præfat. sex dierum Canonica monitione præmissa, Ingressus Ecclesiarum interdicimus in hijs scriptis: Si vero hijs mandatis per alios sex dies præfatos sex immediate sequentes sustinueritis, vos in hijs scriptis monitione canonica præmissa suspendimus a divinis. Verum si præfati Interdicti et Suspensionis sententias per alios sex dies dictos duodecim immediate sequentes, animis, quod absit, sustinueritis induratis, vos extunc prout exnunc, et exnunc prout extunc, hujus monitione canonica præmissa, in hijs scriptis, Excommunicationis sententia, auctoritate Apostolica supra scripta, innodamus. Cæterum cum ad Executionem præmissorum ulterius faciendam nequeamus quoad præsens personaliter interesse, pluribus alijs arduis præpediti negotijs universis et singulis Dominis, Abbatibus, Prioribus, Præpositis, Decanis, Archidiaconis, Scholasticis, Cantoribus, Custodibus, Thesaurariis, Succentoribus, Sacrificis tam Cathedralium quam Collegiatarum Canonicis, Parochialiumque Ecclesiarum Rectoribus, seu loca tenentibus eorundem, Plebanis, viceplebanis, Archipresbyteris, vicarijs perpetuis, Capellanis Curatis et non curatis, altaristis, Presbyteris, Clericis, cæterisque ecclesiasticis quibuscunque dignitatibus, vel officiis constitutis, notariisque et Tabellionibus publicis quibuscunque, per civitates et Diocœses Aberdonen. Rossen. et Moravien., et alijs ubilibet constitutis, et eorum cuilibet in solidum, super ulteriori executione dicti mandati Apostolici atque nostri fiendæ, auctoritate Apostolica supra dicta, tenore præsentium plenarie committimus vices nostras, donec eos ad nos specialiter et expresse duxerimus : revocand : quos nos etiam, et eorum quemlibet in solidum, eisdem auctoritate et tenore præsentium requirimus et monemus primo, secundo, tertio, et peremptorie, communiter, et divisim, diebus, nihilominus, et eorum cuilibet in virtute sanctæ obedientiæ, et sub Excommunicationis pœna, quam in eos, et eorum quemlibet nisi fecerint quæ mandamus, districte præcipien : mandamus, quatenus infra sex dies post præsentationem seu notificationem præsentium et requisitionem pro parte dicti Domini Dougalli principalis, ejus aut eorum alterius de super fact. immediate sequentes, quos dies ipsis et eorum cuilibet, et pro omni dilatione terminoque peremptorio, ac Canonica monitione assignamus. Ita tamen quod in hijs exequendis alter eorum alterum non expectet, nec unus pro alio, seu per alium se excuset, ad vos omnes et singulos supra dictos communiter vel divisim, quibus hujusmodi noster processus dirigitur, nec non ad dictum Prioratum et Monasterium de Bello loco, alias Beulie, et loca alia, ubi quando et quotiens expediens fuerit, personaliter accedant, et præfatas litteras Apostolicas, huncque nostrum processum, et omnia et singula in eis contenta, vobis omnibus et singulis supra dictis conjunctim et divisim, legant, intiment, insinuent, et fideliter publicari procurent, et eundem Dominum Dougallum principalem, vel procuratorem suum prædictum, ejus nomine, in corporalem, realem, et actuallem possessionem, seu quasi dicti Prioratus juriumque et pertinentiarum omnium prædictorum, auctoritate nostra, ymo verius Apostolica prædicta, inducatis et instituatis, et inductum defendatis, amoto exinde quolibet illicito detentore, quem nos præsentium tenore amovemus, et denunciamus amotum, et ipsum Dominum Dougallum principalem ad Regimen et administrationem dicti Prioratus in Spiritualibus et Temporalibus admittatis et recipiatis, ac recipi et admitti faciatis, et procuretis, quantum ad vos pertinet, et sibi tanquam vero et indubitato Priori dicti Prioratus, Reverentiam, Obedientiam et servitia debita et consueta et congruen^t exhibeatis, et quilibet eorum exhibeat, sive exhiberi, quantum ad eos spectat, procuret, ac ipsum in Priorem suum recipiat et admittat, ac recipi et admitti faciat, et sibi ac Procuratoribus suis in Spiritualibus et Temporalibus respondeat pareat et intendat, et responderi, pareri et obediri quantum ad ipsos pertinet, ab alijs faciat et procuret, ac faciat et procuret cum effectu. Et Nihilominus omnia et singula a nobis in hac parte commissa plenarie exequantur, juxta dictarum litterarum Apostolicarum et præsentis nostri processus continentem tenorem. Ita tamen quod nihil in præjudicium dicti Domini Dougalli principalis vel procuratoris sui in præmissis quomodolibet attemptare valeant dicti nostri subdelegati aut homines ejus, seu alij, seu . . . processibus per nos habitis, aut sententijs per nos latis, absolvendo et suspendendo aliquid immutetur. In cæteris autem, quæ eidem Dougallo principali nocere possint, ipsis et eorum cuilibet et quibuscunque aliis potestatem omnimodum denegamus. Et si contingat nos . . . in aliquo procedere, de quibus nobis potestatem omnimodum reservamus, non intendimus propter hoc commissionem nostram hujusmodi in aliquo revocare, nisi de revocatione ipsa specialem et expressam in nostris litteris de verbo ad verbum fecerimus mentionem. Per Processum autem hujusmodi nolumus nec intendimus nostris in aliquo præjudicare Collegis, quo minus ipsi, vel eorum alter, servato tamen hoc nostro processu, in hujusmodi negotio procedere valeant seu valeat, prout eis aut eorum alteri visum fuerit expedire Præfatas quoq. litteras apostolicas, et hunc nostrum processum, et omnia et singula in eis contenta hujusmodi negotium tangent, volumus penes dictum Dominum Dougallum, principalem, aut procuratorem suum remanere, et non per vos seu aliquem vestrum aut quemcunque alium, ipsis invitis, aut contra eorum voluntatem quomodolibet detineri. Contrarium vero facientes, præfatis nostris sententijs, prout in his Scriptis latæ sunt, dicta Canonica Monitione præmissa, volumus subjacere. Mandamus autem copiam de præmissis, si idem petunt et habere debent, petentium quidem sumptibus et expensis. Absolutionem vero omnium et singulorum, qui præfatas nostras sententias aut earum aliquam partem incurrerint aut incurrerit, nobis vel superiori nostro tantum modo reservamus. In quorum omnium et singulorum fidem, et testimonium præmissorum, has præsentes litteras sive hoc præsens Publicum Instrumentum, processum nostrum hujus modi in se continentes sive continens exinde fieri, et per Notarium Publicum infra scriptum subscribi, et publicari Mandavimus, nostrique rotundi sigilli jussimus et fecimus communiri. Datum et actum in capella nostri palatij de Spineto undecimo die mensis Februarii Anno Domini Millesimo quingentessimo, Indictione quarta Pontificatus sanctissimi in Christo, Patris et Domini nostri, Domini Alexandri, divina disponente clementia, Papæ sexti anno nono ; Præsentibus ibidem venerabili in Christo Patre et Domino, Roberto permissione

divina Monasterii de Pluscardin Priore, ac religiosis et . . .
viris Dominis et Magistris Alexandro Priore fratrum Prædicatorum
de Elgin, Adam Forman subpriore de Pluscardin, Thoma Leuinston
Canonica Moraviensi, Andrea de Fores vicario de Abenethy Notario
Publico, Jacobo Brown de Cromdall Johanne Ricardi de Lagan
vicarijs, et Johanne Malcolmi notarijs publicis, Willielmo Stewart,
Henrico et Alexandro Bonkill Donaldo Finlay et Donaldo McCoule
Armigeris, cum diversis aliis testibus ad præmissa vocatis, pariter et
rogatis.

"Et ego Donaldus Thomæ Presbyter Moraviensis Dioccesis,
Apostolica, Imperiali, et Regali auctoritatibus, publicus notarius, quia præmissis receptioni, habitus exhibitioni, pro-
fessionis Emissioni, et receptioni, Juramenti præstationi ac
Inductioni, omnibusque alijs et singulis dum sic, ut præmittitur, agerentur, dicerentur, et fierent, una cum prænominatis testibus præsens interfui eaq., omnia et singula sic
fieri, dici, vidi, scivi, et audivi, et in notam cepi. Ideoque
has præsentes litteras, sive hoc præsens Instrumentum publicum hujus modi Litterarum Apostolicarum, et præsentis
processus tenores in se continentes, sive continens, exinde
confeci, et in hanc formam redegi, signoque, nomine, cog-
nomine, et subscriptione meis solitis et consuetis, una cum
supra dicti Reverendi in Christo patris et Domini, Domini
Andreæ miseratione divina Episcopi Moraviensis, Judicis et
Executoris supra dicti Rotundi Sigilli appensione, de ipsius
speciali mandato, signavi, rogatus et requisitus in fidem et
testimonium omnium et singulorum præmissorum."

Signed under his mark, "Donaldus Thomæ ptr."

Not.—The seal attached to a tag parchment, red upon white
wax, entirely defaced.

This document is the promulgation and execution of the
Bull of Pope Alexander VI. (No. XV.), by Andrew Stewart,
Bishop of Moray, one of the three ecclesiastical personages to
whom it is addressed.

The Bull itself was dated the 7th before the kalends of
March 1497, that is, 23d February 1498, and it is executed in

the chapel of the episcopal palace of Spynie of the date 11th February 1500, that is, 1501.

Bishop Stewart addresses his promulgation to his colleagues nominated by the Pope, the Bishop of Aberdeen, and the Official of Ross, and to the Bishop of Ross, the diocesan of Beauly Priory, and to the Abbot and Convent of Val des Choux, as well as to the Subprior and Convent of Beauly.

Notwithstanding the Pope's nomination of Dougal Rorieson three years before, he had not yet been either admitted in the Valliscaulian order, or invested with the priorate. He was probably the same person as Sir Dugall Rorieson, vicar of Logy-Urquhard in Ross-shire, the parsonages of which formed part of the prebend of the Treasurer of Ross. In 1498, King James IV. presented Master John Monro to the vicarage of Logy-Urquhard (meaning apparently the vicarages of Logy and Urquhart), when it should be vacant by the resignation of Sir Dugall Rorieson.*

It is evident that he was expected to resign the vicarage upon his admission into the monastic order. There was nothing, indeed, to prevent a secular priest becoming a monk, or a monk from holding a benefice. A religious could be instituted in a secular church by leave of the bishop of the diocese and the abbot of his house, and he might live upon his benefice like another rector;† and probably Dougal's accepting the office of prior would not have, *ipso facto*, vacated the vicarage, but he was expected, and doubtless did, resign it, before he made his profession in the palatial chapel of Spynie.

The Bishop of Moray first has read before him at full length the papal Bull, and then, being requested by Dougal to execute it, being satisfied with the candidate's fitness, he admits him as a monk and brother of the monastery of Beauly, clothes him with the habit prescribed by the rule, and then receives his profession as a member of the order. Thus admitted, the bishop next confers on him, and

---

* Reg. Sec. Sig., vol. i., fol. 67, *apud;* O. P. S., ii. 2, p. 548.
† Fosbrooke's Brit. Monach., p. 269.

invests him by the placing of the episcopal ring on his finger with, the office of prior of the house, having administered to him the oath of allegiance transmitted from Rome (No. XVI.).

Then follows a fine specimen of the profuse verbiage of the Elgin official, rivalling the circumlocution of the Roman chancery. Against those who prevent the new prior from exercising all the rights and receiving all the profits of his office—except the Bishops of Aberdeen and Ross, on account of their pontifical dignity—is promulgated Interdict; then Suspension, then Excommunication; and this public instrument, the bishop orders to be confirmed under his round seal.*

All this is done in the presence of the venerable father in Christ and Lord Robert, by Divine permission, prior of the monastery of Pluscardine, and Alexander, the prior of the Preaching Friars of Elgin (Dominicans), Adam Forman, the subprior of Pluscardine, the vicars of Abernethy, Cromdale, and Laggan, and some esquires, and is all attested by a notary public.

It was among the last official acts of the venerable prelate, the great uncle of the king. He died full of years on 29th September following.

This document was a puzzle to the framer of the Inventory of Lovat Writs in 1651, and it is thus inventoried: †

"52. An instrument upon the foundation of certain orders in the Abbacie of Beauly, by the Bishops of Aberdeen and Ross, dated 11th February 1500."

Dougal Roricson being appointed directly at Rome by the barefaced usurpation of a corrupt pontiff, Alexander Borgia, was probably a person of wealth, if not influence. He continued to be Prior of Beauly certainly to 1514, and his priorate was one of interest to the house.

In 1504 he had a great honour conferred on himself and the priory.

---

* This was the seal of office, with the arms of the see, as well as those of the bishop. It is given in plate ii., fig. 2, of the Bannatyne Club edition of the Reg. Moray.
† Dunbar Dunbar MS.

This was no less than the being summoned to attend among the mitred abbots of Scotland in Parliament, as well as the Priors of Dunfermline and St Andrews. He attended on the 11th March 1504, and sat beside the Abbots of Cambuskenneth, of Melrose, and Dryburgh.

The occasion was a momentous one for the Highlands of Scotland. James IV. had applied himself vigorously to introduce law and order into the Highlands. In 1490 he twice rode across the Mounth; in 1493 he was in August at Dunstaffnage, and in October at Mingarry in Ardnamurchan; again in May 1495 he held his court in this remote castle. In the summer of 1498 he was at the newly-erected royal castle of Kintyre. Inverness had been visited by him in the winter of 1497-98.

This year, 1498, died, a recluse in Paisley Abbey, John, Earl of Ross and Lord of the Isles, who fifty years before had succeeded to those great titles and estates. Of his rebellion against or war with James II., his treaty as a sovereign prince with Edward IV., his forfeiture, retirement to the monastery of Paisley, and burial in the tomb* of his royal ancestor, Robert II., it is not necessary now to speak, but it is clear that shortly after his death, James IV. assumed far more personal authority than he had yet exercised over the lordship of the Isles. He proceeded to take steps in 1500 and 1501 to expel the old vassals, who were little likely to bear quietly such usurpation.

Donald Dhu, the grandson of the deceased Lord of the Isles, when an infant had been carried off, and guarded, if not imprisoned, in the castle of Inchconnell. He now escaped, and repaired to Lewis, whose lord, Macleod, embraced his cause. The young heir was, in the course of time, joined by most of the island chiefs; and about the time of the festival of Christmas, 1503, he headed the insurrection which then broke out. He led the islanders and western clans into Badenoch, and wasted it with fire and sword.

The most active measures were taken by James IV. to put

* This tomb is now being restored at the expense of her Majesty.

down the rebellion; the array of the whole kingdom, north of Forth and Clyde, was called out; the nobility of the north were charged to lead their forces against the islanders; and a Parliament was assembled at Edinburgh in March 1504, to which Dougal Korieson, the Prior of Beauly, was summoned.

He must by this time have acquired great influence in the disturbed districts of Ross-shire and Inverness-shire to have had received in his person a dignity which no Prior of Beauly had been favoured with since the Parliament of Brigham in 1291.

The prior and his colleagues made new arrangements for strengthening the royal power over Ross and the Isles. Sheriffs were to be appointed for the north and south isles respectively; whilst Ross, separated from Inverness, was to have a sheriff of its own, whose courts were to be held according to the exigency of the time, either at Tain or at Dingwall.

Two years elapsed before the rebellion was suppressed, and not until the king had personally invaded the Isles in force. Macleod of Lewis was forfeited, his castle of Stornoway besieged and taken; and Donald Dhu, the heir of the Isles, again became a prisoner, and was committed to the castle of Edinburgh, where he lay captive for forty years.

Robert, the Prior of Pluscardine, a witness to this promulgation, was the official of a different monastic order from the Prior of Pluscardine who witnesses Henry of Nottingham's charter (No. V.).

As everything is of interest to the history of Beauly Priory which bears upon the histories of the sister Priories of Pluscardine and Ardchattan—priories of the same order, and founded in the same year as Beauly—I shall ask my readers to go back and trace the story of the House of Pluscardine from its foundation down to an instrument* executed by Robert, the prior, and Adam Forman of Pluscardine, the subprior, who are witnesses to this promulgation of the papal Bull, and which instrument is dated only eight days before it, on the 3d February 1501.

* Family of Kilravock, p. 171.

There are few monastic remains in Scotland which those interested in the history of the past can visit with so much satisfaction as Pluscardine Priory. There are none where more care is taken to protect the buildings from sordid rapacity or wanton injury—to allow Nature to hide the progress of "calm decay" by the veil of evergreen climbers she so bountifully spreads over aged ruins—and to prevent the biting rain and shivering frost from throwing down the stately walls, which still attest the pious liberality of the young pupil of Malvoisin, Alexander II.

In the secluded vale of Pluscardine, in the parish, but at some distance from the city of Elgin, the king placed his foundation for the Valliscaulian brethren in 1230. Elgin was often visited and much favoured by the sovereign; and after the final defeat of the rebel Moraymen in 1229, and the establishment of the new sheriffdoms of Elgin and Nairn, all that was wanted to secure the civilisation of the district was the encouragement of agricultural improvement, and this the king effected by planting there abbeys and priories, those bodies of devoted men, who drained the morass, planted the hill, and cultivated the valley.

It is said that the king not only founded this priory in the parish of Elgin in 1230, but also founded that monastery of Dominicans or Preaching Friars there, in 1233, whose prior is also a witness to this promulgation. A house of Grey Friars, or Franciscans, at Elgin, is said to have been endowed by him in the same year.

The king named the Pluscardine Priory after St Andrew, the tutelar saint of Scotland, and called the Vale of Pluscardine the Vale of St Andrew; the whole valley, about three miles long, of extreme fertility, he granted to them, and also bestowed on them the corn mills of Elgin.

The first extant charter of the king is dated 7th April 1236. A *facsimile* has been photo-zincographed by the Treasury as one of the national MSS. of Scotland.*

As there is not among the Beauly transcripts any copy of

---

* Facsimiles of National MSS. of Scotland, part i., No. xlviii.

the charter of confirmation of John Byset's grant by King Alexander II., it will be useful to give the translation of this charter to Pluscardine, the work in which it is found being expensive, and seldom seen in private libraries.

"Alexander, by the grace of God King of the Scots, to all the men of all his land, clergy, and laity, greeting. Let those present and to come know that we, for the love of God, and for the weal of our soul and of the souls of our ancestors and successors, have given and granted, and by this our charter have confirmed, to God and the Blessed Mary, and to the Blessed Apostle Andrew, and to the Brethren of the Order of Valliscaulium serving and to serve God in the house that we have founded in our forest of Elgin, in the place to wit that is called the Vale of Saint Andrew at Pluscardin, in exchange for the forest of Lanach, which we formerly gave to the same brethren, twenty nets upon Inverspe in free, pure, and perpetual alms.

"Moreover, we give and grant, and by this our charter confirm, to the same brethren, our mill of Elgin, with all the other mills belonging to that mill, and our mills formerly belonging to our castle of Foreys,* and our mill of Dulpothin, in the bailliary of Foreys, so that

---

* It appears from Stevenson's "Documents relating to Scotland," published under the direction of the Master of the Rolls, that in 1291-92, notwithstanding all the traditions about castles in the north, the only castles into which garrisons were placed by Edward I. north of the Spey, were the castles of Elgin, Forres, Nairn or Invernairn, Inverness, Dingwall, and Cromarty. These were the only strong places of sufficient importance for Edward to keep in his own hands. Under the protection of each of these castles, there were, by the time of Alexander III., the following municipalities: The Provost and Burgesses of Dingwall, the Burgesses of Inverness, the Burgesses of Elgin, the Burgesses of Forres, the Burgesses of Cromarty, and the Burgesses of Invernairn. The first charter extant to any of these is that of William the Lion to Inverness.* The next is the charter of Alexander II. to Dingwall, dated 6th February 1227. This gives to Dingwall "omnes libertates et liberas consuetudines quas burgenses nostri de Inverness et in eo manentes habent."† The earliest extant charter in favour of Elgin recognises the existing burgh, which is mentioned as a burgh in King David's charter to Urquhart in 1125, and gives to the burgesses a merchant guild. It is dated at Elgin 28th November 1234, and has William Byset among the witnesses.‡ The

* This and three other charters of the same king are set out in a charter of King James III., dated 16th August 1467, and printed in Bell's Treatise on Scotch Election Law, Edin. 1812, app. xxxv.
† Stat. Acct. Ross-shire, "Dingwall," 1837, p. 219.
‡ Printed in Shaw's History of Moray, Edin. 1775, p. 193.

the aforesaid brethren may have and hold and possess all the aforesaid mills in free, pure, and perpetual alms, with all the multure payable from all the lands from which at the time of this grant we drew multure, or ought to have drawn it if it had been tilled, with their waters and stanks. We will moreover and grant that the aforesaid brethren and their millers take earth, stones, and timber for making the stanks of the aforesaid mill, and for repairing and preserving them without any contradiction or hindrance, in neighbouring convenient and suitable places. We give also and grant, and by this our charter confirm, to the aforesaid brethren, in exchange for twenty-four nets that the monks and the said brethren had by our gift on the water of Findorin for twenty-four pounds, these lands underwritten by the eight marches, and with their just appurtenances, to wit, Fernavan, Thulidoui, Kep, Meikle Kyntessoch, to be held and had by them in free, pure, and perpetual alms; in wood and plain, in meadows and pastures, in moors and marshes, in ponds, mills, waters, and fishings belonging to the said lands, free and quit from every exaction, and service, and demand, and custom, with all suits and pleas in all the foresaid possessions chancing in their court, which we give to them to be litigated and determined, excepting those that specially belong to our crown.

"We will, moreover, and grant that they, in respect of all their proper chattels, be free and quit over all our kingdom from all toll and custom. And all the aforesaid things that they have at present, and that they may in future times acquire by just means in our kingdom, we will and grant that they have, hold, and possess in free, pure, and perpetual alms, according to the tenor and form of the gifts made to them or to be made, as freely, quietly, fully, and honourably as any alms in our kingdom are most freely, quietly, fully, and honourably had, held, and possessed by any religious men. And we have taken the aforesaid brethren and their house, all their men, and all the possessions and goods of them and their men into our firm peace and protection; and we firmly forbid that any one inflict any injury, trouble, or grievance upon them, or upon any one of them unjustly,

earliest mention I have found of the burghs of Forres, Cromarty, and Invernairn, is the insertion among the letters addressed to the King and Queen of Scotland, probably King Alexander III. and Queen Margaret, by Scottish municipalities, of letters from the burgesses of Forres, Cromarty, and Invernairn.*

* National MSS. of Scotland, part i., lxxiv.

upon pain of our full forfeiture; and that any one presume to take poind of them or of their men for any debt unless for their proper debt that they or their men may owe, upon pain of our full forfeiture. But if any one shall have rashly presumed to go against what is aforesaid in anything, let the diocesan in whose diocese this has been done, justly compel, by ecclesiastical censure, him who has done the injury to give satisfaction to the aforesaid monks; and if, on account of his contumacy, he has been tied with the sentence of excommunication, and obstinately resisting has scorned to obey the mandates of the Church, and has remained during forty days under sentence of excommunication, let the bailie of us and of our heirs, in whose bailliary that excommunicated person may be, seize him and thrust him into our prison; which, if that bailie shall have neglected to do after being required three times, the sentence of excommunication shall be enforced by the course of justice. We will, moreover, and grant that as often as injury has been done to the aforesaid brethren or to their men in respect of their lands, mills, or the marches of their lands, their possessions or other things, the bailies of us and of our heirs, when required by them, without waiting for a special royal mandate, do them full and swift justice according to the assize and customs of our kingdom. We charge, moreover, that no one presume to detain unjustly their serfs and those of their lands if found outwith our domains, upon pain of our full forfeiture. Witnesses— William, Bishop of Glasgow, our Chancellor; Andrew, Bishop of Moray; William, Abbot of Dunfermline; Herbert, Abbot of Kelchoch; Ralf, Abbot of Aberbrothock; Gilbert, Abbot of Holy Rood; Patrick, Earl of Dunbar; Malcolm, Earl of Fife; Walter Cumin, Earl of Menteith; Roger of Quinci, our Constable; Walter, the son of Alan, our Steward, and Justiciar of Scotland; Walter Olifand, Justiciar of Lothian; Ingram of Balliol; Roger Avenel; Walter Biseth; Thomas, the son of Ranulf; Archibald of Dufglas; David, the Marischal. At Edinburgh, on the 7th day of April, in the 22d year of the reign of our Lord the King."

The king had been careful, in his grant to the Valliscaulians, to remember their rules, and to give them incomes without labour; as at Beauly, so at Pluscardine, much of the revenues are derived from mills and salmon-fishings. "One grant," says Mr Innes, "of twenty nets fishing at Inverspey may have comprehended the whole fishing of the great river from the ancient bridge downwards."* The maintenance of the ancient bridge, we may remark, was secured by the wise king in 1228 granting property for the purpose of keeping it in repair.

The bishop's charter confirming this in 1237 releases the tithes of the same land to the monks. We print the charter from the Treasury translation:

"To all the sons of Holy Mother Church that shall see or hear these letters, Andrew, by divine permission Bishop of Moray, everlasting health in the Lord,—Be it known unto you all that when our Lord Alexander, the illustrious King of the Scots, had bestowed, in pure and perpetual alms, for the support of the House of the Vale of St Andrew, of the order of Valliscaulium, which he founded in Pluscardin, and for the support of the brothers there serving, and for ever to serve God, the mill of Elgin, with all the mills and other things belonging to it; also the mills of Foreys and of Dulpotin, with all the mills and other things belonging to these mills, from which the churches of Elgin, and of Foreys, and of Dye [Dyke] were wont to draw tithes;† at the instance of our same Lord the King we quit-claimed to the aforesaid house, and to the aforesaid brethren, with the counsel and consent of our chapter and of the rector of the church of Foreys,‡ to wit, the Archdeacon of Moray,§ all the tithes of the aforesaid mills and others, if any happen to have been made within the soke of the aforesaid mills, which the aforesaid mills had at the time of the making of this writing, except the tithes from the profits of the millers holding the aforesaid mills. We have quit-claimed, moreover, to the same house and to the same brethren, at the instance of our same Lord the King, all the tithes that were wont to be paid to us, and that ought to be paid to the Bishops of Moray

---

* Facsimiles of National MSS. of Scotland, Introduction, p. xi.

† It would seem that these churches had the tithes of mills, which are generally vicarial tithes.

‡ William the Lion gave the churches of Forres and Dyke to Richard, Bishop of Moray, who had been his chaplain.

§ Bishop Bricius of Moray erected Forres and Logyn-Fythenach into a canonry, and gave it to the Archdeacon of Moray. This Logie is the Logie near Dumphail, and called Logie Fythenach, or the Woody Logie, to distinguish it from the other Logie.

for ever, from the rents* arising, and that shall arise, from the lands of Fernauan,† Tuliduui, Kep, Meikle Kintessoc,‡ reserving to the mother churches in whose parishes the aforesaid lands are the other tithes pertaining to them. And our Lord the King aforesaid, by bestowing greater gifts, has of his grace benevolently provided an indemnity, and abundantly given satisfaction to us and to our successors, and to the church of Moray. And we have given full satisfaction to the church of Forays and the Archdeacons of Moray§ for those things that belonged to them. In sure and indubitable testimony of the things aforesaid, to this writing along with our seal is affixed the seal of our chapter, together with the subscriptions of the canons. Done in the year of grace one thousand two hundred and thirty-seven.

"✠ I, ANDREW, Bishop of Moray and Canon of the Holy Trinity of Elgin, subscribe. ✠

✠ I, WILLIAM, Precentor of Moray, subscribe. ✠

✠ I, WILLIAM, Chancellor of the church of Moray, subscribe. ✠

✠ I, WILLIAM, Archdeacon of Moray, subscribe. ✠

✠ I, JOHN OF BEREWIC, Canon of the church of Moray, subscribe.✠

✠ I, ANDREW, Canon of Moray, subscribe. ✠

✠ I, WALTER, Canon of Kingussy, subscribe. ✠

✠ I, R., Canon of Duppol, subscribe. ✠

✠ I, JOHN, Canon of Crumbdol, subscribe. ✠

✠ I, WALTER, Subdean of Moray, subscribe. ✠

✠ I, ARCHIBALD, Canon of Croyn, subscribe. ✠ "

* The bishop perhaps refers to the grant to his see by William the Lion of the tithes of the king's can, or rents in kind, but the bishop's charter seems by Pope Urban's confirmation to have been sufficient to grant the corn tithes.

† This is probably Fernway, which, according to Mr Forsyth (Acct. Moray, p. 173), is the original name of the district of Fernoway or Darnaway. This district, or the forest part of it, became the property of Thomas Randolph, Earl of Moray, who is said to have founded Darnaway Castle between 1315 and 1331.

‡ Kintessack is the present name of a locality in the parish of Dyke.

§ Although Bishop Bricius had erected the canonry of Forres and Logyn-Fythenach for the benefit of the Archdeacon of Moray, yet, for some reason, the gift of Logyn-Fythenach required confirmation. This confirmation was enforced as a condition by Alexander in his grant to the bishop, in the month of September 1236, of Finlarg. He grants Finlarg in exchange for the wood called Cawood, and for Logyn-Fythenach, of which latter place the bishop should be bound to make a full grant to William, Archdeacon of Moray, and his successors for ever. This grant had probably been made in the interval between September 1236 and 1237.

In 1239 we have Symon, Prior of Pluscardine, a witness to the charter* by which, among other churches, the church of Fernua, formed out of the Byset parish of Dunballoch, was granted by the Bishop of Moray to the canons of Elgin.

In 1263 Pope Urban IV. granted a Bull to Pluscardine. He, after the example of Gregory, of happy memory, takes the monastery under the protection of the Blessed Peter and himself. He appoints that the monastic order which has been instituted in the monastery according to God and the rule of St Benedict, and the institution of the Brethren of Valliscaulium should for all times be observed there. He confirms the grants made to the house, especially the place where the monastery is situated, with all its appurtenances; the church situated in the town, called Durris (Dores), with the tithes of sheaves of the same place; the right of patronage in the church; the tithes of sheaves in the forests of Pluscardin and Wthutyr; the tithes of the mills placed in the same forests, and of the iron dug in the same; the right of fishing with twenty nets in the Spey; and the mill with the streams, which the monks have in the town called Elgyn. The lands and possessions in the places commonly called Fernauay, Thulidoui, Kep, the Greater Kintessoch, and Mefth, are confirmed; also the land and forest called Pluscardin and Wthutyr. Nobody is to take tithes from their gardens, underwoods, fishings, or meadows. The monks may receive to conversion those flying from the secular power. There are the usual restrictions against leaving the House without the prior's licence; and against any monk or lay brother being surety, and borrowing money; leave to say the holy offices during an interdict; and no prior is to be placed at their head except he who is chosen by the majority. The Bull is dated at Viterbo, 3d July 1263.†

Symon seems to have been a long time prior, for Dominus Symon, Prior de Pluscardine, is witness to a charter by John, the son of Malcolm de Moravia, which Mr Innes puts down as of the date 1284, and which is witnessed by William, Earl

---

* Reg. Moray, p. 35. † Spalding Mis., vol. ii., p. 404.

of Sutherland, and William, Earl of Ross.* In his time the monks of Pluscardine arranged with the burgesses of Elgin, that the monks should have the lands which lay between the two mills of Elgin in lieu of an obligation on the town to repair the mills and stanks, with which the burgh was then burdened. The convention is dated St Nicholas' Day, 1272.† Patrick Heyrock was provost, and Hugo Bisset one of the burgesses ; and Hugo Herock, in 1286, has Simon, Prior of Pluscardine, as a witness to his endowment of the chaplains of St Nicholas and the Holy Cross at Elgin.‡ By 1330 the Heyrocks have become treasurers of the church of Moray, and the controversy between the town and the priory is now as to the multures. The monks are to have the seventeenth vessel or vat of corn in lieu of other multures. §

John, Bishop of Moray, and Richard, Bishop of Dunkeld, in a Cathedral Chapter of the Church of Moray, held on the 10th of October 1345,‖ having before them, summoned by the Bishop of Moray, John Wyse, the prior, Adam Marshall, the subprior, and William of Inverness and Adam Young, monks, of the House of the Vale of St Andrew of Pluscardine, interrogate them, and extract from them this statement— That from the first foundation of the House of Pluscardine, as they have heard from their predecessors and seen in their own time, the Bishops of Moray for the time being, as often as they thought fit, had exercised the right of visitation and correction, institution and deprivation, over the priors and brethren of the House of Pluscardine, and received procurations ; and the prior and monks admitted that they had no exemption or privilege against this right, which was now, and had been from time beyond memory, exercised by the Bishops of Moray. Nor was this all. Sir William de Longo Vico, a monk of the Rennard Valley, of the diocese of Toul, as nuncio of the Order of the Valliscaulians, and proctor of the prior of the House of Valliscaulium in the diocese of Langres, stated that the bishops and diocesan archbishops, as well in

---

* Reg. Moray, 462. † Family of Innes, p. 55. ‡ Reg. Moray, 283.
§ Family of Innes, p. 57. ‖ Reg. Moray, 157.

Germany as in other parts beyond the sea, in whose diocese Houses of the Valliscaulian order were situated, down to this time had exercised, and now exercise, in their dioceses, the right of visitation and correction over these Houses, and received procurations. There were present the Chancellor and Official of Moray, the Chancellor of Glasgow, the Treasurer of Dunkeld, and the canons of Moray, specially called to be witnesses.

The House of Pluscardine had further troubles in connection with their multures. Robert de Chisholm, who was Lord of Quarrywood, near Elgin, refused to pay multures to the prior. The House appealed to the Bishop of Moray, and Alexander Bar, the then prelate, issued a monition to Sir Archibald Douglas, knight, in April 1390, in the following terms :*

"Honourable and Noble Sir,—You and John de Kay, sheriff of Inverness, have determined a certain process in such manner, as God knows, to the grievous injury of the Priory of Pluscardine, and to the great prejudice of the jurisdiction of the Church, which we crave to have by you recalled; for we assert and declare that Alexander, King of Scotland, of pious memory, gifted to the prior and monks of Pluscardine the mills of Elgin and Forres and other mills depending on them, and the mulctures of the lands of those mills which he then received, or ought to have received, as they were for the deliverance of his soul, which mulctures of the lands, when arable, by virtue of the donation, the said prior and monks have received, likeas they yet without dispute receive; and whereas the mulctures of the lands of Quarrywood, in the sheriffdom of Elgin, at that time unimproved, but now reduced to cultivation, belongs and appertains to the mill of Elgin, from which it is scarcely a mile distant; because, if it had been at that time cultivated, the mulctures would, and ought to have been, received by the royal granter."

The complaint, after stating undisturbed possession, with the knowledge and tolerance of Robert de Chisholm, knight, during the preceding reigns, "further asserts and declares that the said Robert had seized and bound a certain hus-

* Reg. Moray, p. 169; Forsyth's Moray, p. 133.

bandman of the lands of Findrassie (Finrossie), to whom the prior had by contract let the said multures, and thrown him into a private prison, by which he directly incurred the sentence of excommunication." The complaint proceeds to show cause why the action could not be determined by the civil, but by the ecclesiastical court, and concludes by threatening to excommunicate the civil judges if they attempted anything further by which the priory might be wronged or the jurisdiction of the Church marred.

On the 16th of April 1390, Sir Thomas, Prior of the House of Pluscardine, records a solemn instrument of protest against the proceedings of Sir Robert de Chisholm.* The prior and the knight, however, attest a charter of John of Dunbar, Earl of Moray, to the burgh of Elgin on the 1st of May 1390, by which the earl discharged to the town for ever the ale of assize belonging to him, as constable of the castle of Elgin.†

Quarrywood is in the parish of Spynie, and is so called from a rich quarry of freestone in these lands. It belonged in 1365 to Sir Robert Lauder, whose grandson, Sir Robert de Chesholme, then Constable of Urquhart Castle (to whom John Randolph, Earl of Moray, had given in 1345‡ the lands of Invermoriston and of Lochletter in Glenmoriston, and Glenurquhart), in January 1365, married his daughter to Rose of Kilravock.§ Shaw wonders that Sir Robert Lauder could be alive when his great-granddaughter was married, but the Lauders of the Bass were a stout race, and he was not only alive, but able to enter into a deed with his grandson in 1366.

Sir Robert de Chisholm's method of taking the law into his

* Family of Innes, p. 65.
† Ib., p. 67. Shaw explains the assize of ale to be the quantity of ale which the burgh was bound to furnish to the earl as constable; and, as Dr Cowell observes, *assisa panis* sometimes signifies a portion of bread, and the Doctor derives the expression "sizar" at Cambridge, from the quantity of bread which those students who had sizarships were entitled to receive. But Dr Cowell explains *assisa panis et cerevisiæ* as the power or privilege of assizing or adjusting the weights and measures of bread and beer; this privilege was one belonging to the lord of a town, and was accompanied with a power of demanding fees and fines, and it is probably this privilege which was surrendered by the earl.
‡ Family of Innes, p. 60.   § Family of Kilravock, p. 37.

hands against the Church was a month after outrageously exceeded by Alexander Stewart, the "Wolf of Badenoch," who burned Elgin and the cathedral on St Botolph's Day, 17th June 1390. It seems that among the Bulls, apostolic letters, public instruments, charters, and other writings burned with the cathedral, were those by which the rights of the Priory of the Valliscaulians at Pluscardine, and its privileges and statutes and foundations, could be manifested. Pope Benedict XIII., in 1404, issued a commission to the Bishop of Aberdeen to inquire for any other copies of the evidences burned, but it does not appear that those of the House of Pluscardine were collected.*

Whether the prior succeeded in rescuing his multures, we cannot ascertain, but the plea of exclusive jurisdiction set up by the Church when the temporal rights of a monastery were in dispute is not likely to have been sustained. In 1388, the appeal of a monk of the Priory of Urquhart in Moray against the investiture of a Prior of Urquhart by the Bishop of Moray, was finally decided by King Robert III. and the clergy in Parliament on the 12th March 1391.†

The mode in which the election of priors and their confirmation by the bishop was managed, is shown by what happened in the Priory of Pluscardine in 1398. Thomas, the head of the House, on the 7th August 1398‡ resigns the priory into the hands of the Bishop of Moray; on the 13th of the same month the senior monk announces to the bishop that Alexander de Pluscardine, one of the monks, was unanimously elected prior; that the *Te Deum* was duly chanted after the election, and that the House in full chapter assembled craved the bishop's confirmation.§ And on the Vigil of the Assumption (14th August) the bishop‖ issues an order that any one opposing the election should appear on the 21st of the same month; and on the 21st the election of Alexander is confirmed by the bishop, reserving to himself and successors the right of annual visitation. As yet no usurpation by the Pope had

---

* Reg. Moray, p. 422.   † Preface, Stat. Eccl. Scot., p. 51, n. (6).
‡ Reg. Moray, 353.   § *Ib.*, 356.   ‖ *Ib.*, 357.

taken place of the rights of the Valliscaulian monks to elect their own prior,—a usurpation which we have seen Alexander Borgia attempt in the Priory of Beauly.

The Priory of Urquhart was founded by King David I.,* and partly endowed by the Abbey of Dunfermline, whose grant the foundation charter confirms. The charter has no date, but is usually stated to be 1125. It is in form a grant to the church of Urquhart and the prior and brethren serving there. The papal Bulls of 1163 and 1182 to Dunfermline include Urquhart and the church of Urquhart among the possessions of the abbey; and in 1234 Pope Gregory IX. expressly confirms it to the abbey as the Cell of Urquhart in Moray, with the church lands and other pertinents.†

A cell might be a grange ‡ or house, with ample farm buildings, erected upon lands at a distance from the monastery to which the cell belonged; there two or three of the monks lived, reaped the crops, collected the rents, and remitted them to the superior House. Thus Pluscardine had a grange and cell of monks in the parish of Dyke,§ who superintended their farm and estate of Grangehill, now Dalvey.‖ At times a cell was an oratory, where a certain number of monks were allowed to retire for prayer and meditation.¶

Urquhart was governed by a prior, who, in 1343, was sufficiently independent to settle the obligation of the priory to pay the expense of serving the chapel of Kilravock;** but in

---

* Reg. Dunf., 15.   † Ib., 151, 154, 156, 175.

‡ Wordsworth has poetically described the office of a cell when a grange, in his poem on the Cell of St Bees:—

> "Who with the ploughshare clove the barren moors,
> And to green meadows changed the swampy shores,
> Thinned the rank woods, and for the cheerful GRANGE
> Made room—where wolf and boar were used to range."

§ Forsyth's Moray, p. 77.

‖ In the beautiful gardens of Dalvey there is a venerable apple-tree, which still blossoms richly, and bears some fruit; it is impossible to ascertain its age, but it is conjectured, with some appearance of truth, that it was planted by the monks of Pluscardine (New Stat. Acc., "Dyke," p. 219).

¶ Ducange in verbo "Cella."   ** Family of Kilravock, p. 112.

1358 the Abbot of Dunfermline asserted that the prior could not be elected without his sanction. In 1429 there is a letter from Columban, Bishop of Moray, authorising the commissioner of the Abbot of Dunfermline—the king's assent having been also obtained to the commission—to inquire into, correct, and reform the priorate and prior of the abbot's cell of Urquhart, on account of some crimes come to the ears of the abbot.*

The bishop at the same time addressed a letter to the Prior of Urquhart, Sir Andrew Raeburn, informing him that the abbot intended, by his commissioner, to hold a visitation of the priory, and requiring the prior to attend it.† What faults the Prior of Urquhart had committed does not appear, nor the result of the visitation. Great care was taken in the rules of the Benedictine order that cells should not lapse into places where monastic discipline was neglected.

Some twenty-five years later the charms of the Priory of Pluscardine excited the cupidity of a principal officer of the House of Dunfermline. The transaction which followed and gratified the covetous sacristan of Dunfermline is by Shaw and Forsyth attributed to the vices of the Pluscardine monks.

"The monks of Pluscardine," writes Shaw, "becoming vicious, the priory was reformed and made a cell of Dunfermline." "The Convent of Pluscardine was free from episcopal jurisdiction," says Forsyth, "but becoming licentious, soon after 1460 the white monks were expelled, the black were introduced, and the priory made a cell of Dunfermline." The property of the House had dwindled, and the priory church and priory buildings had become ruinated in 1398, for the election of Alexander proceeded on his being expected to defend the possessions and to repair the church and dwellings of the monks.‡ John Benale, Prior of Urquhart, whose convent of brethren seems to have consisted of two monks, in 1454 petitions Pope Nicholas V.§ that he would unite the priories of Urquhart and Pluscardine. The petition stated that these

---

* Reg. Dunf., 167. † Ib., 282, 283. ‡ Reg. Moray, 356.
§ Theiner, Mon. Vet. Scot. et Hib., p. 391.

two priories were conventual, curative, and elective, and were acknowledged to be foundations of kings of Scotland; that by reason of wars, mortalities, and other calamities, the income of the priories had so diminished that they were unable to keep up a prior in each House with a decent and competent number of religious men, or to keep the buildings of each house in proper order, or to maintain Divine service; so that in Pluscardine there were generally not above six monks, in Urquhart two only. The petition stated that Pluscardine was a dependent member of the Priory of Valliscaulium in the diocese of Langres in France, and on account of the great distance of Pluscardine from Valliscaulium, and other inconveniences, it was unable to be visited by the Mother House or her substitutes, or to obtain any help from her, and that it would be desirable it should be wholly separated from the Priory of Valliscaulium, and that the Priory of Urquhart, which depended on the Monastery of Dunfermline of the order of St Benedict, were annexed and united to Pluscardine.

The Pope, on the 12th of March 1454, issued a commission to the Abbot of Lindores and the Chancellor and Treasurer of Moray, stating the petition of the Prior of Urquhart, and authorising them to inquire into the truth of its allegations, and the consent of the king being obtained, to carry out the union. The papal Bull requires the commissioners to assign some proper compensation for the change to the Priory and Order of Valliscaulium. It asserts that Andrew Haag, Prior of Pluscardine, had resigned on a pension of £12, and appoints or authorises the commissioners to appoint John Benale prior of Pluscardine.

On the 8th of November 1454,* the Abbot of Dunfermline granted a commission to William de Boys to receive the professions into the Benedictine order, of the monks of Pluscardine.

John, who was then appointed prior, was apparently a person of importance, for Elizabeth, Dowager-Countess of Moray, executing a deed† at Forres on 20th May 1455, says, "The

* Reg. Dunf., 333.   † Miscellany of Spalding Club, vol. iv., p. 130.

said Elizabeth, Countess of Morra, in absence of her own sele, has procurit the sele of a worshippful fader, Done John Benolda, Prior of Pluscardine;" a curious instance of the translation of the " Dominus."

In November 1456 the exchange is completed; on the 7th[*] there is a commission of the Abbot of Dunfermline to William de Boys, the sacristan, to visit the Priory of Pluscardine; it is addressed to John de Benaly, and on the same day,[†] on William de Boys' resignation, John de Benale is made Sacristan of Dunfermline. On the 8th there is a letter from the Abbot of Dunfermline to the Abbot of Kinloss,[‡] informing him that John de Benaly had resigned the Priorate of Pluscardine, and requesting him to confirm the new prior if elected.

With his commission of visitation in his pocket, the influence of William de Boys was enough to procure his election, and in 1460 we find him named William de Boys, Prior of Pluscardine and Urcharde.[§] He did not allow the rights of his House to be violated, for in 1463 he obtained a declaration from the Chancellor of Moray that the church of Dingwall in Ross-shire, with all its fruits, belonged to the Prior of Pluscardine. How long he continued does not appear, but in 1500, Robert is the Prior of Pluscardine. On the 3d February 1501, this person executed a deed, printed in the book of Kilravock,[||] which is interesting, not only from the rarity of any documents of the convent of Pluscardine, but also from its throwing some light on the subject of mills and multures, so constantly mixed up with the Valliscaulian priories.

" The erecting the machinery of a corn-mill," says Mr Forsyth,[¶] " could not formerly be undertaken by any person in a rank inferior to a baron, a bishop, or an hereditary sheriff." The Pluscardine House, by this deed, thirl all the growing corn of their lands of Penyck[**] to the mill of the laird of Lochloy, " but the annexation of the foresaid corns to the

---

[*] Reg. Dunf., 337.   [†] Ib., 339.   [‡] Ib., 339.   [§] Ib., 353, 354.
[||] Family of Kilravock, p. 171.   [¶] Forsyth's Moray, p. 131.
[**] Pennik was given to the Abbey of Dunfermline by David I. (Reg. Dunf., 14), and by the Abbey to the Priory of Urquhart at its foundation (Reg. Dunf., 17).

foresaid myll till indure ay and quhill we or oure successors thinks it speidful to big ane myll of our awin, or caus ony vther to big in our name a myll to grund our foresaid tennantes corneys." It concludes thus :

" And this contract was maid at Pluscardin undir owre common seill, with our subscriptiones manualle, the thride day of Februar in the yere of God a thousand and five hundreitht year.

" Ego, ROBERTUS, prior ad suprascripta subscribo.
Et ego, ADAM FORMAN, ad idem.   Et ego, JACOBUS WYOT, ad idem.
Et ego, ANDREAS BROUN, ad idem. Et ego, JOHANNES HAY, ad idem.
Et ego, ANDREAS ALAIN, ad idem. Et ego, JACOBUS JUSTICE, ad idem."

No. XVIII.

COMMISSIO VISITATIONIS MONASTERII DE ARDQU-
HATTAN DATA PRIORI DE BELLO LOCO PER
JACOBUM QUARTUM PRIOREM SEU GENERALEM
VALLIS CAULIUM DIOCŒSIS LINGONENSIS.—ANNO
1505 [1506].

Ex Autographo.

"Frater Jacobus Quartus Prior Vallis Caulium Venerabili in Christo nobis præcarissimo Priori nostro Monasterij de Beuling in Diocœsi Rossensi in Scotia Salutem. Et proximorum utilitati ex caritatis fervore diligenter intendere nostræ superioritatis officium nos incessanter excitat et inducit, ut ad ea per quæ Monasteriorum nobis subjectorum status in utroque regimine salubriæ suscipiat incrementa solerter intendamus. Hinc est quod vobis, de cujus providentiâ zelo et discretione plenam in Domino gerimus fiduciam, Monasterij nostri de Ardquhattan in Diocœsi Argadiæ, nobis et nostro Monasterio Vallis Caulium immediate subjecti, visitationem omnimodam damus et committimus, dantes vobis auctoritatem et nostram plenariam potestatem ibidem, quotiens opus fuerit, in capite et in membris visitandi, reformandi, corrigendi, emendandi, instituendi et destituendi, quandocunque, secundum Domus et Ordinis Statuta, visitationis reformationis, correctionis emendationis institutionis et destitutionis Sarculo indigere cognoveritis. Et si contingat, quod dictum Monasterium de Ardcattan, per cessionem, mortem, vel alias viduare pastore, in electione futuri præsideatis, conventui licentiam eligendi conferatis, electam personam si sufficiens et ydonea fuerit, et in Ordine nostro professa, instituatis, installetis, et in possessionem realem et actualem ipsius Monasterij ponatis et inducatis. Si vero jus providendi, nobis, ratione nostræ Superioritatis, devolvatur, auctoritate nostra paterna, supradicto Monasterio de personæ prædictis qualitatibus qualificatæ provideatis, cæteraque omnia et singula circa præmissa et ea tangentia faciatis et exequamini, quæ faceremus et exequeremur, si præsentes essemus, Salvis per omnia nostri Ordinis et Papal institutis, confirmatione tamen penes nos reservata; omnibus dicti loci personis districte præcipiendo, quatenus vobis in omnibus præmissis et eorum dependentijs pareant et obediant tanquam nobis, præsentibus usque ad nostram specialem revocationem in suo vigore permansuris. Datum in nostro prædicto Monasterio Vallis caulium sub appensione Sigilli nostri die septima mensis Maij Anno Domini Millesimo quingentesimo sexto."

   Not.—The seal wants. It has been oblong on green wax stamped on the paper.

This document is a commission, dated the 17th May 1506, from the General of the Valliscaulian Order, the Prior of Val des Choux, in Burgundy, addressed to the Prior of Beauly for the visitation of the Priory of Ardchattan, in Argyle.

The commission runs to this effect :

"James Quartus, Prior of Valliscaulium, to the venerable and most loved in Christ, Prior of our Monastery of Beuling, in the diocese of Ross, in Scotland, greeting. With a sense of the duty of our superiority and of our obligation to see to the sound condition of the monasteries subject to us, and of your prudence, zeal, and discretion in the Lord, we give and commit to you the visitation of our Monastery of Ardchattan (Ardquhattan), in the diocese of Argyle, immediately subject to us and our Monastery of Valliscaulium ; and we give this with full power of visiting, reforming, correcting, amending, instituting, and depriving, as occasion may require, both in the head and the members, whenever, according to the statutes of the house and of the order, you shall find there is need of the hoe (*sarculo*) ; and if it should happen that, by resignation, death, or otherwise, the said Monastery of Ardchattan (Ardcattan) should be deprived of its shepherd, you, the Prior of Beauly, are to preside at the election of a new one, allow the convent the liberty of electing him ; and if a proper person, professed in our order, should be elected, you are to institute, install, and induct him into the real and actual possession of the monastery ; and if the right of providing a head should devolve upon us by reason of our superiority, then you are by our fatherly authority to provide for the said monastery a person qualified as before mentioned, as if we were present; but, in all things, without prejudice to the institutes of our order and the Papal Regulations, reserving, nevertheless, confirmation to ourselves. Given in our monastery of Valliscaulium, our seal being affixed, the 7th of May 1506."

What state of things existed at Ardchattan when this commission was issued by the head of the order, or what had reached his ears, we cannot tell. The priorate, we know, had become vacant in 1502, and there may not have been another prior appointed since.

There had apparently grown up, since the simple rules laid down by Viard for the discipline of the order, laws and customs regulating the relations in which the general of the order stood to the houses, other than the chief house, of which he was the prior. These were probably similar to those in which the Abbot of Citeaux, the General of the Cistercian Order, stood to the other Cistercian abbeys.

Notwithstanding the usurpation of Alexander VI., the prior-general still adheres to the rule of the order, election of the head of a house by the members of that house, and asserts, probably in the event of non-election within a given time, that the patronage would lapse, like the patronage of a secular advowson, to himself as the superior of the order.

The commission introduces to us two monasteries both intimately connected with the Priory of Beauly, and both requiring some notice; the Mother House of Val des Choux, in the diocese of Langres, in Burgundy; and the House of Ardchattan, in Argyle, the only other priory besides Pluscardine, of the Valliscaulian order in Scotland.

The Monastery of Val des Choux was situated about ten miles from Chatillon-sur-Seine, at the head of a glen watered by a small stream, which flows a little above Vanvey into the Ource, a tributary of the Seine.

It was in Burgundy, a name which suggests the sunny land of the golden grape, studded with abbeys and castles, the homes of the most illustrious orders and of the noblest knights. Citeaux, Clairvaux, and Clugny, those magnificent foundations whose monasteries extended throughout all Europe, were all Burgundian houses. But the Priory of Val des Choux did not vie, and its rules forbade it to vie, with the splendour of their pride.

Although nominally in Burgundy, it was in the poorest district of that province, and where the soil is least generous; the aspect of the vale where it stood, shut out from the sun by hills, which bound it to the south and west, must have been always gloomy and cold. The spot was selected by the founder as a hermitage, and it could never have been divested of that character. The house is spoken of in 1710,[*] 1728,[†] and 1739,[‡] as still existing, but small trace of it now remains, and the pilgrim who would visit the site must search for it in the Forest of Chatillon. Its position had little to recommend it as a residence, and it would seem that when the storm of the Revolution drove away its inmates, and cast down its walls, the spot relapsed into the state of primeval forest in which it was found by Viard, when he first sought its wooded recesses six centuries before its fall.

In our account of the foundation, we have followed Helyot; later writers have been more precise, and have named Otho III.[§] as the Duke of Burgundy who founded the House of Val des Choux. His title to this honour has been questioned by the historian of the duchy,[||] but upon insufficient grounds.

Viard seems to have taken the name of Guido, on his elevation to the post of prior, probably out of compliment to Guido, the Archbishop of Rheims, the " G. elect of Rheims " mentioned in the Bull of Pope Innocent III. Viard is named as prior, it is said, by the archbishop in his charter confirming

---

[*] Buonanni Ordini Religiosi, Rome 1710, part iii., No. 4, "Vallis Caulium sita est *in silvis* inter Divionem et Augustodunum."
[†] Gallia Christiana, vol. iv., p. 742.
[‡] Planche's Hist. de Bourgoyne, vol. i., p. 379.
[§] Gallia Christiana, vol. iv., p. 743.
[||] Planche's Histoire de Bourgoyne, Dijon 1739, vol. i., pp. 379, note, 448.

the foundation of Val des Choux, dated 1204, and appears to have been prior in 1213.

St Marthe * gives a list of fourteen priors after Viard, the fourteenth being this Jacobus Courtois, who was certainly prior in 1472, though when he first became so is not recorded.

The relation between the Mother House and the other priories in the Order of Valliscaulium seems to have been of the same character as existed in the rules of the Carthusian Order. They were all priories, but the prior of the Mother House was General of the Order.

The Scottish priories of Beauly, Pluscardine, and Ardchattan, although members of the House of Val des Choux, were not in the situation of the alien priories of England, or the cells of abbeys in England and Scotland. The Valliscaulian priories were members of the Mother House, because the head of the Mother House was head of the order; but they held their possessions quite independently of the Mother House, and paid no rent or acknowledgment to it. They elected their own prior from their own body, and the bishops of their respective dioceses being their visitors, they obtained confirmation of the election from the bishop, although they sought also apparently to obtain confirmation from the prior-general.

The prior-general, however, as well as the bishop, had a right of visitation, and of depriving the priors of the subordinate houses for any violation of the rules of the order. Probably the visitorial powers of the bishop were directed to preserve general ecclesiastical discipline, while those of the prior-general were intended to keep up the peculiar discipline and rules of the order.

One of the principal rules of the order was that the priors of the subordinate houses should attend the chapters of the order, which were held at Val des Choux, and also most probably at the House of St Lieu in Dijon, which was called the Petit Val de Choux, and which was much more accessible than the great house in the Forest of Chatillon.

* Gallia Christiana, vol. iv., p. 744.

St Marthe records that a successor of Prior Courtois held general chapters in 1525, 1526, 1527, 1529, 1533, 1536, and 1541. The concordat of Francis I. and Leo X. in 1516 gave the king the privilege of nominating to the bishoprics and vacant benefices of the first class, abolishing the Pragmatic Sanction, under which every cathedral church chose its bishop, and every monastery its abbot.* This change was felt at Val des Choux; the king nominated the prior in 1585, and again in 1595, although the nominee of the Crown in 1595 had already been elected by the monks. The result of this violation of the rules of the various monastic orders in France was the profligate appointment by court favourites of persons to benefices as sinecures.

Helyot, in his account of the Valliscaulian order,† says, Cardinal Vitri, from whom he takes his account of their rules, is mistaken in thinking they followed the institute of the Cistercians; the mistake, however, was frequently made. In fact, the Valliscaulian rule resembled rather the rule of the Chartreuse, in the separation of the abodes of the brethren; whilst it imitated the Cistercian system, in making them have a common table. Chassanæus, indeed, writing in 1579,‡ speaking of the small revenues of the Valliscaulian priories and the few brethren in each house, says it would be better that they were entirely brought under the rule of the Cistercians, since they wear their dress.

This event seems at last actually to have taken place when at Sept Fonds a new reform of the Cistercian order was carried out by Dom. Dorothee Gallowitz, who was elected abbot of Sept Fonds in 1757, and who afterwards become Prior of Val des Choux, and induced the members of that order to enter into the Reformed Cistercian Rule.

The consequences of the vast revenues of the French monasteries being applied to keeping in luxury and idleness the creatures of a profligate court, were seen at the very commence-

---

* Mosheim's Ecc. Hist., vol. iv., p. 14, ed. Maclaren.
† Helyot, vol. vi., p. 178.
‡ Catalogus Gloriæ Mundi, Francf. 1579, p. 119.

ment of the French Revolution. Nothing could be urged in favour of such a system, and the usurpations of Francis I. were the indirect cause of the confiscations of the National Assembly.

Dom. Dorothee survived till 1790, when on 13th February the Assembly suppressed the religious orders, and abolished the obligation of monastic vows, devoting their property to the service of the State, and charging the communes with the maintenance of religious worship. Many religious took advantage of the law, and the last year of the last Prior of Val des Choux must have been embittered at the destruction of all his hopes. And it must be remembered that he and such as he were the salt of the earth to France amidst the corruptions of those fearful times.

The site of Val des Choux is marked on the War Office map of France of 1843. Apparently nothing remains of the monastic buildings. Too distant from a town to become a barrack or a magazine, and too gloomy to attract the taste of a purchaser, the spot seems to have relapsed into its primitive condition of forest; and the only traces of the existence of the house seem to be the large fish ponds which afforded to the brethren a plentiful supply of their lenten and fast-day food.*

So much for the governing house of the order, from which the commission for visitation proceeded.

We will now pass on to the house which was the subject of the visitation, and

" In pilgrimage we wend our way,
To lone Ardchattan's abbey grey."

The visitor who passes from Oban to Connel Ferry, and walks up the northern shore of Loch Etive, will find himself, after going about four miles, in the estate of Ardchattan, a district perhaps naturally not more beautiful than many in the picturesque county of Argyle, but singularly cared for and tastefully developed. The hills are clothed with wood, leaving between them and the water-side stretches of cultivated,

---

* The House of Sept Fonds, sanctified by the priorate of Dom. Dorothee, has lately been restored to its original pious uses.

smiling ground. Passing the parish church, which is such an effort at Gothic as the skill of half-a-century since could be expected in so remote a district to produce, he comes to Ardchattan Priory, a specimen very rare in Scotland of the domestic buildings of a conventual establishment, preserved and continued from being the residence of the prior of the monastery to becoming the manor-house of the laird ; everything in perfect keeping—stone gables and buttresses—whilst the windows are themselves a history, from the Early English lancet of the thirteenth century to the sash of the eighteenth and the revived mullions of the nineteenth, and all points of vantage crowned with the holy emblem of the cross.

Let us take a hasty glance at its history.

In the Scottish chronicler's account of the year 1230, after stating the foundation of Pluscardine and Beauly, he adds : *
" Duncan Mackowle founded in this year the monastery of Ardchattan."

The remains of the priory church attest the accuracy of the date. The piscina in the south wall of the chancel is of pure Early English character. The priory seal also seems from its impression to have been a work of the thirteenth century.

Who was Duncan Mackowle?

Highland scholars † and Highland peasants tell us that MacCoule and MacDougal are the same name. In 1512 we have MacDougal of Dunolly recorded as MacCowle. Duncan M'Cowle, the son and heir of Alexander M'Cowle of Dunnoly, is entered as being buried at Ardchattan. ‡

The founder being Duncan MacDougal, in 1231, a little further inquiry will identify him.

Somerled, in the time of David I., expelled the Norwegians from Argyle, and became, under the Scottish monarch, the Lord of Argyle. He married the daughter of Olaf, the Nor-

---

* Extracta e Cronicis Scotiæ, p. 93.
† Campbell's West Highland Poetry, vol. iv., p. 27.
‡ His. Acc. of Clan Gregor, p. 44. This young man was killed by Colin M'Eno (M'Ean) of Barbreck (Chronicle of Fortirgall, in Black Book of Taymouth, p. 116).

wegian King of the Isles; and the eldest son of that marriage was Dougal. He, on his father's death in the battle of Renfrew, in 1164, succeeded to the Sudreys, the southern portion of the islands, as his mother's heir, and to Lorn as his share of his paternal possessions of Argyle, and founded the house and clan of MacDougal of Lorn.

Dougal left two sons—Dugall Scray and Duncan—who appear in the Norse sagas under the title of Sudereyan Kings.* In 1230, it seems Dugall Scray was taken prisoner by the Norwegians, and Duncan was then the only one of his family who retained any power in the Sudreys.

This Duncan, the son of Dougal, was the first who adopted the name MacDougal; as Duncan de Lorn, witnesses a charter of the Earl of Athol;† as Duncan de Ergalita, signs the letter and oath to the Pope of the nobles of Scotland on the treaty of Ponteland in 1244;‡ and was doubtless the founder of Ardchattan.

It was probably as a peace-offering to King Alexander II., and his chief adviser, William Malvoisin, that Duncan of Lorn founded the priory.

The king had, in 1221, made himself master of the whole of Argyle; and although he had not included Lorn in his new sheriffdom of Argyle, yet he made Duncan MacDougal hold it of the Crown instead of the Lord of the Isles; and the surest way of cementing the union was by bringing it ecclesiastically as well as politically into connection with the rest of Scotland. At this time, therefore, instead of the nominal subjection of Argyle to the bishopric of Dunkeld, there was constituted the bishopric of Argyle, whose seat was Lismore, an island close to the mainland where Ardchattan lies, and the placing near it a priory linked with the sister priories of Beauly and Pluscardine served to rivet the union of ecclesiastical strongholds which would bind the country and people to the Crown and Church of Scotland.

* Skene, ii. 49. † Cart. de Cupar, 9.
‡ Matt. Paris, 1244, ed. Wats. John Byset the younger, as we have seen, also signed this with Duncan MacDougal.

Alexander II., in 1243, compassionating the poverty of the bishopric of Argyle, granted to the bishop the church of Killean, in Kintyre.* In 1249, the king died in the island of Kerrera, just off the coast of Lorn. By 1251, Duncan Mac-Dougal must have died, as in that year Lord Ewin, the son of Duncan of Argyle, grants lands in Lismore to the Bishop of Argyle.

In 1296, Pieres, the Prior of Ercattan, and the whole convent, swore fealty to King Edward I.;† but the prior did not attend with his brother priors of Pluscardine and Beauly the Parliament of Dreghorn in 1290. It had, however, been well endowed either by the founder, or, as Father Hay implies, by the kings of Scotland; for in Boiamond's Taxation of 1274, where the bishopric of Argyle is valued at £293, the Priory of Ardchattan is valued at £200, the same valuation as the Priory of Beauly.

Its endowments included salmon fishings, the shell-nets, " the fishings of the Prior Schotts at the mouth of the Water of Aw," just where the tide enters into the river Awe, and where the salmon is found in the greatest abundance and most perfect flavour and condition; and of Port Verran at the head of Loch Etive, and the teinds of the salmon and herring caught between the Connel and the head of Loch Etive or in the Water of Aw.

The priory does not seem to have been endowed with mills or multures, but the monks were secured from the temptation to break their rule and cultivate their land for subsistence by endowing the priory with the tithes, or portions of the tithes, of the churches of various parishes.

These were Ardchattan itself, by its name of Ballibodan or Kilbodan, Kilninver, Kilbrandon, in Seil; Kirkapole, in Tiree; Kilmonivaig, in Lochaber; and Kilmarow, in Kintyre.

Of these, Ardchattan was completely appropriated, and no vicar endowed, the monks apparently doing the parochial duties. Kilbrandon had a vicar who lived at Seil. The priory seems to have had only a portion of the tithes,

* Reg. Mag. Sig., lib. xiv., No. 389.   † Ragman Roll, p. 117.

whilst there still remained a rector in each parish of Kilmonivaig and Kilninver, the advowsons of which rectories belonged to the priory. In Kilmarow they had a portion of the tithes only, the church of Kilmarow being appropriated, in 1251, to the bishopric of Argyle.* The exact condition of Kirkapole, in Tiree, is very obscurely indicated; but probably the priory was *only a portioner* of tithes in this parish, the rectory of which was appropriated to the bishopric of the Isles. The island of Tiree belonged to John of Lorn, Lord of Argyle, in the fourteenth century.†

Father Hay says of the founder: " He joined on to the church dwelling-places moderate indeed, and such as in a short time could be set up; there the fathers, sighing for the habitations of their heavenly country, despised the comforts (*hospitia*) of their present life."

" Privileges," he adds, " are said to have been granted to the holy house by the pontiffs of Rome and the kings of Scotland. The place given to the devout monks was marked out, instead of landmarks, by fixed crosses." ‡

It is probable this alludes to what would be a great boon to the wild tribes who dwelt in the neighbourhood of Ardchattan, the right of sanctuary within the girth of Ardchattan. We have seen that this right was to a limited extent given to Pluscardine by Urban IV. " No one," says Pope Alexander, in his Bull to Kinloss § (A.D. 1174), " is to presume to take away a man within the ambit of your church or within your granges." The sacred marks of the bounds were those within which the refugees were free; what the precise rule at Ardchattan was, we know not; but at Hexham ‖ there were three lines of refuge—the third being the Frid-stol, the seat of peace itself, where even the sacrilegious and the traitor could find a safe asylum.

---

* Reg. Mag. Sig., lib. xiv., No. 389.
† Hailes' Annals, 2d ed., vol. iii., p. 281.
‡ Father Hay's Scotia Sacra, MS., Adv. Lib., p. 203. The father's Latinity belongs to the kind called by Ducange *infimus*.
§ Book of Kinloss, p. 106.   ‖ Appendix, No. XV.

For two hundred years no mention is made in the pages of the annalist of the Priory of Ardchattan. "Bene vixit, qui bene latuit," was a monastic proverb; we will hope it was so. The local historian indeed tells us that Robert Bruce held a parliament here—one of the last, he adds, at which the business was conducted in the Gaelic language.* Bruce's parliament in Lorn, even after his defeat of the Lord of Lorn must have been a mere mockery of a national assembly, and probably was a court only at which he received the homage in their native tongue of the vanquished Highlanders.

Just a trace of the existence of the priory occurs in 1470; but there is no record relating to it until this commission for visitation in 1506. At the time of this visitation, it is suggested that the quiet of the monastery proceeded from the utter decay of its monastic discipline, and from the conversion of its holy precincts into a mere inheritance of a family of priors.

In England, at the close of the twelfth century, it is on record that a parish church in Norfolk descended from father to son, from parson to parson, without any presentation.† In the early part of the thirteenth century we have the Pope complaining to the Bishop of Coventry that when priests and clergymen, holding churches and benefices with cure of souls, died, their sons presumed, sometimes with violence and armed force, to take possession of these churches and benefices, and as of hereditary right (*et jure quasi hæreditario*) to retain them.‡ In Scotland, in the diocese of Glasgow, in the same age, says Mr Robertson,§ sons formally claimed their fathers' churches as of hereditary right.

In the remote district of Lorn, it is suggested in the "Origines Parochiales Scotiæ," there might be seen, towards the end of the fifteenth century, a convent descending from

---

* Anderson's Highlands, p. 310.
† Selden's History of Tithes, cxii., sec. 4.
‡ Hist. Letters of Henry III., p. 560, app. 41.
§ Pref. to Stat. Eccl. Scot., p. ccvi. Mr Robertson seems to have had little sympathy with the system of family livings.

father to son, in the case of this Priory of Ardchattan. At that time the district was ecclesiastically little subject to external influence.

Robert, Bishop of Argyle, who had sequestrated some churches in Argyle, belonging to the monks of Paisley, seems, in 1491, to have repudiated the jurisdiction, and defied, even to excommunication, the decision of the Pope.* The king wisely tried to put Robert's successor, David, Bishop of Argyle, above the temptation to attack the churches appropriated to Paisley, by appropriating some more churches to the bishopric, grounding his bounty in 1508 on the poverty of the bishopric, "situated among wild and untamable tribes."

The writer of the "Origines Parochiales Scotiæ" says,† "about the end of the fifteenth century, the priory seemed to have been ruled in succession by Somerled or Somherle Macdougall, and his two sons, Duncan and Dougal, the last of whom died in 1502, and who are all buried within the church." This seems an extraordinary state of things, reviving, in the fifteenth century, the practices of the twelfth, and we had better examine the evidence on which it rests.

It is founded on the figures and inscriptions on two tombstones, now within the ruined church of Ardchattan Priory.

Dean Howson‡ could not read the inscription in the Gothic character on the one, except the words *Ardchattan* and *apud Ardchattan*. The stone is broken, and "the fracture," he says, "passes near the figures in the date, but it is certainly either 1400 or 1500. I observed that one end of the stone tapered as if it had stood in a socket; and on turning it over, I found figures which convinced me it was the shaft of a cross. These figures are extremely grotesque. One is a lion, and the other some nondescript creature in a rampant position, like the lion at Mycenæ, and enclosing a galley between them."

The writer of the "New Statistical Account"§ thought he was able to read the inscription. He says: "The following

---

* Reg. de Passelet, p. 154.   † O. P. S., "Ardchattan," p. 148.
‡ Trans. Camb. Camden Soc., 1845.
§ New Statistical Account, "Ardchattan."

letters appear in the old Saxon character: 'Funallus Somherle Macdougallus, Prior de Ardchattan, MCCCCC.'"

I examined the stone in September 1874, and by the kindness of Mr Sutherland, the Free Church minister, I have obtained a rubbing of the inscription. One thing only is clear, that the date is 1500.

The accounts given of the other tomb differ.

Dean Howson says: "It has six figures in relief, each under a crocketed canopy of that peculiarly stiff form which at once fixes the date of the tomb to be not very long anterior to the Reformation. Above these are two female figures, and between, the effigy of Death, with a toad between the knees. Below the armed figures, and between them, an ecclesiastic. The inscription runs round in Roman letters, 'Hic jacent M. Duncanus et Dugallus, hujus monasterii Priores, una cum eorundem patre et matre quorum Dugallus istius monumenti fabricator, obiit 1502.'"

In "Ancient Reliques," vol. ii., Lond. 1813, is an engraving of the tomb. It is there stated: "It contains an inscription in Latin, translated as follows: 'Here lies Macdougal and Duncan, also Dougal, their successor, the first two of whom descended from the same father and mother; but Dougal, who erected this monument, was by a former mother. He died in the year 1502.'"

Lastly, in the account of the monuments at Ardchattan, by Dr Rogers,* we get the description, which states that the monument represents "two dignified churchmen in monastic costume, a warrior in mail armour, and two weeping nuns; between, a human skeleton. The following inscription, in old Irish characters, occupies the sides and margin: 'Hic jacent nati Somerledi Macdougall Duncanus et Dugallus, hujus monasterii successive priores, una cum eorundem patre matre et fratre Alano, quorum Dugallus hujus monumenti fabricator, obiit Anno Domini MCCCCII.'"

These are the circumstances upon which the statement in

* Monuments and Monumental Inscriptions in Scotland. Grampian Club, vol. ii., p. 6.

the " Origines Parochiales" of the descent of the priorate from father to son, is founded.

It is upon these also, I suppose, that the suggestion of the Rev. Mr Fraser of Ardchattan was given to Dean Howson in this note: " It is a melancholy thought that so much of evil was mixed with so much that was good. Nor is this thought arbitrarily suggested or wilfully called up by an angry dislike of monastic institutions; but on the contrary, forced into the mind by documentary evidence of the state of the religious house shortly before the time when the Scottish Reformation, in rebelling against the evil, did not spare the good of former generations."*

Whatever the facts, clearly the prior who died in 1500 could hardly be the father of two priors, the eldest of whom died in 1502, without some special notice of such a mortality.

But taking the tomb of 1500 to be the first of the two brothers who were priors, and the five figures on the other tomb to commemorate the five persons mentioned in the inscription, the story is plain enough.

From a careful examination I made in September 1874, I found the inscription as given in the " New Statistical Account" to be correct, except that the word " hujus" is " istius," but I satisfied myself that the so-called two nuns are the priors in their cowls and monks' robes. The two armed figures below are their father and brother Alan; and the dignified ecclesiastic between them is the lady their mother in the full-dress costume of the period. The armed figure of the father shows that he was not the prior, and that the priorate had not descended from father to son. It passed from brother to brother, and the priors were probably often of the same family; if, in pursuance of a right reserved to the founder, Duncan MacDougal, on the original foundation, or even, if by usage, the MacDougal family had the power of nominating the prior, a power not infrequently given to founders, then the whole thing is explained, and nothing would be more natural than that a member of the MacDougal family should

* Camb. Camden Soc., 1845.

be constantly elected as prior upon the nomination of the founder's heir.

Certainly few places were more tempting to repose, than the Priory of Ardchattan; and it cannot excite surprise if from time to time the patron appointed a son or a brother to the post of its head. The arrangement seems to have been made that the church and prior's house should face Loch Etive, and the open country to the south, one of the most beautiful scenes in Argyleshire; nor did the sense of ownership which the continuance of the headship in one family fostered fail to make the possessors more and more careful to add to the pleasantness and profitableness of the place. Its very description in the old charters when dissolved, tells a tale of care and cultivation; the " manor or place of old called the Monastery or Priory of Ardchattan, with the buildings, greens, office-houses, gardens, and orchards, as well within the Inner Precinct or stone fence of the said former monastic place as in those other gardens within the outer precinct and fence, commonly called the Thornedykes and Hedges of the said monastery of Ardchattan."

This description is from a deed of 1697, but in 1602 the description is, "The manor or place of Archattane, called the priory, with the houses, mansions, buildings, greens, office-houses, gardens, and orchards, lying within the inner precinct of the monastery, and also within the outer precinct or hedges of the priory." And yet some Anglicising Scotsmen would persuade us that the hawthorn hedge was an introduction at first planted in Scotland by Cromwell's soldiers, as if the party of ruffians, calling themselves English soldiers, who burned the house of Ardchattan in 1654, could be the planters in its gardens of

> "The hawthorn bush, with seats beneath the shade,
> For talking age and whispering lovers made."

The trees that are now round the priory ruins attest the fitness of the soil and climate for their growth: among them an ash-tree, 3 feet from the ground, is 9 feet 10 inches in growth, and a plane or sycamore 9 feet 6 inches; these probably relics of the monks' planting. Between the priory and the point where the hill rises abruptly from the plain, is a wide extent of pasture ground, level, green, and richly luxuriant; it is called the "Monks' Garden."

We shall add a description of the architecture of Ardchattan Priory church when we give the particulars of the Beauly Priory buildings.*

Before passing to the next document transcribed, we may mention that the papal Bull which we print hereafter, as promulgated in 1514, was dated in July of this very year 1506.†

Among the storms of civil war which raged in Ross-shire and the Isles between 1498 and 1506, it is likely that the Priory of Beauly may have suffered from one or other of the contending parties. Thomas, Lord Lovat, their immediate neighbour, was specially associated by the king with the Earl of Huntly to put down the rebellion.

It was probably in consequence of the injury which the priory had suffered, that Prior Dougal, who had influence with the Roman Court, obtained from Pope Julius the Bull dated in July 1506, and promulgated in 1514.

---

* The name Ardchattan is derived from St Cathan the bishop, the uncle of St Blane. To St Cathan were dedicated the church of Kilchattan in the island of Lunig, opposite the coast of Lorn, and other churches, but his reputation in the Highlands led to the adoption of his name by a whole clan. "The Clan Chattan," says the learned and accurate Mr Robertson, "was peculiarly a ghostly tribe. It took its distinctive appellation from a saint, that kinsman of St Blane who was patron of Aberuthven in Strathern, and gave name to Ardchattan and Kilchattan in Lorn, to Kilchattan in Bute, to Kilchattan in Gigha, and to other churches in the West Isles" (Appendix to pref. Spalding Miscellany, vol. v., p. 74).

† This same year (1506) King James IV. granted to David, Bishop of Argyle, the royal escheats and fines of Argyle and Lorn.

No. XIX.

LITTERA FRATRIS JACOBI COURTOIS GENERALIS
ORDINIS VALLISCAULIUM IN BURGUNDIA PRIORI
DE BELLO LOCO.

Ex Autographo [1506].

"Nos Frater Jacobus Courtois, humilis Prior Prioratus Monasterij Beatæ Mariæ Virginis Valliscaulium, Caput sive Generalis dicti ordinis Valliscaulium, situati in Ducatu Burgundiæ juxta Castillon supra Senam, Notum facimus, quod die datæ præsentium comparuit in dicto nostro Prioratu quidam Scotus Presbyter nomine Gulielmus Tomson et certas litteras papireas, non signatas, nulloque Sigillo munitas, de data diei decimi mensis Novembris novissime elapsi, nobis præsentavit. Quas quidem litteras, sic nobis per præscriptum Dominum Gulielmum ex parte carorum et dilectorum nobis in Christo fratrum Prioris et Conventus Beatæ Mariæ Virginis de Bello loco in Scotiâ situati in Diocœsi Rossensi præsentatas ad longum vidimus ac legimus et ad vos super contentis in hujusmodi vestris litteris respondendum nobis videtur: quod doletis et conqueritis, quod Reverendus in Christo pater Dominus Episcopus Rossensis aut ejus Officialis vult ad volunt: vos aut supradictum Monasterium visitare, nec non in eodem Monasterio seu Prioratu vestro, jura visitationis ac procurationis solita et consueta capere et levare, et quod eidem non vultis obtemperare, dicentes, vos esse exemptos ab hujusmodi visitatione, prout vobis videtur, quia Valliscaulium religio, nec non omnia Monasteria ejusdem sunt exempta a Jurisdictione Episcopi. Quod non est verum. Quapropter, et ne vos litibus seu processibus involvatis, notum vobis facimus, et certificamus, quod non habemus in partibus Galliæ, nisi tredecim parvas domus ordinis Valliscaulium locatas et situatas in quinque Dioccesibus—Videlicet, Lingonen. Educn. Senonn. Trecen. et Verduncn. in Lothoringia a quibus

Episcopis aut eorum Commissarijs sumus singulis annis visitati, et capiunt expensas et provisiones a nobis; que de re vobis insinuamus, ut in hac materia uti velitis bono consilio.

"Item desideratis habere copiam authenticam Institutionis et Confirmationis ac privilegiorum nostri jam dicti ordinis Valliscaulium, quod pro nunc non est possibile, ut relatu dicti Domini Gulielmi percipere poteritis, quia omnes dictæ Confirmationes et Privilegia in Nostro Thesauro apud Divionem consistunt, et ad ipsas, propter instans festum Dominicæ Nativitatis, ac adversam nostram valetudinem illo accedere minime possumus. Et vos, Domine prior, non valemus satis mirari, quo Privilegij titulo munitus potestis regere, et gubernare dictum Prioratum de Bello loco, et alia Monasteria ex eo dependentia, eo maxime attento, quod huc nunquam venistis aut misistis, pro vestrâ institutione et confirmatione dicti Prioratus ac ejus membrorum habendi. Quare vos monemus sub pœnis ordinarijs in nostro ordine factis et declaratis, quatenus vos recipiatis, seu compareatis in Capitulo nostro, quod celebraturi sumus in Festo Inventionis Sanctæ Crucis, proxime venturo, aut Festo Johannis exinde proxime insequenti, quia illic vobis monstraturi sumus Confirmationem Statuta et Privilegia ordinis, favente Altissimo, cui precamur, ut vobis et religiosis vestris det lætitiam, nos nihilominus vestris orationibus commendantes. Dominus Prior quoque, Prædecessor vester novissimus, nobis promisit, quod ipse aut ejus Procurator de quadriennio in quadriennium comparerit in nostro Capitulo generali: Concessimusque eidem Priori aut ejus Procuratori de gratia nostra speciali, et quia longe a nobis, sive in longinquis partibus estis constituti, terminum comparationis hujusmodi de sex annis ad sex annos. Ipse tamen Prædecessor vester aut ejus Procurator, neque vos aut persona pro vobis, minime comparuistis, seu comparuerunt, in nostro Capitulo prædicto, qua re de vobis contentos nos reddere non debemus; Quanquam etiam idem vester Prædecessor seu ejus Procurator nobis promiserit mittere [pisces] Salmones nuncupatos, ex partibus, seu rivis et aquis vestris, apud oppidum Brugen. sive Valenthinen. ubi commisimus Mercatores, qui dictos pisces reciperent, et nobis apud Divionem deferrent, non tamen unquam aliquid ab eodem Prædecessore aut suo Procuratore exinde percepimus; sed quia præfatus Dominus Gulielmus præsentium lator asseruit nobis, vos esse virum tantæ nobilitatis, veracitatis ac bonæ religionis, credimus quod, favente

Altissimo, non solum pro Prædecessore sed et pro vobis hâc æstate proxime futurâ, rationem estis reddituri. Scriptum seu datum apud Valliscaulium die decima octava mensis Decembris anno Millesimo quingentesimo sexto. In testimonium affixiones Sigilli nostri et signi manualis præsentibus appositi.

"Sigillat. V^{is} necnon subscript. et Signat. Sic, Courtois.

"Not.—In dorso litterarum, hujusmodi erat superscript. talis.
Dilectis nostris Atque bene Amatis Dominis Priori et Conventui Beatæ Mariæ de Bello loco diocœsis Rossensis in Scotia.

"Translatio facto est de lingua Gallica in Latinam non mutando rei substantiam, collataque est præsens copia sic translata cum suo originali per me Johannem Bertin Notarium Apostolica et Imperiali Auctoritatibus ac Venerabilis Curiæ Episcopalis Tornacens. publicum, et concordant. Teste signo meo Manuali. Ita est Joh. Bertyn p^{ls} N^{rius}."

This instrument is a translation into Latin from the French of a letter from the same James Courtois, the Prior of Valliscaulium, from whom the last document we have printed proceeded.

The translation is by John Bertin, notary public, of the episcopal court of Tournay; but the mistakes of the transcriber are most glaring, such as "Bivio" for "Divio," and "Fornacensis" for "Tornacensis."

It is dated the 18th of December 1506, about six months later than the commission to visit Ardchattan, and is in answer to a letter from the prior and convent of Beauly, dated the 10th of November 1506.

On a winter's morning late in December a stranger presented himself at the gateway of Val des Choux. He was not a monk, he was not a pilgrim, but a travelling priest. By travelling priests most of the communication of those days was kept up, especially that spread of public opinions and feelings among the common people, for which, in the absence of a public press, we should otherwise be unable to account. He was received, as all strangers would be, gladly, and he was the bearer of this letter written at Beauly in the preceding month.

The prior-general now gives his titles more in full. He styles himself Brother James Courtois, the humble prior of the priory of the monastery of the Blessed Virgin Mary of Valliscaulium (the head or general of the said order of Valliscaulium), situated in the duchy of Burgundy, near Chatillon, on the Seine. He states that on the day of the date of his letter, a Scottish priest, named William Tomson, made his appearance in their priory, and presented certain paper letters, unsigned and unsealed, dated 10th November preceding, which letter, so presented to him by the said Sir William, on the part of the dear and much-loved brethren in Christ, the prior and convent of the Blessed Virgin Mary of Beauly, in Scotland, situate in the diocese of Ross, the prior-general had seen and read in full, and to them concerning the contents of the letter he thinks this answer should be sent: That whereas they lamented and complained that the Bishop of Ross or his official claimed the right of visiting their monastery of Beauly, and of taking and levying in their said monastery or priory the accustomed rights of visitation and procuration, and they were not willing to submit to the bishop, but maintained that the rule (*religio*) of the Valliscaulians and the monasteries of the order were exempt from the jurisdiction of the bishop, which is not true; therefore, in order that they might not involve themselves in suits and proceedings, the prior-general informed them that in France the order had but thirteen small houses, situated in the five dioceses of Langres, Autun, Troyes, Sens,* and Verdun in Lorraine, and that these were visited every year by the bishops or their commissaries, who took expenses and provisions from them, wherefore the prior-general suggests that, in this matter, the prior and convent of Beauly should be well advised.

The prior-general continues, that whereas they desired an authentic copy of the institution and confirmation, and of the privileges of the order, this was not then possible, as he would

* The transcriber has Benonn.

understand from the report of the said Sir William, for all the said confirmations and privileges lay in the treasury at Dijon, and the prior-general, on account of the approaching feast of the Lord's Nativity and his own ill-health, could not go thither. The prior-general proceeds with a more direct address to the head of the monastery from which had come the letter he is answering, in these words:

"And, Sir Prior, we are not able sufficiently to wonder by what title of privilege fortified, you are able to rule and govern the said Priory of Beauly, and the other monasteries dependent upon it, most particularly considering this, that you have never come or sent to this house for your institution and confirmation of the holding of the said priory and its members, wherefore we admonish you under the ordinary penalties, made and passed in our order, that you present yourself or appear in our Chapter, which we are about to celebrate at the coming feast of the Invention of the Holy Cross (May 3, 1507), or the feast of John immediately following (June 24, 1507), because there we shall show you the Confirmation, Statutes, and Privileges of the Order, by the favour of the Most High, to whom we pray that He may give joy and gladness to you and your religious, nevertheless commending ourselves to your prayers. Moreover, the Lord Prior, your immediate predecessor, promised us that he or his procurator would appear in our General Chapter at intervals of four years, and we conceded, of our special grace, to the same prior or his procurator, that, on account of the distance, the term of appearance should be extended to intervals of six years; but neither he, your predecessor, nor his procurator, nor you, nor any person for you, has appeared in our said chapter, for which reason we ought not to rest satisfied concerning you; and, moreover, although your same predecessor or his procurator had promised to send fish, called Salmon, from your parts, or waters, or rivers, to the town of Bruges, or Valenciennes, where we commissioned merchants to receive the said fish, and transmit them to Dijon, we have never received anything on that account from the same predecessor, or his procurator; but the said Sir William, the bearer of this letter, has assured us that you are a man of such nobility, veracity, and of good religion, that we believe that, by the favour of the Most High, not only for your predecessor, but also for yourself, you will render account this next coming summer. Written or dated at Valliscaulium, the 18th day of December 1506. In witness, the affixing of our seal and sign-manual is appended to these presents."

The signature is the surname only—"COURTOIS." *

A note is added that the translation is from the French into the Latin, not changing the substance, and that the copy translated is compared with the original by John Bertin, the notary-public we have mentioned.

The old prior-general had now been for at least thirty-five years Head of the Mother House and the Order, and his infirmities might well have prevented his journeying to Dijon in the winter of that part of France.

He was, it would seem, under the impression that the Priory of Beauly had some lesser houses dependent upon it; but this does not appear to be the fact. Pluscardine had, in 1454, ceased to be a monastery of the Valliscaulian order, and had become a Benedictine house, dependent on the Abbey of Dunfermline; nor whilst it observed the rule of Viard is there any trace of its having been in any way subject to Beauly. The prior-general himself had just before placed Ardchattan, the only other house of his order in Scotland, under the control of the Prior of Beauly, by issuing to him a special commission to visit it, but this is the only instance recorded of any act of supremacy of the Ross-shire priory over the Argyleshire house.

The prior-general was naturally anxious that the Prior of Beauly should not raise, on the subject of episcopal visitation, a contention, which was contrary to the practice of the order. The Valliscaulians neither were nor claimed to be exempt from episcopal jurisdiction.

In the year 601 Gregory the Great (himself for some time the inmate of a monastery) held a council, in which, among many regulations favourable to the independence of monks, rules were laid down, by which the bishop was precluded not

---

* Of course this was not Quartus. The name originally may have been Courthose; Robert, eldest son of William of Normandy, was Robert Courthose.

only from all interference in their temporalities, and all exercise of jurisdiction over them, but even from the celebration of the Divine office in their churches. But this regulation was not observed; and afterwards the contrary rule was the rule of the Church; the bishop, as the ordinary, had jurisdiction over the monasteries as well as all other ecclesiastical establishments in his diocese; special immunities were required to exempt monasteries from episcopal visitation; and, in Germany, there is not an instance of such exemption till the time of Pope Hildebrand.*

There was no such exemption in the confirmation, by Pope Innocent III., of the constitutions of Viard; and we have seen that the "Register of Moray" contained the record of the appearance, before the chapter of Moray, of monks of Pluscardine, and of the proctor of the Mother House of Val des Choux, who distinctly repudiated the plea of independence for Valliscaulian priories from diocesan bishops' control, and denied that such independence had ever been claimed by the order. The "Register of Moray" contained also an entry of the Bull of confirmation of Pope Innocent. That register, Prior Dougal Rorieson seems not to have consulted; and as half a century had elapsed since a Valliscaulian house had been within the diocese of Moray, there was little reason to suppose information would be derived from the records of that bishopric.

The prior-general says that there were, in 1506, only thirteen small houses of the order in France.

Miræus,† who writes in 1614, and Helyot, who writes in

---

* Waddington's History of the Church, p. 412.

† Orig. Benedict. Colon., 1614. The British Museum copy has a book-plate, with a motto which is very happy. The plate represents a person in an ecclesiastical habit seated in a library, with this legend:

"IN TALI NUNQUAM LASSAT VENATIO SYLVA."

This would have delighted Sir Richard Hoare, the historian of Wiltshire. He said to the late learned antiquary, Mr Joseph Hunter, that no pursuit was so fascinating as archæology, except fox-hunting. Those antiquaries who have assisted in drawing the fine coverts of Stourhead, will appreciate the comparison of the owner.

1714, state that there were about thirty priories of the order of Val des Choux in Burgundy, particularly mentioning Vallis Benedicti, near Autun, and Vallis Crescens, near Sedan.* If this number is correct, it must have increased after the time of Prior Courtois.

The right of holding Chapters of the Order, if vested in a priory which was the head of an Order, gave to such a priory the title of a Capitular or Chapter priory, which distinguished it from a priory which was subject to an abbey.†

The exemption which Prior Courtois had given to the Prior of Beauly, from attending the Chapter of the Order more frequently than six years, was analogous to the practice of the Cistercian order as to the abbots of Cistercian monasteries in Scotland, who were exempted from attending the General Chapter of the Order, at Citeaux, oftener than once in four years.‡

William Tomson had come from Beauly to Val des Choux in forty days. He could not have performed the journey entirely on foot in the time; and was probably not a pilgrim—not one of those whose departure, taking wallet, cloak, cap, and staff, on their journey to Rome, is several times recorded in the Protocol Book of Glasgow.§ He must have come by sea, and probably from Inverness to Flanders, and then on foot, using the hospitality of convent after convent, until he arrived at Val des Choux. And by the same route he must have returned, as he was the bearer of the letter from Prior Courtois, for this was translated in the diocese of Tournay, in Flanders, although the translation may have been sent on by another hand.

The Salmon which Prior Hugh Fraser had undertaken to send to the Mother House, was partly a compliment and partly a due. Some slight acknowledgment of dependency in money or kind, was probably customary, from the inferior

* Appendix, No. XVI.
† Stevens' ed. of Dugdale's Monasticon, vol. i., pp. 20-29.
‡ *Ib.*, vol. ii., p. 29.
§ Diocesan Registers of Glasgow. Grampian Club, vol. i., p. 489.

houses of the Valliscaulian order to the Head House; a trace of this we found in the compensation to be awarded to Val des Choux, on the change of order at Pluscardine; and, here again, we have a slight recognition of the due, but, as we have seen, the position of the Scottish priories of this order was much more independent of the Foreign House, than that of the Alien priories in England.

This notice of the trade between Beauly and Bruges in salmon is interesting, and shows the extent to which the practice of sending these splendid fish then prevailed. Inverness was long anterior to this period evidently a colony of busy merchants, whose names, from the earliest date, indicate their Flemish or Saxon descent. Its exports of hides, herring, salmon, malt, etc., were known in the ports of the Continent, even on the shores of the Mediterranean. Boece, who was Principal of King's College, Aberdeen, soon after 1500, states that in ages long before, a concourse of German merchants annually resorted to the town of Inverness for the purposes of trade, bringing with them the manufactures of their own nation, and taking away in return quantities of skins and other products of the Highlands; but that owing to the frequent burnings and plunderings to which the town had been subjected, its prosperity had been greatly impaired in his time. Even for some years subsequent to the final union of Scotland with England, the merchants of Inverness carried on their import trade with the ports of France and Holland.*

We have interesting details, about the date of this letter of the prior-general, of the trade between Scotland and the Low Countries, from the accounts, which have been brought to light by Mr Cosmo Innes,† and published by the Treasury, of Haliburton, a Scottish merchant residing mostly at Middleburgh, but carrying on business at the fairs at Berri, Bruges, and Antwerp, from 1493 to 1503.‡

* Anderson's Highlands, ed. 1842, p. 89; Statist. Account, Inverness, 1842, p. 23.
† Innes's Scotland in the Middle Ages, p. 241.
‡ Ledger of A. Halyburton. H.M. General Register House, Edin. 1867.

The shipping employed in the trade with Scotland was partly Scottish, and we find that the import into Flanders included a large quantity of salmon. The first account with the Duke of Ross, who was Archbishop of St Andrews, commences with £43, placed to his credit for the produce of his teind salmon. The Bishop of Aberdeen exported salmon. Another exporter sent large quantities of skins, and got in return awms of Rhine wine and tuns of Gascon claret (the claret cost £4 the tun), with two butts of Malvissy from Jan Burg.

No. XX.

PRÆSENTATIO AD ECCLESIAM DE CONUETH PER PRIOREM DE BELLO LOCO ANNO 1612.

Ex Autographo.

"Reverendo in Christo Patri et Domino Andreæ Dei et Apostolicæ Sedis Gratia Episcopo Moraviensi, Commendatorique de Pettinwym Dryburgh et Cottinghame in Angliâ, Sancti Andreæ et Eboracensis Diocœsium, vestri humiles et devoti oratores, Prior et conventus Belli Loci Ordinis Valliscallium Rossensis Diocœsis, reverentias cum omni mansuetudine et honore debitas. Ad Vicariam perpetuam Parochialis Ecclesiæ de Conueth Moraviensis Diocœsis de jure et de facto vacantis per decessum quondam Domini Donaldi Watsone Presbyteri, ultimi vicarij et possessoris ejusdem, ad nostram præsentationem, totiens vacare contingerit, vestramque collationem, de jure et de facto spectantis, dilectum nostrum Dominum Nicholaum Brauchine Presbyterum, vestræ Reverendæ Paternitati, animo non variandi, duximus præsentandum, prout tenore præsentium præsentamus; eandem Reverendam Paternitatem antedictam humiliter exortando, quatenus, dictum Dominum Nicholaum nostrum præsentatum prætextu veræ præsentationis ad perpetuam Vicariam prædictam, vel ejus legitimum procuratorem, cum omnibus suis juribus, decimis, oblationibus, emolumentis, et suis justis pertinentijs admittere, illamque sibi conferre, et ipsum in eodem investiri mandare, aliasque et alia facere et exercere, dignemini, quæ ad officium vestrum pastorale in hac parte incumbunt. In cujus rei testimonium sigillum commune nostri Capituli præsentibus est appensum apud locum nostrum Belli Loci die undecimo Mensis Maij Anno Domini Millesimo quingentesimo duodecimo."

  Not.—The seal red upon white wax, representing a St John baptizing Christ, both straight. In a niche under them a monk bareheaded, praying. On the circumference, which is oval, is, "S. commune conventus S^{ti} Johannis Baptistæ de Bello loco." The tag of parchment.

This instrument is another presentation to the vicarage of Conveth. Donald Walters—that is, Walter's son—seems to have acquired, whilst vicar of Conveth, the corrupted but more euphonious surname of Watson;* and Conway, a name forcibly reminding us of its origin, has now again resumed its older form of Conveth.†

It was Donald Walteri whose presentation we have printed No. XIV., which was dated 1493. The presentation before us is to the perpetual vicarage ‡ of the parish church of Conveth, in the diocese of Moray, now vacant by the decease of the late Sir Donald Watson, priest, the last vicar and possessor of the same.

The Bishop Andrew of Moray now, is a different person from the Bishop Andrew of Moray of 1493. The former Bishop Andrew was Bishop Andrew Stewart, son of the Dowager Queen of Scotland, Jane Beaufort, and Sir James Stewart of Lorn ; the present Bishop Andrew is Andrew Forman. He was a good specimen of a thriving churchman in those times, a great pluralist, and adds to his title of Bishop of Moray that of Commendator of Pittenweem, Dryburgh, and Cottingham in England, of the dioceses of St Andrews and York.

Pittenweem was a priory of Canons Regular, in Fifeshire. It was first a cell of Reading, and afterwards of St Andrews. In that old priory a life was passed extending to our days, of one who, in striking contrast to Andrew Forman, was " a bishop of a primitive type "—Bishop David Low.§

Dryburgh in Teviotdale, the wealthiest house of the Præ-

* Appendix, No. XVII.

† There seems at Tynemouth Priory to have been a feudal service called the Conveyes, which was performed by entertaining the tenants of the priory at Christmas-tide. See Gibson's Chronicle of Tynemouth, vol. i., p. 140.

‡ Appendix, No. XVIII.

§ Bishop Low lived at Pittenweem for sixty-five years. He was the last survivor of the Scottish Episcopal clergy, who declined to pray for the reigning family till the death of Prince Charles Edward in 1788 (Scottish Nation, iii, 716).

monstratensian order in Scotland, was founded in 1150 by Hugh de Moreville, Constable of Scotland, and Beatrix de Beauchamp, his wife. Its beautiful ruins are now the resort of pilgrims from all parts of the civilised world, as the burial-place of Sir Walter Scott.

Cottingham in England was a priory of Augustinian canons, otherwise called Haltem Price, in the East Riding of Yorkshire, about five miles from Hull. The expression Commendator of a monastery is not usual in the case of English houses, and some authors suppose Bishop Forman to have been Commendator of Coldingham ;* but we have the bishop on 1st April 1509 as Commendator of Pittenweem and Cottingham in England, presenting to chapels, and his seal to the letters of presentation has these titles on its legend.† His name does not occur in the list of priors of Cottingham, given by Burton or Dr Hutton‡ from the registers of the Archbishopric of York.

Bishop Forman in 1514 was translated to the archbishopric of St Andrews, with the power of a legate *a latere*, and the promise of a cardinal's hat ; not being a cardinal, he could not be an actual legate *a latere*. In 1516 he was made Commendator of Dunfermline. He was also Archbishop of Bourges, in France, by the gift of King Louis XII., which greatly increased his resources. His arms were emblematic of his ecclesiastical voracity : "A chevron between three fishes *hauriant*," an epithet which, as heralds tell us, signifies their position, as if they were refreshing themselves by sucking in the air.§

The most interesting part of this transcript is the note of the seal of Beauly Priory. The seal is red upon white wax, representing a St John baptizing Christ, both straight. In a

* Preface to Book of Dryburgh, Bannatyne Club.
† Anderson's Family of Fraser, appendix.
‡ Dugdale's Monasticon, last edition, vol. vi., p. 519. This may have arisen from his never having been formally instituted to the priory by the Archbishop of York, or never having performed the duties of the priorate, but I have no doubt he received the salary.
§ Porny, Elements of Heraldry, Lond. 1795.

niche under them a monk bareheaded, praying. On the circumference, which is oval, is: "S. COMMUNE CONVENTUS S^{TI} JOHANNIS BAPTISTÆ DE BELLO LOCO."

This is a different seal from that which is described by Mr Laing,* as used in 1571. His description is, "The Virgin and Child sitting within a niche ; below is a monk praying. Inscription not legible."

We may here mention the seals of the two other Scottish Valliscaulian priories.

The seal of Pluscardine† was a very singular design emblematic of delivering souls from Purgatory, with the legend : "SIGILL. CONVENTUS VALL. ——— ANDREE IN MORAVIA."

The seal of Ardchattan‡ represents St John Baptist in his coat of hair with the legend : "SIGILL. CONVENTUS DE ARDKATTAN IN ARGADIA."

Sir Nicholas Brauchine, the presentee, had been rector of Uig, in the barony of Trotternish, in the Isle of Skye, a parish united after the Reformation to the parish of Snizort. In 1512 King James IV. presented Sir Donald Rede to the rectory of Wig in Trouternes, vacant by the demission of Sir Nicholas Brachan.§

Sir Nicholas Brauchine did not apparently long retain the vicarage of Conveth, for among the Lovat Writs of 1652,‖ we have :

"82. A presentation by James, Bishop of Moray, to Mr Kenneth Mackenzie of the vicarage of Conveth, dated the 27th June 1518."

This frequent change shows the poverty of the vicarage of Conveth. This was the natural result of the tendency of all church rulers in Scotland, before and after the Reformation, to depart from the principle of giving the parish minister the parish tithes. It is laid down again and again by Popes and general councils, and edicts of kings of Scotland and statutes of the Scottish Church, that the tithes of a parish

---

* Laing's Scottish Seals, ii., No. 1110.
† *Ib.*, No. 1113.
‡ O. P. S., "Ardchattan."
§ Reg. Sec. Sig., vol. iv., fol. 201.
‖ Dunbar Dunbar MSS.

belong to the minister of the parish, "decimæ debentur parocho."

The Priory of Beauly took for its own use the great tithes of the parishes of Abertarff, Comar, and Conveth, and allowed to the vicars of Abertarff and Conveth, and the parochial chaplain or perpetual curate of Comar, small incomes for their maintenance, though to them alone, by original right, belonged all the tithes of those parishes. And it must have followed from this, that either the vicars were men very little elevated above the lowest rank of their parishioners, content with a bare subsistence and unable to afford the charities and hospitalities which are at once the bulwark and the privilege of the parish priest; or they were men looking out for a change, and who accepted these vicarages as steps to higher and more adequately endowed preferment.

We shall see that when the Reformation came there was no improvement in this respect; when the rectorial and vicarial tithes were alienated to the use of laymen, the covetousness of the nobles exceeded the avidity of the monks.

Among the Lovat Writs inventoried in 1652 there is an entry as follows:

"75. A presentation by the Bishop of Moray to Sir Donald Braichie to be vicar of Beauly, dated the 11th of May 1512." *

This must be the instrument before us mis-described by the ignorance of the maker of the Inventory, but doubtless the same.

There is indeed in the same Inventory a mention of a vicarage of Beauly, as follows:

"68. A presentation by the Prior of Beauly to Sir Donald Dow of the vicarage thairof, dated the 7th of May 1512."

But this is probably a presentation to the other vicarage in the gift of the priory, that of Abertarff, as there is no trace of any vicarage of Beauly, which was not a parish, but merely a village gathered round the monastery and within the parish

* Dunbar Dunbar MSS.

of Kilmorack and diocese of Ross; and the Bishop of Ross, and not the Bishop of Moray, would have been the bishop to whom the presentation of a vicarage of Beauly would have been made. Comar, the only other church which besides Abertarff and Conveth belonged to Beauly, was never provided with a vicar; and as this inventoried presentation is dated only five days before the presentation to Conveth, we are led to conclude that the appointment must have been to Abertarff.[*]

We may resume the history of the heirs of our founder.

William de Fenton of Beaufort of 1403 and 1416, shortly before 1422 was succeeded in all his estates, including Baky Castle and Beaufort Castle, by his son, Walter de Fenton of Beaufort.

Walter de Fenton of Beaufort is so described in 1438, and as being then dead, and he left, as we have seen,[†] four daughters co-heiresses; but, according to the custom of Scotland, the eldest daughter took the castles of Baky and Beaufort, as a portion of her fourth share, and accordingly we find him succeeded at Beaufort by his eldest daughter Margaret. She in 1439 married Walter Ogilvy.

Walter Ogilvy was the son of Patrick Ogilvy of Auchterhouse, and in 1444 styles himself Walter Ogilvy of Beaufort. He was the bailiff—that is, the steward—of the lands of the Abbey of Arbroath. His sister, Marjory, married Alexander, second Earl of Crawford, and in 1445 Walter Ogilvy was wounded and taken prisoner in defending the monastery from an attack by his brother-in-law, the earl, who was also severely wounded. The chroniclers say Walter was smothered by his sister, the countess, exasperated at her husband's wounds when she heard that the surgeons *could* cure her brother.[‡]

---

[*] In 1536, Sir Magnus Vaus was vicar of Abertarff (O. P. S., vol. ii., p. 450), and in 1560 James Dow (Shaw's Moray, "Abertarff").

[†] *Supra*, p. 98.

[‡] Extracta e variis Cronicis Scotiae: "Et Ballivus captus Fynecon ducitur, et dum concepit Comitissa quod sponsus comes morti proximus fuerat, accessit ad cameram ubi erat Ballivus vulneratus jacens, qui et ipse frater erat Comitissæ, et dum intellexit quod chirurgicorum arte impensa convalere potuit, superposito lecto

Margaret de Fenton had by him two sons, Alexander Ogilvy, who was afterwards Sheriff of Forfarshire, and Walter Ogilvy.

She married again, her second husband being David Lindsay of Lethnot, and was a widow in 1461; she had by David Lindsay a son, David Lindsay, and four daughters. She was living in 1493.*

Janet de Fenton was unmarried in 1449, but afterwards married Sir James Douglas or de Douglas of Railstone. Henry her son's style "of Culbirnie," was taken from Culbirnie, near Beaufort.

I think that another daughter was also named Janet, and had the distinction of junior attached to her name. She was in 1471 married to William Hakket or Hacket, was his widow in 1487, and appears to have died in 1491, when her share seems to have descended to Margaret de Fenton, David Narne of Sandfurde, and Henry Douglas.

The fourth daughter's name has not survived, but she was either the wife or mother of, and her share came to, David Narne of Sandfurde.

The second son of Countess Marjory and Alexander, second Earl of Crawford, was Walter Lindsay, a man of great energy and unscrupulous ambition, and for forty years under the style of Walter Lindsay of Beaufort, he occupied an important place in the history of the great family of Crawford.

James II. of Scotland, by a charter † dated 7th November 1458, grants and confirms to Walter Lindsay of Kinblathmount "terras baroniæ de le Arde et Beucfort," which had belonged by hereditary right to Margaret Fenton of Baky, and had been resigned by her into the king's hands in favour of Walter Lindsay; he was her first husband's nephew.

A fourth portion of the barony was all that passed by this

---

plumali enim, ut aliqui ferebant, ad interitum acceleravit." The "good countess," as she was afterwards called, did not agree with the sentiment of the wife of Intaphernes, "ἀδελφεὸς ἂν ἄλλος οὐδενὶ τρόπῳ γένοιτο" (Herod. Thalia, 119), or of Antigone (Soph. Antig., 909).

* For these particulars, see the Crawford Case, by Mr Riddell, and Lives of the Lindsays, by Lord Lindsay.

† In the Haigh Muniment Room, Crawford Case, p. 145.

grant, but Margaret, as the eldest daughter, had the manor and principal messuage, the castle of Beaufort, as a "*præcipuum,*" as the Scottish lawyers say. This would give the title of Beaufort (and the principal superiority) preferably to Margaret Fenton and her successors, and she conveyed it to Walter Lindsay.

Walter Lindsay adopted the style of LINDSAY OF BEAUFORT, and continued it all his life; he died about 1494. His eldest son, Sir David Lindsay, on 13th May 1495, as his heir, was given sasine by Duncan Macintosh, captain of Clan Chattan, Sheriff of Inverness-shire, "of the lands" of the barony of the Aird and Beaufort, by the delivery of earth and stone at the old Castle of Beaufort (" apud veterem Castrum de Beaufort ").

Sir David Lindsay adopted for a time the title of Lindsay of Beaufort, but in 1498, conveying Beaufort Castle and the estate to the Earl of Argyle, he dropped that title, and styled himself Lindsay of Edzell.*

Patrick Ogilvy of Calyebroche had, or claimed to have, in 1485 a fourth of Baky and the Aird. He may have been another son of Margaret Fenton by her first marriage, or he may have been not so related, but have purchased a share from one of the other sisters. He seems in 1501 to have conveyed a portion of the Aird to John Ogilvy.†

Hugh, the first Lord Lovat, the descendant of the founder through Janet Fenton of 1416, in his old age seems to have left the management of his affairs to his eldest son Thomas, and Thomas followed up the acquisition of the outlying parts of the Fenton property, which had been made in 1416, by purchasing the bulk of the Fenton estates from the co-heirs of Walter de Fenton.

On 21st October 1498, Thomas, while his father, Hugh, Lord Lovat, was yet alive, purchases the lands of Fopachy in the parish of Kirkhill from this Patrick Ogilvy of Calyebroche or Kilbrovock.

* Claiming through him, the present Earl of Crawford recovered that peerage in 1845.
† Laing's Scottish Seals, vol. ii., p. 131.

On 29th January 1497-8, Sir David Lindsay of Beaufort sold to Archibald, Earl of Argyle, his fourth part of Quhilbrune (Culbirnie), with the castle and fortalice thereof, the two Moys, Balcrum, Conwich Mor, Sanevalle in Glen Conwich, Eskadale, Arderoyn, Kyneriche, Moncref, Appathy, Nelston, and of the superiority of all and sundry the lands in the lordship of Beaufort, belonging hereditarily to the said Sir David Lindsay of Beaufort, Knight, lying in the lordship of Beaufort.*

Henry Douglas, who styles himself Henry Douglas of Bartlan, in 1499 conveys Montloth to Thomas Fraser.†

Lord Thomas, in 1501, succeeded his father Hugh as Lord Lovat, and married Janet Gordon, the daughter of Sir Alexander Gordon of Midmar, brother to the Earl of Huntley, and it is said that the earl renounced in favour of this Thomas, Lord Lovat, all right he had to Stratherrick, the old Byset property on Loch Ness.

In 1510 John Ogilvy, the grantee of 1501 from Patrick, is still portioner of Beaufort; but in June 1511 he seems to have sold the two Moys, Ardrannach, and others, to Thomas, Lord Lovat, who acquired from Henry Douglas (now styled of Culbirnie) in 1509, the Douglas share of the lands of Culbirnie with the castle of Bewfort.‡

Beaufort Castle, though giving a title to Margaret Fenton and her husband and the overbearing Lindsays, Walter and Sir David, yet was probably deserted since the partition of the estates which belonged to it among the heirs of Walter de Fenton.

Nor was the heir of Erchless Castle and the Chisholm third of the barony of the Aird idle ; John Haliburton of the Aird or Kinrossie was succeeded by James Haliburton, who styles

* Thanes of Cawdor, p. 87.

† Anderson, p. 72, says the deed is dated 15th June 1499, and that it is to Thomas, apparent heir to Hugh, Lord Lovat, but he gives as an authority the Lovat Case, 1730, which, however, gives no date in 1499, and speaks of Thomas as Lord Lovat.

‡ This is stated as "Castle of Bewlay," in the Lovat Case, 1730, and as being in the Register, lib. 17, No. 53, but the reference is incorrect.

himself of Gask, and to him in 1512 King James IV. granted certain lands in the barony of the Aird (Ard) and the lands of the two Erchless (Arcles), in the earldom of Ross, and erected them into the free barony of Erchless, together with, among others, the lands of Kirkton and Ingliston in the barony of Aird.

At the same time, in 1500,* Wylandus, or Wiland, Chisholm has Comer, and in 1513 he gets this barony of Comer in Strathglass erected in his favour by King James IV. This barony consisted of those portions of the earldom of Ross which lay opposite the lands of Comerkirktoun. Who Wyland Chisholm was is not clearly proved, but probably he was a descendant of one of the sons of Margaret del Ard mentioned in 1401,† that is, of a brother of Thomas de Chisholm of 1403. Another brother probably founded the family of Chisholm of Cromlix in Perthshire.

* Family of Kilravock, p. 169. † *Supra*, p. 94.

No. XXI.

BULLA JULIJ II[DI] PONTIFICIS ROMANI ROBERTO FRESELL DECANO ET OFFICIALI ROSSENSI MISSA IN FAVOREM PRIORIS DE BELLO LOCO 18vo DIE JANUARIJ ANNO DOMINI 1513.

"Robertus Fresell Decanus et Officialis Rossensis, Judex et Executor ad infra scripta, a Sede Apostolica, cum nonnullis alijs in hac parte nostris collegis, cum illa clausula; 'Quatenus si non omnes hijs exequendis potueritis interesse, duo aut unus vestrum ea nihilominus exequantur,' specialiter deputatus, Universis et singulis Ecclesiarum Rectoribus, Vicarijs perpetuis, Curatis et non Curatis, cæterisque Capellanis, Tabellionibus, et Notarijs publicis, per Diocœses et Civitates Rossens. et Moraviens. ac alias, ubilibet constitutis, ac illi vel illis ad quos seu quem præsentes nostræ Litteræ pro earum executione pervenerint, Salutem in Domino. Et mandatis nostris, ymo verius Apostolicis, firmiter obedire, ex parte Venerabilis in Christo Patris Dougalli Prioris Belliloci et Conventus ejusdem Ordinis Vallis Caulium Rossensis Diocœsis, Litteras quasdam, Sanctissimi in Christo Patris, et Domini nostri, Domini Julij Divina providentiâ Papæ II[di] Sanas, integras, non rasas, cancellatas aut abolitas, aut in aliqua sui parte suspectas, sed omnibus prorsus vitio et suspicione carentes, ut nobis prima facie apparuit, reverentiâ quæ decuit, noveritis recepisse, hujus modi sub tenore.

"JULIUS EPISCOPUS servus servorum Dei, dilectis filijs Priori Burgen. et Archidiacono Sancti Andreæ Ecclesiarum, et Officiali Rossensi, Salutem et Apostolicam Benedictionem. Significarunt nobis dilecti filij, Prior et Conventus Monasterij per Priorem soliti gubernari, Belliloci, ordinis Vallis Caulium, Rossensis Diocœsis, quod nonnulli iniquitatis filij, quos prorsos ignorant, Decimas, Census, Fructus, Redditus, Proventus, Terras, Domos, Possessiones, Grangias, Casalia, Maneria, Prædia, Viridaria, Vivaria, Ortos, Campos, Virgulta, Prata, Pascua, Nemora, Sylvas, Molendina, Stagna, Lacus, Piscaria, Aquas, Aquarum decursus, Arbores, Arborum fructus, Ligna, Postes, Trabes, Plantas, Vini, bladi, frumenti, ordei, avenæ, siliginis, olei, leguminum, Auri, argenti monetati, et non monetati quantitates, Calices, Cruces, Ornamenta Ecclesiastica, Jocalia, Cassias, . . . Coclearia, Vasa argentea et deaurata, vitrea, cuprea, ferrea, stannea, plumbea, lignei, Pannos laneos, lineos, sericos, lectos . . . coopertoria . . . Pulvinaria, Curtinas, Ferramenta, mappas, manutergia, domorum utensilia, vestes, tunicas, sudaratores, mantellas, cappas, caputia, equos, jumenta, boves, vaccas, oves, porcos, capros, et alia animalia, Libros, Literas autenticas, Instrumenta publica, Contractus, Documenta, Cedulas, Recognitiones, Obligationes, Registra, Testamenta, Codicillos, Protocolla, Cartas, Rotas, Debita, Tradita, Legata, Pecuniarum Summas, Jura, Jurisdictiones, et non nulla mobilia et immobilia Bona ad dictum Monasterium legittime spectantia, temere, malitiose occultare et occulta detinere præsumunt, non Curantes de Præfatis Priori et Conventui exhibere, in animarum suarum periculum, et ipsorum Prioris et Conventus non modicum detrimentum. Super quæ dicti Prior et Conventus Apostolicæ Sedis remedium implorarunt. Quocirca discretioni vestræ per Apostolica Scripta mandamus, quatenus omnes hujusmodi occultos detentores Decimarum Censuum et aliorum Bonorum prædictorum pro parte nostra publice in Ecclesijs, coram populo, per vos vel alios moneatis, et infra competentem terminum, quem eis præfixeritis, omnia Priori et Conventui prædictis a se debita restituant, et relevent, ac de perpetratis plenam ac debitam satisfactionem impendant. Et si id non adimpleverint infra alium competentem Terminum, quem eis ad hoc peremptorie duxeritis præfigendum, extunc in eos generalem Excommunicationis sententiam proferatis, et eam faciatis ubi et quando expedens videritis, usque ad satisfactionem condignam solemniter publicari. Quod si non omnes hijs exequendis potueritis interesse, duo aut unus vestrum ea nihilominus exequantur. Datum Romæ apud Sanctum Petrum Anno Incarnationis Dominice Millesimo quingentesimo sexto, quarto nonas Julii Pontificatus nostri anno tertio.

" Post quarum quidem Literarum præsentationem, ostentationem, et lecturam sic ut præmittitur factas, fuimus per Dictum venerabilem Patrem in dictis Litteris, principaliter nominatum, debita cum Jnstantia requisiti, quatenus ad Executionem earundem juxta traditam sive nobis directam formam in eisdem procedere curaremus, et processum in forma decernere. Nos igitur Robertus Judex et Executor præfatus attendens hujus modi requisitionem justam fore, et rationi consonam, volensque mandatum Apostolicum nobis in hac parte commissum reverenter exequi ut tenemur; vobis igitur Universis et singulis supradictis, in virtute sanctæ obedientiæ, et sub pœnis Suspensionis et Excommunicationis, quam vel quas in vos vel vestrum quemlibet ferimus in his scriptis, nisi feceritis quod mandamus, districte præcipiendo mandamus, quatenus ad hujus modi mandatum nostrum ymo verius Apostolicum exequendum, alter vestrum alterum non expectet, sed omnes et singulos Decimarum, Censuum, Fructuum, Reddituum, Proventuum, Terrarum, Domorum, Possessionum, Grangiarum, Casalium, Prædiorum, Maneriorum, Viridariorum, Vivariorum, Ortorum, Camporum, Virgultorum, Pratorum, Pascuorum, Nemorum, Sylvarum, Molendinorum, Stagnorum, Lacuum, Piscariarum, Aquarum, Aquarum Decursuum, Arborum, Lignorum, Plantarum, Vini, bladi, frumenti, ordei, avenæ, siliginis, olei, leguminum, Auri, argenti, monetati et non monetati, et aliorum bonorum mobilium et immobilium, verum suprascriptorum, occultos detentores, occupatores, concelatores, impeditores, ac præfata facientes, adhærentes, consilium auxilium favorem nec opem præbentes, ferentes, et non revelantes, auctoritate nostra, ymo verius Apostolica nobis commissa, et qua fungimur in hac parte, palam, et publice in Ecclesiis de quibus ubi, quando et quotiens expediens fuerit, et pro parte dicti Requirentis fueritis requisiti, seu alter vestrum fuerit requisitus, Requiratis et Moneatis, quos nos etiam tenore præsentium requirimus et monemus, Primo, Secundo, Tertio, peremptorie communiter et divisim, eisdem et eorum cuilibet, in virtute sanctæ obedientiæ, et sub pœnis excommunicationis, mandamus quatenus infra novem dierum terminum post Requisitionem et Monitionem hujusmodi, eis et eorum cuilibet a vobis loco nostro factas, et postquam præmissa ad eorum notitiam devenerint, quem terminum eis et eorum cuilibet, primo, secundo, et pro tertio termino ac monitione canonica eis, et ipsorum cuilibet assignamus et vestrum quilibet assignat, res, bona et mobilia prædicta in præmissis Litteris apostolicis et contentas et contenta, dictis Dominis conquerentibus reddant et restituant, ipsosque detentores, occupatores, impeditores & concelatores, declarent, et occulte revelent, ac de præmissis omnibus et singulis plenam et debitam satisfactionem impendant. Quod si forte infra hujusmodi novem dierum terminum, requisitionibus et monitionibus hujusmodi nostris, ymo vero Apostolicis non paruerint, omnes ipsos et quemlibet ipsorum, dictis novem diebus elapsis, in his scriptis Excommunicamus, et vos similiter excommunicatos publice et solemniter denunciatis. Et si dicti Raptores, Occupatores, Detentores, Impeditores, et Cancelatores dictam Excommunicationis sententiam pertinaciter sustinuerint, et ad emendam non venerint, omnes ipsos et quemlibet ipsorum, octo diebus inde sequentibus elapsis, in eisdem scriptis Aggravamus. Præterea si prædicti Malefactores dictas Excommunicationis et Aggravationis sententias nostras, per alios octo dies, corde et animo, quod absit, sustinuerint induratis, omnes ipsos et quemlibet ipsorum, dictis octo diebus elapsis, in hijs scriptis Reaggravamus, et quos vos vel vestrum quilibet Excommunicatos Aggravatos Reaggravatos a nobis auctoritate nostra, ymo verius Apostolica, Campanis pulsatis, Candelis accensis, et demum in terra projectis et extinctis, in Ecclesiis vestris palam et publice denunciatis. Absolutionem vero omnium et singulorum, qui dictas sententias incurrerint nobis et Superiori nostro tantum modo reservamus. Et quid inde feceritis, nobis fideliter significetis et rescribatis. Ut autem præmissa facilius ad omnium et singulorum quorum interest aut interesse poterit, notitiam devenire valeant, et ne aliquis de hujusmodi præmissis aliquam ignorantiam pretendere possit, volumus et decernimus Copiam præsentium ad valvas quarumcunque Ecclesiarum, et aliorum locorum affigi et affixam dimitti. Quam si quis amovere vel lacerare præsumpserit, præfatis nostris sententijs, prout in hijs scriptis latæ sunt, ipso facto volumus subjacere. In quorum omnium fidem et testimonium præmissorum, has præsentes litteras sive hoc præsens publicum Instrumentum, hujus modi Litteras Apostolicas in se continentes sive continens, exemplare fieri et per Notarium publicum subscriptum subscribi et publicari mandamus, nostrique sigilli appensione jussimus et fecimus communiri. Datum et Actum in loco Consistoriali Rossensi decimo octavo die mensis Januarij anno Domini Millesimo quingentesimo decimo tertio secundum computum Ecclesiæ Scoticanæ Indictione secunda Pontificatus Sanctissimi in Christo Patris et Domini nostri Domini Leonis, Divina favente Clementia Papæ Decimi anno primo, præsentibus ibidem Honorabilibus viris et Dominis et Magistris, Cantore Rossensi, Ancelmo Roberti Succentore Rossensi et Johanne Fresell Canonicis Rossensibus, et Wilielmo Spyne Præposito de Tana et Donaldo Red vicario de Hyltane

Notarijs Publicis cum diversis alijs testibus ad præmissa vocatis et separitim rogatis.

" Et ego Andreas de Sancto Claro, Presbyter Aberdonensis Diocœsis, Publicus Apostolica Auctoritate Notarius, quia prædictarum litterarum Apostolicarum publicationi et lecturæ, nec non processus et . . . Decreto et fulminationi, cæterisque omnibus alijs et singulis, dum sic, ut præmittitur, agerentur, dicerentur et fierent, una cum prænominatis testibus præsens interfui, eaque omnia et singula sic fieri vidi, scivi et audivi, ac in notam cepi, ideoque has præsentes litteras, sive hoc præsens publicum Instrumentum, manu alterius, me alijs præpedito negotijs, scriptas, hujus modi litteras Apostolicas in se continentes, exinde confeci, et in hanc formam publicam redegi, signoque, et subscriptione meis solitis et consuetis signavi, et subscripsi, una cum appensionne sigilli dicti Domini Judicis et Executoris, rogatus et requisitus in fidem et testimonium omnium et singulorum præmissorum."

Not.—The tag parchment; no seal.*

Placed on the edge of the wild Highland country of Wester Ross and Inverness-shire, the Priory of Beauly was likely to suffer from any invasion of the more settled parts of the north, by the rough tribes who gave allegiance to the Lords of the Isles. For protection against such danger, threatened in the spring of 1506, by the expiring efforts of Donald Dhu's rebellion in the Isles, Prior Dougal had applied to Rome and obtained a Bull of Excommunication against any plunderers of the priory, dated the 4th before the nones— that is, the 4th—of July 1506.

The document now printed, although entitled a Bull of Pope Julius II., dated 18th January 1513, is in fact the promulgation in 1514, by the Dean and Official of Ross, of the Bull of 1506.

The Bull is a perfect specimen of the common forms, as lawyers call them, of the Roman chancery, intended for the

---

* The original transcriber of this document added to it Latin notes respecting Leo X. and Julius II., which we have printed in the Appendix, No. XIX. He speaks of the disputations excited by Luther still going on at the time he wrote, and we may assume, therefore, that his transcript was made before 1560.

latitude of Italy and not of Scotland. It speaks of the supposed plunder of quantities of wine, oil, and winter wheat; and in its long list of costly furniture, and rich plate, and household effects, it recalls the splendour of the proud Abbey of Monte Cassino rather than the frugal poverty of the humble Priory of Beauly.

One article alone is mentioned of which Beauly seems to have possessed a store, and that is books (*libros*), for we have some indications of the literary character and pursuits of its inmates.

The Wardlaw MS. speaks of George Dawson as prior in 1505. This is clearly a mistake, the prior was then as now Dougal Roriesou, but George Dawson may have been sub-prior; and when the MS.* speaks of him as a man most obliging in educating gentlemen's children in the priory, which was the only school in "our" north,† it states the general system prevailing in the priory, which is confirmed by the more detailed accounts of the education afforded there under Prior Reid.

Nor is this all: the first Earl of Cromarty wrote in the MS. of the "Regiam Majestatem," now in the Advocates Library, the following memorandum:

"This book, belonging to the monastery of Beaulie, comeing to my hands in a bad cover, I have keept it by me above thirty years, and having caused bind it, I present it to the library belonging to the honourable society of advocates in Edinburgh. These things are remarkable in it, that this belonging to that priory long before the Reformation, and consequently many years before Sir John Skene was born," etc.

Mr Innes‡ says that the book belonged to the priory of the Chartreux of Perth; but the Earl of Cromarty, as we know from Mr Hugh Rose, the family historian of Kilravock,§ had

---

* Findon MSS.

† This prior, George Dawson, the MS. says, invented the ordinary farewell drink at parting, called the Deoch Durris; but if the writer's reading had extended to William of Malmesbury, he would have known that the stirrup-cup was a fashion as old as the Heptarchy, as the murder of Edward the Martyr, at the gate of Corfe Castle, tells us.

‡ Acts of Parliament, Scotland, i., pref.; Notices of MSS., Cromartie MSS., ix.

§ *Supra*, p. 29.

access to the charters of Beauly Priory, and although mistaken in thinking that this MS. came from Beauly, must have known that the priory had a library and collection of books, from which he obtained some MSS., even if not this particular one.

The Bull states that the prior and convent of the monastery, of wont governed by a prior of Beauly, of the order of Vallis-caulians, in the diocese of Ross, complained to the Pope that some sons of iniquity, whom they knew not, had rashly presumed to conceal, and keep concealed, possessions, real and personal, of which there is a vast enumeration, and utensils, and clothing, and muniments of title, and therefore the Pope requested the Prior of Burgos (*Priori Burgen.**), the archdeacon of the churches of St Andrews, and the Official of Ross, to announce publicly in the churches before the people, that these unknown holders of the convent's property were to bring it in to the prior, or if this was not done, any two or one of the commissioners were to pronounce general excommunication against the person or persons unknown.

In the seventh year after the issuing of the Bull by Pope Julius, Robert Fresel, the dean and official of Ross, at the instance, as he says, of Dougal, the Prior of Beauly, proceeds to promulgate it, recites it, repeats its warnings, threatens excommunication with bells and candle, and directs this monition to be affixed to the church doors throughout Moray and Ross.

---

* Few words have given me more trouble than these two, "Priori Burgen." The literal meaning is the "Prior of Burgos;" and there are many instances in the preceding half-century, in Theiner, of foreign ecclesiastics being joined by papal Bulls, with Scottish prelates, in commissions indicating that their co-operation was only nominal; they may have been at the Roman court at the time of granting the commission, and never left it, neither acting or being expected to act. The transcriber could, if the words were really "Edinburgen." have miscopied it; but no prior at Edinburgh is known by such a title. The Dominican monastery at Edinburgh was indeed the monastery of the burgh of Edinburgh, but the prior is styled "Prior Fratrum Prædicatorum burgi de Edinburgh" (Collegiate Churches in Midlothian : Bannatyne Club, p. 90). The priories at St Andrews were within the city (*civitas*) of St Andrews, St Andrews being never called a burgh. Unless the original Bull is entered at the Vatican, the correct reading must, I fear, remain unascertained.

The official executes and dates his monition in the Consistorial Place of Ross on the 18th January 1513, according to the computation of the Scottish Church, that is, in fact, the 18th January 1514,* the second indiction, and the first year of Pope Leo X. (Julius II. having died on 20th February 1513), there being present the chanter of Ross; Anselm, the son of Robert or Robertson, the sub-chanter of Ross; and John Fraser, canon of Ross; and William Spiny, provost of Tain; and Donald Reid, vicar of Hilton. The provost of Tain was the provost of the collegiate church of Tain, founded, in September 1481, by Thomas, Bishop of Ross.

Beauly may have suffered during the rebellion suppressed in 1506. After this there was quiet until the unfortunate event at Flodden, on the 9th September 1513, when Thomas, the Master of Lovat, the eldest son of Thomas, Lord Lovat, was killed, and where it is said the rashness of the Highlanders caused the defeat of the royal army.

Donald, the eldest son of Alexander de Insulis of Lochalsh, is said to have been knighted on the field of Flodden; he escaped, and turned the general confusion to good account by proclaiming himself, two months after, in November 1513, Lord of the Isles.

He then with a large force of Highlanders, among whom were Alexander Macranald of Glengarry, and Weland Chisholm of Comer, expelled the garrison, and seized the castle of Urquhart, on Loch Ness, plundering and laying waste, at the same time, the adjacent lands, which, with the castle, were then held of the Crown by John Grant of Freuchy.

Truly it was time for the Prior of Beauly to make use of all ecclesiastical protection he could muster, and therefore we can understand why in the winter of 1513-14 he insisted on the dean and official of Ross publishing the Bull of protection, and issuing the monition we are now illustrating, which the official accordingly did on 18th January 1514, in the Consistorial Place of Ross.

And here let us pause to notice for a while the cathedral

* Appendix, No. XX.

church whose Dean is the person by whom and whose Consistory is the place where this publication was announced—the Church of Ross, the church of the diocese, in which Beauly Priory was situated, and to which it owed subjection.

As you wind along the seashore, below the cliffs of Avoch, you see before you on the sky-line a long high range of building, crowned with a bell-tower, standing high above the town of Fortrose: this is the Cathedral Church of Ross.

Wherever the Norman built a cathedral, he reared it aloft over the surrounding houses. Every one who first sees Canterbury or Durham, Salisbury or Lincoln, must feel the matchless effect of these noble structures, hung high in air, over the whole mass of the other buildings of the place; the first glimpse of the distant city shows only the tower or spire or lofty roof of the great church. Michael Angelo raised the stupendous dome of St Peter's far above the Capitoline Hill, changing Rome from an imperial into a sacred metropolis: Old St Paul's towered high over London, long before Wren built the Dome, to overhang the city, and elevate as well as chasten the tone of the Great Mart. All these were in their several fashions humble but pious efforts to follow the example of the Inspired Builder, who placed the temple of Jehovah on Mount Zion above the palaces and towers of Jerusalem, so that the Holy City might stand out at first sight as the joy of the whole earth, the city of the Great King.

Very little is recorded of the early history of the bishopric of Ross. Let us take the account of the learned Dr Reeves :*

"The origin of the church of Rosmarky, or Rosmarkin, as it is called in ancient records, is ascribed by tradition to St Boniface, surnamed Queritenus, a foreigner, who lived in the seventh century, and whose legend in the Breviary of Aberdeen identifies him with Boniface the Fourth, who died 615. But this fiction sets the entire history of the Pope at such flagrant defiance that it is unworthy of refutation or further notice. The name of St Boniface, however, has from an

---

* Canon Reeves' Memoir of the Culdees, sect. v., "Rosemarkie," p. 45.

early date been associated with the church of Rosmarky, both on seals and in records, and his day is set down in the Scotch calendars at the 16th of March. The day of his festival, and his *alias* name, Queritenus, instead of Italy, point to Ireland, as the quarter from which the founder of this church came; and we may with safety conclude either that Boniface was an assumed name, or that the memory of some later ecclesiastic who was so called has been confounded with that of the Celtic founder.

"In the Irish calendars of Tamhlacht and Marian Gorman, under the above-named day, the 16th of March, is found the commemoration of Curitan, Bishop and Abbot of Ros-mic-Bairenn, who, beyond all reasonable doubt, is the Queritenus de Rosmarkyn of the Scotch.

"We may therefore assume that the church of Rosmarky, which in course of time became the cathedral of the diocese of Ross, was an Irish foundation; and if the conjecture of the calendar of Donegal, that this Curitanus was the bishop of that name who attended the Synod of Birr under St Adamnan, be correct, its origin belongs to the latter half of the seventh century."

Silgrave's[*] catalogue designates the society at Rosemarkie as Keledei, and it is probable that soon after the foundation of the canon clerics by St Chrodegang about 760, the society at Rosemarkie adopted his rule. How these canon clerics became secularised and degenerate from that rule, and just when they lost the spirit of the name of Cultores Dei, or Culdees, adopted its use, is shown clearly by Dr J. Robertson.[†] Then came Margaret, the niece of the saintly Confessor, who had entertained for fourteen years her husband, King Malcolm; and she and the king brought the Church of Scotland into harmony with that of England. Her son David extended the reform to the Culdee colleges; among these, to Rosemarkie. There probably, as at Dunkeld, Brechin, and St Andrews, was a lay abbot, who transmitted the benefice and title as a heritage to his children; and an ecclesiastical prior, who performed perfunctorily enough the religious services.

[*] Henry of Silgrave's Chronicle, MS. Cott., printed in Scalacronica, p. 241, and quoted in Pref. to Book of Deer, p. 89.
[†] Preface to Stat. Ecc. Scot., p. ccxii., *et seq.*

The first time a bishop is mentioned is in a charter by King David I. (*c.* 1126)* to the Abbey of Dunfermline, where Macbeth, a witness, signs himself "Rosmarkensis Episcopus;" and the universally received opinion is, that David in this case, as at Dunkeld, Dunblane, Dornoch, and Lismore, took the prior or ecclesiastical head of the Culdee college, and made him the bishop, and the college would be his council or chapter.

The property of the lay abbot was, I conceive, only partially recovered by King David for religious uses; the remainder was retained by the lay abbot, with probably the name Gilleanrias (the modern Gillanders), the servant of St Andrew.

Wynton gives† the name of Gyllandrys-Ergemawche among the earls who besieged Malcolm IV. in Perth in the year 1160. Mr Skene suggested ‡ that Ferchard Macintagart, the son of the priest, was the son of this Gilleandres. This Macintagart was able to give great assistance to Alexander II., was knighted by him, and made Earl of Ross; and it easily accounts for the power, position, and names of himself and his suggested father, if we suppose that they were successively the lay abbots of the Culdee college of Rosemarkie.

Macbeth was "Episcopus Rosmarkensis." Simeon, the successor of Macbeth, between 1147 and 1160, signs himself "Epis. de Ros." § In 1161 Gregory is consecrated Bishop of Rosemarkie. ‖ A few years later, in March 1188, in the Bull of Pope Clement III., which is the Magna Charta of the independence of the Scottish Church, we have among the nine episcopal sees recognised in the Church of Scotland, the church of Ross, "Ecclesia Rossensis." ¶ Six of the nine bishoprics—St Andrews, Glasgow, Dunkeld, Dunblane, Brechin, and Aberdeen—take their title

* Reg. Dunf., p. 4. † Wynton, bk. vii., c. 7, line 1388.
‡ Skene's Highlanders, vol. ii., pp. 223, 224. I prefer this his early opinion to Mr Skene's more recent suggestion that Farquhard was the son of the farmer of the church lands of St Maolrubhe, in Applecross. See his edition of Fordun, appendix ii. 434.
§ Reg. Dunf., p. 7. ‖ Chronica de Mailros, p. 78.
¶ Robertson's Pref. Stat. Con. Scot., p. xxxix.

from the town where the cathedral church stood, but the three northern sees of Moray, Ross, and Caithness are named, as Bishop Leslie in 1578* points out in the case of his own cathedral church of Ross, not from the town, but from the province.

This peculiarity does not exist in the case of any existing English bishopric; it is only to be found in the anomalous case of that bishopric which is neither English, Scottish, or Irish, the diocese of Sodor and Man.

But in regard to Ross, there is this further anomaly: Down to the Norman Conquest, in many of the English dioceses also, the bishop was not called from the cathedral city, but from the country at large, or from the tribe that inhabited it. Thus the bishop in Somerset was not called the Bishop of Wells, but the Bishop of the Sumorsætas, the tribe from which Somersetshire takes its name; and the practice both in the northern parts of Scotland and the western districts of England, probably arose from the division of those parts among sovereign and independent princes, who, on the first foundation of a bishop, appointed him for the whole principality; thus the Bishop of St Andrew's earliest title was Bishop of the Scots. It is most remarkable, therefore, that the bishop who first assumes the style of Bishop of Rosemarkie, where his cathedral stood, should afterwards be entitled the Bishop of Ross.

The bishopric of Ross was from its erection co-extensive with the earldom of Ross, but the earldom then only included Cromarty and Ross proper; it was not till 1221 that North Argyle was added to the earldom, on the forfeiture of the claimant of the lordship of the Isles, which included on the mainland North Argyle or Wester Ross.

The great peculiarity of the see of Ross and its relation to the earldom is this, that all the churches of the earldom seem to have been given to the Bishop of Ross; and that when North Argyle was added to the earldom of Ross in 1221, it seems that all the churches of North Argyle were added to the diocese and given to the bishop.

* Leslæus De Gestis Scotorum, p. 25, edit. 1678.

I say given to the bishop, although I believe that if the grants and confirmations were found, we should find they were given to the church of Rosemarkie, and what the legal effect of this was, in these irregular times, is not quite clear; but at first the canons of these old cathedral foundations seem to have had no property distinct from that of the bishop.* The bishop, when there was an existing rector at the time of the grant of a church to the see, could not disturb him; only on the next vacancy of the church the character of the benefice was changed. The parochial duties would be performed, if the church was at a distance from the cathedral, by a stipendiary vicar; and the rectory, the whole endowment of the church, would be at the disposal of the bishop, who would, until he made another arrangement, be himself the rector, but for the benefit not of himself only, but of the members of the cathedral generally.†

When in 1227‡ the Bishop of Ross, dealing with the stone of wax, devoted to the use of the cathedral church of Ross by Beauly's founder, John Byset, gave it to the cathedral church of Elgin, he, the bishop, was himself a canon of the cathedral, and the other members of the chapter of Rosemarkie were only the dean, the treasurer, and the archdeacon, with four canons.

The cathedral church of the Bishop of Ross was at that time the church of St Peter of Rosemarkie.

In 1235§ Pope Gregory IX. gives leave to the Bishop of Ross (Robert) to found new canonries in the church of Rose-

---

* Freeman's Cathedral Church of Wells, p. 33.

† At first there was only one church in each diocese, viz., at the place where the bishop and his clergy resided and performed all divine offices (Ayliffe's Parergon, p. 167). In it the bishop placed those who were to assist him in such duties, and after the parochial system was established, the bishop retained a portion of the clergy to assist him in the performance of divine service and other duties in his cathedral, and also as his council, from whence sprung the bodies called deans and chapters (Bishop of Ossory *v.* Dean of the Cathedral Church of St Carnie, Kilkenny, reported in Brit. Mag., xxix. 687).

‡ *Supra*, p. 27.   § Theiner, p. 32.

markie, to endow them, and to increase the endowment of the four existing canons.

In July 1238 * the same Pope addresses a special letter to Robert, Archdeacon of Ross, reciting that the archdeacon had, previously, no certain prebend in the church of Rosemarkie, and that the bishop had, with the consent of the chapter, endowed the archdeaconry with the church of Forthirdin (Fodderty) and the chapel of Lesselin (Lochslyn?), and also the lands and the tithes of corn of the churches of Ederdover (Eddyrdor, Killarnan), and Langibride (Logie Wester),† and Lemnalare (Lumlair), belonging to him, as appeared by the letters of the bishop and chapter; and the Pope confirmed the grant.

In February 1256,‡ Pope Alexander IV., by his Bull, confirms the institution by the Bishop of Ross of new officials and their endowment, when we find a complete establishment of the following officials: Dean, endowed with tithes of Andresser (Ardersier) and Kelmur (Wester), except those of half of Aleyn; Precentor, tithes of Kenneythes (Kinnettes) and Suthy (Suddy); Chancellor and Treasurer had, with the dean and precentor, equal shares in tithes of Rosemarkie and Cromarty; treasurer had tithes of Urcharde and Legidibride (Logie Wester); Archdeacon was now restricted to tithes of Fortherdi and Edordor, except half of Aleyn; the Subdean, tithes of Thayne and Eduthayne; Sub-chanter, the church of Bron (Brahan) § and tithes of Inverferan (Ferintosh or Fairburn). ‖ The bishop's prebend was the tithes of Nigg and Tarbat; and all the churches of Argyle (*i.e.*, Wester Ross or North Argyle), when vacant, were to be

---

* Theiner, p. 38.

† This name, which in the next Bull is made Legidibride, was then the name of Logie Wester. Its church was probably dedicated to St Bridget or St Bride. The church stood on the right bank of the Conan at a place anciently known as Logyreth, or Logywreid. There was in Perthshire a parish called Logiebride.

‡ Theiner, p. 69.

§ This was the then name of the parish of Urray; it is an early form of Brahan.

‖ Some of the lands of Fairburn were afterwards called Kyrk Farbrone, but the lands of Ferintosh may be those meant.

common churches; the greater dean * was to be elected as at Salisbury.

These churches of North Argyle, thus given by the bishop to the common use of the chapter of Ross, are specified in a lease from Queen Mary in 1567,† by which she leases to the bishop the parsonages and vicarages of the common churches of Kintail, Lochalsh, Lochcarron, Gairloch, Applecross, and Lochbroom.

Lumlair was thus taken away from the archdeacon, and formed the separate prebend of a canon, who was called the rector of Lumlair.

It must have been about the date of this Bull, and at the period of the enlargement and endowment of the cathedral chapter, that the site of the cathedral church was changed from Rosemarkie to Fortrose. The contribution of John Byset (*supra*, p. 24) to the church of St Peter of Rosemarkie was probably to the new church. No records have come to my knowledge establishing this fact, but the construction of the Under-croft and Chapter-house which still remain, with their dog-tooth mouldings and pure Early English lancet windows, points to the fact of the Chapter-house being built not later than 1250. We must remember that before the wars of Bruce, the styles of architecture in England and Scotland were contemporaneous and identical. The rest of the existing remains of the cathedral church of Ross are of the Decorated and Perpendicular periods.

The only portions of the Church mentioned in the Beauly charters are the Consistorial Place of Ross, the place in which the charter we are now illustrating was executed, and "the aisle of the most blessed Virgin Mary within the cathedral church of Ross," which is the place appointed, in the next document printed, for the meeting thereby summoned.

It will be interesting to discover, if we can, the position of these parts of the Church.

We have very few references in records to the cathedral church. In 1338, Sir Andrew de Moravia, Lord of Avoch, died in Ross, and was buried in the "Kyrk cathedyrale of Ros-

* See *supra*, p. 42.   † Reg. Sec. Sig., vol. xxxv., fol. 109.

markyne."* In 1451 a production of charters takes place in the chapel of St Nicholas in the cathedral church of Ross: in presence of Andrew of Monro, Archdeacon of Ross, commissary of Bishop Thomas, and auditor of consistorial causes, and of other witnesses, including two chaplains, John Ross, Lord of Balnagowan, produced certain charters, of which a transcript was then made.†

From the production taking place before the Auditor of consistorial causes, and from the transcript being made there—evidently showing that the place was used as a court or office—it seems probable that the "consistorial place of Ross" and this chapel of St Nicholas are identical.

In August 1564 Queen Mary, with her court, spent some days at the Chanonry; and as Bishop Henry Sinclair, in his return to the collector of thirds, not later than 1564, mentions his payments to the vicar of the choir, and his expenses in order to keep up the house and place of Chanonry, it is clear that no destruction had then been done to the cathedral buildings; but in the north, when the Regent Moray was gone, the protection which the ecclesiastical buildings had received from him was withdrawn.

The Regent Morton, who did not hesitate to take to himself the temporalities of the see of St Andrews, in spite of Knox, assisted his confederates to similar spoliation; and in the name of the infant king, grants, in 1572, to the treasurer, William, Lord Ruthven, the very lead on the roof of the cathedral church of Ross.

He granted the whole lead wherewith the cathedral church of Ross is covered, as well principal church as choir and aisles thereof, "ellis tyrvit, tane of, and disponit upoun, as to be intromittit with, and in place unhandellit,"‡ formerly belonging to the bishop and canons, but now in the king's hands, through the forfeiture of the bishop (Bishop Leslie) for treason and

---

* Wynton's Cronykil, ii. 215; Fordun, ii. 328.
† Balnagown Charters, O. P. S., "Kilmuir Easter," p. 462.
‡ Some spoliator had already begun to strip off the lead: "tyrvit," *stript*, from *tirer* (Sibbald's Glossary, Edin. 1802).

lesemajesty, and "throw being of the said cathedrall kirk no paroch kirk, bot ane monasterie to sustaen ydill belleis." *

The dilapidation now began in earnest, and the lead being taken off the nave and choir of the church, which was probably not vaulted with stone, the roof would be soon destroyed by a few Ross-shire winters. Something was done to repair and rebuild it after the restoration of Episcopacy, under Patrick Lindsay, about the year 1615 ;† and the ruin was not complete even in 1649, for the inhabitants of the Chanonrie that year represented to Parliament that the cathedral church had lain waste since the Reformation, and prayed that it should be declared a parish church. It is probable that the complete dilapidation of the body of the church was effected by using it as a quarry for Cromwell's citadel of Inverness, the foundation of which was laid in 1652-3.‡

The remains now standing are a south aisle to the nave, and the chapter-house or sacristy on the north side of the chancel. The church itself, nave, and choir or chancel, has completely disappeared.

The aisle remaining is about 100 feet long inside, having a groined roof with stone vaulting, and forms an exquisite specimen of Scottish Gothic architecture.

The minister of Wardlaw, writing after 1661, speaks of the tomb of Bishop Fraser, which now exists on the north side of this remaining aisle, being "extant still on ye north side of ye church [Ross], opposite to ye great door."§ This is the exact description of the position of the tomb at present, and implies that there was in the writer's time nothing to the north of the tomb, so that by 1661 the nave and choir were gone.

The foundations have been within the last few years laid

* Reg. Sec. Sig., vol. xl., fol. 106.

† "My hart ryses at the newes of a ryseing cathedral at Rosse ; in the words of the Psalmist : 'The glorious majestie of the Lord our God be upon it; prosper the worke, O prosper it'" ("Letter from John Carse to Patrick Lindesay, Bishop of Ross, 10th January 1615 :" Letters and State Papers of the Reign of King James VI., Abbotsford Club, 1838, pp. 248, 249).

‡ *Cf.* Old Statistical Acct., vol. xi., pp. 341, 342 ; New Stat. Acct., Ross and Cromarty shires, p. 351.

§ Findon MSS.

open by the direction of Her Majesty's Commissioners of Works, and the result is that the ground plan of the cathedral can be accurately ascertained. It has been carefully drawn and engraved by the Edinburgh Architectural Association.*

The whole church was about 185 feet long internally; the choir about 85 feet long, and the nave 100 feet; its width 25, but this was extended by the width of the aisle to the nave; the width of the upper part of the aisle being 20 feet, and of the lower part of the aisle 14.

Let us see if we can find the place of the aisle of the Blessed Virgin.

The foundations of a block of building at the east end of the chancel which is supposed to be the base of the high altar, are only 6 feet from the east wall, so that there was no room for a Lady Chapel in the ordinary position of that chapel to the east of the high altar, and the only aisle that ever existed was that on the south side of the nave.

This aisle is divided, like the south aisle to the nave at Melrose,† into two parts, the eastern part being wider than the other; and the east window must have been magnificent, and consisted of five lights. It is wide in proportion to its height, and must, as Mr Neale remarks, have afforded great scope for throwing up the altar beneath; there is here a piscina in the south wall for use with the altar, and a credence table or awmry on the north side.

As there are, as we have said, no aisles except this long aisle divided into two, in which there are no places for altars except under the eastern window, or across the whole space of the aisle

---

* Mr Neale described (Ecclesiological Notes, p. 53), what remains as the south aisle to chancel and nave. It turns out that it is the aisle to the nave only; but in justice to my old class-fellow I must say that Mr Muir's conception of the plan of the building, which he says Mr Neale has strangely misapprehended, is much further from the truth than that of the late Warden of Sackville College. Mr Muir says "the building originally consisted of choir and nave, with a north aisle to both, but no south one; a slender spire-capped tower on the south engaged to, and having an entrance from, the choir; and a detached chapter-house on the north-east" (Characteristics, p. 68).

† Rickman's Gothic Arch., ed. iv., p. 200.

at some other part, and as the Lady Chapel is always placed in a position to the east, I think that the aisle of the Virgin must have been the easternmost and wider part of this aisle. It is interesting to inquire when this was built.

The architecture of the westernmost part contains adaptations of older windows and doors, which were seldom adopted in the purest period of Decorated architecture, to which the eastern window belongs, as may be well seen from the drawings published by the Association; and I, examining the buildings in 1873, discovered on looking at the vaulting in the first bay west of the Bell tower—the point of division of the aisles—and which bay belongs to the narrower and westernmost aisle, that the boss in the centre of the vaulting has carved on it a shield on which is the coat of arms "*on a bend, three buckles,*" the well-known coat of Leslie. Nor does the matter end here: on carefully observing the boss in the centre of the second bay from the west end of the westernmost aisle, I discovered carved on it a shield bearing "*a bull's head caboshed,*"* that is, a bull's head without any part of the neck, and full faced. This is the coat of arms of John Bullock, who was elected bishop in 1420.† As the first connection of the name of Leslie with Ross is Eufamia, the eldest daughter and heiress of William, fifth Earl of Ross, marrying, in 1366, Walter de Leslie, and as she only succeeded her father in 1372, the insertion of the arms of Leslie shows that this part of the aisle was not built till after that date, and the insertion of the arms of Bullock shows that it was not completed before 1420.

Before the war of independence, the correspondence of styles between England and Scotland was so close that I

* Neither of these heraldic bosses are noticed in the Architectural Association's publication; this appeared in 1873, from drawings by Mr A. R. Scott. These drawings contain many minute details of the groined roof, including the mouldings, but omitting all the bosses.

† The seal of this bishop is engraved by Mr Laing, vol. ii., pl. ix., fig. 4. His name has been supposed to be Turnbull, but Mr Brady's extracts prove it to have been Bullock (Brady's Episcopal Succession in England, Scotland, and Ireland, 1400-1875, p. 143, "Ross;" from Vatican Consistorial Records, Rome, 1876).

should have thought it improbable that the eastern and wider half of this south aisle could have been built after 1372; but when the connection with England was broken, the change of style which took place in England was not adopted in Scotland, and in that country the Decorated or Middle-pointed style seldom passed into the English Perpendicular style, but rather into the French Flamboyant style. So we may well believe that the eastern part, as well as that which contains these authentic marks of date, was built after 1372.

The Wardlaw MS. speaks of Bishop Fraser being buried in the Lady Ross's own chapel; and modern writers[*] state that the canopied monument on the second bay from the east window is that of a Countess of Ross, that the date is 1330, and that she was the foundress of the cathedral.

No Countess of Ross, before Eufamia Leslie, had the independent means to execute such a work as even to build this aisle, for, as to the cathedral itself, there is nothing to lead us to suppose this was not of the same date as the Chapter-house. Eufamia certainly had the vast property of the earldom, and may have commenced the building of the aisle in 1372; but it is not likely that she would have inserted the arms of Leslie, those of her first husband, Walter de Leslie, without her own arms, those of Ross. He died in February 1382.[†]

She afterwards, before July 1382, married Alexander, the Wolf of Badenoch. During the troublous period of her second marriage, she would have neither the means nor the leisure to complete the whole work; and it is, I conceive, only after the Wolf's death in 1394, that the westernmost part of the aisle could have been begun. She then exercised all the rights, and was in full and independent possession of all the property of the earldom; and to this period may be attributed the completion by her of the easternmost and wider part of the existing aisle, the part which we have suggested is the aisle of the Virgin, or the Lady Chapel.

[*] New Stat. Account; Neale, Ecc. Notes, Edin. Architect. Assoc., 1873.

[†] At Perth, February 27, 1382 (Kalendar of Ferne, and Ane Breve Cronicle of the Earlis of Ross).

Her first husband, Walter de Leslie, was buried at Perth; her second husband, the Wolf, at Dunkeld. The latter died, not, as we have stated from the inscription on his tomb, on 24th July 1394, but on the 20th February 1394.*

The countess, on his death, took the veil, and became abbess of the convent of Elcho; and we may well assume that she then, as an act of expiation, renewed the pious work of building the chapel-aisle in Ross Cathedral. The stains of murder and sacrilege and filial disobedience were to be washed out. Her father, Earl William, in that very convent of Elcho, half a century before, had assassinated Reginald, Lord of the Isles. Then in his old age the Nemesis overtook the earl, and he complains to the king how she, his heiress-daughter, had, against his will, married Walter Leslie, and how they, the daughter and son-in-law, had wrung from him grants of all his lands† in Buchan. Lastly came the avenger to her; and in her turn, when she was exposed to the brutality of her ruffian husband, the Wolf, she must have felt herself verily guilty concerning her father.

She died before 1398. The place of her burial is not mentioned, but it is probable she was buried in the cathedral of Ross, and that the canopied tomb, near the east window, which tradition calls the tomb of the Countess of Ross, is hers.

Whether she inserted the boss, with the shield of Leslie on it, is uncertain. On her marriage ‡ with her second husband in 1382, she had a beautiful seal engraved, displaying her own shield of the earldom of Ross between the escutcheons of Leslie and Buchan, her successive husbands;§ but although she uses this same seal when, acting as Countess of Ross, on

* *Supra*, p. 93. Correct date given in New Stat. Acc., "Dunkeld."
† "Querimonia Willelmi Comitis de Ross, Roberto Regi, June 24, A.D. 1371" (Antiq. of Aberdeen and Banff, vol. ii., p. 387).
‡ Nisbet, vol. ii., p. 299, describes this seal as attached to a charter of Walter de Leslie and the countess dated 20th June 1375, noting that "the other shield on the left wing had three garbs;" but this discrepancy is not alluded to by Mr Innes or Mr Seton.
§ Seton's Heraldry, p. 268, plate xii., fig. 5.

8th August 1394* she makes a grant to her most dear brother, George Lesley of Rothes, yet as Abbess of Elcho, in June 1394, she places over the coat of Lindsay, the founder of Elcho, only the arms of Leslie, and uses the simple legend—" S. EUFAMIÆ LESCLE ABAS." † Yet it seems more probable that her son, Alexander Leslie, Earl of Ross, erected her tomb, and inserted his own arms of Leslie in the vaulting of the lower aisle, which was completed by Bishop John Bullock during the troubles which beset the earldom after Earl Alexander Leslie's death in 1402 (May 8, at Dingwall).

Where, then, was the chapel of St Nicholas, the consistorial place of Ross?

The only other chapel I have found mentioned within the cathedral is the chapel of St Boniface.

Now, I should suggest that this was the narrower and lower or western part of the aisle, and that on account of the aisles divided by the Bell tower being dedicated respectively to Our Lady and St Boniface, Bishop Tulloch dedicated the existing bell, which he placed in the tower, to St Mary and St Boniface.

The chapel of St Nicholas, then, was probably the crypt, or rather Undercroft,‡ under the chapter-house; certainly better adapted for a consistorial office than either of these two chapels open to the nave; in the crypt there are evident traces of an altar having existed. If the chapel of St Nicholas had been a mere side chapel or recess between the piers, it would not have been large enough for the purpose of an assembly of people, as in 1451 were collected; and there were never, as we can now see from the foundations of the whole cathedral being laid open, any aisles or subsidiary buildings to it, other than the undercroft and chapter-house to the north, and the aisle now existing to the south.

Alexander, Earl of Ross, the second of the line of the Isles, is said to have died at Dingwall in 1449, and to have been

* Book of Kilravock, p. 122.
† Laing's Seals, vol. ii., p. 200. On the authority of Mr W. Fraser.
‡ It is not strictly a crypt, because it is above ground. There are similar undercrofts to the chapter-house at Wells, and the chapter-house at Llandaff.

buried in the Chanonry of Fortrose on the 8th of May 1449.* There is no tomb now remaining which can be claimed as his : three only exist, the canopied monument of the countess, and two others, one west and the other east of hers,† both episcopal ; the east one probably Bishop Cairncross's, as the westernmost is that of Bishop Fraser, which the Wardlaw minister says was opposite (near) the great door. Bishop Fraser's tomb corresponds in style as in date to that of Sir Kenneth Mackenzie, in Beauly Priory. On the north side of Bishop Fraser's tomb there is a low recessed arch, which was probably used for the purposes of an Easter sepulchre—it is not large enough for a tomb. I observed at St Duthus' Church, at Tain, on the north side, a similar recess.

Before parting with the subject of the cathedral of Ross, we may as well illustrate a passage in the next document we print, in which passage Thomas Stephens, a chaplain of the cathedral church of Ross, records that he served a citation on James, Bishop of Ross, and the dean and the chapter of the same, being present faithfully at their stalls.

What was the chapter of Ross ?

In 1227 the Bishop of Ross releases his rights in Kiltarlity with the consent of his chapter and clergy, and the clergy as well as the canons subscribed the charter.‡

The subscriptions are as follows : Robert, Bishop of Ross, and canon ; Henry, Dean of Rosemarkie ; William, treasurer of Rosemarkie ; Robert, Archdeacon and canon of the Church of Ross ; Edward Beket, canon of Ross ; Archibald, canon of Ross ; Maurice, parson of Kincardine ; James, vicar of Alness ; Adam Bur, parson of Alness ; Bryden, vicar of Tain ; John, vicar of Contin ; Mathew, parson of Lochbon (Urray); Donald, vicar of Locunethereth (Logiewreath, Logie Wester); William Poer, parson of Lemnelar ; Jerome, parson of Culicuden ; Thomas, parson of Sudy ; Andrew, parson of Keltierny (Kiltearn) ; Andrew, vicar of Arterbert (Tarbat); Maurice,

---

* Chronicle of the Earls of Ross.
† Buried in Cathedral (Smyth's Chron. of Kinloss, p. 10).
‡ Reg. Moray, pp. 81, 82.

canon of Rosemarkin and parson of Ardrosser; Peter, canon of Moray and Ross.

Vicars are not usually members of a chapter; and the vicars subscribing represent the parochial clergy simply. The parsons of Kincardine, Alness, Urray, Lumlair, Cullicudden, Suddy, and Kiltearn may, even then, have had some capitular position.

In 1238 Lumlair was appropriated to the archdeacon, but in 1255 it was restored to a separate rector. That year Urray was appropriated to the sub-chanter, and Suddy to the precentor, so that these two parsonages were extinguished.

In 1588[*] we find that the following arrangement had existed at the date of the act of annexation as to certain churches. The churches of Kilmuir (Wester) and Ardersier were possessed by the dean; Killearnan and Fodderty by the archdeacon; Tain, Edderton, Cullicudden, Kincardine, Alness, and Roskeen, by the subdean; Logie (Wester) and Urquhart by the treasurer; Suddy and Kinnettes by the chancellor; Kilchrist and Kilmorack by the precentor; Urray by the subchanter; Rosemarky and Cromarty, one-fourth of each belonged to the dean, treasurer, chancellor, and precentor.

We know that the six western churches were common to the whole chapter; and thus it appears that, of the whole thirty-five parish churches in the diocese of Ross, only Avoch, which belonged to Kinloss Abbey; Dingwall, which was originally a chapel in the royal castle (*supra*, p. 125), and belonged to Pluscardine; and six others—Kilmuir Easter, Kiltearn, Logie Easter, Lumlair, Contin, and Kirkmichael—were not specifically appropriated to the bishop and chapter, or members of the chapter.

As regards these six, there were rectors as well as vicars; and all these rectors had manses belonging to them round the cathedral close at the Chanonry,[†] and doubtless stalls in the choir.

---

[*] Lords Appeal Cases (1814), x. 637.

[†] Possibly, with the exception of Contin, whose vicar seems to have had a manse in the Chanonry.

OF THE PRIORY OF BEAULY.   201

The chapter therefore at this time consisted of the bishop and the seven officials—the dean and subdean, the treasurer, the archdeacon, the precentor and sub-precentor, and the chancellor—four canons of the old foundation, the Abbot of Kinloss as rector of Avoch, and the six rectors we have named—in all, nineteen persons, to whom, severally or collectively, every parish in Ross was appropriated.

Every member of the chapter, by the Bull of 1255, was obliged, on being installed in the choir, to take an oath of perpetual residence, and also to have a vicar who had a lower place in the choir, and who ultimately was selected for his skill in chanting, and supplied any deficiency of his lord, the canon, in that respect, being a vicar-choral.*

The choir of 85 feet was not too long to provide stalls for the canons and seats for the vicars-choral. Some of the chaplains also were stallars.

Other chaplains would have no regular place in the choir. Their duty was to perform masses in their several chapels, which were, in this cathedral, all recesses or side chapels, except the Lady Chapel and the chapels of St Nicholas and St Boniface.

I have the satisfaction of concluding this digression with a valuable list of the bishops of the diocese of Ross, far more perfect than any hitherto published, for which I am indebted to the kindness of Major-General Allan.†

LIST OF THE BISHOPS OF ROSS IN SCOTLAND—ROSMARKENSIS—DE ROS—ROSSENSIS—from A.D. 1128 to A.D. 1596, May 31.

1. MACBETH, Celtic priest (perhaps head of the old secular college of Keledei, of Irish foundation, at Rosmarkny), " Rosmarkensis Episcopus," between A.D. 1128 and 1138.

---

* In 1561 the bishop paid £20 "to the vicar of choir in the chanonry" (O. P. S., "Rosemarkie," 569); the dean paid 20 marks yearly to "the lad of the choir, for his fee;" the precentor's "chorister in the chanonry" had 21 marks yearly "for his fee" (*Id.*, pp. 587, 588); the Abbot of Kinloss paid £6, 13s. 4d. "to the stallar of the Kirk cathederale of Ross, quhilk stallar is for the parsonage of Awache" (Records of Kinloss, p. 159).

† I believe we may soon expect from the general's pen, to which, in 1840, we owe the account of the abbey of Fearn in the " New Statistical Account," a complete history of the bishopric of Ross, under the title of " Fasti Rossenses."

2. SYMEON, "Episcopus de Ros," and "Sancti Petri in Ross," after A.D. 1147 and before A.D. 1150; apparently successor of Macbeth, and *died* before A.D. 1161.
3. GREGORY, *consecrated* Bishop of Rosmarkin A.D. 1161; present at general council of Lateran A.D. 1179, March, as "Episcop. de Ros;" *resigned* (?) about A.D. 1190, and *died* A.D. 1195.
4. ROGER I., "Episcopus de Ross" about A.D. 1190, and apparently the Cistercian prior of Manuel; resigned or died A.D. 1194.
5. REGINALD, *dictus* "Macer," monk of Cistercian Abbey of Mailros; *elected* "Bishop of Rosmarkyn" A.D. 1195, Feb. 27; *consecrated* September 10 following, "Epis. Rossensis," and *died* A.D. 1213, December 13.
6. ROBERT I., chaplain of King William the Lyon; *elected* "Episcopus de Ros" A.D. 1214, about November; *died* before A.D. 1256, February (certainly after A.D. 1238).
7. ROBERT II., chaplain of King Alexander I., "Episcopus Rossensis" before A.D. 1256, February 9 (perhaps some years), and *died* before November 1272 (but is also said to have died A.D. 1270, being succeeded by *Robert, Archdeacon of Ross*, who sat for two years only?).
8. MATTHEW, sub-chanter of Ross; *elected* bishop; *confirmed* A.D. 1272, December 28, by Pope Gregory X., and *consecrated* by him at Orvieto; *died* at general council of Lyons A.D. 1274, May or June.
9. ROBERT III., de Fyvine, Archdeacon of Ross; *elected* bishop; *confirmed* by P. Gregory X. A.D. 1275, April 8, and *cons.* in Scotland; *died* A.D. 1295.
10. THOMAS I., de Dono Dei (Dundemore), canon of Ross, and chaplain to Card. Bp. of Ostia; *elected*, but *nominated* Bp. of Ross by Pope Boniface VIII. A.D. 1295, November 18; *died* in or before A.D. 1325 (*sup.* p. 80).
11. ROGER II., Bishop of Ross about A.D. 1326, and before March A.D. 1328; *resigned his see* "*voluntarily* for reasonable causes" A.D. 1350; date of death unrecorded.
12. ALEXANDER I., Archdeacon of Ross; *nominated* bp. by P. Clement VI. A.D. 1350, November 3; *cons.* before March following; *died* A.D. 1371, between February and May.
13. ALEXANDER II., Kylquhous (de Culchws), canon of Ross; *elected*, but *nominated* by P. Gregory XI. A.D. 1371, May 9, and probably *cons.* at Avignon; *died* A.D. 1398, July 6.
14. ALEXANDER III. (Kilbuines?), Bishop of Ross after A.D. 1398, July, and before A.D. 1404; *sitting* A.D. 1416, March 17, and *died* apparently in that year, or early in A.D. 1417, when *vacancy*.
15. LLEWELYN Bifort, formerly Bp. of Bangor, in North Wales; *trans.* to church of Ross in Scotland by Pope Martin V. A.D. 1418, February 14, but must have *died* in the same month at Constance (while attending the general council there as "Ludovicus Bangorensis" A.D. 1416; *cons.* after A.D. 1408).
16. GRIFFIN, Bishop of Ross, and Papal Nuncio to Scotland, A.D. 1418, March 1, from P. Martin V.; *resigned*, and *trans.* to see of Hippo *i. p. i.* by same Pope A.D. 1423, February 1; *died* before A.D. 1433.

17. JOHN I., Bullock; *nom.* by Pope Martin V. to vacant see of Ross A.D. 1423, February 1, but styled "Bp.-elect-confirmed of Ross" A.D. 1420, July 16; *died* after September A.D. 1439.
18. THOMAS II., de Tulloch, Bishop of Ross A.D. 1440; *confirmed* by Pope Eugene IV. October 14; *cons.* before April 3 following; *died* A.D. 1463, before October.
19. HENRY I. (Cockburne?), Bishop of Ross A.D. 1463, "elect-confirmed" October 19; *cons.* before August A.D. 1464, and *died* A.D. 1477, before August 16 but after April A.D. 1476.
20. JOHN II., Wodman, Prior of Augustinian Monastery of Canons Regular in Isle of May; Bp. of Ross A.D. 1477; *confirmed* by Pope Sixtus IV. October 16; *res.* or *died* A.D. 1478.
21. THOMAS III. (Urquhart?), Bishop of Ross A.D. 1478, October (but difficulties about date of succession here); *sitting* A.D. 1480; *died* after September 12, A.D. 1481, and before March following.
22. WILLIAM Elphinstone, Official of Lothian, Bishop of Ross A.D. 1482; *elect and confirmed* by Pope Sixtus IV. before March 18; but, before consecration, *translated* to see of Aberdeen by same Pope A.D. 1483, after April 13 and before November 20.
23. THOMAS IV. (Hay?), Bishop of Ross A.D. 1484; still *sitting* A.D. 1487; but *resigned*, or *died*, A.D. 1492, before March, perhaps end of A.D. 1491.
24. JOHN III., Guthrie, Bishop of Ross; *nominated* by Pope Innocent VIII. A.D. 1492, March 26; *died* before July A.D. 1494 (when the see was *vacant* till A.D. 1498).
25. JOHN IV., Fraser (or Frisaile), Dean of Collegiate Church of Restalrig, Bp. of Ross A.D. 1498; "postulate" February 8; *nom.* by Pope Alexander VI. March 15; *cons.* before January 3 following; *died* A.D. 1507, February 5, at his see.
26. ROBERT IV., Cockburne, councillor of King James IV., Bp. of Ross A.D. 1507, before August; *translated* to see of Dunkeld by Pope Clement VII. A.D. 1524, April 24; and *died* there, A.D. 1526, April 12.
27. JAMES Hay, Abbot of Cistercian monastery of Dundrennan, Bishop of Ross A.D. 1524; *nominated* by Pope Clement VII. April 24; *cons.* after February A.D. 1525; *died* A.D. 1538, shortly before December 15.
28. ROBERT V., Cairncross, Abbot of Augustinian monastery of Holyrood, Bp. of Ross A.D. 1539; *nominated* by P. Paul III. April 14; *cons.* before June 23 following; *died* A.D. 1545, November 30, at his see.
29. DAVID Paniter, canon of Glasgow, *postulate* Bp. of Ross A.D. 1546, before October, but *nom.* by Pope Paul III. A.D. 1547, November 28; and *cons.* at Jedburgh (or Linlithgow?) A.D. 1552, November; *died* at Stirling A.D. 1558, October 1.
30. HENRY II., Saint Claire, Dean of Glasgow, *postulate* Bp. of Ross A.D. 1558-59; *nom.* by Queen Mary; *conf.* by Pope Pius IV. A.D. 1561, June 2; and *consecrated* in that year? *died* at Paris A.D. 1565, January 2.
31. JOHN V., Lesley, canon of Aberdeen, and commendatory Abbot of Lindores;

nom. by Q. Mary Bishop of Ross A.D. 1566, April 20; *admitted* to temporalities of see A.D. 1567, January 21; *conf.* by Pope Gregory XIII. A.D. 1575, April 22; and *consecrated* at Rome (probably on Sunday following? April 24). Exiled from Scotland from A.D. 1568, and imprisoned in England till A.D. 1574, January. *Translated* by Pope Clement VIII. to see of Coutances, in France, A.D. 1592, December 16 (with retention of his bishopric of Ross). *Died* at Augustinian monastery of Guirtenburg, near Brussels, in Flanders, A.D. 1596, May 31, aged sixty-eight years; and interred there, with monument and inscription. Last Catholic Bishop of Ross; a learned historian, divine, and jurist in both canon and civil law.

NOTE.—The authorities for the above list are derived from the various chartularies, Acts of Parliaments of Scotland, Kalendar of Ferne, MS. at Dunrobin, Africa Christiana, Theiner's Vet. Monumenta, Godwin De Præsulibus Angliæ, Hardy's Le Neve, Chron. Mailros, Turnbull's Fragmenta Scoto-Monastica, Roger de Hoveden, Thomas Walsingham, Consistorial Records in Vatican Library, Archæologia Scotica, and other sources, both printed and in MS., too numerous to specify separately in this brief notice; but it is believed that all the dates may be relied on, as far as general accuracy is now attainable, in the absence of contemporary records or diocesan registers of the bishopric of Ross, of which no traces remain, or have been hitherto discovered.

No. XXII.

PRÆCEPTUM SYLVESTRI, APOSTOLICÆ SEDIS NUNCII ABBATIBUS DE KYNLOS ET DE FERNE, PRO NOBILI ET POTENTI DOMINO HUGONI FRASER DE LOUETT. 1532.

"In Dei nomine Amen. Per hoc præsens publicum instrumentum cunctis pateat evidenter, quod Anno Incarnationis Dominicæ, Millesimo quingentesimo tricesimo secundo, mensis vero Aprilis die vicesimo sexto, Indictione quintâ, Pontificatus Sanctissimi in Christo Patris et Domini nostri, Domini Clementis, diuinâ Providentiâ Papæ, Septimi, anno ejus nono. In mei Notarij Publici et testium Subscriptorum præsentiâ personaliter constitut. Robertus permissione divinâ Abbas Monasterii de Kynlos et Donaldus eâdem permissione Abbas de Ferne Cistertien. et Præmonstraten. Ordinum, Moraviensis et Rossensis Dioccæsium, Judices auctoritate Apostolica ad infrascripta specialiter deputati; universis et singulis Sanctæ Matris Ecclesiæ filijs ad quorum notitias præsentes litteræ pervenerint, Salutem in Domino. Noveritis nos litteras Domini Sylvestri Dorij Lucanensis Sanctissimi Domini Nostri Papæ Capellani, causarum Sacri Palatij Apostolici auditoris, ad invictissimum Principem Jacobum Scotorum Regem illustrissimum, ejusdem Domini Papæ et Sedis Apostolicæ Nuncij, suo sub sigillo Cerâ rubeâ Albæ impressâ, filis rubeis sericis, more Romanæ Curiæ, dependentibus, sanas siquidem et integras, non rasas, non abolitas, nec in aliqua sui parte suspectas, sed omni prorsus vitio et suspicione carentes, nobis per nobilem et potentem Dominum Hugonem Fraser de Lovett, principalem in ipsis litteris principaliter nominatum, præsentatas. Nos cum quâ nos decuit reverentiâ noveritis recepisse, hujusmodi sub tenore.

"Silvester Dorius Lucan. Sanctissimi Domini Papæ Capellanus, Causarum Sacri Palatij Apostolici Auditor, ad invictissimum Princi-

pem Jacobum Scotorum Regem illustrem ejusdem Domini Papæ et
Sedis Apostolicæ nuncius, discretis viris de Kinloss et de Ferne
Cistertiensis et Præmonstratensis ordinum, Moraviensis et Rossensis
Diocœsium, Abbatibus salutem et sinceram in Deo caritatem.
Ea quæ pro Ecclesiarum quarumcunque commodo vel utilitate pro-
vide facta fuisse dicuntur, ut firma perpetuo et illibata persistant,
cum a nobis petitur, libenter ex commissa nobis facultate mandamus
roborari. Sane ex parte dilecti nobis in Christo Hugonis Fraser de
Louet Laici Moraviensis Diocœsis, filij et hæredis quondam Thomæ
Fraser de Louet, nobis nuper oblata petitio continebat, quod dudum
recolendæ memoriæ Robertus, dum in humanis ageret, Episcopus
Rossensis, cum pleno assensu et consensu Decani et Capituli
Ecclesiæ Rossensis, ac matura deliberatione præhabita, desiderans
ejusdem Ecclesiæ conditionem efficere meliorem, omnes et singulas
terras de Kirktoun et Kilmoricht una cum le Craig et piscaria
ejusdem vulgariter le Ess de Kilmoricht [nuncupata], cum omnibus
suis pertinentijs jacentibus in Comitatu Rossiæ, infra vicecomitatum
de Innernes, et ad dictam Ecclesiam legittime pertinentes et spectantes, dicto quondam Thomæ Fraser, suisque hæredibus et assignatis,
prout jacent in longitudine et latitudine, cum omnibus Libertatibus,
Commoditatibus, Proficuis et Pertinentijs. Reddendo inde annuatim
decem libras, sex solidos, et octo denarios usualis monetæ regni
Scotiæ, videlicet quinque libras sex solidos et octo denarios ejusdem
monetæ pro quatuor barellibus Salmonum secundum communem
æstimationem annuæ piscationis dictæ le Ess, et quadraginta solidos
præfatæ monetæ pro antiqua firma dictæ villæ et le Craig de Kilmoricht, et tres libras prædictæ monetæ in augmentationem annui
rentalis in certis terminis tantum expressis, ea tantum adjecta con-
ditione sive lege, quod Thomas, hæredes, et assignati prædicti de
et super terris hujus modi cum omnibus pertinentijs per Robertum,
et per sæpe exeuntem Episcopum Rossensem et Capitulum præfatos,
in omnibus et per omnia, contra omnes mortales, warrantisari, ac-
quietari, ac in perpetuum defendi deberent et tenerentur, dedit, concessit, assignavit, et in feodi firmam dimisit, prout in instrumento
publico sive letteris patentibus ejusdem, sua manuali subscriptione,
et Sigillo Communi dicti Capituli, minutis desuper confectis, dicitur
plenius continere. Cum autem sicut eadem subjungebat petitio,
datio, concessio, assignatio, in evidentem ejusdem Ecclesiæ cesserint
et cedant utilitatem, cupiatque dictus Exponens, qui ejusdem Thomæ

filius et hæres existit, illas in quæcunque inde secuta pro illorum substantia firmiari, Apostolicæ confirmationis munimine roborari. Ideo supplicare fecit humiliter Exponens præfatus, sibi super hijs de opportuno remedio mature provideri. Nos igitur terrarum situationes, confines, valores et limites ac instrumenti seu litterarum prædictarum, aliorumque hic latius exprimendorum tenores et compendia præsentibus pro sufficienter expresse habentes, ac attendentes, et in hijs quibus Ecclesiarum procuretur utilitas, favorabiles esse debemus, atque benignum ad infra scriptas per litteras dictæ Sedis, ad quorum insertionem minime tenemur, et quibus nobis indulgetur, quod nostra assertio in omnibus et per omnia sufficiat, proinde ac si earundem litterarum tenores de verbo ad verbum in litteris per nos exponend. inserti forent, sufficienti facultate muniti, discretioni vestræ conjunctim demittimus, tunc si vocatis vocandis, et juris torma, alijsque solemnitatibus in similibus requisitis debite observetis, dationem, concessionem, et dimissionem hujusmodi in evidentem dictæ Ecclesiæ utilitatem cessisse, et eadem reperientes, super quibus vestram conscientiam oneramus, easdem dationem, concessionem et dimissionem, ac prout eas concernunt, omnia et singula in dictis instrumento seu litteris contenta, alias licita et honesta, auctoritate Apostolica qua fungimur in hac parte confirmetis et approbetis, supplentes omnes et singulos tam juris quam facti defectus, si qui intervenerint in eisdem. Non obstantibus Apostolicis, ac in provincialibus et in synodalibus concilijs editis generalibus vel specialibus Constitutionibus, nec non omnibus illis quæ in litteris nostræ facultatis concessum fuit non obstare, cæteris contrarijs quibuscunque. In quorum fidem præsentes fieri et per nostrum Secretarium subscribi, sigilliqua nostri appensione fecimus communiri. Datum Edinburgi Sanctæ Andreæ Diocœsis in domo habitationis nostræ residentiæ Anno Incarnationis Dominicæ Millesimo quingentesimo tricesimo primo juxta stylum regni Scotiæ die vicesima sexta mensis Februarij, Pontificatus prælibati Sanctissimi Domini nostri Domini Clementis Papæ Septimi anno nono.

"Post quarum quidem litterarum Apostolicarum præsentionem et receptionem nobis, et per nos, ut præmittitur, factas, statim requisiti fuimus, per dictum nobilem Dominum Hugonem, quatenus ad executionem hujusmodi litterarum Apostolicarum procedere dignaremur. Nos attendentes hujusmodi requisitionem fore justam et rationi consonam, volentes Mandatum Apostolicum exequi, et justitiam partibus exhibere, ut tenemur. Quocirca universis Dominis Abbatibus, Prioribus, Præpositis, Decanis, Archidiaconis, Cantoribus, Thesaurijs, Sacrificis, Rectoribus, Vicarijs perpetuis, et Curatis Ecclesiarum, ac Notarijs ac Tabellionibus publicis, præcipue per Diocœsem Rossensem, ubilibet constitutis, et nostris, immo verius Apostolicis firmiter obedire mandatis, stricte præcipiendo mandamus, quatenus visis præsentibus statim et indilate citetis legittime Reverendum in Christo patrem in Dominum Jacobum Miseratione divina Episcopum Rossensem, Decanum et Capitulum ab una, dictum Hugonem Fraser Dominum de Louet ab altera, omnesque alios et singulos seu communiter et divisim interesse habentes, seu habere putantes, primo, secundo, tertio, et peremptorie, unico tamen contextu pro triplici edicto, quos nos etiam tenore præsentium citamus, ut compareant coram Nobis in insula Beatissimæ Virginis Mariæ infra Ecclesiam Cathedralem Rossensem de vigesima octava mensis Augusti proxime futura, hora Causarum, ad videndum et audiendum dationem, concessionem et dimissionem omnium et singularum terrarum de Kirktoun· de Kilmoricht cum le Craig et piscaria ejusdem, vulgariter le Ess de Kilmoricht nuncupata, per quondam recolendæ memoriæ Robertum, dum in humanis ageret, Rossensem Episcopum, cum pleno assensu et consensu Capituli Ecclæsiæ Rossensis, quondam nobili et potenti Domino Thomæ Fraser Domino de Louet, suis hæredibus et assignatis, patri Domini Hugonis, in feodifirma factas, plene coram nobis esse et fuisse in evidentem utilitatem dictæ Ecclesiæ, et in augmentationem rentalis cessisse et cedere, et quatenus est ita dictum feodum seu feodifirmam Auctoritate Apostolica, prout de jure, per nos confirmari, ac alia contenta in hujusmodi litteris fieri et debere, prout in eisdem præcipitur et mandatur, cum intimatione, quod sive in dicto citationis termino comparuerint, sive non comparere curaverint, nos nihilominus in dicto termino procedamus, prout justum fuerit, et ordo dictaverit rationis, sua contumacia non obstante, certificantes eisdem quod dictis die et loco producant coram nobis dictas infeodationes et omnia alia jura quibus uti voluerint in hujusmodi causa; cum simili intimatione. Insuper citetis Reverendum Dominum Alexandrum Munro, Joannem Duf, Donaldum Duf, Hugonem Thomæ, Maldonyth Macego, Johannem Clerk et Johannem Brechen, Alexandrum Forbes—quod compareant coram nobis dictis die et loco ad perhibendum fidele testimonium veritati in hujusmodi causa, sub pœnis Excommunicationis in Laicos et Suspensionis a divinis in Presbyteros. In quorum omnium et singulorum fidem et testimonium præmissorum, præsentes litteras, sive præsens Publicum Instrumentum exinde fieri, et per Notarium Publicum subscribi, nostrisque Sigillis jussimus et fecimus appensis communiri. Datum et actum in hospitio Roberti Waus infra Burgum de Innernes hora quasi sexta post meridiem, vel eocirca, sub anno, die, mense, Indictione et Pontificatu quibus supra; præsentibus ibidem Venerabilibus viris Magistris et Dominis Willielmo Paterson Subdecano Moraviensi, Andrea Cuthbert Vicario de Verlau, Johanne Roy Rectore de Bullesky, Honorabilibus Viris Johanne Waus Domino [de] Lochsliny, Angusio McCulloch de Tarrell, Roberto Waus Burgensi de Innernes et Roberto Malcomi Notario Publico cum diversis aliis ad præmissa vocatis pariterque rogatis.

"Et ego vero Magnus Waus Moraviensis Diocœsis Presbiter, sacra auctoritate Notarius, quia prædictarum litterarum dicti Domini Sylvestri Darij Lucanensis, Sanctissimi Domini nostri Papæ Capelani, Causarum Sacri Palatij Apostolici auditoris, &c., dictis Dominis Judicibus ad infra et supra scripta specialiter auctoritate Apostolica, ut præmittitur, constitutis, præsentationi, receptioni, et præsentis citationis concessioni, eorundem Judicum suprascriptorum sigillorum appensioni, cæterisque omnibus et singulis, dum sic ut præfatur, dicerentur, agerentur, et fierent, una cum prænominatis testibus præsens interfui, eaque omnia et singula sic fieri scivi, vidi et audivi, ac in notam sumpsi, et exinde hoc præsens publicum instrumentum, aliena manu, me alijs arduis occupato negotijs, fideliter scriptum redegi, signavi, subscripsi, et publicavi sub meis signo et subscriptione in fidem et testimonium omnium et singulorum præmissorum rogatus et requisitus manualibus solitis et subscriptis.—Waus.

"Undecimo die mensis Augusti anno Domini Milesimo quingentessimo tricesimo secundo, Ego Thomas Stephens Capellanus Ecclesiæ Cathedralis Rossensis, suprascriptum Reverendum in Christo Patrem Jacobum Rossensem Episcopum, Decanum, et Capitula ejusdem, apud eorundem Stalla devote præsent. citavi, præsentibus Dominis Johanne Spens, Alexandro Spens, Jacobo Yong Capellanis cum diversis alijs.—Thomas Stephens *manu propria.*

"Decimo tertio die mensis antedicti, anno ut supra, Ego Johannes Scot Notarius publicus suprascriptos Dominum Alexandrum Munro, Johannem Duf, Donaldum Duf, Hugonem Thomæ, Maldonyth

M&c Ego, Johannem Clerk, Johannem Brechen, et Alexandrum Forbes, personaliter apprehensos tenore præsentium ad comparendum in Ecclesia Cathedrali Rossensi, ad effectum ut supra, citavi. —*Teste manu propria Ita est* Johannes Scott."

> Not.—At the syde is " Magnus Waus notarius publicus," with a big M and a V for paraph. above and under " Veritas est Vita :" Waus.
> There are two Seals appended to the Instrument, the one red upon white wax, representing Our Lady in a niche crowned with an antick crown, standing and clothed with a long robe and pled, holding on her left arme our Saviour. On the dish—"SIGILLUM ROBERTI ABBATIS DE KYNLOSS." The other seal is round, of red upon white wax, and represents a Virgin sitting and crowned, holding on her lap and right arm a babe. On the circumference of the seal—"SIGILLUM COMMUNE MONASTERII B. MARIÆ DE FERNE." Both tags parchment.

In 1531, Pope Clement VII., warned by the blows aimed daily at his power by Henry VIII. in England, sends Silvester Darius, high in office at the Vatican, as Apostolic Nuncio to Holyrood, to confirm and enlarge the privileges accorded to Scotland by Rome.

From this Nuncio proceeds this document we now print, which, although among the Beauly charters transcribed by Macfarlane, does not relate to the Priory itself, but only to a transaction of one of the heirs of the Founder.

Before we enter upon an explanation, we may as well continue the account of those heirs down to its date.

Thomas, Lord Lovat, made no further acquisitions than we have mentioned of the property of the founder from his co-heirs. He is said, in what is called the Culduthel MS. by Mr Anderson (p. 76), which MS. appears to have been full of inaccuracies, to have had, by his second marriage, a son Robert, who married Janet Gelly, the heritrix of Braky in Fife, and to have purchased the estate of Braky Kinnell. We should have hardly been justified in mentioning this Robert

Fraser, but that the same MS. states that he was killed at the water of Beauly by the monks of Beauly. If this is true, it was probably in some dispute about the salmon fishing.* Thomas, Lord Lovat, died on 21st October 1524, and was succeeded by his son Hugh, Lord Lovat.

It is said Lord Thomas died at Beaufort Castle; but this is doubtful. Beaufort Castle itself, if inhabited, belonged in property to the Earl of Argyle. The conveyance, indeed, of Culbirnie from Henry Douglas in 1509 (*supra*, p. 175), included a claim to the hill on which the castle of Beaufort stood; and the service of Hugh, Lord Lovat, to his father in 1524, extends to "Culbirnie, with the mount of the castle of the same called Beaufort." It was not till 1542, however, that Hugh, Lord Lovat, got a feu-charter of the lands of Beaufort from the Earl of Argyle. The House of Lovat seems to have been, in Lord Thomas's time, the residence of the family.† He was buried in the Priory of Beauly.

Hugh, Lord Lovat, married a daughter of the chief of the Grants, the widow of Halyburton of Pitcur, and used the connection thus formed with the descendants of the Chisholm co-heirs of the founder of Beauly, to acquire much of the Chisholm portion of the Byset property. In 1528 he induced George Halyburton of Gask to convey to him the lands of Ingliston (Englishtown) and Kingslie (Kingillie), now in the united parish of Wardlaw and Fernua; and in 1529 he got James Halyburton of Gask to give up to him the whole barony of Erchless created in 1512.

Lord Hugh also gets confirmed to him the old Kiltarlity church right of salmon fishing, which had been so hardly

---

* We have, in the Wardlaw MS., a story of the monks killing a gentleman of the Lovat family with a cross bow, who was fishing within their bounds; but this is stated to have occurred in the priorate of Walter Reid after 1558.

† In his time, the House of Lovat is said to have suffered by a fire, which burned down the chapel of St Lawrence, which was on the east corner of the house. In this fire, Roderick, a younger son of Sir Kenneth Mackenzie and Agnes Fraser of Lovat (*supra*, p. 105), afterwards Roderick Mackenzie of Fairburn, who probably built the Tower of Fairburn now standing, is said to have rushed through the flames, and brought out his uncle's charter chest and other valuables, for which he was rewarded with a present of a bonnet and pair of shoes (Anderson, p. 74).

gained by the first Fraser of Lovat in 1380.* The Lovat Inventory of 1652 contains the entry of a precept given by Robert, Bishop of Moray, for giving of sasine to Lord Lovat, as heir to Thomas, Lord Lovat, of the half lands of Kincalartie and fishing of Ess, dated 25th September 1526.†

The monks, as we have seen, are stated to have had the fishings on the river from the sea, that is, the Firth,‡ to the cruives above the Ford of Dunballoch—the cruives, namely, above the spot where now stands the Lovat§ or Beauly Bridge, built by Mr Telford. Unless their right included the Wardlaw half of the river, they would not have paid, as they did, tithes of fish to the church of Wardlaw. Their right extended across the river, or they could not have erected the cruives.

Above these cruives, where the priory right of fishing ended, the right of fishing appears to have belonged, before the foundation of the priory, to the churches of Kiltarlity and Kilmorack. This requires some explanation, which will make intelligible the transaction recorded in the document now printed.

"The church [of Kiltarlity] standeth," says the learned historian of the province of Moray, writing about 1760, " on the bank of the river, a mile above the lower end of the parish, near three miles S.S.W. of Kirkhill, six miles N.W. of Urquhart, and about a furlong E.N.E. of Kilmorack church, that standeth on the opposite bank."‖ The site is just on the east side of the present wooden bridge below the lower falls of Kilmorack.¶ The site of the present parish church of Kiltarlity is distant from the river. A church was built there in 1763,** and the change of site must then have been made.

---

* *Supra*, p. 70. † Dunbar Dunbar MSS., No. 57.

‡ In the Beauly Firth, the fishing seems to have belonged to the riparian proprietors, thus the grant of Englishtown and Kingillie of 1528 is "cum lie yairs et piscationibus."

§ "At Lovat Bridge," says Southey, in his Journal of a Tour with Mr Telford in 1819, "we turned aside, and went four miles up the river along the Strathglass road, one of the new works, and one of the most remarkable, because of the difficulty of constructing it, and also because of the fine scenery it commands" (Life of Telford, by Smiles, Lond. 1867, p. 95).

‖ Shaw's Moray, ed. 1775, p. 145.   ¶ Ord. Map. Inverness-shire, x. 6.

** New Stat. Acc., "Kiltarlity."

The Kiltarlity church land right of fishing extended only to the half of the river which was within the parish of Kiltarlity and opposite the church lands. It, however, certainly included the fishing of the Ess or Fall, perhaps the whole of the Lower Fall. The other half of the river was in the parish of Kilmorack, and adjoined the church lands of Kilmorack, which church lands, and the fishing in the river adjoining them, are the subject of the grant proposed to be confirmed.

The salmon fishing was the most important subject included in the grant, and seems to have formed part of the endowment of the church of Kilmorack, and that even before the foundation of Beauly Priory.

The church of Kilmorack stands upon the heights (*le Craig*), whose barrier has been broken through by the river, which there forms the upper falls or Ess of Kilmorack. Immediately below the Falls are pools of great resort for the salmon, and the fishing here is most valuable. Probably the right being attached to the church lands and glebe, extended only half across the river; the other half belonging to the opposite parish of Kiltarlity, and being called on that side also the Ess or Fall. Or the higher falls may have been the Ess of Kilmorack, for the higher falls are associated with steep craigs; and the lower falls, where is less steepness, may be the Ess or Fall pertaining to the church lands of Kiltarlity.

The priory having the fishing from the cruives to the Firth, it seems probable that the church of Kilmorack was endowed with the salmon fishing before 1230, or the grant of fishing in the Forne (Farrar) given to the monks by John Byset, and confirmed by the Pope,* would have included, at least, all the fishings up to the boundary of their lands, the burn or rivulet of Breakachy or Teanassie.†

The precentor of Ross had undoubtedly the rectorial tithes of Kilmorack as part of his prebend; but it seems doubtful whether the Bishop of Ross ever granted to the precentorship the whole endowment of the church of Kilmorack.

In 1515 Master John Calder was the precentor of Ross, a

* *Supra*, No. I. † Appendix, No. XXI.

considerable man of the Cawdor family, who provides a dowry for his kinswoman * when she marries Rose of Kilravock, and was not likely to allow any interference with or usurpation of his rights; but in 1515, without any reference to John Calder, Thomas, Lord Lovat, seems to have obtained from the Bishop of Ross alone a charter of the Kirklands of Kilmorack.† This was probably only a lease.

In 1521 the same Bishop (Robert) of Ross granted to him and his heirs the same land by the description of the lands of the Kirktoun of Kilmorack, with the Craig and fishing of that town, commonly called the Ess of Kilmorack, belonging to the church of Kilmorack, for the yearly payment of £10, 6s. 8d.,—namely, £5, 6s. 8d. for four barrels of salmon, according to the common valuation of the yearly fishing called the Ess, and 40s. as the old rent of the Kirktoun and the Craig, with £3, in augmentation of the rental.

The grant in fee in 1521 was a dangerous attempt to violate the recently made law of the Church; the fifth Lateran Council, summoned unwillingly by Pope Julius II., had, on the 5th of May 1514, strictly prohibited all kings, princes, and lords to seize or sequestrate ecclesiastical property, except by permission of the Pope.

No Nuncio had come to Scotland since the grant, but in 1531 Silvester Darius, one of the Pope's chaplains, and auditor of Palace causes, came as Nuncio to Edinburgh. The opportunity was seized by Hugh, Lord Lovat, to request the Pope's confirmation, through the Nuncio, of the grant of the church lands of Kilmorack to his father. The Nuncio acceded to the request; and this document is the record of some steps in the transaction.

On the 26th April 1532, Robert, Abbot of Kinloss, and Donald, Abbot of Fearn, judges appointed by apostolic authority, testify that they have inspected the letter of the Nuncio, sealed in the Roman manner, presented to them by Hugh, Lord Lovat. They set forth the letter which authorises them—upon the allegation that Robert, Bishop of Ross, with

* Reg. Mag. Sig., lib. xx., No. 154.   † Laing's Seals, vol. ii., p. 187.

the consent of his dean and chapter, desiring to benefit the condition of his church, had granted to Thomas, Lord Lovat, lands and others to the effect foresaid—to confirm and approve of the said grant. The letter is dated at Edinburgh, in the house of the habitation of the Nuncio's residence, in the year 1531, according to the style of the kingdom of Scotland, the 26th day of February; and after reciting the letter, the two judges summon and cite James, Bishop of Ross, and the dean and chapter, on the one hand, and Hugh, Lord Lovat, on the other, to appear before them in the aisle of the most blessed Virgin Mary within the cathedral church of Ross, on the 28th day of August then next, to enable the judges to inquire into the propriety of the grant; and they also cite eight men, some laymen and some priests, there to attend, as jurors on the inquiry.

The instrument is dated in the inn (*hospitium*) of Robert Waus, in the burgh of Inverness; present, the sub-dean of Moray; Andrew Cuthbert, vicar of Wardlaw; the rector of Boleskine; John Waus, Lord of Lochslin; Angus M'Culloch of Tarrell; the said Robert Waus, and Robert Malcomson (*Malcomi*), notary public. It is attested by Magnus Waus, priest of the diocese of Moray, notary.

The citation, on the 11th of August 1532, by Thomas Stephens, chaplain of the cathedral church of Ross, of James, Bishop of Ross, and the dean and chapter of the same, being present faithfully at their stalls, is testified by the subscription of Thomas Stephens.

The citation, on the 13th August 1532, by John Scot, notary public, of the eight jurors to appear in the cathedral church of Ross, is testified by the subscription of John Scot.

Attached to the instruments are the signature and motto of Magnus Waus and the abbatical seal of Abbot Reid, and the common seal of the Monastery of Fearn.

Magnus Waus was a thriving churchman of a lower class than Archbishop Forman, but apparently he accumulated as many church offices. He appears in 1523 as parish clerk of the church of Inverness, and chaplain of St Peter in the same;

1525, as vicar of Dalcross and commissary of Inverness; 1536, rector of Y or Ey in Lewis, vicar of Abertarff, commissary of Inverness, and chaplain of St Catherine's chapelry there; and also in 1542, provost of the College Church of Tain.

Still stands on the shore of the loch of Slyn the castle of Lochslyn, the old dwelling of the witness John Waus of Lochslyn; it is in the parish of Tarbat, and consists of two towers 60 feet high, and respectively 38 and 20 feet square. Here was born the first Earl of Cromarty, whose researches as an antiquarian we have had occasion not unfrequently to consider.

The seals attached to the instrument are interesting. That of Abbot Reid is probably the same seal which is engraved in the Book of Kinloss, as attached to a charter granted by this abbot and his convent in 1537.* The Macfarlane transcriber has not given the full legend, which is, "Sigillum Roberti Abbatis Monasterii de Kynlos;" and although he faithfully notes the plaid (*pled*) flowing behind the Virgin's robe, he yet omits the armorial bearings of Reid—a stag's head erased—which are placed under the figure.

The seal of the abbey of Fearn is used by Abbot Denoon instead of his own seal. The convent seal attached to a deed of 1577 is, "A front figure of the Virgin, sitting with the infant Jesus in her arms; on the sinister side a pot, with lilies, and the legend: 'SI. COMNE CAPITULI ET CONVENTUS MONASTERII DE FERNE.'"†

We have at some length already enlarged on the Virgin's Aisle of the cathedral of Ross, the place where the Nuncio's commission is to be finally executed, and now we ought to direct particular attention to the persons to whom it is addressed.

One of the judges and commissioners was Donald, Abbot of Fearn. The time would fail us were we to dwell on all that these names suggest: the man—Donald Denoon—ascended the steps of the abbot's throne through the ashes of Patrick

---

* Records of Kinloss, pref., p. 64.
† Laing's Scottish Seals, vol. ii., p. 200.

Hamilton, the first of Scotland's martyrs; the place—Fearn, the only monastery save Beauly in Ross-shire, founded by Farquhar, the first Earl of Ross, where the White Canons of St Norbert kept alight the lamp of learning for three hundred years; but their connection with Beauly is not intimate enough to justify our entering on their long and interesting history.*

The other judge and commissioner was Robert Reid, Abbot of Kinloss, the most distinguished ecclesiastic whose name is linked with that of the Priory of Beauly.

As the traveller walks up the venerable avenue of lofty and aged elms which leads to the western door of the Priory church, the towering gable attracts his attention; and as he stands at the great door itself, he can see above it, on a shield, the initials R. R., and below them, a stag's head, with a bishop's crosier issuing in front of the antlers.†

These are the initials and armorial bearings of Robert Reid, Bishop of Orkney, Abbot of Kinloss, and Prior of Beauly, one of the first Lords President of the Court of Session, and the first founder of the University of Edinburgh.

Robert Reid, according to Ferrarius, his biographer, and the historian of Kinloss,‡ was born at Akynheid, in Kenneder. His father was killed at Flodden field. His mother was Bessie Schanwell. He was educated and made M.A. at the University of St Andrews, and resided with his uncle, Robert Schanwell, official of that see. He afterwards went to the University of Paris, where he studied civil and canon law.§ He was in 1525 sub-dean of Moray,|| and in 1526 he was selected by Abbot Chrystall as his successor at Kinloss.

In 1527 he went to Rome, in order to get the formal approbation of the Pope to his appointment as abbot, and found it just reeling under the sack of the Constable Bourbon. At last,

* Appendix, No. XXII.

† The stag's head is couped, but on the seal of 1537, and as sculptured on the abbot's house at Kinloss, it is erased (Records of Kinloss, pref. lxi.).

‡ Records of Kinloss, by Dr Stuart, *passim*.

§ Dr George Mackenzie's Scottish Writers, vol. iii., p. 47.

|| "A.D. 1525.—Maister Robert Reid, Subdene of Murray, was a member of the University of St Andrews" (Lyon's Hist. of St Andrews, vol. ii., p. 232).

getting his diplomas signed, he in the early part of 1528 came back to Paris, and there met with this Ferrarius, a Piedmontese; a little after Easter he came to London by Dieppe and Rye,* and so to Scotland and Kinloss.

In the autumn he went from Kinloss to Edinburgh, and there was received into the Cistercian order by the Bishop of Aberdeen, and assumed the Cistercian habit; at the Franciscan or Grey Friars' church, he was anointed abbot by the same prelate, and on the 2d of August came to Kinloss, and received the vows of obedience from the monks.

In the year 1530 he received *in commendam* the Priory of Beauly, where, says his biographer, he daily did things worthy to be remembered by posterity.

No sooner had James V. attained twenty-one than he, in 1532, instituted "ane college of cunnyng and wise men" for the administration of justice in all civil actions, and thus established the Court of Session.

Among the persons selected for one of the Senators of the College of Justice and judges of the Court of Session, was Robert Schanwell, the instructor of Robert Reid; but he preferred that his nephew, Robert Reid, should take his place, which accordingly Reid did at the first meeting of the Court of Session, and ultimately became Lord President of the Court.

In 1533 Abbot Reid was sent by James V. with William Stuart, Bishop of Aberdeen, ambassador to Henry VIII., and appears to have gone on to Rome in 1534. In 1535 and 1536 he was sent ambassador to France, to negotiate the king's marriage with Mary of Guise.

In 1537 he took five youths into the profession of the Valliscaulian order at Beauly, whom he added to two who had recently professed there, and in the same year he collected materials for constructing the nave of the Priory Church at Beauly.

He sent John Person, a Cistercian monk from Kinloss, to Beauly, to be the instructor of the novices there. Apparently

* Rye harbour has been long ago choked up, and Rye, which was once destroyed by the sea, is now two miles from it (Lyell's Geology, 9th ed., p. 316).

young men of family in the neighbourhood were also educated at Beauly. We shall see that the education of Alexander, second son of Hugh, Lord Lovat, and his successor, seems to have been carried on there, but Abbot Reid could only have given an occasional superintendence to it.

He was now one of the chief counsellors of the king, on account of his knowledge of civil and municipal law. He appointed John Grant of Freuchy, the head of the house of Grant, his bailiff at Kinloss. In 1540 he brought from Dieppe in France, a town which we shall afterwards have to mention in connection with his history, to Kinloss, William Lubias, as gardener, who greatly improved the abbey garden by planting fruit trees of the best kinds, and grafting many more; the improving labours of Lubias extended, Mr Forsyth says,* over the whole of the low part of Morayshire, which since that time has been distinguished for its fruits, particularly for its apples. He did not neglect, as we shall see, the gardens or orchards of Beauly Priory.

Ferrarius says that Abbot Reid in 1540 built the nave of the church of Beauly magnificently, and covered it with oak tiles. This date is probably incorrect; at all events, the work was not completed till he was a bishop, as his coat of arms on the building has the addition of the episcopal crosier, a distinction it did not bear whilst he was only Abbot of Kinloss. Ferrarius adds to this statement about the bishop's building the nave, the following paragraph: "The bishop elegantly repaired the bell tower, which had been struck by lightning;" but it was in January 1541 that this accident to the bell tower of Beauly took place.

"On the 2d of January 1541, there raged a most great and vehement wind, with enormous rain, which wind destroyed the bell tower of Beauly, and the bells † thereof." This is the account of John Smyth, the contemporary chronicler of Kinloss.‡

---

* Forsyth's Moray, p. 352.   † Appendix, No. XXIII.

‡ Smyth's Chronicle, Book of Kinloss, p. 11. Smyth seems to adopt the Roman style, and to begin the year with 1st January.

On the 5th April 1541, Reid was selected by King James V. as successor to the Bishop of Orkney, and in his letter to the Pope recommending the abbot, the king expressed his hope that the Cistercian dress of Robert being wholly abandoned, he would be allowed by the apostolic see to adopt the episcopal dress by which he would be able more conveniently to move about in the king's company, and amongst the Orkney Islanders. He was created bishop on 27th November 1541, and consecrated in the Franciscan or Grey Friars' church at Edinburgh on the first Sunday in Advent 1541.

That same year he went to Orkney, and on his return he brought the five junior monks of Beauly to Kinloss, that Ferrarius might instruct them in learning, whose names as Latinised by Ferrarius are: Dominus Thomas Tognius, dominus David Dason, dominus Joannes Crawford, dominus Jacobus Pont, dominus Gilbertus Gray. They stayed, Ferrarius says, at Kinloss three years, during which time he lectured to them on various books, among which are not only Aristotle, Cicero, and Virgil, but the work of Erasmus on " Plenty," and the two " Rhetorics of Melanchthon."

The death of King James V. in 1542 produced troubles which induced Ferrarius to desire to leave Scotland and go back to France. In 1544, Ferrarius says, Bishop Reid pulled down the old and rickety buildings of the priory at Beauly, and erected a spacious and handsome house with six vaulted rooms on the ground floor. This was that " palace and principal buildings of the messuage in the place of the Priory of Beauly erected by the late Robert, Bishop of Orkney, and prior of the said monastery, on the east side of the church of Beauly,"* of which the keepership was granted in 1571 to Lord Lovat.

Doubtless here was also a garden worthy of the palace, and Lubias, the French gardener, would take care to stock it well with apples and pears. Of the palace no trace now remains, but the spot where once the bishop's garden smiled is marked by very ancient trees, an apple and a pear. The pear-tree is a jargonelle pear; one branch only is now alive, but the

* Book of Kinloss, app., p. 97.

original stump is 8 feet 4 inches in circumference. The apple-tree is still standing, its trunk is 6 feet in circumference,* of a size rarely to be found save in "the most fertile of English valleys," Taunton Dean.†

On the departure of the bishop for Orkney in August 1544, Ferrarius tells us, he begged the bishop, Alexander Cumming of Altyre then being present, to examine Ferrarius's effects and see that he took away nothing but what was his own; the bishop told him he might not only take away his own things, but any of the bishop's that he liked. Ferrarius, however, declined the favour, and said he would only take those books he had brought with him from France to Kinloss.

The presence of Cumming of Altyre is explained by the fact that this year, 1544,‡ Robert Reid's bailie, John Grant of Freuchy, constitutes "my weil beluvit and traist friend," Alexander Cumming of Altyre, his bailie depute.

The voice of scandal, notwithstanding, attacked the Piedmontese, and in this way: when the five monks of Beauly returned to their own priory, their tutor did not suffer them to leave without giving them some few little books, one of which, the "Lives of Plutarch," was then in the possession of Adam Elder; and Adam not only refused to give the book to the young Beauly monk, Thomas Togny, but said that Ferrarius did not possess a single book which was not bought with Abbot Reid's money.

Ferrarius prints the letter he thereupon wrote to Thomas Togny at Beauly; and as monkish Beauly correspondence is rare, although it is given by Dr Stuart in his "Records of Kinloss" (pref. p. xvii.), it will be well to insert it here: §

"I am not much astonished at what you write of Adam Elder. I thought, however, that in these days, when he drinks milk and

---

* These were the sizes as measured by me on 23d September 1873.

† There is in one of the orchards at Thornfaulcon, on the edge of this vale, "rich with orchards" (Macaulay, Hist., i. 585), an apple-tree, whose trunk is six feet in circumference, and its head proportionally large.

‡ Forsyth's Moray, p. 23.

§ This translation is somewhat varied from Dr Stuart's.

water, he would not make himself such a fool; but he goes on, I see, always like himself. The argument by which he defends himself against giving up my books is of a similar stamp to the man himself —weak in the loins—for it does not necessarily follow that books belong to another, although his name be written on them; just as you and your colleagues, for nearly three years, wore the cowl of the Cistercian order, when you were of a different profession:* for a good part of the books have the name of Abbot Thomas affixed to them by Sir James Pont, when they really belonged to Abbot Robert. Besides, it is untrue that all the books were acquired with the abbot's money, for before I ever knew the abbot I had many books at Paris, and brought more with me at my first coming to Scotland than the abbot himself. Then, while engaged at court, I bought not a few books at Edinburgh with my own money; and what I procured at Paris during the last four years, many at Kinloss can attest who saw those which I brought with me at my second coming; and if all is taken into account, you may conclude that almost a half of the books were bought with my money. Is not the money my own which I had before I came to know the abbot? or which I afterwards acquired through my own industry? more truly mine than what Adam diverts to his own use, without leave of the abbot, by selling cabbages from his garden. I indeed am of no profession but that of Christ, and what my industry brings to me is my own; but what a monk acquires is not for himself, but for his monastery.

"That I have frequently put the name of the abbot on the books arises from the love which I bear to him, as though I wished all things belonging to friends to be held in common. But I ask you with what front, with what face, does Adam daily approach the altar in such manifest and perverse falsehood? May Christ grant that hereafter he may judge more candidly of our affairs; and in the meantime take care, through your Sub-Prior, again to claim the Plutarch which at your departure I, with a good title, bestowed upon you."

In October 1544 † Bishop Reid made a new foundation of

* In fact it would seem the dress of the Valliscaulians differed from that of the Cistercian habit, although it is usually said they wore the same habit (*supra*, pp. 8, 10; Appendix, No. XXIV.).

† Wallace's Account of Orkney, Lond. 1700, p. 83. As the details of this foundation illustrate admirably those of Rosemarkie and Elgin, I have reprinted Wallace's Account in the Appendix No. XXV.

the chapter of Kirkwall—seven dignitaries, seven canons or prebendaries, thirteen chaplains, a sacrist, and six choristers. His predecessor, Robert Maxwell, had, says Dr Wallace, caused found and made "those excellent bells that are in the steeple of the cathedral"—"a set of as excellent and sweetly-chimed bells as are in any cathedral of the kingdom:"* and thus nobly furnished to be the light and lustre of those dark islands, was left by Reid, "the glorious church of St Magnus the Martyr."†

At the time Ferrarius wrote, Thomas Haistie was sub-prior of Beauly.‡ In 1543, Sir Thomas Haistie, a monk of Beauly, found surety before a civil court for his appearance, to answer being art and part in the oppression done to Master Gawin Dunbar, treasurer of Ross, in coming upon him, with the bishop and his accomplices in the cathedral church, in laying hands upon him, and in cruelly wounding him to the effusion of his blood.§ This is the charge in the language of criminal pleading; whether anything took place beyond a scuffle between the bishop of Ross and his followers and the treasurer of Ross does not appear. The bishop was Robert Cairncross, who died in 1545, and, Smyth says,‖ was buried in the cathedral church of Ross.

This same year (1544) Beauly Priory saw a sad funeral procession enter the restored church, bearing the bodies of Hugh, Lord Lovat, and his eldest son, killed in a clan fight.

Such a specimen of civil warfare showed the weakness of the government, and astonished the ambassador of Henry VIII.

It arose in this way: the Clanranald estates were in 1542 given by charter to Ranald, the son of a former chief by his second wife, a daughter of Lord Lovat. This Ranald was fostered by his mother's relatives, the Frasers, and thence

* Dr Wallace's idea of a fine peal was modest. They seem to have been only three, now happily remaining (Muir's Characteristics, p. 91).
† Neale's Ecclesiological Notes, p. 72.
‡ Records of Kinloss, app. to pref., p. 48.
§ Pitcairn's Criminal Trials, vol. i., p. 328.
‖ Smyth's Chronicle, Records of Kinloss, p. 10.

called Ranald Galla, or the Stranger. By the assistance of the Frasers, Ranald was put into possession; but John Moyderlach, who was the bastard son of Ranald's elder brother, and had been put in prison by James V. in 1540, procured his discharge; and being again acknowledged as chief of the clan, he expelled Ranald from Moydart, and forced him to take refuge with Hugh, Lord Lovat.

Not content with this, the Clan Ranald, with the assistance of the Macdonells of Keppoch and the Camerons, invaded the country of Lovat; they ravaged Abertarff and Stratherrick, and even attacked the lands of Urquhart and Glenmorriston, which had recently become the property of the Laird of Grant, the brother-in-law of Lord Lovat. They also possessed themselves of the strong castle of Urquhart, which the Grants had bought of James IV.

The Earl of Huntly, the lieutenant-general of the north, with a numerous force, among which were four hundred of the Frasers, the flower of the clan, assembled to drive back the invaders; Lord Lovat was there and the Laird of Grant.

At the approach of Huntly the Highlanders retreated, and the earl penetrated as far as Inverlochy, and Ranald took possession of Moydart. Huntly then returned. On arriving at the point where the Spean joins the Lochy, his forces separated, he and the Grants taking the line of the Spean and the Spey, Lord Lovat going straight to the Aird by Loch Lochy and Abertarff.

No sooner was Huntly gone than Lovat, marching up the south side of Loch Lochy, saw a superior force of Highlanders marching up the north side, in seven companies, with displayed banners, to intercept him at the head of the lake (Kin-Lochy), and there they met and fought.

Just after the commencement of the action the Frasers were joined, to the great grief of their chief, by his son, the Master, a youth of great promise, lately returned from being educated in France. It is said that he had been expressly charged by his father not to join this expedition, and had remained at home; but, roused by the taunts of his step-mother, Janet

Ross of Balnagowan, who wished to get rid of him, the gallant youth chose twelve trusty followers, and set out in search of his father and clan, whom he met at the head of Loch Lochy, in time to join in the fray.

The battle was almost the last, and certainly the bloodiest of the clan fights in the Highlands.

It began with the discharge of arrows at a distance, but when their shafts were spent, both parties rushed to close combat, and attacking each other furiously with their two-handed swords and axes, a dreadful slaughter ensued. Such was the heat of the weather, it being the month of July, that the combatants threw off their coats and fought till nightfall in their shirts, whence the battle-field received the name of "Blair-na-Leine," or the Field of Shirts. All the Frasers were killed, it is said, except James Fraser of Foyers, who was severely wounded and left for dead, and four common men.

The bodies of Lord Lovat, his son, the Master, and Ranald Galla, who had all fought with the utmost bravery, and only yielded to superior numbers, were a few days after the battle removed by a train of mourning relatives, and interred in the church of the priory of Beauly.*

For two hundred years, and down to 1746, the inscription over Hugh Lord Lovat's tomb was visible. "Hic jacet," so it is said it ran, "Hugo Dominus Fraser de Lovat, qui fortissime pugnans contra Reginaldcrios occubuit Julii 15, 1544."†

Bishop Reid was a great encourager of learning. We have seen what he did at Kinloss, we shall see what he did for Edinburgh. At Kirkwall he built St Olaus' Church and a large court of houses, to be a college for instructing the youth of that country in grammar and philosophy.‡

Honours and offices crowded upon this remarkable man; he seems especially to have been linked with the fortunes of the infant Queen Mary. She in 1548 was sent to France for her education, and he seems, from his previous visits there,

---

* Gregory's Highlands and Islands, 162.
† Anderson's Fraser Family, p. 81, quoting MS. in Adv. Lib., 220.
‡ Wallace's Orkney, p. 97.

well fitted for the offices he filled in relation to the royal person. In 1549 he became Lord President.*

In 1553 he must have resigned the abbacy of Kinloss in favour of his nephew, Walter Reid, as Smyth's Chronicle is as follows: On the 6th of April 1553, Walter Reid, Abbot of Kinloss, received the obedience of the monks, and on the 16th of the same month he received solemnly and honourably the episcopal blessing on his appointment as abbot in the monastery of Kinloss from Bishop Reid, in the presence of many noble men, as the Lairds of Innes, of Duffus, of Walterton, and Ochterellane.

His appointment doubtless included the priorate of Beauly, held by his uncle with the abbacy.

It is probable that the accustomed forms were gone through at Beauly also, and the pupils of Ferrarius were doubtless quite ready to elect the nephew of their patron to the headship of their house.

It seems doubtful whether Walter Reid was then of age; probably not, and his duties would be performed at Beauly by the sub-prior.

In 1554 Bishop Reid was appointed one of the curators of Queen Mary, and countersigned the infant queen's discharge to the Duke of Chatelherault.

In 1556 he was at Inverness with the queen regent.†

He placed his nephew, the abbot, Walter, under the tuition of Adam Elder, who had incurred the wrath of Ferrarius, but was employed by the bishop in the office of instructor of the novices both at Kinloss and Beauly; and about 1556 the tutor and his pupil were sent by the bishop to Paris, in order that the abbot might be instructed in Greek, Latin, and philosophy.

In December 1557 he was appointed one of the commissioners of the Estates of Scotland to go into France, and there negotiate the marriage of the young queen with the Dauphin.‡

---

* 24th Feb. 1549, Acta Dom. Conc.

† Gregory's Highlands and Islands, p. 186.

‡ Keith, Appendix XIX. The young queen signed the commission at the castle of Fontainebleau (*apud Castrum Fontes Bleaudi*).

Elder published in Paris in 1558 some chapter discourses, partly those delivered at Kinloss and Beauly, and partly composed at Paris, with a view to future delivery.

Among those not yet, I think, delivered, must be reckoned the one containing an address to his pupil, the abbot, and a eulogium on his patron, the bishop, which is printed by Dr Stuart in the "Records of Kinloss." * It contains allusions to the preacher having just resigned the office of pedagogue, or, as we would now call it, travelling tutor ; and it is quite clear that, between the period of his being made tutor at Paris, and his publishing these discourses, Elder had not returned to Scotland. The epistle dedicatory is dated the 1st January 1558.

The same year, 1558, Bishop Reid, now Lord President of the Court of Session, was despatched by the Estates of Scotland to France as one of their commissioners, to consent to the marriage-contract, and witness the marriage of Mary to the Dauphin on the 19th of April 1558.

There he would meet Abbot Walter, and his tutor, Adam Elder, and Walter would become acquainted with the rest of the commissioners, and particularly with the half-brother of the queen, James Stewart, afterwards the Regent, then Commendator of St Andrews, whom we find on the 28th of April 1558 signing with Bishop Robert Reid an address to the Dauphin.†

On his return Reid and the Earls of Cassillis and Rothes were all taken ill at Dieppe, and died there after a few days' illness, the bishop on the 6th September, the Earl of Rothes about two days after, the Earl of Cassillis on the 14th of the same month, ‡ not without suspicion of their patriotism causing their removal by poison.

Dr Mackenzie states that the bishop settled two considerable funds to be given yearly, the one for the maintenance of gentlemen's sons at the Universities of Aberdeen, St Andrews, and Glasgow, "that had good spirits," but had not whereupon

---

* Records of Kinloss, p. 69.
† Keith's History, Appendix, book xxxi., p. 21.
‡ Keith, book i., p. 65.

to prosecute their studies. The other was for the education of young gentlewomen who were left unprovided for by their parents.* I am especially bound to state, that to the liberality of Bishop Reid is owing the foundation of the University of Edinburgh. He left 8000 marks for that purpose, whereby the magistrates of Edinburgh were enabled in 1581 to purchase from the last provost of the Kirk of Field, the site where the first buildings of the university were afterwards erected.

To so great and good a Scotsman no monument or memorial was ever erected in his native land, and it was left to our day and to a foreign hand to mark his last resting-place by a simple inscription.†

It is difficult to leave so interesting a personage as Bishop Reid; and I believe my readers will excuse me for giving as a summary of his life and character, an extract from an article in the *Quarterly Review*, which bears intrinsic evidence from the knowledge, and still more the scholarly feeling and cultivated taste it displays, that it proceeded from the pen of Mr Cosmo Innes :

"Robert Reid, the son of a good gentleman, who fell at Flodden field, was one of a band of regular churchmen, zealously attached to the faith of their fathers, but no less zealous to purify it from error and superstition. With that view they laboured the reformation of the monastic houses; and, as a first step, tried to restore, by means of foreign teachers, the decayed learning of the Scotch cloister. Reid, at his own expense, brought over an Italian, who taught philosophy and the classics to the young monks and noviciates of his abbeys of

* Mackenzie's Scottish Writers, Edin. 1722, vol. iii., p. 27.

† In 1870 there was set up in St James's Church at Dieppe, under the superintendence of M. l'Abbé Cochet, inspector of historical monuments of the Seine Inferieure, a tablet in copper, which bears the following inscription : "To the memory of Robert Reid, Bishop of Orkney, President of the Scottish Parliament, Deputy-Commissary of Scotland at the marriage of the Queen Mary Stuart. Died at Dieppe, September 1558. Buried in the Chapel of St Andrew (commonly called Chapel of the Scots). Requiescat in Pace." The tablet is destined to perpetuate the remembrance of an historical fact, which was not known at Dieppe until M. l'Abbé Cochet brought it to light in an article which appeared in the *Vigie de Dieppe* in June 1870 (*Journal Officiel*).

Kynloss and Beaulieu in Moray, and has left a minute record of his prelections. Our abbot secured also the services of a foreign artist—*pictorem in arte sua egregium*—(antiquarian reader, his name was *Andreas Bairhum !*) to adorn not only the church of Kynloss, but the abbot's apartments, which last were done in fresco. He brought from France a gardener, who exercised his delightful art ungrudgingly for the benefit of the whole province as well as for the monastery. Moreover, he collected a great library at a time, be it remembered, when the books were MSS., or printed volumes almost as costly, and, with a fitting care for his collection, he built a vaulted fire-proof gallery at Kynloss for its reception. When promoted to the bishopric of Orkney (1541), his goodness found a wider field. He was frequently employed on distant embassies, and brought home splendid testimonials of the favour of foreign states and princes. He was made one of the judges of the newly-established Court of Session, and soon its president. Without neglecting his duties as a servant of the Crown, he was assiduous in his care of his diocese. He carried into those remote islands the same zeal for the Church and taste for the refinements of domestic life which had distinguished him when Abbot of Kynloss. He made sumptuous additions to the bishop's palace at Kirkwall, and to that venerable cathedral, still entire, for building which all Christendom is said to have paid a tax. He made a new foundation of the chapter, augmenting the number of prebendaries, and assigning ample funds for their maintenance. He built a college at Kirkwall for instructing the youth of his diocese in grammar and philosophy; and, amid all these cares of the good bishop, he found means to leave a munificent endowment for a projected college at Edinburgh. Than such a prelate, religious, learned, and fostering learning, loving the arts, and encouraging them, religion has no shape more dignified and amiable. If we view him, moreover, as the statesman, conversant with courts and the favourites of princes, carrying to those wild isles the manners and usages of civilised life, we may understand some part of the blessed influence such a bishop exercised over such a diocese" ("Ecclesiastical Antiquities of Scotland," *Quarterly Review*, vol. lxxii., p. 379, see pp. 393, 394).

But to return to the instrument we are illustrating.

The meeting summoned by it seems to have taken place, and the confirmation of the grant of the church lands and fishings of Kilmorack to have been conceded, for we find the next Bishop of Ross grants a charter of the Kirkton of Kilmorack to Alexander, Lord Lovat, in 1545.*

This was the son of the slaughtered Lord Hugh, by that Janet Ross of Balnagowan, who had hurried her stepson, the heir, to the battle of Kin-Lochy. Alexander succeeded on his father's and elder brother's death in that conflict. The family annalist says of him, "The charge of his lordship's education had been entrusted to Robert Reid, who lived in a style of great magnificence in Beauly, where he had built a mansion-house. Several young men of rank were under his paternal care at the same time."

How this may be is not clear, but it is certain that Alexander, Lord Lovat, received a better education than the other chiefs, his neighbours.

He was a "gentleman, clerklike," for among the signatures to the general bond of manrent to the Earl of Huntly at Elgin, 7th December 1544, he writes his name "Alexander Fraiser, Lord Lowet," whilst his neighbours, the chief of Mackenzie and the Chisholm, sign respectively, "Jhone Mackenzie of Kyntaill, with my hand on the pen, led by Mr William Gordon, notar," and "Johne Chislome of Cummyr, with my hand at the pen, led by the said Maister James, notar publick."†

Alexander, Lord Lovat, before 1555, married Janet, the daughter of Sir John Campbell of Cawdor. Ten years before the battle of Kin-Lochy (Blair-na-Leine), she had been contracted to marry the eldest grandson of Ewen Cameron of Lochiel. Two years after the battle Ewen Cameron's head was set over the gate of Elgin after he was tried and beheaded for the slaughter of Lord Lovat and his son. Somehow, his grandson, though he became chief of the clan in 1552, missed the wife that had been provided for him, and she became the wife of the son and brother of the avenged Lovats, and of the heir of the House which had sustained so heavy a loss at Lochiel's hands.

* Laing's Scottish Seals, vol. ii., p. 187.
† Spalding Club Miscellany, iv. 213.

In 1557 Lord Lovat chose the reverend father in God, Robert, Bishop of Orkney, as one of the arbiters in a question between himself and his mother, and in December of that year he died, universally regretted.

Before the date of the next document we print, the storm of the Scottish Reformation had begun; many ardent Reformers sincerely denounced the "friars as enemies to God's Gospel," * whilst the estates of the monasteries were naturally objects most attractive to the cupidity of those who cared little about the new doctrines: the example of England in monastic spoliation was contagious; there, in 1536, the lesser monasteries were suppressed, and the greater abbeys in 1539.

Bishop Reid, if he had lived, might have diverted the course of the monastic properties by securing, as Wolsey did, to some extent, a large appropriation towards the establishment of colleges and schools. The very year Reid died, friendly articles of reformation were proposed by the Scottish clergy themselves; and within six months after his death, in March 1559, a General Provincial Council was held of the Scottish bishops and clergy in the Dominican, or Black Friars', monastery at Edinburgh, amongst whose resolutions are provisions for the visitation of monasteries and nunneries, and for enforcing the canon, which enjoined that every monastery should send one or more monks to a university.

Prior Walter Reid, probably just after the death of his uncle, but at all events in 1558, returned to Scotland, and sat in the Parliament, assembled on the 29th November 1558, as the mitred Abbot of Kinloss.

Walter Reid was very likely one of those "young abbots, priors, deans, and beneficed men," mentioned by Bishop Lesley,† who, dreading or disliking the discipline of the Old Church, as promulgated by the canons of 1559, assisted at the overthrow of the Catholic religion.

It appears that he was the general legatee and executor of

* See in Keith, p. 65, declaration signed 16th March 1557-8, by (amongst others) James Stewart.
† Bp. Lesley's Hist. of Scotland, p. 271.

Bishop Reid; and it is notorious that the payment of the bishop's bequest of 8000 marks, to found a college at Edinburgh, was long deferred by Abbot Walter.*

The acquaintance he must have formed in Paris with the future Regent, then, like himself, an ecclesiastic, probably led to his being selected to take a principal part in the changes that followed. As Abbot of Kinloss and lord of Parliament, Walter Reid, in 1560, was appointed one of the lords of the articles, and concurred in framing the famous Act of 24th August 1560, forbidding the celebration of the mass. His signature stands high in the list appended to the Solemn League and Covenant in 1560.

On 10th February 1561, he, acting as Abbot of Kinloss, showed his complete adoption of the principle of the Scottish Reformation by, at one and the same moment, sanctioning the marriage of churchmen and alienating the property of the Church, for he then commenced the dilapidation of Kinloss by giving the lands of West Grange, part of its possessions, to his sister, on her marriage with Alexander Dunbar, the Sub-chanter, and afterwards Dean of Moray.† Walter himself, abbot and prior though he was, carried out his principles with a will, and afterwards married Margaret Collace, a daughter of the House of Balnamon.

Spottiswoode, and Keith and Robertson ‡ on the authority of Spottiswoode, tell us that, in May 1561, the Convention of

* "It [the University of Edinburgh] originated in a bequest made in 1558 by Reid, Bishop of Orkney, to the town council of Edinburgh, for the erection of a college. The money was at first retained by the Abbot of Kinloss. After a delay of five years, the council, on the faith of ultimately obtaining the bequest, purchased part of the present site of the university. Queen Mary lent her assistance, granting a charter of presentation to some confiscated church property; but building was not commenced till 1581. In the following year, King James VI. incorporated the university by royal charter, increasing the grants of Queen Mary" (Edinburgh Almanac, 1876, p. 738).

† Records of Kinloss, pref. lxx. I ought, in justice to Walter's conduct as executor of his uncle, to mention that there is also secured to his sister, on her marriage, "the one thousand merks, the quhilke the said Katherine hes, *siller in her awne hand*, left to tocher be ane reverend fader in God umquhile Robert, Bischopp of Orkney, her fader brither."

‡ Spottiswoode, p. 174; Keith, p. 503; Robertson, ed. 1821, vol. ii., p. 46.

Estates, considering every religious fabric as a relic of idolatry, passed sentence upon them by an act in form; and that persons the most remarkable for the activity of their zeal were appointed to put it in execution: James Stewart, the Prior of St Andrews, was to put it in force in the north. "Abbeys, cathedrals, churches, libraries, records, and even the sepulchres of the dead, perished in one common ruin."

This Act of Convention has never been printed, nor is it known to exist; and certain it is that the Prior of St Andrews did not put it in force in the dioceses of Moray or Ross, and I doubt its ever having been formally passed.

On the 19th August 1561, Queen Mary, at the age of nineteen, returned to Scotland. That same year, in December, a Convention of Estates was held.

A great majority of abbots, priors, and other heads of religious houses, had, with Walter Reid, changed their religion, but retained their offices and emoluments. The Convention proposed, and the queen in council ordained, in February 1561-2, that an exact account of the ecclesiastical benefices throughout the kingdom should be taken, and commissioners were appointed for that purpose. The present incumbents, to whichever party they belonged, were allowed to retain possession: two-thirds of the whole revenue were reserved for their use, the remaining third, called the Assumption of thirds, was annexed to the Crown; and out of this the queen undertook to assign a sufficient maintenance for the Protestant clergy.

The queen visited Inverness in September 1562, but she did not pay that visit to Beauly, to which we have alluded, at that time. "From Stirling," writes Randolph to Cecil, "she taketh her journey as far north as Inverness, the furthest part of Murray; a terrible journey both for horse and man; the countries are so poor, and the victuals so scarce." *

Mr Chalmers, in his "Life of Mary," gives, from a diary of the places where she dined and slept, the houses where she passed each day; and I can discover no trace of her having gone

* Chalmers's Q. Mary, vol. i., p. 77.

beyond Inverness. By the kindness of Mr David Laing, I have printed an abstract of the diary, found among Mr Chalmers's papers.* The diary itself, though stated by Mr Chalmers to be in his library, is missing.

She left Old Aberdeen on 1st September, and her sleeping places were as follows: Buchan, 1st September; Grange, 2d; Balveny Castle, 3d; Elgin, 4th-7th; Kinloss Abbey, 8th; Darnaway Castle,† 9th and 10th, holding a Privy Council there on the 10th; on the morning of the 11th, she goes to Inverness; she slept that night in the town,‡ but in that night the castle of Inverness was taken by her troops, and its captain, Alexander Gordon, who presumed to hold it out for the Earl of Huntly, was hanged next morning: she slept at Inverness, but whether in the castle or the town does not appear, 12th, 13th, 14th; and on the 15th she went to Kilravock Castle,§ and slept there; Darnaway Castle, 16th; Spynie Palace, the seat of the Bishop of Moray, 17th and 18th; Cullen, 19th; Shire Town (Banff), 20th; Gight, 21st; and returned to Aberdeen on 22d September—all performed on horseback by a young lady of twenty. ‖

The adhesion of Abbot Reid to the Reformed party doubtless preserved the Abbey of Kinloss from being rabbled, and enabled him to offer the use of it to her Majesty.

Meanwhile the commissioners appointed by the Act 1561 for taking an account of the revenues of the Scottish Church

* Appendix, No. XXVI.

† Randolph says, "The place called Tarnway was ruinous, saving *the House*, which is very fair and large, built like many that I have seen in England" (Chalm., i. 304).

‡ Tradition says it was in a house at the end of the bridge.

§ The abstract of the diary says Quittra, whilst Mr Chalmers himself (vol. i., p. 86) says Kilravock. Kilravock Castle had been just enlarged by the Black Baron of Kilravock, who built, in 1552, a manor-place beside his narrow old tower (Innes's Family of Kilravock, p. 209). He was an important personage, Justice-Depute in that quarter, and receives, both from Queen Mary and from her brother, letters, dated at Aberdeen, on their return from the north in October 1562; but Mr Innes, although he prints these letters, does not allude to the queen's visit to the castle.

‖ Randolph must have found out now that it was not "a sick, crazed woman" he had to deal with (Robertson, vol. iii., p. 279).

were not idle, and we have the results of their inquiry into the possessions of the Priory of Beauly.

We find the following account in the appendix to Keith's "Church History" as from the collector's books of the thirds in the Laigh Parliament House, dated 1562:

"*Reformed Cistercian Priory of Beauly in the Shire of Ross.*— Money, £136, 13s. 4d. Bear, 14c. 2b. 3f. 3½p. Oats, 7b. 3f. 3½p. Mairts, n. 10. Muttons, n. 20. Poultry, 21 doz.* Salmon, 2 lasts 6 barrels."

We shall afterwards give the actual return to the controller, but it may be desirable just to ascertain the actual value of this income.

The high estate of the Scottish coinage had grievously fallen since John Byset's time, and in 1567 the pound weight of silver was coined into £18 Scots; but this depreciation of the coin made no difference, except in intercourse with foreign countries, as the prices of food at home were in the same currency.

In the same collector's books we have the converted prices thus: Mairts of Aberdeen, £2, 13s. 4d. the piece; ditto of Beauly, £2 the piece; ditto of Orkney, £1, 6s. 8d. Muttons of Aberdeen, nine shillings the piece; ditto of Kinloss, six shillings the piece. Poultry of Aberdeen, four shillings the dozen. So that the money rent of £136, 13s. 4d. would represent at Beauly seventy head of cattle; not that this was the market price, but the customary equivalent. In the bishopric of Brechin, salmon let for £1 a barrel, and in the bishopric of Aberdeen, £4 a barrel.

Keith, writing in 1734, says that in 1587 £100 went as far as £700 now; but surely the effect of the discovery of America was so far exhibited in 1587 as to make this statement exaggerated.

* Keith puts the poultry thus: "C., 21 doz.; S., 24 d.," explaining below that C. means the collector's books of the thirds in the Laigh Parliament House, 1562, and S., the book of assignation, 1594. The S. puzzled Maitland, who, in his "History of Scotland," p. 258, says: "24 dozen of S.; what is meant by 'S.' I know not, unless it be *scrafish !*"

We shall now give the actual return of the collector of thirds to the controller:

"THE RENTALL OF THE PRIORIE OF BOWLYNE, baith of the maillis, silver, fearmis, teindis, martis, wedderis, and utheris dewties, as efter followis: The rentall of silver—Item, in primis the silver maill of the barronie of Bewlyne, with the maynis of the samin, extendis to lxi lib.—Item, the kirkis of Convith and Cumer sould pay in silver in the yeir the sowme of xxxiii lib.—Item, the kirk of Abirtarf sould pay in silver the sowme of xlii lib.—Summa of the haill silver in maillis and teindis extendis to i⁰ xxxvi lib. xiiis. iiiid. The rentall of the victuall of the said pryorie—Item, in the haill victuall of the barronie of Bowlyne, with the maynis of the samin, extendis to iiii ch. victuall.—Item, the kirkis of Conveith and Cummer in victuale extendis to vii ch. xi bs.—Item, the twa mylnes of Bowlyne sett for ii ch. viii bs. meill and malt.—Summa of the haill victuall extendis to xiiii ch. iiii bs. victuale. The rentall of aites—Item, the haill aitis of the said baronie, viii bs. The mairtis—Item in mairtis, x mairtis. The muttoun—Item in wedderis, xx wedderis. Item in pultrie, xxi dussane. As for the fishing of Bowlyne, it is vncertane, sumtyms les, sumtymis mair, and vther tyms verie lytill; and thir twa yeiris bygane hes scarslie giwin ii last vi barreillis. And sua the haill priorie of Bewlyn extendis yeirlie in silver, victuale, and wedderis, aitis, mairtis, pultrie, and salmond, as efter followis: Summa of the silver, i⁰ xxxvi lib. xiiis. iiiid. Summa of the victuall, xiiii ch. iiii bs. victuale. Summa of the haill aitis, viii bs. Summa of mairtis, x mairtis. Summa of wedderis, xx wedderis. Summa of pultrie, xxi dosan. Summa of salmond, ii last vi b. Thir ar the thingis that are to be deducit of the money, salmond, and victuallis, aboue specifeit, payit as efter followis: Item in primis to be deducit be payment maid to the aucht brethir for their habit silver, ilk bredir havand in the yeir xls., quhilk extendis to xvi lib. Item, thair is to be deducit for the said viii brethir for thair flesh and fish in the yeir, ilk brother havand for thair flesh iiid. in the day, for thair fish ilk day, iid., extending in the yeir to xxix lib. xiiiis. viiid. Item, for the Lordis of the Seit contributioun yeirlie, iiii lib. iiiis. Item, Master Alexander McKenzie, for his yeirlie pensioun quhilk he has of the said pryorie, and provydit thairof in Roome, xiii lib. vis. viiid. Item, to the officiar of Bowlyne, yeirlie, for his fie, quhilk he hes dureing his lyftyme, xxvs. viiid.

Item, thair is to be deducit for the said aucht bretheris drink in the yeir, v ch. xii bs. victuale. Item, for thair breid in the yeir, lvii bs. iii fir. i pc. Item, for the officiaris fie, i b. Item, thair is to be deducit for officiaris fie, i b. Item, thair is to be deducit for the teind-fish of the kirk of Warlaw, iii bs. 3 barrell salmond—summa of the haill victuallis and salmond, deducit as is abouc written, extendis to lxiiii lib. xiiis. of silver, and x ch. x bs. iii fir. i p. victuale, iii bs. 3 b. salmond; and sua restis to the prior lxxii lib. xvid., iii ch. iii bs. iii pc. victuale, and of salmond, ii last ii b. ½ b. salmond. Memorandum, that the kirk of Conveith was wont to pay for the vicarage thairof the sowme of xxvii lib. xiiis. iiiid., and now gettis na payment of the samin.

"W., Abbot of Kinloss.

"Memorandum, to tak the salmond, the thrid, not as it is rental-lit, bot as it givis, for this rental is manchlitt. Remember, my Lord Comptrollar, and speir the rental of thir twa, Kinlos and Bewlyne, for they are suspitious anent the fishing."

This rental we print from the "Origines Parochiales Scotiæ;" it is there given as from the Book of Assumptions, but it does not appear in that record in the Register House.* The concluding paragraph seems to have been repeated in the rental of the Abbey of Kinloss, which has this conclusion:

"OUT OF THE FISCHEING OF BEWLIE,

Remember, my Lord Comptrollare, to speir the rentall of thir twa Kinlos and Bewlie, better, for thay ar suspitious anent the fische-ingis." †

Let us examine this account in detail.

We see now how the rental given by Keith is made up: of

* Per Mr Walter Macleod.

† Records of Kinloss, p. 163. The suspicions which the collector had as to the correctness of the returns as to the salmon fishing do not appear to be well founded. The fishings of the Beauly and of the Findhorn were probably then "vncertane," as they now are. The quantities of salmon and grilse caught on Burghead and Roseisle fishings in the Findhorn district in 1861 and 1862 were 10 tons 16 cwt. and 19 tons 19 cwt. respectively; so in 1867, 9 tons 17 cwt.; in 1868, 16 tons 17 cwt. (Scotch Salmon Fishery Inquiry Report, 1871, app. p. 99). So at Beauly, from 1839 to 1848, there were 14,639 salmon and 42,152 grilse, whilst from 1809 to 1818 it was, salmon, 30,823, and grilse, 54,352 (Lords' Report on Salmon Fisheries (Scotland) Act, 1860; Evid. 1201, 1202).

the £136, 13s. 4d., the money rent (silver maill) of the lands of the barony of Beauly was £61 ; the churches of Conveth and Comar paid £33, and the church of Abertarff £42 ; as the rental is said to be made up of rent and tithes (*maillis* and *teindis*), we may suppose that the money payments from the churches were either rents or compositions for the tithes in kind, and not rents for the glebe lands of those churches.

The payments in grain include payments from the churches of Conveth and Comar, which were probably in respect of the glebe lands of those churches, but there are none in respect of Abertarff.

Conveth, or Conway, we have seen, was an ancient parish, existing in 1221 (*supra*, p. 22). Out of it was taken, in 1226, the parish of Kiltarlity (*supra*, p. 24) ; the patronage of Conveth belonged, in 1258, to John Byset the younger, the son of our Founder; and between that date and 1274 it had probably been granted to the monks of Beauly, who, before 1274, had endowed a vicar there, with a stipend of five marks and a half—or £11 of our coinage, with silver at 60s. a pound— each mark being two-thirds of a pound of silver (*supra*, p. 53).

The rental informs us that this stipend had been increased to £27, 13s. 4d. (with silver at 360s. a pound, it is more correct to say reduced) ; for it states that the Kirk of Conveth was wont to pay for the vicarage thereof, £27, 13s. 4d., but now [the vicarage] gets no payment of the same. We shall see that this was speedily remedied.

The church of Conveth was dedicated, it would seem, to St Lawrence*—its ruins still remain in the valley of Glenconveth. The notion that these are the ruins of a nunnery is incorrect, though it has the authority of the valuable "Guide" of Messrs Anderson. "Glenconveth," say they, "takes its name from a nunnery, the foundations of which, in the centre of the valley, are still visible."†

This is the first occasion where we have explicit mention of the church of Comar. This church of Comar must have

---

* Ancient Church of Scotland, p. 291.
† Anderson's Guide to the Highlands, ed. 1842, p. 524.

been endowed in the parish of Conveth, after the parish of Kiltarlity had been taken out of Conveth; and not only after 1275, when the very careful Taxation of Boiamond discloses no mention of the church of Comar, but after 1350, when the church and vicarage of Conway are mentioned, but no church of Comar.*

Comar had an endowment in land; for we find the kirk land of Comar mentioned in 1576, and for this it was probably indebted to the Fentons, as in 1416 they had not only the lands of Comar-Kirktown but also all the other Byset lands, lying on the south side of the Glass, in the old parish of Conveth, viz., the davochs of Guisachan and Buntait.†

The monks of Beauly must have concurred in this good work of erecting a church at Comar, and thus providing a resident minister for the upper portion of Strathglass; and they must have arranged that the chaplain who served the church of Comar should have a portion of the vicarial tithes of Conveth. At the same time it is difficult to understand how the church of Comar could have had any land, which, after its endowment, became the property of the Priory of Beauly.

The church of Comar was founded before 1416, because the lands round it had by that time acquired the title of Comar-Kirktown, and were granted under that name, by William de Fenton, in the marriage-contract of his sister, as we have seen (*supra*, p. 96). It must have been founded by one of those Williams de Fenton, who appear in 1359, 1384, and 1403 (*supra*, pp. 88, 92, 95). William de Fenton of 1359 must have been the same person with the William de Fenton who endowed the chaplain of Baky with land;‡ and it is likely he also endowed the chaplain of Comar—"the liberal deviseth liberal things."

This church, in 1576, is dealt with as a parish church, but it was probably only a parochial chapelry. A district out of

---

* Reg. Moray, p. 305.   † *Supra*, p. 23.
‡ *Supra*, p. 76. This endowment of Baky was confirmed by King David II. in 1362, and dated in 1361 (Reg. Mag. Sig., 25).

the parish of Conveth was probably attached to it, and naturally Guisachan and Buntait, which with Comar-Kirktown are conveyed in 1416, would form parts of this district. The inhabitants of this district would have the rights of baptism and sepulture at the parochial chapel of Comar, whose minister would be the parochial chaplain, nominated by the vicar of Conveth, or nominated by the Fentons and their successors, with his approval.

No entry is made in the lists of procurations and synodals of the church of Comar. The church of Conway pays the same procurations and synodals in 1350 and 1400, and no mention is made of any payment by the vicar of Conway or the church of Comar.

Procurations were the sums paid to the bishop on his visitations, and were the substitute for the expenses originally incurred by each parish, of entertaining him and his suite on those occasions. They were also payable to an archdeacon or rural dean, if such dignitary had the right of visitation, which does not appear to have been the case in the province of Moray. Synodals were the payments made by the clergy who attended the synods or diocesan meetings at the cathedral, the metropolitan church of the province. The vicar of Conway and the parochial chaplain of Comar, if bound to appear at visitations, which the zeal of the visitor seldom extended to each separate church, had no payment to make, their liabilities, in that respect, being covered by the payment made by the priory, as representing the rectory of the mother church of Conway; and I doubt whether these stipendiaries were entitled to appear at synods of the clergy, in the province of Moray.*

The church of Abertarff is the other church which was appropriated to our priory. The omission of any grain rent from the church of Abertarff is explained by the circumstance that the church of Abertarff had no glebe land belonging to it, at the time of its appropriation to Beauly, by

* Amongst the clergy who concurred with the Bishop of Ross, in the release to the Bishop of Moray in 1227, are vicars (*supra*, p. 199).

our Charter No. II. (*supra*, p. 33). The arrangement we referred to (*supra*, p. 34), as taking place between the Bishop of Moray and Thomas de Thirlestane in 1225, deprived the church of its glebe. It was then agreed that the half davoch of land, which the Bishop of Moray asserted to belong to the church of Abertarff, should be given up to Thomas de Thirlestane and his heirs, except one full toft and croft for the church of Abertarff and every rector of it. This toft and croft was no doubt given up by the priory to the vicar, on their endowment of the vicarage of Abertarff, between the appropriation and 1274.

Let us trace the history of these three parishes a little further down.

In 1567 an Act was passed that "the haill thirds of the haill benefices of this realm sall now instantlie, and in all times to come, first be paid to the ministers."*

A commission, called a Commission of Plat, was appointed to carry these provisions into effect.

We have among the items of the Inventory of 1651:

"55. A tack of the teind sheaves of the parish of Conveth, by the Abbot of Kinloss to Lord Lovat for nineteen years."

"74. A tack, by the Abbot of Kinloss to Hugh, Lord Lovat, of the lands of Conveth for nineteen years."

These leases are probably by Abbot Walter, and that of the

---

* 1567, c. 10. In the same session an Act—1567, c. 12—was passed, by which provostries and prebends of collegiate churches, altarages, and chaplainships were reserved to patrons, in order that they might present to such benefices bursars or poor students, at such university as the patrons chose to name. This is the only legislative provision for advancing education and learning out of the Church revenues. It was exercised by King James VI. by devoting chaplaincies belonging of old in common to the canons of Ross to entertainment at the university of young students. One of these, Thomas Davidson, the son of Patrick Davidson, Ross Herald in 1574, was to be received under the care and discipline of the principal master of Sanct Leonardis College, within the University of Sanctandrois. In 1586 another Thomas Davidson gets a chaplaincy—Saint Lawrence in Ardefaill, perhaps the chapel of Allangrange (*supra*, p. 82)—to entertain him, being a bursar in the College of Cambridge, in England, at the said college, for his better education, in vertew and guid lettres (O. P. S., "Rosemarkie," 584, 585).

teind sheaves, probably the instrument to which the seal is attached (*supra*, p. 170), being a tack of the teinds of Conveth to Hugh, Lord Fraser of Lovat, by Walter Reid, Abbot of Kinloss and Prior of Beauly, A.D. 1571. Though granted for nineteen years only, they were no doubt usually renewed upon favourable terms.

In 1573 the clergy were promised by the Regent Morton that the stipend of each parish should be paid out of its own tithes, and under the Commission of Plat the stipends were modified in 1574.

We have the modification in 1576 of the stipends to the churches of Conveth, Comar, and Abertarff, as follows:

"*Conveth.*—Mr John Fraser, minister. His stipend, the haill tua pairt of the priourie of Beauly, newlie providit to him.

"   Reidar at Conveth. His stipend, xx merkis, with the kirkland, to be payit out of the thrid of the Priorie of Bewlie, etc.

"*Cummer.*—   Reider at Cummer. His stipend, xx merks, with the kirkland, etc.

"*Abertharff.*—James Duff, minister. His stipend, lxx li., and the kirkland of Boleskine, quhairof he is parsone."*

The incumbent must have been the Prior of Beauly at the passing of the order in Council of 1561, and also of the Act of 1567, and as Fraser gets the two-thirds of the benefice, which, by the order in Council of 18th February 1561, was reserved to the incumbent, he has the prior's rights. James Duff or Dow is entered in the register before, under Dores (Durris):

"*Durris—Boleskine—Abertharff.*—James Duff, exhorter, xx li., and xx li. mair for Abirtarff, sen November 1569.

"*Durris—Boleskin.*—James Duff, Reidar, xx li."

In 1581 an Act of Parliament, c. 100, was passed, that every parish should have its own minister, and c. 101 was passed prohibiting any dilapidation by grants of tithes.

In 1617 an Act passed enabling the Commissioners of Plat

* Register of Ministers, Maitland Club, p. 65.

to modify entirely out of the teinds of the parishes a perpetual local stipend, which should override the grants of tithes to the Lords of Erection, and all other laymen who had received grants of tithes. The provision was not very luxurious: 500 marks was the minimum stipend (£27, 15s. 6d. sterling). In order, however, to compensate the lessees of tithes, power was given to the commissioners to prorogate or extend their leases if they were compelled to pay more stipend than the amount of the reserved rent.*

The nineteen years' lease of the corn tithes of Conveth, by Abbot Walter Reid to Hugh, Lord Lovat, expiring in October 1576, Mr John Fraser, Prior of Beauly, on 13th October 1576, granted a lease of those tithes to Simon Fraser, Master of Lovat,† at a rent of 80 marks, for his and his heirs' lives, and for nineteen years after.‡ He also granted a similar lease of the vicarage teinds of Conveth.

On the same day a tack of the teind sheaves of Abertarff was granted by the same John Fraser, Prior of Beauly, to the same Master of Lovat, for the same term, at the rent of 63 marks.§

* Archbishop Spottiswoode says: " For what augmentation soever was granted, the same was recompensed to the givers by prorogation of their former leases for a number of years, and thereby the Church more damnified than bettered " (p. 364). The archbishop was, I conceive, much mistaken ; the Act of 1617 is the Bill of Rights of the Kirk of Scotland ; the principle that the first charge on the tithes was the maintenance of the clergy was by it clearly established, and to the Church it was matter of indifference who got the surplus, whether the tacksman, or the Crown, or its grantees ; and the rule thus laid down in 1617 was adhered to, when, in 1690, all teinds not previously granted away were given to the patron ; the obligation of providing for the minister was then again expressed, whilst the tacks granted after 1617 generally contained a clause, throwing the burden of augmentations on the tacksman, so that there was no room for any claim of prorogation. The enforcing the principle of maintaining the parish minister out of the parish tithes, coupled with the provisions for valuing or commuting the tithes introduced by Charles I., has made the average endowment of the parish minister in Scotland more advantageous to himself and less burdensome to the people than in England, where the condition of Vicars and perpetual Curates has been the shame of the Church, and their right to a maintenance out of the great tithes appropriated by the monasteries persistently denied.

† He was then four years old.

‡ Appendix, No. XXVII. § Appendix, No. XXVII.

Shaw says, "James Dow, vicar, sold the vicarage of Abertarff to the Tutor of Lovate about the year 1570; and, for want of a living, Abertarff was annexed to Boleskine."* There was no Tutor of Lovat in 1570, nor till 1577, but Shaw may have been informed of the tack which was made by the vicar of Abertarff of his teinds, on 31st March 1580, to Thomas Fraser of Strichen, then tutor of Simon, Lord Lovat.†

The commissioners had other powers which they exercised too freely. They had the power of uniting parishes. Calderwood says:‡ "They united sometimes two, sometimes three, kirks into one. The bishops consented to these unions to currie the favour of noblemen and gentlemen, or for gaine, for by these unions multiplication of stipends was spared."

Short as the operations of this commission were, and few as were the decrees pronounced by them, unfortunately, among the small number of parishes whose stipends were awarded throughout Scotland, were included the seven parishes which we have seen so nearly connected with the Priory of Beauly—Abertarff, Boleskine, Fearnua, Kirkhill, Kiltarlity, Conveth, and Comar.

Scant justice was done to the claims of the clergy and the people, and at the instance of Simon, Lord Lovat, § who had acquired leases of the tithes of all these seven parishes, and the rights of the Priory of Beauly over Abertarff, Conveth, and Comar, the seven parishes were reduced to three.

Boleskine was a parsonage, that is, a parish where the rights of the rector to the whole of the endowment of the benefice, glebe as well as tithes, and tithes great and small, remained in full force, not diminished by episcopal or capitular or monastic usurpation. It was in the patronage of the Bishop of Moray, and was included in the grant of patronages of that bishopric to Lord Spynie by James VI. in 1590,‖ the land of Boleskine being part of the episcopal barony of Kilmylies.

---

* Shaw's Moray, p. 363.   † Anderson's Family of Fraser, p. 178.
‡ Calderwood's History, p. 697.
§ It should be mentioned that he exercised "unbounded hospitality."
‖ Forsyth's Moray, p. 90.

The patronage of Abertarff belonged to the Priory of Beauly, but it was only a vicarage, as appears from the extracts already given.

In 1569 the vicarage of Abertarff was held by the parson of Boleskine, James Dubh (Dhu) or Dow, and he appears to have been also appointed exhorter and reader at Durris, the parish at the north end of Loch Ness, which belonged to the cell of Urquhart (*supra*, p. 135).

This temporary joint holding of Abertarff and Boleskine was made perpetual on 14th July 1618, and the lease to Lord Lovat extended for 101 years after its expiration (as events happened, till 1766), though the permanent union of the parishes was most injudicious, " there being a hill seven miles long intervening between the inhabited districts of the two parishes, and the greater part of the intervening space being, from its height, frequently impassable in winter." †

The uniting of Fearnua and Wardlaw was effected on 14th July 1618, so that instead of two ministers—one for each parish, and each with the legal salary—one only was allowed for the two parishes.

But the worst case was the union of Comar and Conveth and Kiltarlity, and the destruction of the pious work of the founder of Beauly Priory. Comar was the upper part of Strathglass, on one side of the river only indeed, but stretching up and including Guisachan, and some twenty miles above the church of Kiltarlity; Conveth was separated from Comar by high hills, and stretches away to Glenurquhart; three ministers with three stipends then existed. We have quoted from the register for 1576 the names and provisions for the ministers at Conveth and Comar—we have also this entry in the register : ‡

"*Kintallartie.*—Johnne Wricht, reidare at Kintallartie. His stipend, the haill vicarage," § etc.

---

* Appendix, No. XXVIII.
† New Stat. Acct., "Inverness-shire," p. 91.
‡ Register of Ministers, Maitland Club, p. 94.
§ This is the only notice of the vicarage of Kiltarlity (*supra*, p. 26).

But three ministers' stipends were too great a burden, and so on the 3d July 1618,* these three parishes were united, and one stipend of 520 marks provided for one minister.

The result of this forced abolition of what would have been so many strongholds of the Reformed religion was, as might have been expected, that the ancient faith still kept its hold on the people, whose right to have a teacher of religion provided for them, and maintained out of the tenth of the produce of their labour, was so rudely violated.

Abertarff and Strathglass, left to their own voluntary efforts, adhered to the Catholic faith. Shaw speaks of the large number of Catholics in those districts in his time. A missionary since 1739, supported from the royal bounty, at Fort Augustus, still supplies the place of the parish minister of Abertarff, who had there a pleasant glebe and ancient church; and the writer of the "Statistical Account," in 1831, states that the number of Papists in that parish is 318,† the whole population being 1873. "The mission of Strathglass," says the minister of Kiltarlity in 1841, "has a district, nearly one-half of the population of which belongs to the Roman Catholic faith;"‡ but the missionary, with his three preaching places, could not occupy the position of the resident incumbent of Comar.

Nor was this all. The Act of 1696, establishing schools in Scotland, took for its stand-point the parish, and appointed that there should be one school in every parish supported by the heritors. Such a provision was a delusion for parishes like the united parishes of Abertarff and Boleskine, and of Conveth, Comar, and Kiltarlity; and the first school established by voluntary efforts in the province of Moray, that of the Christian Knowledge Society, was placed in Stratherrick in 1708, whilst the upper portions of the modern parish of Kiltarlity have been supplied with the means of education from voluntary efforts mainly, until the evil in this respect of the work of the Plat in 1618, demanded and obtained in 1870 a legislative remedy.

* Appendix, No. XXVIII.   † Stat. Acct., "Inverness-shire," p. 62.
‡ *Id.*, p. 500.

The rental being stated, the next items are the deductions from the rental before the thirds were to be calculated.

These deductions throw a good deal of light on the state of matters in the priory.

The first deductions are the payments to be made to the brethren of the house.

There were eight monks who each received 40s. a-year for habit-silver or clothes-money. Their garments were of wool, no linen, and consisted only of a close-fitting gown, resembling the modern cassock, and a tippet or scarf, with a cloak, when they went out of doors, and sandals. No shirt, no drawers, no stockings. We may compare their dress with their neighbours. At Kinloss, which was a Cistercian house, with a costume almost the same as the Valliscaulians, the allowance was 50s. a-year for their habit-silver.

Each monk at Beauly had, for his flesh meat, 3d. a-day, and for his fish, 2d. a-day. The more luxurious Kinloss monk had 8d. a-day for meat, but the same daily (2d.) for fish. This rate of payment must have assumed as many fasting days almost as Viard prescribed, considering that the pound of silver was then coined into £18, each penny being only the sixth of a penny sterling. The allowance for bread is given as a yearly allowance: at Beauly, for all the monks—at Kinloss, for each monk, of so many bolls, firlots, and pecks, of bear and oats. The delicate habit of allowing the monks of Kinloss white bread was introduced about 1500 by Abbot Thomas Chrystal, who gave them 32 ounces of wheaten bread each daily, instead of oatcake;* but no provision for continuing this seems to have been made.

They lived on their allowances in kind: cakes of bear and oatmeal for bread; bear malted and brewed for drink; their allowance for drink exceeded that for bread.† Such luxuries as the Kinloss brethren had a slender provision for

---

* "Mos fuit ante, lato pane, hoc est lagano ex avenis ad ignem super laganario formato monachos vesci" (Ferrarius in Hist. of Kinloss, p. 29).

† The hospitable Lord Simon expended an equal quantity of meal and malt, seven bolls of each per week (Anderson, p. 102).

—of £12 among thirteen monks, to supply fire, butter, candle, spice, and Lenten meat—were not allowed to the inmates of Beauly, but they had their fine old gardens to make up the deficiency of their allowances.

The contribution for " the Lordes of the Seit," yearly £4, 4s., is the same kind of payment as was made out of the revenues of the Abbey of Fearn to the College of Justice.* The expression, " Lords of the Seit," became afterwards the present form " Lords of Session."†

Bishop Reid, as we have seen, was one of the first Senators of the College, and he doubtless assisted the king as much as he could in getting the tax on ecclesiastical benefices for the support of the College agreed to by the Pope, and confirmed by the General Provincial Council at Edinburgh in 1536. Among the prelates of the Church, the archbishops, bishops, abbots, priors, and prioresses, who contribute to the tax, we find " the Priour of Bewling, iv li. ivs."‡ The sister Priories of Pluscardine and Ardchattan are rated—Pluscardine at £17, 4s., and Ardchattan (Ardquhottarne) at £4, 4s.—showing something of the same relative proportion of property to each priory as existed at Boiamond's Taxation, three hundred years before.

The yearly pension to Mr Alexander Mackenzie, which was provided to him in Rome, is an instance of the then recent usurpation of power over monastic revenues assumed by the Pope, who gave pensions out of them.

The officiar of the priory was the ground officer. Beauly does not seem to have been burdened with a bailie until afterwards. The bailie or steward was an important person. The office was often held by a neighbouring proprietor. Thus at Fearn, Ross of Balnagowan was bailie of the abbey ; § and at Kinloss the Laird of Grant was the bailie, with Cumming of Altyre for his bailie-depute. The fee of the bailie of Kinloss was £14, 6s. 8d., whilst that of the officiar was in

* O. P. S., vol. ii., part ii., p. 438, "Tarbet in Ross-shire."
† In Act 1543, c. 9, a pension is mentioned to "the Seit of Sessioune and College of Justice."
‡ Miscellany of the Bannatyne Club, vol. ii., pp. 51, 53.
§ O. P. S., vol. ii., part ii., p. 437.

money, £1, 6s. 8d., but a boll a-month for his bread and drink, his less fortunate brother in our priory only getting a boll in the year.

The last deduction is for the teind fish of the kirk of Wardlaw.

In 1221, as we have seen (*supra*, p. 22), our founder, John Byset, released to the Bishop of Moray the advowson of the church of Dunballoch. The bishop immediately established a vicar there; and when the parish of Fearnua was taken out of Dunballoch, and the site of the church was changed from Dunballoch to St Mary's Hill or Wardlaw, this vicar became the vicar of Wardlaw (*supra*, p. 26). The vicar of Wardlaw was a witness to the promulgation of the Nuncio's letter in 1532.

The tithe of fish was a vicarage tithe,* and the person entitled to the tithe of fish in the parish of Wardlaw was the vicar of Wardlaw, who, being a resident minister, would perhaps not have leased it, but received it in kind.

The circumstance that the only deduction in respect of tithe fish is that payable to the church of Wardlaw is remarkable, because Wardlaw had only the half of the river from Dunballoch to the sea; the other half, being in the parish of Kilmorack, would be tithable to the vicar of Kilmorack.

It would seem, however, that the vicar of Kilmorack had been negligent in asserting his rights to tithe of fish against Beauly Priory; for when the Bishop of Ross became entitled to the rights of the chantry of Ross in the church of Kilmorack, he, in 1636, raised an action against Lord Lovat, for the tithes of fish in the Beauly, which Lord Lovat could only and successfully defend, by borrowing the tack of the vicarage teinds of Kilmorack, prorogated in 1618.†

The vicarage of Wardlaw and the parochial chaplaincy of Fearnua were still separate benefices; and as to Fearnua, there is this entry in the Register of Ministers, 1576:‡

* Teind-fish were found to appertain to the vicar of the parish, Haddington, 5th July 1610.
† Chisholm MSS.
‡ Register of Ministers, Maitland Club.

"*Fernway.*—Andro Makphaill, minister. His stipend the haill common kirk of Fernway, extending to xi li. vis. viiid."

The great tithes of Wardlaw were leased on the 10th of June 1585, by George, Bishop of Moray, with consent of the dean and chapter of the cathedral church of Moray—being ten persons—to Simon, Lord Fraser of Lovat, at the rent of £40, for the lives of himself and any heir nominated by him, and the life of the survivor, and for nineteen years after. This lease was confirmed by Alexander, Bishop of Moray, in 1607; and the vicarage and small tithes of Wardlaw were leased, in 1617, by Alexander, Bishop of Moray, to the same Lord Simon for life, and to his heirs-male for nineteen years after, at the rent of £4.

The Act of Prorogation of the Tack of the Teinds of Conveth (Appendix, No. XXVIII.), mentions a prorogation of a tack of the teinds of the parish of Fearnua. This is probably the tack mentioned in the Inventory of 1652 [*] as:

"66. Tack of the Teinds of Lowat, sett to Dame Janett Campbell and her heirs for her life time, and nineteen years, be Mr Andro Makphail, daittit 10 Feb^{ry} 1579."

The maker of the Inventory must have misdescribed this document. The lands of Lovat were in the parish of Wardlaw, of which Donald Dow was minister.[†] This is the lady who was destined for Lochiel, but married Alexander, Lord Lovat (*supra*, p. 230), and her heir would be Lord Simon.

The parishes of Wardlaw and Fearnua were united by the Commission of Plat, on 14th July 1618. The church of Fearnua seems to have been dedicated to a saint named Corridon, according to the Wardlaw MSS.;[‡] and the light of Christi-

---

[*] Dunbar Dunbar MSS.

[†] Anderson's Family of Fraser, p. 100, citing Reg. of Decreets, 78, fol. 321; in Register, p. 64, "*Wardlaw.*—Donald Dow, minister; his stipend, xl lib."

[‡] At p. 112, according to the Findon MSS. This seems to be the same name as is Latinised in Queritenns (*supra*, p. 185), and to point to St Boniface of Rosemarkie as the patron saint of Fearnua; but the histories of the Celtic saints of Scotland and Ireland and Wales are yet to be written. We are persuaded that many saints lived even in Scotland before St Columba, though they have not had their lives written by the sacred hand of Adamnan, nor their names recorded in the Chronicle of St Bede.

anity, which had been burning there, dimly it may be, for four hundred years, was suddenly extinguished by this Commission for the Plantation of Kirks.*

On the 18th July 1618, the commissioners provided a stipend of 620 marks for the minister of Kilmorack, the parish of our priory, payable as to 465 marks out of the parsonage or rectorial tithes, by George Monro of Tarrell, principal tacksman of the chantry of Ross, and as to 155 marks, by the tacksman of the vicarage teinds; and the lease was prorogated as compensation for the charge.†

And now to return to the year 1562, the date of this rental.

Queen Mary, in 1563, hunted and took her summer journeys in the west and south-west of Scotland; but her brother James, the new Earl of Moray, came north to Inverness late in the autumn, with his two brothers, to hold courts and consolidate his power, and there first put in execution the new Act against witchcraft, sorcery, and necromancy, by burning two old women as witches.

On the 15th October 1563, Campbell of Cawdor was served heir before him as sheriff-principal by a jury, including of the family of the founder of the priory, William Fraser of Struy, uncle of Hugh, Lord Lovat, now a minor; Hugh Fraser of Guisachan, whose father had died fighting beside his brother Hugh, Lord Lovat, at the battle of Lochlochy; Alexander Chisholm of Comar; and Kenneth Mackenzie of Kintail.

It was probably in 1564 that Queen Mary paid that visit to Beauly Priory, the memory of which is preserved in local tradition.‡

She left Edinburgh on 22d and Perth on 31st July, and proceeded to Athole to the hunting; she then passed the Mounth into Badenoch, and thence to Inverness, and from Inverness to the Chanonry of Ross.

* Appendix, No. XXIX.

† George Monro had married Mariot M'Culloch, the heiress of Angus M'Culloch of Tarrell, one of the witnesses to No. XXII. The vicarage tack then belonged to Duncan Bayne of Tulloch, who, in 1628, assigned it to Alexander Chisholm of Comar.

‡ *Supra*, p. 7.

She was certainly in Ross-shire in August, for Maitland writes to Cecil in September acknowledging receipt of Cecil's letter of the 8th ult. "at that time they were in Ross." *

She was on her return at Gartly, where there was a castle belonging to the Earl of Huntly, on the 24th of August;† at Dunottar on the 5th September;‡ and at Dundee§ on the 9th September.

Mr Chalmers suggests, with considerable probability, that her object was to inquire into the nature and value of the earldom of Ross, which she meant to settle upon Darnley, ‖ whom she had determined to marry, and she would naturally go to Dingwall, which was the head of the earldom, the castle of Dingwall being its manor-place.

Going to Dingwall from Inverness, she must have passed by Beauly; and it was therefore, probably, on a bright morning in August 1564 that she opened the window at the prior's house, and looking out on the gardens,¶ eulogised the beauty of the spot and the appropriateness of its name.

Abbot Walter would have preserved the priory from any injury; and the queen's experience of his hospitality at Kinloss in 1562 would induce her more readily to avail herself of it at Beauly in 1564.

The queen's progresses in 1562 and 1564 were according to the fashion of her royal ancestors. Lesley, speaking of the progress of James IV. and his queen in 1505, says: "For the use observed in Scotland was at that time, as it was many years before, that the king, the queen, and their court travelled for the most part of the year through the realm, and lodged in the abbey places, or with the bishops and prelates, where

* Letters Domestic, Queen Eliz., 1564.
† Letter from Q. Mary to Q. Elizabeth in Calendar of State Papers, Elizabeth, 1564, dated Gartly, 24th August 1564.
‡ Chalmers, vol. i., p. 116.
§ Labanoff, vol. i., p. 221, Q. Mary to the Duke of Savoy.
‖ She, when preparing for her journey, told her servants she was going into Argyle. Inventories of Mary Queen of Scots, p. 149: "*July* 1564.—Plus a Baltase 11 pieces d'estamine blanche pour mettre a un coffre pour porter au voyage que la Royne fait en Arguylle." She had gone to Argyle in 1562.
¶ Appendix, No. XXX.

they were well entertained certain days; and at their departure, the bishop or abbot, master of the place, gave a purse to the king, and another to the queen, with certain quantities of gold contained therein, which extended yearly to a great sum."*

In 1566, Hugh, Lord Lovat, although not of age, was served heir to his grandfather; he got seisin of the lands of Kinmylies from the Bishop of Moray in March 1567; this included Kintallartie, "cum piscaria de Ess,"† the salmon fishing of the Falls of the Beauly.

Mary, the queen, was now compelled to resign her crown in favour of her infant son, on 24th July 1567; and the power of the kingdom was actually exercised by her brother, the Regent Murray.

We can only glance at Mary's escape from Lochleven, and her gathering up those Scotsmen who cared for the good old cause and the Catholic Church: then came the fatal battle of Langside, and that gallop from the field on the 13th of May 1568, of sixty miles,‡ till she descended at the Abbey of Dundrennan, and received from the abbot that hospitality which, whatever faults they may have had, was always shown by the Abbeys and the Priories of Scotland.

---

* Lesley's Hist. of Scotland, 1505. † Dunbar Dunbar MSS.

‡ It seems hardly possible that Mary could have ridden so far, but she expressly says in her letter to Elizabeth from Workington, on the 17th of May, that she had accomplished this distance the first day: "Car je n'ay chose du monde que ma personne comme je me suis sauvée, faysant soixante miles a travers champs le premier jour, et n'ayant despuis jamaiss osé aller que la nuit" (Autograph letter from Queen Mary to Queen Elizabeth in the British Museum, Cotton Collection, Caligula, c. i., fol. 65), printed by Prince Labanoff, vol. ii., p. 77: "She was of tall stature and large size." Chalmers, i. 129, says: "Of the largest size of women." Dr J. Robertson (Inventories, pref., p. cxx.) speaks of "her large stately figure." She was fond of exercise, and capable of great exertion. Her gallop of forty-five miles, at five in the morning, on 2d July 1565, from Perth, through Kinross to Queensferry, and then to Callander House, and her forty miles' ride from Jedburgh to Hermitage Castle and back, on the 16th October 1566, show the power she possessed of making long and rapid journeys on horseback; at the same time, this ride to Dundrennan, prolonged into the night, must have been very trying to her, for of a previous night ride she writes, on 15th March 1566, "We are so tyrit and ewill at eise quhat throw rydding of twenty milles in five hours of the nycht" (Inventories, pref., p. xxxi.).

No. XXIII.

TACK OF SOME OF THE LANDS OF BEWLY BY WALTER, PRIOR OF BEWLY, TO JOHN AND ALEX^R CLERKS, 19 NOV^R 1568.

Ex Autographo.

"Be it kend till all men be yir present Lettres, ws, Walter, Abbot of Kinloss and Prior of Bewlie, with express consent, assent, decrete, and determinatioune of our Breyir and Conuent of oure said Abbay and place of Bewlie, being chapturlie gaderit, and yairwith riplie aduisit, the utilitie and profite of us and our saide Abbay, forseyne and considerit, and for gude and thankful serwice done till ws and our predecessours in tyme byegane, to haue sett and for maill lattin, and be ye tenour heirof settis, and for maill letts to our louit seruent John Clerk in Bewlie, and failying of him, to Alexander Clerk his lauthefulle sonne, and to ye langer Livar of yame twa, yair airs and assigneis, of na grater dygre nor yame selfis, All and haill ye Auchtant pairt of owr toune and landis of Reyndoun, lyand within ye Baronie and Priourie of Bewlie and Sherifdome of Inuernesse: Togiddir with all and haill ane pace [of] land callit John Clerks land, lyand betwix our said Abbaye and place of Bewlie, betwix the twa getis, Eist and West, ascendant up fra the Croft, callit Alexander Writhtis croft, to ye get passand Eist and West throch ye Cuthill, as ye said auchtant part and pate [pace of], callit John Writhts [Clerks] land lyes in lenth and braid, occupit yis lang tyme bygane, as ye samyn is as yett at yis present tyme, be ye said John Clerk, with yair pertinaintis: Togyddir with killhouse, barne, toftis, waystis, and byginnis, usit and wont, with power to ye said John, and Alexander his sonne, yair airs and assigneis of na grater degre nor yame selfis, to brew and sell ye malt yat grouis to yame selfis, prouiding yat ye samyn be not hurt nor prejudice to ye priuilege of owr principall

OF THE PRIORY OF BEAULY. 255

Aillehowse in tyme comyng, for all ye dayes, termes, and space of Nyntyne yeiris nixt, and immeditly following ye feist of Witsoundaye in ye yeire of God one thowsand five hunderid and saxtie aught yeiris, quhylke Feist, God willing, sall be ye said Johnnes, and Alexander his sone, yair Entries to and in ye saidis auchtant pairt of Reyndoun and Pate [pace of] land callit Johne Clerks land, with yair howses, toftis, croftis, yairds, Kille, Barne, Ailehouse, and pertainentis; and to bruick, joyse, occupie, mannure, and possesse ye samyn, induring ye said space of nintyne yeris, frelie, quyetlie, rele, and in pace, butt ony obstacle, impediment, or agayne calling of yis our assedatioune, or lice of tack in ony tyme cuming, during ye said space of nyntyne yeris. Payand yairfor yeirlie, ye saids John Clerk and Alexander Clerk, his sone, yair airs and assigneis, of na graiter dygre nor yame selfis, till ws and our successouris Priors ot Bewlie, viz., for ye said auchtent part of Reyndoun, the soume of twelff shillings six pennies usual money of the Realme, twa bollis twa pekkis ferme, ane firlet aitis, ane quarter of Mart, thre quarters of Mutoun, sax pultrie, ane Kid, with twinty four eggis for ane penny; and for ye said pate [pace of] land callit John Clerks land, yeirlie, four pounds money forsaid, ane dousane of Pultrie, ane   to ye water, and ane huick in heiruest, Extending to the haill in muney to the soume of foure punds twelff shillings and sax pennies, usuel muney of yis Realme, to be payd at twa usual termis in ye yeir, Witsundaye and Martimes, be equall portiounes; and ye saids ferme, custumis, and dewties yierlie, at termes equal and wount, togiddir with arrage, carrage, and dew seruice, conforme to our rental of sameikle land, use and wount; and we foirthwith, ye said Walter, Abbot of Kinloss and Prior of Bewlie, for ws and our successouris Prioris of Bewlie, sall warrand, mentaine, and defend yis our Assedatioune and Lettre of Tack of ye saidis auchtent pairt of Reyndoun and pace of Land, callit John Clerks land, with Killhouse, Barne, Byggings, toftis, croftis, yairds, and pertaynentis, with comun pastur, fre ische and entre, with all fredums, aysiamentis, and commodities pertayning to ye saids lands,   for all ye days and termis of nintyne yeris, aboue mentionat, to ye said Johne Clerk and Alexander Clerk, his sone, yair airs and assigneis forsayds, contrair all Mortill as Law will: Prouiding alwais that, give it sall happin, the said Johne, and Alexander his sone, yair airs & assigneis forsayds, to faylzie in gude and thankfull payment making of ye saids Maillis, fermis, Custumes, and Dewties, yeirlie and termlie, as said is, swa yat ye termis rynn togiddir successively unpeyit, yan in yat case, yis present Assedatioune and Lettre of nintyne yeris tack to be null, inualidat, of na force, strenth or effecte in ye selff, but ony foryer process of law.— In Witnesse of ye quhilke thyng, to yis our present Assidatioune and Lettir of tak subscriuit with our hand, with ye subscriptionnes manual of our said Conuent, in signe and taking of yir consents, our commoune Saill of our Chapture of Bewlie is to hungyn. At Kinloss, the nynteine day of Nouember, ye yeir of God ane thousand fiue hundereth saxtie aught yeiris, befor yir Witnessis, Adam Dundass, Archibald Inness, and John Jaradic,* and uyers diuers present.

    1. WALTERUS, Abbas de Kinloss.
    2. Ego, Dominus JOHANNES PALENDI,† subscribo.
    3. Ego, DAUID DAUISONE, Subscribo.
    4. Ego, Frater JOHANNES CRAWFURDE, Subscribo.
    5. Ego, JACOBUS ROX, Subscribo.
    6. Ego, Dominus THOMAS TUYNAM, Monachus, Subscripsi.
    7. Ego, GEORGIUS MORAY, subscribo," etc.

    Not.—The tag parchment, and no seale. The abbot's and monks' names subscribing scarce legible. On ye bak of the charter, in a recent and distinct hande: "Tack ol some of the Lands of Bewlie, &c.—before yat in the body of the charter they appear to have been granted to John and Alexander Clerks."

This document is the last, in date, of those transcribed by Macfarlane. It is a lease, by the prior and convent of Beauly, of part of the property of the House. It is dated the 19th November 1568, and at Kinloss, although it is stated to be with the consent of our brethren and convent of our said abbey and place of Beauly, being chapterly gathered. It commences in a like form with the deed by the prior and convent of Pluscardine in 1501 (*supra*, p. 139), which runs thus: "Be it kende till all men, be this present writ, ws, Robert, be the permission of God, Prior of Pluscardine, and

    * Probably Paradise. John Paradise, a servant of the abbot, is a witness to a charter by him at Kinloss, in 1565 (Records of Kinloss, p. 154).
    † Probably "Roland."

the convent of the samyn, chaptourlie gaderit, riplie auisit, our utilitie and profitt considerit;"* and in 1559, when Walter and his monks, as abbot and convent of Kinloss, give a precept to their bailiff, to deliver possession of lands leased, they recite, " Forsamekill as we, with avyis, consent, and assent of the said convent, being chaptourlie gaderit, and ryeplie aduisit heirvpon." †

The term granted is for nineteen years, from Whitsunday 1568, which feast was to be the entry. The lessees are John Clerk, whom failing, to Alexander Clerk his son, their heirs and assignees, "of no greater degree nor themselves." So the Countess of Crawford's lease of the Castletown of Rait, in 1572, is to David Hay, his heirs, assignees, and sub-tenants, "of no higher degree nor himself;" ‡ and even Dallas, in his "Styles" (A.D. 1693), inserts, as an ordinary form of tack, the letting to a tenant, "his heirs and sub-tenants, of no higher degree than himself."

" It was the most material of circumstances for the proprietors of land, in ancient times, to have nobody round them but friends, vassals, and tenants, composing what was termed their following;"§ and to secure this, the restraint upon assignment and sub-tenancy was inserted.

The subjects let are the auchtant (eighth)|| part of the lands of Rheindoun, within the Barony and Priory of Beauly, and a pace (piece) of land called John Clerk's land, lying between our said abbey and place of Beauly, between the two gates east and west, ascendant up from the croft called Alexander Wright's croft, to ye gate¶ passing east and west through the Cuthill, and with the kilnhouse, barn, and alehouse. Power is given to the lessees to brew and use the malt grown, providing that the same should not hurt the privilege of our principal ale-house in time coming. The rent is, for the eighth of Rheindoun, 12s. 6d. money, two

* Family of Kilravock, p. 171. † Records of Kinloss, p. 151.
‡ Family of Kilravock, p. 261.
§ Ross's Lectures on Law of Scotland, vol. ii., p. 482.
|| Not eighteenth, as suggested in O. P. S., " Kilmorack."
¶ "Gate" here means road, and not entrance.

bolls two pecks ferme—this probably implies bear—and one firlot oats, and one-quarter of a mart or ox, three-quarters of a mutton or wedder sheep, sax poultrie, ane kid, with twenty-four eggs for a penny; for the pace of land, £4, a dozen poultry, and ane [oar (?)] to the water, and ane hook in harvest.

In respect of this service in kind, the lease was like the leases referred to by Mr Loch, in his account of the improvements in Sutherlandshire.* The money rent was to be paid at the two feasts of Whitsunday and St Martin's in winter—that is, St Martin of Tours; the rent in kind once a-year, with a provision for forfeiture of the lease on non-payment of the rent, so that the terms run together successively unpaid.

It is subscribed by Walter Reid and Sir John Palendi (Roland), David Davison, Brother John Crawford, James Rox, Sir Thomas Twynam, monk, and George Moray. Of these, David Davison, John Crawford, and Thomas Twynam, had been all pupils of Ferrarius in 1540-43.

The common seal of our chapter of Beauly is said to have been added, but it was not attached at the time of transcription.

The bear was used instead of barley for malting—a practice peculiar to Scotland,† and provided for in the Acts imposing the Malt Tax. The kilnhouse was used not only for drying the oats before making oatmeal, but also for making the bear into malt. This malt the lessees were allowed to sell, but apparently not to brew into ale for sale; the privilege of selling ale being reserved to the principal ale-house of the priory. The principal ale-house of Beauly must, in those times, have been an important hostelry. Here was the principal road into Ross and the north. The ford of the Beauly river was called the Stock-ford of Ross, and was the spot where, according to Wynton, Alexander I. had finally defeated the High-

* Loch's Lord Stafford's Improvements, 1820, app. i.
† In 1738, the "Account of the State of Scotland," published in London, says: "Besides barley, they have great quantities of beer or bigg, which makes good bread but better malt, and of this they make good bread, broth, ale, and beer."

landers, in 1116; and the fairs of Beauly,* which have survived to our time in addition to the monthly Muir of Ord market, required, and doubtless obtained, under the statute of James I., an ample hostelry, having stables and chambers, and provision for man and horse †—in bread, meat, and "ale" —according to the statute of 1424.

Ale is again mentioned in the statute of 1535, respecting inns; but I find no mention of whisky (*aqua vitæ*) until 1591.‡ It was a common drink in 1622.§ By 1690, a cen-

---

* Cross Fair, established on 3d May, the Feast of the Invention of the Holy Cross (*supra*, p. 97), is said, by the MS. historian of the Frasers, to have been established also by Lord Hugh, who fell at Kin-Lochy; he adds, that he procured an Act of Parliament for a weekly fair, every Wednesday; he mentions also, the Fair of St Mauricius (festival, September 22), at Downie—this was the patron saint of Dunballoch parish (*supra*, p. 22); All Saints (November 1), at Kilmorack; and Michaelmas (September 29), at Beauly (Anderson, p. 80).

It will be remembered that the MS. of 1728 states (*supra*, p. 28) that, before the foundation of the priory, there stood a chapel of St Michael on its site. In fact, whatever customary fairs might have been held, the weekly market was first established by Act of Parliament in 1685 (Acta Parl. Scot., vol. viii., p. 574). It runs thus:

"Warrand to Hugh, Lord Fraser of Lovat, for ane yearly fair at the Mure of Lovat, and a Weekly Mercat at Beauly.

"Our Soveraigne Lord and Estates of Parliament, considering that the Mure above Lovat, belonging to Hugh, Lord Fraser of Lovat, lies conveniently for fairs and mercats to the ease of His Majesty's lieges, and advantage of the place: Therefore, our said Sovereign Lord, with advice and consent of the said Estates of Parliament, gives and grants to the said Hugh, Lord Frazer of Lovat, his aires and successors, ane free fair in the yeare, To be holden upon the eight day of August, to continue for the space of   days; with ane weekly mercatt on   , at the Town of Bewly, with power to the said Lord Lovatt and his foresaids, or any other whom they shall appoint, To uplift and exact all tolls, customs, and other casualitys belonging to the saids fair and weekly mercat, and apply the same to ther own proper use; and to enjoy all other privileges, libertys, and immunitys therewith appertaining, sicklike and as freely as any other subject has done or may doe, in the like case."

† See note 1 to Marmion, canto iii., "The Hostel or Inn." Act 1424, c. 25.

‡ Sketches of Early Scottish History. Though there is plenty of wine—Alicant, Bastard, Muscadine, and Cyprick—in the House of Petty in 1513, there is no whisky. See the inventory, Family of Kilravock, p. 188. In 1591 a mutchkin (quarter pint) of *aqua vitæ* (whisky), was 6s.; French wine, 6s. 8d. a pint; Spanish wine, 20s. a quart; and ale, 2s. a quart, whisky being twenty-four times as dear.

§ Appendix to Burt's Letters, vol. ii., p. 245.

tury after its first mention, the practice of distilling it had become so common, that Forbes of Culloden was amply compensated for a loss of £54,000 Scots, by being allowed to brew *aqua vitæ* from the grain of the barony of Ferrintosh, at a duty of £266, 13s. 4d. Scots;* and by 1720, the practice of drinking it had increased to such an extent, that Burt says, "Some of the Highland gentlemen are immoderate drinkers of usky—even three or four quarts at a sitting."† I am afraid they corrupted their inferiors. The invention of distillation by Raymond Lully, just after the foundation of our priory, was not, it is said, taken much advantage of in Scotland prior to the Reformation. Colonel Stewart of Garth says, writing in 1822: "It was not till the beginning, or rather towards the middle, of the last century, that spirits of any kind were so much drank as ale, which was formerly the universal beverage. Every account and tradition go to prove that ale was the principal drink among the country people; and French wines and brandy among the gentry. . . . Whisky-house is a term unknown in the Gaelic. Public-houses are called *Tai-Leanne*—that is, ale-houses."‡

Here ends the roll of charters transcribed by Macfarlane.

We have printed them in their chronological order; but this is not the order in which they are transcribed; that is best indicated by the table of contents prefixed to the transcripts, probably by Macfarlane. There is first this entry:§

"In hoc volumine continentur
Diplomata Prioratus de Bello loco
a Pag. 369, ad Pag. 443."

And there is afterwards the following table of contents or list of the *diplomata*:

Fol.
1. Carta Willielmi Byseth de Ecclesia de Aberterth facta Fratribus de Bello loco ordinis Vallis Caulium.—Ex autographo, ... 369

---

* The brewhouse of Kinkell or Ferrintosh, is mentioned in 1584 (O. P. S., vol. ii., p. 549).
† Vol. ii., p. 161.   ‡ Sketches of the Highlanders, vol. i., p. 196, note.
§ Adv. Lib. MSS., Diplomatum Collectio, vol. xi., 35, 2, 4.

2. Carta Willielmi de Fenton Domini de Beuford de duabus
Marcis singulis annis percipiendis de Molendino de Beuford fratribus de Bello loco, ... 370
3. Carta Patricij de Grahame de parte sua de Altyr facta
Fratribus de Bello loco in Excambio pro Multuris de
Loueth, &c.—Ex autographo, ... 372
4. Bulla Alexandri Papæ 6^{ti} Andreæ Moraviensi Episcopo de
Prioratu de Beaulieu in favorem Dougalli Roderici Clerici
ad annum 1500 XI^{mo} die Februarii.—Ex autographo, . 374
5. Forma Juramenti Prioris B. Johannis Baptistæ de Bello
loco Cistertiensis ordinis Rossensis Diocœsis sub Regula
Valliscaulium a summo Pontifice nominati, . . 390
6. Bulla Julij II^{di} Pontificis Romani Roberto Fresell Decano
et Officiali Rossensi missa in favorem Prioris de Bello
loco 18vo die Januarii Anno Dom. 1513, . . 392
7. Tack of some of the Lands of Bewly by Walter Priour of
Bewly to John and Alex^r Clerks, 19 Novr 1540-1568, . 400
8. Præceptum Sylvestri, Apostolicæ Sedis Nuncii Abbatibus
de Kynlos et de ferne, pro nobili et potenti Domino
Hugone Fraser de Louett, ... 403
9. Bulla Gregorij Papæ Priori de Bello loco ordinis Valliscaulium Rossensis Diocœsis.—Ex autographo, . . 412
10. Carta Laurentij Militis, filii Patricii Janitoris de Innernes
Priori de Bello loco 1255.—Ex autographo, . . 413
11. Carta Magistri Henrici de Tottyngham Priori de Bello
loco 1274.—Ex autographo, ... 414
12. Carta Andreæ de Boscho Domini de Edirdor facta Fratribus de Bello loco ordinis Valliscaulium Anno 1278.—Ex
autographo, ... 417
12. Carta David de Innerlunan de terra de Ouchterwaddalle,
seu Orach-teroadal, ex Dono Gillechrist Magilledufti
Fratribus de Bello loco.—Ex autographo, . . 418
13. Carta Johannis de Urchard Vicarij de Abbertherff Priori
de Bello loco de quieta Clamatione Decimarum Salmonum de Abbertherff 1340.—Ex autographo, . . 420
14. Collatio Ecclesiæ parochialis de Conueth ad Conventum
de Bello loco spectant per Willielmum Episcopum Moraviensem Anno 1480.—Ex autographo, . . . 421
15. Commissio Visitationis Monasterij de Ardquhatten data

Priori de Bello loco per Jacobum quartum Priorem seu generalem Vallis Caulium Diocœsis Lingonensis Anno 1505.—Ex autographo, ... 424
16. Bulla Alexandri Papæ sexti pro Dougallo Roderici Clerico Rossensis Diocœsis de Prioritata de Beaulieu ordinis Valliscaulium Anno 1497.—Ex autographo, . . 425
17. Bulla Gregorij XI. Papæ Priori et Conventui Belli loci ordinis Valliscaulium, ... 431
18. Carta Andreæ Moraviensis Episcopi de Decimis Garbarum et Salmonum Parochiæ de Abertarf.—Ex autographo, . 432
19. Præsentatio ad Ecclesiam de Conueth per Priorem de Bello loco anno 1512.—Ex autographo, . . . 434
20. Præsentatio ad Ecclesiam de Conuay per Priorem et Conventum de Bello loco Anno 1493.—Ex autographo, . 436
21. Littera Fratris Jacobi Courtois Generalis ordinis Valliscaulium in Burgundia Priori de Bello loco.—Ex autographo, ... 437
22. Carta Dominæ Ceciliæ Byseth Fratribus Valliscaulium de Bello loco de tertia parte terræ suæ de Altir.—Ex autographo, ... 441

The headings of all these transcripts, except five, state that they are *ex autographo;* one only of these five (No. XXI.), appears to have been transcribed by Macfarlane, from a copy; and there is nothing to lead us to suppose that the transcripts were made from a Chartulary or Register of Beauly.

It is to be feared there is little hope of satisfying the expectations arising from the language from time to time held by Scottish antiquarians respecting the records of Beauly. Mr Cosmo Innes wrote in 1861 : " The Register of the Priory of Beauly of Benedictines of Vallis Caulium, the foundation of the old family of Lovat, is still hid in some northern charter-room. It has not been seen since the days of Sir George Mackenzie, who quoted its contents. Copies of a few of the priory charters are preserved."* Mr Brichan says :† " The records . . . of the Priory of Beauly and the

---
* Sketches of Early Scottish History, 1861, p. 21, note.
† Preface to part ii. of vol. ii. of Orig. Par. Scot.

Abbey of Fearn, the former of which were extant in the seventeenth century, cannot now be found; the principal materials of their scanty early history existing in copies of some Beauly charters, preserved by Macfarlane, and in the original of, at least, one of the later Fearn charters, preserved at Balnagown." Dr Stuart says:* "The registers of the following religious houses cannot now be traced, although some of them were quoted by writers of the last century. . . . XI. Beauly."

The origin of these statements must be the mention by Rose of Sir George Mackenzie of Tarbet's "report," as to the foundation deed of Beauly Priory (*supra*, p. 29). I have been unable to find any reference to the Register, or Chartulary, or Records of Beauly in any printed work, of either Sir George Mackenzie of Roschaugh or the Earl of Cromarty, nor in any of the Rosehaugh MSS. in the Advocates Library. There is a general belief that every monastery had its chartulary or register—that is, a book in which the charters relating to the house were transcribed for preservation; but this was not always the case. We know that the charters of Cambuskenneth were not registered in a chartulary: the register printed, was made in 1535, by royal authority, at Cambuskenneth; down to that time the charters and evidents belonging to the abbot and convent were kept in the abbey; what was the practice there, was often that of smaller monasteries, like Beauly; and we may be pretty confident that a Chartulary or Register of Beauly, in the strict sense of the term, never existed.

All we can hope for is, that the priory charters, described by the minister of Wardlaw (*supra*, pp. 16, 17), or copies of them, may yet be discovered.

We can hardly part with the charters without carrying on the history of the Priory down to the present time; its subsequent annals are short and simple enough; they mainly consist of the account of the acquisition of its lands by Hugh, Lord Lovat, and of the state of its existing remains.

* First Report of Commission on Historical Manuscripts, appendix.

Lord Hugh did not attain his full age till after May 1568; before that time, in 1567, he signs, or authorises his name to be attached to the Bond of Association, which Murray procured after the queen's abdication.* Notwithstanding this, we find him of the queen's party in July 1568, after the defeat of Langside.

In June 1569, the regent and his Privy Council sat at Inverness; and after his assassination, in January 1569-70, his widow writes to Rose of Kilravock: "Thair is mony a noble man has promessit to be my friendis in thay pertes, sik as my Lord off Huntlie, my Lord Atholl, my Lord Lovatt."†

The Earl of Huntly, son of that earl who had been killed on the queen's visit to the north in 1562, had been quickly received into her favour, appointed to the charge of the castle of Inverness by her, and after the death of the Regent Murray, constituted her lieutenant in the north. He was supported by the Earl of Athole, and was very anxious to get together as many friends as he could, against those who, under the patronage of Elizabeth, had, on the 12th July 1570, appointed Lennox, Regent of Scotland. Lord Huntly was then at Aberdeen, endeavouring to concentrate all his strength; and on the 26th and 27th of July 1570, he treats with the more powerful people in the north. On the 26th he makes terms with the young Lord Lovat.‡

Lovat took the opportunity to get Huntly's assistance in securing the possession of the Priory of Beauly, and they enter into a solemn contract;§ the earl "binds and oblesses him to assist, fortifie, and maintaine the said Hew, Lord Lowat, in all his honest, lauchful actions and causes, as he happens to have ado, and requires the s^d Erle thereto; and also sall, at his uttermost, labour and procur the Abbot of Kynloss, to gif and set in feu-farme, to the said Hew and his

---

* Crawford's Officers of State, app. 442.

† Family of Kilravock, p. 252.

‡ In the "Estimate of the Scottish Nobility" for 1577, printed for the Club in 1873, under "The Lord Loval" is, "This Baron is of goode lyvinge and power in the North, allied and a dependaunt vpon the Erle of Huntley."

§ Appendix, No. XXXI.

aires, all and haill the landis and mainis of Bewlyne, with the salmond fischeing * thereof."

The next day Huntly writes to Kilravock, informing him of the summoning of a Parliament at Linlithgow on the queen's behalf, on the next month; and as a rebellious faction had lately gone about to treat a new pretended form of government, established in the person of one who has sworn and professed his obedience to a foreign prince, he begged Kilravock, accompanied with his honourable household, kin, friends, and tenants, "bodin jn feir of weir," to meet him at Cupar, on the 12th day of August, with twenty days' provision.

The Wardlaw minister states, that it was by the influence of Abbot Walter Reid's wife, that he was induced to agree to grant the property of the Priory of Beauly to Lord Lovat, and that she was connected with Lord Hugh through his grandmother, Janet Ross of Balnagowan. "My Lord Lovat," says this reverend gossip, "takes occasion by familiarity with Sir Walter's lady, and broaches his resolution to her, of feuing the barony of Beauly; she assured him that his lordship would be preferred to any whomsoever in the bargain, and that she would secure her husband of all importunities that might assault him upon that head; she actually effected and guided him so, that the next time Lovat paid a visit to Sir Walter, they came to such an agreement, that a minute of sale was drawn up betwixt them and subscribed; and John, Earl of Athole, and Mr John Campbell of Calder, were both witnesses to the paper, so that all was out of doubt and hazard for the future." †

* This is the first time that the noble fish, whose capture constituted the value of the fishings of Forne three hundred and fifty years before, and which had caused the lord and lady of Beaufort in old time to brave excommunication and interdict, is expressly named as comprised in them. It had been discovered to be a royal fish, *inter regalia*—a jewel of the crown—and needed, crown lawyers said, to be expressly named, to pass to a subject. We have seen enough to show that, if the Highlander "never held it theft to take a tree from the wood or a fish from the water" (Family of Kilravock, p. 241), the property in salmon fishings was, from the earliest times, regarded as of great value: at Abertarff they are expressly named in 1242 (*supra*, p. 38).

† Findon MSS.

The manner of carrying out the transfer of the property was peculiar. There was a feu-charter of the barony of Beauly—a charter making hereditary the office of bailie of the barony or regality of Beauly; and the creation of a new office, that of constable and keeper of the Palace in the place of the priory of Beauly erected by Bishop Reid, which office was also made hereditary.

The feu-charter of the barony is by the prior and convent to Lord Lovat. We have from the "Records of Kinloss" a note of it, which, when collated with the Act of Parliament of 1584 confirming it, is as follows:

"Charter by Walter, abbot of Kinlos and prior of the monastery of Bewlie, in favour of Hugh, Lord Fraser of Lovat, of the barony, town, and lands of Beulie,*—namely, the village and lands of Ardingrask [Ardnagrask], Rewindown [Rheindoun], Incherorie [Inchrorie], Alter [Altyre], Craigscorie [Craigscorry], Platchayth [Platchaig], Grome [Groam], Fernelie [Farley], with the forests and woods; Thaynok [Teachnuick], with the pendicles,—namely, Owrcroarss, the Relict [Ruilick], and Grenefauld [Greyfield], with the cottage of the same; the lands of Vrquhany, with the woods; the half Davoch; the lands of Lie Boycht and Conharbrie; third part of Meikle Culmulang [Culmil]; third part of Eister Glen of Conveth; fourth part of the lands of Faynblair [Fanblair]; Lie Ferriehouse, with its croft; Lie Amonth or Ainocht [Annat]; Lie Auldtown, called the Common pasture; Thacfreshe [Teafrish], with the cottage; the lands called Lie Mason's land; the lands called Johane Clerk's Land; a croft called M'Hucheon's Croft, and common cottage; the dominical lands called the Mains of Bewlie, with the yards and orchyards belonging to the Priory, and the pertinents and crofts of the said lands and lordships; a croft called Dean James Pape's Croft; a croft called Merschellis Croft; a croft called M'Alesteris Croft, then occupied by Sir David Dawson; and also the two mills called Thaynok [Teachnuick] and Bewlie Mills, with the thirled multures of the whole barony of Bewlie, and of all the lands above written, with their sequels; and also the whole salmon fishing on the water of Forne, marching from Cairncot to the sea, or anywhere else on the said water between the salmon fishings of the said noble lord, Hugh,

* We insert the present names in brackets.

Lord Fraser of Lovat, from Kilmorak to the sea, with the cruives and other commodities lying within the Priory of Bewlie and shire of Inverness: To be held of the granter and his successors, in feu-farm fee and heritage for ever, for rendering to the granter and his successors, viz., for the toun and lands of Ardingrask, £4, 6s. 8d. Scots, and 8s. 4d. for each boll of 12 bolls of farm victual, 3s. 4d. for each boll of 2 bolls of market wheat [oats], 30s. for each mart of 2 custom marts, 5s. for each of 4 custom sheep, 16d. for each kid of 8 custom kids, 16s. for each dozen of custom poultry, and 8d. for custom eggs. For the said town and lands of Rawindown, etc., £5 : £6, 3s. 4d. for 16 bolls of farm victual, 6s. 8d. for 2 bolls of custom wheat [oats], £3 for 2 custom marts, 20s. for 4 custom sheep, 11s. 4d. for 8 kids (price of each, 16d.), 16s. for 4 dozen custom poultry, and 8d. for custom eggs. For the said town and lands of Inchrorie, 43s. 4d. : 33s. 4d. for 4 bolls of farm victual, 3s. 4d. for 1 boll of custom wheat [oats], 30s. for 1 custom mart, 10s. for 2 sheep, 5s. 4d. for 4 kids, 8s. for 2 dozen poultry, and 4d. for custom eggs. For the said town and lands of Alter, 56s. 8d. : 50s. for 6 bolls of farm victual, 3s. 4d. for 1 boll of wheat [oats], 30s. for 1 mart, 10s. for 2 sheep, 5s. 4d. for 2 kids, 8s. for 2 dozen poultry, and 4d. for custom eggs. For the town and land of Craigskorrie, 43s. 4d : 33s. 4d. for 4 bolls of farm victual, 3s. 4d. for 1 boll wheat [oats], 30s. for 1 mart, 10s. for 2 sheep, 5s. 4d. for 4 kids, 8s. for 2 dozen poultry, and 4d. for custom eggs. For town and land of Platchayth, 43s. 4d. : 33s. 4d. for 4 bolls victual, 3s. 4d. for 1 boll wheat [oats], 30s. for 1 mart, 10s. for 2 sheep, 5s. 4d. for 4 kids, 8s. for 2 dozen poultry, and 4d. for custom eggs. For town and lands of Grome, 56s. 8d. : 33s. 4d. for 4 bolls farm victual, 3s. 4d. for 1 boll wheat [oats], 30s. for 1 mart, 10s. for 2 sheep, 5s. 4d. for 4 kids, 8s. for 2 dozen poultry, and 4d. for custom eggs. For the town and lands of Fernlie, 56s. 8d. : 33s. 4d. for 4 bolls farm victual, 3s. 4d. for 1 boll wheat [oats], 30s. for 1 mart, 10s. for 2 sheep, 5s. 4d. for 4 kids, 8s. for 2 dozen poultry, and 4d. for custom eggs. For the town and lands of Tharknok, £5. For Wrquhanye, 53s. 4d. For the said half davach lands, 40s. : 33s. 4d. for 4 bolls farm victual. For the Boytht, 26s. 8d. For Conharbrie, 13s. 4d. For third part of Mekel Culmulyne, 40s. For third part of Eister Glen of Conuetht, 40s. For fourth part of Faynblair, 16s. 8d. For Lie Amonth, 26s. 8d. For the Ferrie hous and croft, 20s. For Lye Aldtoun,

26s. 8d. For Tharfreysche, 20s. For the Masonis lands, 40s., and 16d. for 1 kid or lamb. For Johane Cwkis [Clerk's] lands, £4, and 4s. for 1 dozen poultry. For M'Huchonis croft, 26s. 8d. For the Mayns of Bewlie, 40s. : £3, 6s. 8d. for 8 bolls farm victual, 3s. 4d. for 1 boll custom wheat [oats], 30s. for 1 mart, 10s. for 2 custom sheep, 5s. 4d. for 4 kids, 8s. for a dozen poultry, and 4d. for custom eggs. For dene [Dean] Jame Papis Croft, 46s. 8d. For Merchellis Croft, 6s. 8d. For M'Alesteres Croft, 10s. For the mills of Tharknok and Bewlie, £16 : 13s. 4d. for 40 bolls victual. And for the salmon fishings on the water of Forne, 50s. for each barrel of 30 barrels of salmon; with duplication of the said silver duties of the whole foresaid lands at the entry of each heir; and the said lord and his heirs rendering one suit or personal presence at one of the prior's head courts, to be held at Bewlie every year, after the feast of Pentecost.—Dated at Bewlie and Petlathie respectively, 6th and 12th November 1571.

> "WALTER, Abbas a Kinloss, ac commendatarius de Bewly.
> Ego, Dompnus JOHANNES ROLAND, subscribo.
> Ego, Dompnus THOMAS TWYNAM, subscribo.
> Ego, dominus IOHANNES CRAUFORD, subscribo.
> Ego, dominus DAUID DAUSON, subscribo."

We can now see the extent of the endowment of the priory.

Ardnagrask and Rheindoun, I conceive, are the lands of Ouchter Waddale (Outer Tarradale), granted by Charter No. VI. (*supra*, p. 60). They are now in the parish of Urray, and were in the parish of Kilchrist before its union with Urray.

Tarradale belonged to Gillichrist Macgilliduffi about 1235 (*supra*, p. 61). He, by descent, was the son of one calling himself Gillie Duffi, the servant of Duff, that may be of Duff, Earl of Fife, one of the seven earldoms of Scotland; and he took for his name that of *Gilliechrist, the servant of Christ*, and showed his attachment by erecting his property of Tarradale into a parish, building a church for it, and dedicating it to his Saviour, calling it *Kilchrist, the Church of Christ*.

The other lands, except those in the parish of Conveth, coincide in extent with the description of the foundation charter in the Wardlaw MS. (*supra*, p. 16), as extending from Outer Tarradale to the burn of Teanassie (*Rivulus de Breckach*). They are the whole of the low grounds of the parish of Kilmorack from the bounds of the parish of Urray to Teanassie, and include the line of hills above Beauly and the Beauly valley in Kilmorack parish, running from the heights of Rheindoun (the King's Hill) along the ridge which takes its name of Farley (Fearnly) from the alders (*Fearn*) that crowd over the shallows of the lovely river as it emerges from the pinnacled rocks of the entrance to the Dhrium, and which ridge has been again in our day clothed with wood by the most zealous planter in the north,* and the Priory Hillground finishes with the Hill of the deer forest of Urchany.

The lands in the parish of Conveth, which are included in this charter, are the third of Meikle Kilmoling (Culmil), the third of the Easter Glen of Conveth (Convinth), and the fourth of Fyndblair (Fanblair), all lands now in the parish of Kiltarlity. The mode of acquisition of these lands by the Priory does not appear by the transcribed charters, but some indication of the period when they must have been given to the monks appears from their description.

They are described as *thirds* and *fourths* of lands; they could not have been part of the kirklands of Conveth, if that church was granted to the priory by John Byset the younger, as is possible (*supra*, p. 53), as before his time the Bysets were owners of the entirety of those lands; and it seems much more likely that the thirds of Kilmoling and Easter Glen of Conveth were granted by some of the three co-heirs of the Bysets after 1259 (*supra*, p. 54), and that the fourth of Fanblair was granted after 1438 by one of the four co-heirs of Walter de Fenton (*supra*, p. 98).

As we find no mention now of any lands being thirled to the mills of Beauly except those comprised in the barony of Beauly, the lands of which barony were all in Kilmorack

* The late Lord Lovat: his neighbour, the late Alexander William Chisholm, M.P., followed his example, and planted the great wood at Erchless in 1834-37.

parish, except these third and fourth parts of lands, which
were in Conveth parish—if the grant of multures by the
Founder to the monks is correctly given in the Wardlaw MS.
(*supra*, p. 17)—it is probable that these Conveth lands were
granted in exchange for some of the multures of lands in Conveth parish * after the fashion of the exchange of Patrick
Graham effected by Charter No. IX.

For some reason, a separate charter seems to have been
taken of these Conveth lands, though they are included in the
charter of the barony. This separate charter is doubtless the
same as that inventoried in 1652 as No. XV., though the
writer styles the lands as of " Kilmorra." †

Farley and Urchany, we may observe, are granted—Farley
with the forests and woods, and Urchany with the woods.
The monks probably encouraged the clothing of those heights
with timber and trees, protecting the arable lands from the
winds that sweep down from the mountain range of Beneva-
chart (nearly 3000 feet in height).

The name Dean James Pope's croft indicates a croft once
occupied by James Pope (*dominus Jacobus Pop*), one of the
junior monks sent to Kinloss in 1540 to be taught by Ferrarius (*supra*, p. 220). James Pope seems to have been afterwards dean, perhaps of the priory, though we have no other
notice of the office. The occupation of this croft by him, and of
another by the monk David Dawson, one of his fellow-pupils,
who still survived, with what Ferrarius says about Adam Elder
and his garden produce (*supra*, p. 222), indicates a departure
from the pristine rules of common work for the common good.

The last subject conveyed is the prime jewel of the whole
setting, the salmon fishings in the waters of Forne, that is,
the salmon fishing granted by the Founder to the monks
under the title of the FISHINGS OF FORNE (*supra*, No. I.,

* It may be that " Kenniath," mentioned among the lands of which the multures were granted, is really "Conveth."

† The separate charter is noted, without date, by Dr Stuart (Records of Kinloss, p. 97), and the entry No. 15 in the Inventory is "ane charter be the Abbot
of Kinloss to Hew, Lord Fraser of Lowet, of ye lands of Kilmorra, daitit ye
day of   " (Dunbar Dunbar MSS.).

p. 15), and extending from Cairncot* to the sea. These, added to the fishings of the church lands of Kilmorack and Kiltarlity, already acquired by the Lords Lovat, secured the whole lower fishings of the river Beauly, with the cruives.

The charter is signed by Walter Reid, who styles himself "Abbas a Kinloss ac commendatarius de Bewly," and four monks, who sign, each with the prefix of *dominus*—John Roland, Thomas Twynam, John Crawfurd, and David Dawson. These are doubtless four of the six monks who signed the lease to the Clerks three years before; and three—Twynam, Crawfurd, and Dawson, were old pupils of Ferrarius thirty years before.

It seems that the feu-duties or ground rents made payable by this charter were the then existing rents payable by the then tenants of the priory, converted into money when not money rents, and this conclusion is arrived at from comparing the lease No. XXIII. with this charter. By the charter, Rheindoun pays £5 in money, 16 bolls of farm victual, 2 bolls of custom oats,† 2 custom marts, 4 custom sheep, 8 kids, 4 dozen custom poultry, and fourpence for custom eggs; now this is just the rent payable by the Clerks multiplied by eight: nor is this all, Johane Cwkis lands, by the charter, pay £4 and 4s. for one dozen of poultry; John Clerk's land, by the lease, pays £4 in money and a dozen of poultry.

* The Cairncot was probably some point or cottage opposite the cairn of which the minister of Wardlaw speaks. He says the mother of Hugh Fraser of Lovat, who is recorded in 1367 (*supra*, p. 89), intended to have built a stone bridge over the water of Beauly, for which purpose a great heap of stones was collected, "still to be seen in ye river, called Cairn-na-baintighearna" (the Lady's Cairn), but was prevented by her death from executing the work. The spot would probably be not far from the cruives, where the boundary lay between the monks' rights of fishing and the churchland rights belonging to Kilmorack and Kiltarlity.

† Dr Stuart calls this custom wheat, but if he had had experience of Rheindoun husbandry he would have suspected the true correctness of his reading. The 2 bolls of custom (wheat) are really eight times the "one firlot aites," payable for an eighth of Rheindoun. A boll of wheat in 1591 was estimated at five marks, or £3, 6s. 8d., while a boll of oats was only estimated at £1, 10s. (Family of Kilravock, p. 278).

The services exigible by the lease were of course of no use to the superior, and no equivalent for them is given by the charter.

And we may also compare with advantage the feu-duty reserved by the charter, with the rental of 1562, and we shall find that the feu-duties reserved by the charter for money payments amount to the same as those given in the rental;* so the chalders of victual are 4 in the rental, and by the charter 4, less 2 bolls; for the custom oats (not wheat) 8 bolls; the marts the same, and the sheep the same, and even the poultry exactly the same; of kids it appears the collector of thirds took no account.

The two mills of Beauly are put in the rental as sett (let) for 2 chalders 8 bolls meal and malt, which is no doubt the same rent as the 40 bolls victual for the mills of Tharknok and Bewlie.

Notwithstanding the suspicions of the comptroller, it was thought better to take the salmon at the quantity given up as correct to him, 2 lasts six barrels, or 30 barrels—a last being 12 barrels.

The other charter, dated the same day, is noted by Dr Stuart as follows :

"Charter by Walter, abbot of Kinloss and prior of the monastery of Bewlie, in favour of Hugh, Lord Fraser of Lowatt, for certain great sums of money, and for other reasonable causes, of the office of constable and hereditary keeper of the palace and principal buildings of the messuage in the place of the Priory of Bewlie, erected by the late Bishop of Orkney and prior of the said monastery, on the east side of the church of Bewlie ; also, of the office of hereditary bailie, within the bounds of the lands of the said priory, with the power of ministering justice, of apprehending and punishing malefactors according to law, of holding courts, etc., etc., within the bounds foresaid : To be held of the granter and his successors in feu and heritage for ever, rendering for the said office of constable and keeper foresaid, two silver pennies, in name of blench farm at the feast of Pentecost, if asked ;

* In fact the money rent by the charter is only £59, 10s., whilst the rental gives £61 ; but the number of marts in the rental is only 10, whereas in the charter it is 11, and the commuted price, £1, 10s. makes up the deficiency.

and for the office of bailiary, two pence of the usual money of Scotland, in name of blench farm, at the said feast, if asked. Dated at the monastery of Bewlie and Petlathie respectively, 6th and 12th November 1571." *

It was probably a real advantage to Lord Hugh to get the excellent house erected by the bishop. Lord Hugh seems to be residing at Beauly, and dating his deeds there, in May 1573 † and November 1575. ‡

It seems that before this time Lord Lovat had lent Abbot Walter, on the security of the barony of Beauly, 4500 marks, had paid him in November 1571 4500 marks more, and that he was bound to complete the purchase by paying a third 4500 marks at Whitsunday 1572, or else the charter of November 1571 was only to be a security.

The minister of Wardlaw says that it was of importance in those times to get the prior's charter confirmed by the Crown, which was not then a matter of course; but Lord Lovat had just married Elizabeth Stuart, daughter of the Earl of Athole. We will let the chronicler tell the story:

"The Lord Lovat and his lady design to go south in May: in the very interim of preparing and making ready for the journey, a sudden disaster and indisposedness seized upon my lady, so that she could not travel. He was loath to leave her, but she told him she might recover, but occasions lost were irrecoverable. He wondered what might be under this reply and ambiguous sentiment, and asked her seriously what she meant. She told him that Colin Mackenzie of Kintail was still his competitor, and he might be too cunning for him, as she feared that he and his party were contriving a plot to apply to and prevail with the regent, their relation, anent the right of Beauly; the court was changeable, courtiers flexible, donations and pactions alterable. He yields to her advice, and presently takes horse, and, at Inverness, is informed that Colin of Kintail had taken the start of him, and was gone on the journey south. Lovat, being well acquaint with the road, cuts short, and arrived by a day's journey before him at Edinburgh, some saying they were a night in one and the same lodging, or perhaps in one town on the way, unknown to one

* Records of Kinloss, pp. 96, 97.' † Family of Fraser, p. 86. ‡ *Ib.*, p. 99.

another. But, be sure, Lord Lovat had his intelligence of the other's motions, and made but short stay in any part till he came to his journey's end; and, in short, he secured his object and got his right of Beauly through the seals before Mackenzie came to Edinburgh. The day after, they met together in the open street, and the whole matter came above board, and Kintail found himself outwitted." *

In point of fact, the charters of confirmation under the Great Seal of these charters of the prior and convent of November 1571 were granted on 14th February following, February 1571-2.† The regent was then Lennox.

We have the note of a receipt on 30th April 1572:

"Discharge by Walter, Abbot of Kinlos and Prior of Bewlie, to Hew, Lord Fraser of Lowet, for 4500 merks contained in a reversion made by the said lord to the said abbot, for redemption of the lands, mains, fishings of Bewlie, and their pertinents, in case of non-payment of the said sum before the feast of Whitsunday next, the said 4500 merks being complete payment of 13,500 merks promised by the said lord to the said abbot for the feu of the said lands, mains, and fishings of Bewlie. Dated at Dundee, 30th April 1572."‡

Lord Lovat seems to have got some of the money paid to the prior in November 1571 on a wadset to the Countess of Crawford, Janet Campbell, his mother's sister,§ and some of the money paid in May 1572 on a security to David Waus of Leith, a merchant, who took salmon (fifty-six barrels), full red and sweet, at Lammas 1573, of Lord Hugh, probably in payment of interest, and who exchanged with his lordship salt for salmon.‖

Lord Hugh conveyed away Rheindoun the same year in June to Bain of Tulloch, and Ardnagrask was also shortly afterwards conveyed away. It is probable that the energy displayed by Lord Hugh in the acquisition of Beauly was due to the zeal of his wife.

It seems that this 13,500 marks, or £9000, was mainly paid

* Findon MSS.
† Dunbar Dunbar MSS., 1652; Inventory, Nos. 16 and 44.
‡ Records of Kinloss, p. 98.
§ Dunbar Dunbar MSS.; Inv., Nos. 81 and 71. ‖ Family of Fraser, p. 87.

for the house of the prior, and the difference between the rental and the actual value, which would be paid on the existing leases being renewed : as the process of getting the full benefit of the priory's rights over the parishes, whose rectories she had appropriated, was not yet accomplished.

And now Walter, the prior, having taken his 13,500 marks out of the property of the priory by selling it under a feu-rent to Lord Lovat, was content to give up the office of prior to a Fraser, doubtless a faithful and obedient vassal of the chief.

On the 29th April 1572,* the day before his receipt of the last instalment of the purchase money, Walter Reid executes a procuratory of resignation into the hands of the king of the benefice, priory, and monastery of Beauly, in favour of Mr John Fraser. The Earl of Mar was then the regent; and on his death on the 29th October 1572, it was thought advisable to obtain a new resignation, which was signed by Walter Reid on the 25th November, the day after the Earl of Morton was elected regent.† He, anxious to conciliate the Huntly party, followed up the resignation, by directing, in the name of the king, on the 8th January 1573, a precept to the superintendent of the churches within the diocese of Ross, to instal Mr John Fraser in possession of the Priory of Beauly, the said Mr John Fraser being found by his ordinary of sufficient literature and ability for the said priory.

Mr John Fraser, within a few months after his presentation, executed a new charter of conveyance of the barony of Beauly to Lord Lovat on 8th June 1573 and in June 1575, a charter of the Dominical lands and the salmon fishings, on which sasine was duly given.‡

It seems probable that this Mr John Fraser was the vicar or minister of Conveth (*supra*, p. 242) ; Mr John Fraser, the minister, takes the priory's portion of the Conveth living, and then grants to the Master of Lovat all the leases § which we have before specified, including that of the vicarage of

---
* Records of Kinloss, p. 98. † Lovat Titles, Dunbar Dunbar MSS., No. 26.
‡ Dunbar Dunbar MSS., Lovat Titles, Nos. 6, 7, 9, 25, 31.
§ *Supra*, 243; Appendix, No. XXVIII.

Conveth, which, although he professed to grant as prior, yet it could not have been effectual except as granted by the vicar.

Hugh, Lord Lovat, died in January 1577; and Simon, his infant son, in his sixth year gets sasine of the lands of Beauly on 10th November 1578, and a confirmation under the Great Seal of the charter of Prior Walter Reid on the 10th August 1579.

The collector-general of Thirds, Robert, Lord Boyd, seems to have taken the hint given by the local collector as to the doubtful accuracy of Prior Walter's return of the produce of the fishings, to have improved on it, and to have questioned the right of the young lord's tutors to limit their payment in respect of Beauly to a third of the feu-duty reserved by the charter of November 1571, which we have seen was equivalent to the rental given up by Prior Walter to the collector; but Lord Boyd was unsuccessful.

The principal Tutor of Lovat was Thomas Fraser of Knockie (afterwards of Strichen), his uncle, the founder of the Strichen family, which in 1816, just 240 years after his tutory began, succeeded to the estates of his ward.

Strichen upheld the rights of his ward against all comers, and got a decree of the Court of Session against Lord Boyd, declaring that the third of the benefice of the Priory of Beauly was to be considered a third of the feu-rent reserved by the charter of Prior Walter.

This decision confirms the view we have already taken, that this feu-rent corresponded to the actual rent paid by the tenants of the priory; the benefit of the transaction lay in the reversionary profit expectant on the determination of the leases of the occupying tenants, in the acquisition of the palace or prior's house of Beauly, and in the secured power of obtaining those beneficial leases of the appropriated rectorial tithes of Abertarff and Conveth, which were immediately granted by the new prior. Some hold was also got in this way over the glebe lands of Conveth and Comar; the kirklands mentioned in the register of 1576—which hold seems to have prevented their falling to the Crown by the Act of Annexation.

In 1584, by an Act of Parliament, the King and Estates, reciting the good service done by the deceased Hugh, Lord Fraser of Lovat, and his son and heir, Simon, then Lord Fraser of Lovat, confirmed the charter of Prior Walter, the sasine following given to the said Hugh, and the other sasine given to his heir Simon, and the charter of confirmation of 1579; directing the third to be paid according to the infeftment, together with the decreet against the collector-general to pay only according to the infeftment; and ordaining the third to be paid after the rate and quantity of the feu-duty; and ordering the said decreet, given by the Lords of Session, to have the force of a decree of Parliament.*

The reference to good service done by the boy lord is a mere form of the lawyer who drafted the Act of Parliament; Lord Simon was only twelve years old,† and at King's College, Aberdeen, which he left without the knowledge of his tutor, in July 1586, and wrote to his tutor six months after, from the north of Ireland, that he was visiting there. The person with whom he was staying was Sorley Buy, who styled himself Lord of the Route, and is named with Macangus M'Onell of the Glens, as witnesses to a bond of interdiction, executed by Lord Simon, in September 1587. The connection between them was the marriage of Janet Campbell, Lord Lovat's grandmother, to Donald Macdonald.

Thus, three centuries after John Byset, the founder of our priory, retired to Ireland, and obtained from Henry III.‡ a grant of the lands, some of which were now possessed by the Macdonalds of the Route and the Glens, claiming under John Byset's Irish descendants §—his most important descendant in the Highlands took refuge with them. The youth's mother

* Acts of Parl. Scot., iii., p. 356.
† In the "Estimate of the Scottish Nobility, 1683," the entry is: "Louet.— Hew Fraser, a childe of xii yeres of age, sonne to her that is now Lady of Arran, ane auncient house, and of good power of Hilandmen in the North."
‡ *Supra*, p. 46.
§ Appendix, No. VIII.

may have driven him to this, for his tutor seems to have upheld the position of his ward against her and her infamous husband, the Earl of Arran.

The writer of the Wardlaw MS. says the tutor's first act of kindness was to reinstate in their cells the monks of Beauly who had been dispossessed by Act of Parliament, and to see a provision assigned them for the remainder of their days.* There was no Act of Parliament dispossessing them except the Act obtained by the tutor himself, but this act of kindness was done before its date. The kindness was probably confirming the allowances mentioned in the rental. If dispossessed, they must have been so treated by the new prior or Hugh, Lord Lovat, but without any warrant, as the charters of Prior Walter do not include the priory buildings.

In 1587, the year which saw the judicial murder of his mother, King James procured the Act for the general annexation of the Church lands to the Crown. This included all that belonged to the Priory of Beauly which had not been granted to the Lovat family, and the feu-rent.

The Wardlaw MS. tells us of another act of the good tutor:

"While the Tutor of Lovat was thus discharging the duties of his important trust, his paternal cares were nearly overturned by the following incident: It happened that no marches were settled between the priory lands of Beauly and their neighbours to the north.† The Laird of Kintail having an eye upon these, assembled his vassals, with the intention of appropriating them to himself. The tutor, hearing of this disturber of the general peace of the country, rendezvoused his followers at Beauly. The Laird of Foulis, his staunch friend, advanced to the banks of the Conan with three hundred men, to support his cause. Alarmed at the intrusion of so formidable an array into his territories, Mackenzie had recourse to pacification; and the terms being such as were consistent with their rights, the tutor drew off his forces, and all differences were forgotten."‡

It was probably a part of these terms that the young lord

* Family of Fraser, p. 92. † The line of hills mentioned *supra*, p. 269.
‡ Family of Fraser, p. 93.

should marry Catherine, daughter of the Laird of Kintail, which he did when he was not more than seventeen years old. The entry as to him in the " Present State of the Nobilities in Scotland, 1592," * is : " Lovatt . . . Frasir . . . Prot. of 23 yeres; his mother, Stewart, aunt to Atholl; his wife, the Laird of Mackenzie's daughter." Again, in 1602, the entry is : " The Lord Lovet, callit Fraser: Protestant, of small action." † He built the castle of Dalcross in 1620. ‡

It is said that in 1626 Sir Alexander Fraser of Doors having lost his lady, came to visit Lord Lovat, and died, whilst his guest, in May that year, and was interred in St Catherine's aisle in Beauly Priory, his lordship's own burial-place. Lord Lovat died in April 1633, and was buried, it is said, in the priory church.§

We may assume that Crawford and Twynam would not have added, the one the word "friar," and the other the word "monk," to their names, in 1568, unless they had still retained the Catholic faith ; they were both monks in 1540, if not in 1557. Half a century elapsed before the Act of Annexation in 1587; till that time the brethren at Beauly were entitled to reside in the priory buildings, although they were forbidden by the Act 1567 to say mass in the priory church.

Perhaps the pupils of Ferrarius still gave some instruction to some of the young gentry of the north, as before the Reformation (*supra*, pp. 182, 230), seeing that for a time nothing was done to supply the place of the monastic schools. ‖ The Act of Annexation excepted church property granted for the entertainment of masters and students in colleges, but it completed the destruction of the provision for primary education that existed in the monasteries, which the profuse grants of the abbots and priors had begun.

In 1587 Simon, Lord Lovat, was an exile in Antrim, and the tutor, Strichen, managed his estates. As long as the tutor lived, the monks would not be disturbed. He appears in 1611

* Estimate of Scottish Nobility, p. 70. † *Ib.*, p. 78.
‡ Family of Lovat, p. 169. § *Ib.*, p. 101.
‖ Appendix, No. XXXII.

to have buried his wife in the priory church. He himself died in 1612. By the time of the death of Lord Simon in 1633, the last monk of Beauly would have disappeared.

There are no remains of the priory buildings except the church, and some fragments clinging to the walls of the church, from which it would appear that the priory buildings were attached to it at the south-west end of the nave, and at the south end of the south chapel or aisle. The buildings probably formed a square, having the south wall of the nave, which is eighty feet long, for one side of it, and were two stories in height at the points of connection with the church. There was a cloister against the nave, which was sixty feet long on that side, and this cloister probably ran round the whole square enclosing the Cloister Garth.

The general arrangement may be understood from the annexed sketch of ground plan, where the dotted lines indicate the priory buildings, and the lines the existing remains of the priory church.

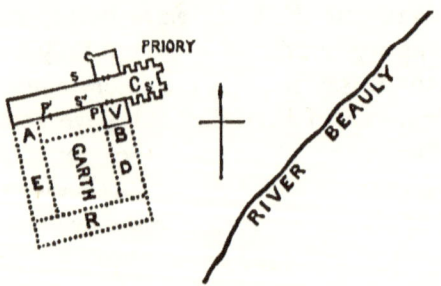

Scale—208 feet to an inch.

And now we may inquire into the actual extent of the restoration of the church, which was executed, according to Ferrarius (*supra*, p. 219), by Bishop Robert Reid.

Before we examine the traces afforded by the building itself, we may obtain help by the account Ferrarius gives of his patron's architectural work in Orkney.

Bishop Reid, the Piedmontese tells us, greatly enlarged Kirkwall Cathedral, the cathedral church of Orkney, adding three pillars (piers) to the former fabric, and decorating the entry with a magnificent porch.

Mr Neale, speaking of Kirkwall Cathedral, mentions * that Bishop Robert Reid, who succeeded in 1540, is said to have erected the three Romanesque western pillars of the nave, and the First Pointed western porch, and he adds : †

"Popular tradition says that Bishop Reid added the new bays, and was prevented by the progress of the Reformation ‡ from vaulting them in, but granting that in his new piers he did imitate the old work, and that this is one of the few instances in which Third Pointed restoration fell back on Romanesque, he would not have imitated First Pointed in the new portions of his aisles, and Middle Pointed in his west window; nor could he, if he would, have made the beautiful western porch a gem of First Pointed ; add to which, that, as I am fully satisfied, the vaulting has been complete, and then pulled down, not left incomplete."

Now I have faith in the contemporary account of the bishop's friend and companion, Ferrarius, and we shall find, on examining the architecture of the priory church at Beauly, that it is probable the bishop extended both the cathedral church and the priory church in the same fashion.

The ground plan will help the reader to understand the priory church of Beauly.

From the wall, at the eastern end of the choir or chancel, C, down to a point about fifty feet from the western door, the work is pure Early English work, of the style which was prevalent in England and Scotland in the year 1230, and for thirty or forty years following it.

This no doubt is the original work executed after 1230, and in the lifetime of John Byset and his son, and it corresponds to the earliest work at Pluscardine, and to all that remains of the church at Ardchattan.

Even here there is a difference between the easternmost,

* Ecclesiological Notes, p. 101. † *Ib.*, p. 103.
‡ The progress of the Reformation could not affect the bishop's work.

and presumably the first, work—that to the east of the transepts, and that to the west of them. The earlier windows are not foliated. The later windows on the north side are trefoil headed above the mullion, and on the south side there is the remarkable feature of three windows externally spherically triangular, but the opening for light trefoil-shaped—a style nearly resembling windows of the same date at Westminster Abbey (where the spherical triangle encloses a foliated circle), and in design like some at Pluscardine, and which style was adopted by the architect, in order to leave room for the cloisters below, although the cloisters were probably roofed with wood, resting on the corbel stones, still to be seen in the wall.

There is a beautiful double piscina, S', in the south wall, executed in the very best style of the Early English period, and under the east window is an awmry. The remains of the east window show that it must have been altered after the original erection of the choir; this is a large window, with a fragment attached to the spring of the window arch, which shows that the head must have been filled in with tracery. This implies a window of the style of Scottish architecture which prevailed after the Baliol wars were over.

The Wardlaw MS. speaks of the wife of the first Fraser of Lovat as filling the east window of the priory church with baken glass. It puts the first Lovat much too far back; but there may have been some true tradition of this beautifying the choir. The style of the east window would correspond with work done between 1367 and 1384, when Hugh, the first recorded Fraser of Lovat, was in possession; and it is not improbable that he or his wife took down the combination of separate lancet windows, which would form the east window of the Early English period, and inserted one large window of several lights, with the head pierced by flowing tracery, and full of stained glass.

The side windows of the choir have over them a bead moulding forming an arcade, and resting upon small corbels, which seem now to be simply balls.

So little remains of Ardchattan Priory that it is only a trace here and there which indicates the period of its erection. What is left appears to be the chancel of the church, with an aisle or chapel on the north side, and in the south wall of the chancel there is a piscina or ablution drain under an arch, with a credence table, which arch is ornamented with the Early English toothed ornament. The east windows of the chancel are gone. At the end of the chancel are some remains of strong piers, which suggest a central tower there. The "Old Statistical Account" of 1793 says: "What now remains of the priory is converted into burying-ground, in which are two monuments in niches in the walls. Each has a stone coffin, and one of them is ornamented with a font and inscription in the Runic character. On two gravestones are effigies of priests in their pontifical robes, with inscriptions in the same character." There appears to be an Early English lancet window in the prior's house, and in the church there are no indications of buildings of a later period.*

In Pluscardine, the Early English style marks much of the building, as may be seen from Mr Billings' engravings, in his handsome work on "Scottish Architecture."

At Beauly there is still on the first floor at A a fireplace and a garde-robe, which is continued to the ground, and close to which are the vestiges of a staircase. There is said to be a drain running from this point in the direction of the Beauly. This fireplace had the chimney standing above it at the times that Cordiner and Cardonnel took their views of the priory.

At B there is a door which must have led to the priory buildings in that direction; and there are masses of stone, showing that the walls were pulled down to this point. The tradition of the village is that here was the Infirmary. Probably the Dormitory was at D—a continuation of the same

---

* General Hutton inserts, in his MSS. in Brit. Mus., an extract from a letter of August 1798 by a lady, who had just visited Ardchattan Priory. She says: "The place has been destroyed by the possessor for the sake of the stones, much to the regret of the inhabitants. The old tombs, therefore, are almost the only remains of what it once was" (B.M., Add. MSS., 8142).

building with steps leading down into the South chapel or vestry, for the use of the brethren at midnight and early prayers.

At R would be probably the Refectory, and at E the entrance to the priory. At P and P' there are doors from the cloister into the church, probably processional doors.

The South chapel, V, is by some supposed to be the St Catherine's Chapel mentioned in the Wardlaw MS. (*supra*, p. 279) as where Sir A. Fraser of Doors was buried when on a visit to Simon, Lord Lovat. It was probably the Vestry or place where the vestments were kept, as it must have been too low for divine service, and there is now no trace of an altar there.

The North chapel or aisle is said by tradition to have been the Chapter-house, and also St Catherine's Chapel. It was quite large enough to contain the brethren of the house when "chapterly gathered." It had a stone-groined roof, with ribs springing from corbels, and these are of later work, apparently, than that of the choir.

Hugh Fraser of Lovat, who married Janet Fenton in 1416, is said to have built the north work of the church and the Chapel of the Holy Ghost. The wall on the north side, which divides the North chapel from the nave, appears to be continuous with the wall of the nave, and so is the wall on the south side; although there is a large arch opening into the South chapel of later construction, it seems to have been an opening into the upper part of the transept only, which was divided horizontally into two floors, the lower being little more than seven feet high. The north work of Hugh Fraser must have been the north transept, with the turret at its north-west corner, up which is a stair, and which was probably a bell-turret for the bell summoning the chapter.

The Chapel of the Holy Ghost was external to the present church, and the piscina or water stoup, S, still remains in the external wall of the nave, twenty-two feet from its junction with the north transept, showing that the altar of the Chapel was near this spot, at right angles to the piscina; and this altar would probably have been to the east, for, in 1416, the practice of having side altars facing the north or south was not common. On examining the external walls, we find traces of the extent to which this Chapel of the Holy Ghost went; it seems to have ended easterly, just beyond the piscina, so as not to darken the beautiful two-light windows of the nave, and to have extended westerly to the then depth of the nave.

The alterations made by Prior Mackenzie (*supra*, p. 105) were simply confined to piercing the walls between the transepts and the nave, to afford room for his own tomb, and for his brother, the Knight of Kintail's tomb.

It is perfectly clear that the latest alteration in the church was a very extensive addition, amounting to a lengthening of the nave by upwards of thirty feet below the present door, P', leading into the cloisters.

The windows in this western part of the nave are poor and late imitations of the Early English work at the east end. The two on the north side are clumsy single-light windows; whilst of the two on the south side, the western one is a two-light window of debased workmanship, and the other is ill-shaped but large, as if to throw increased light, suggesting the position of a rood loft: so the windows in the western gable itself are, if to be considered Gothic at all, only a base kind of Romanesque-Gothic.* But the internal arrangements of the nave show not only the fact, but the reason of its prolongation.

Not far above the junction of the prolonged walls there is a double piscina, S", and awmry, showing that at this point there must have been an altar stretching across the church. The work of this piscina is a faithful, but yet ineffectual, imitation of the pretty piscina in the choir.

* Captain White, R.E. (Proc. S. A. Scot., June 13, 1870), maintains that this western gable is Early English work. He says it "is almost an exact counterpart, only in miniature, of the window arrangement in the west front of Wells Cathedral, which is known to be Early English." Whatever may be said to the similarity of the window arrangement of the two fronts, I fear that the shade of Bishop Josceline would arise if the comparison were extended to the workmanship.

I take it, Bishop Reid extended the choir of the church from the transepts down to the point where he erected a new altar, probably for the use of the villagers of Beauly, whilst he increased the space for the monks, the brethren of the choir, and, as a memorial of his work, he put up his initials and arms on the outside of the new western gable.

One of his objects probably was to extend the space for processions at the greater festivals. There may have been a western bell-tower before,* and the cloister square was probably not extended. The upper floor, however, at A in the plan, was most likely added by the bishop; and the room there may have served for the residence of the sub-prior.

Precisely the same desire to afford longer space for processions would have induced him to prolong the nave of the cathedral at Kirkwall. He had, on becoming bishop, largely increased the chapter of the cathedral by instituting a complete set of officials, on the scale of the most liberal establishments of England and Scotland (*supra*, p. 222; App., No. XXV.).

It appears by his work at Beauly that the bishop was not unskilful in imitating the early and simpler style of Gothic; and I conceive that he added the three western bays to Kirkwall Cathedral, whilst he probably reinserted there the Early English western door which had stood in the western gable before he pulled it down, to prolong the nave. In fact, the construction of the western gable of Kirkwall Cathedral, as engraved by Mr Billings (vol. iii., plate 44), seems to indicate that the great portal had been removed from a thicker wall than that in which the transomed window above it is placed; and there is a somewhat unadorned and inartistic triangular projection brought out to make the wall below thick enough to receive the great portal.

Simon, Lord Lovat, was succeeded by his son Hugh, whose retour gives the feu-rent of Beauly at £211, 15s.† This does not correspond accurately with the rent reserved by the charter of 1571; but on comparing that with the return in the

* *Supra*, pp. 93, 219.   † Inq. Ret., Inverness-shire, May 19, 1635.

MS. in the Register House of the charge of the Temporalitie of Kirklandis, north side of the Forth, we find that Lord Simon's rent had been slightly augmented, and slightly varies from the charter, which omits the interesting item of "The common brew-hous in money, xvis.," found in the return.

On the 22d December 1639, King Charles I. granted the Priory of Beauly to the Bishop of Ross.* The effect of this was to give the bishop the feu-rent of £211, 15s., to make him the superior of the lands, and to vest in him the property of the priory church and priory buildings, other than the prior's house built by Bishop Reid, which was detached from the monastery proper. The Bishop of Ross was at that time also entitled to the feu-rent of £10, 6s. 8d., payable by Lord Lovat, in respect of the kirklands and fishing of Kilmorack (*supra*, Charter No. XXII.).

Cromwell's citadel at Inverness, which is said to have been partly built out of the ruins of the Cathedral of Fortrose (*supra*, p. 193), is reported to have laid the Priory of Beauly under contribution for stone. The rights of the Bishop of Ross would be then vested in the Government, and the property of the priory buildings would belong to Cromwell as Lord Protector.

On the Restoration, the Bishop of Ross resumed his rights over the priory; for example, in 1688, James, Bishop of Ross, as superior, with consent of his chapter, as having right to the Priory of Beauly by grant from King Charles I., confirms a charter of Rheindoun,† part of which lands were leased to John Clerk by the Charter No. XXIII.

The buildings would be used without licence from bishop or chapter as a quarry for stone; and most likely Hugh, Lord Lovat, who, about 1665, is said to have erected a mansion-house at Beauly, and to have demolished the House of Lovat, for the sake of using its oak rafters for his Beauly house, took largely of the priory buildings for the purpose. He may have only enlarged the prior's house at Beauly.

In 1691, on the abolition of Episcopacy, the feu-rent, and

* Hutton's MSS. in Brit. Mus., Add. MSS., 8144, p. 142.   † Chisholm MSS.

the church and priory buildings, if any remained, reverted to the Crown, of whom the Lovat family would hold the Beauly lands, until their forfeiture in 1746.

We hear nothing more of Beauly Priory until Pennant, in 1769, inserts the entry: "August 17. Ford the Bewley, where a salmon fishery, belonging to the Lovat estate, rents at £120 per annum. The country on this side the river is called Leornamonach, or the Monks' land, having formerly been the property of the Abby of Bewly."* On his return from Ross-shire, August 29, he enters: "Pass near the Abby of Beaulieu, a large ruin; cross the ferry, and again reach Inverness,"† with a note, "Founded about 1219, by Lord Patrick Bisset, for the Monks of Vallombrosa."

Pennant's allusion was followed up by the Rev. Charles Cordiner, Episcopalian minister at Banff, who published his "Antiquities" in 1780, and dates one of his letters to Pennant, "Abbey of Beaulieu, June 10th." We may quote his description, as showing the reviving interest even then in ecclesiastical antiquities in Scotland:

"Round this ruined monastery at present, nothing but rural images invite attention. The venerable boughs of aged trees cast their shade on either hand. Within all is silence and desolation. Decaying monuments of saints and heroes are but as 'the clouds of other times,' and give a transient solemnity to the recollection of past ages. The thought of these courts having often echoed with the glad *Te Deums* of thousands who, along with their temple, are now mouldering into dust, deepens the veneration which these hallowed ruins inspire.

"The whole floor of the abbey is crowded with tombstones of various ages, many of them, I should suppose, nearly co-eval with itself, which was built in the thirteenth century. The most ancient of these appear to have been the lids of stone coffins. On each is a large cross, orna-

* Pennant's Tour in Scotland, Chester, 1771, p. 140.
† *Ib.*, p. 161. His entry of the then price of provisions at Inverness is interesting: "Beef (22 ounces to the pound), 2d. to 4d.; mutton, 2d. to 3d.; veal, 3d. to 6d.; chickens, 3d. to 4d. a couple; fowl, 4d. to 6d. a piece; goose, 12d. to 14d.; ducks, 1s. a couple; eggs, seven a penny; salmon, of which there are several great fisheries, 1d. to 1½d. per pound."

mented with various flowerings, sometimes with swords, and other emblems, at the side; and, as there is not along with these any vestige of letters, it is a tacit acknowledgment that writing was little practised at the time when these monuments were carved; for, as many of them must have been cut under the eye, and by the direction, of the clergy, and as monasteries were in this country the first seats of learning, and where the fine arts were principally studied and encouraged, it must place the era of these stones at least five hundred years back. At the same time, a degree of neatness and elegance, which prevails both in the design and execution of the carvings, implies a refinement in taste and progress in the arts at that period, which certainly had much declined in later ages. In the vaults of the abbey there are some remains of bodies found in the stone coffins. On the lids of these are warriors, well carved and in fine relief; these have *Latin* inscriptions in old characters round the margin, which seem to be dated in the fifteenth century, but are in general so much defaced, it is impossible to copy them.

"A few of the most distinct figures on the older gravestones are marked in the foreground of the view of the abbey."

He gives two views of the ruins; and one of the figures in the foreground deserves attention: it seems to be a representation of the then state of a large tombstone now lying on the north side of the chancel: this has on it a figure in armour, and an almost illegible inscription, of which, however, the words "SIMON DUS. DE LOVIT"* may be distinctly made out.

This must be the monument of Lord Simon, who died in 1633, or of a more interesting person—Simon, who is supposed to have been the predecessor and elder brother of Hugh Fraser of Lovat of 1367 (*supra*, p. 89).

On the one hand, as Captain White remarks,† the correct style, after the elevation of the family to the peerage, was "Dominus Fraser de Lovat;" and this very style is given as the inscription on the tomb in the Priory church of Hugh, Lord Lovat, who fell at Kinlochy (*supra*, p. 225). On the other hand, the only existing memorial is much more likely to be that of the last Fraser of Lovat who was buried there,

* No other words can be relied on except "obilis vir."
† Proc. S. A. Scot., June 13, 1870, p. 456.

than of the first; and the whole cutting is so obliterated that we can place little reliance on the supposed details of the armour, such as the "roundels" on the shoulders, on which Captain White relies for attributing an earlier date to it than 1633.

Armour was used down to 1633;* and the helmet, in the form of a conical steel cap or bascinet, though, strictly speaking, of the thirteenth and fourteenth centuries, is almost invariably the monumental type of helmet of every age in the North of Scotland.† We have certainly this form of helmet on the monument of Sir Kenneth Mackenzie, A.D. 1491 (see frontispiece), and on the armed figures on the monument of the Macdougals at Ardchattan, A.D. 1502 (*supra*, p. 153). The heraldic bearings on the stone are, on one side the head, a shield quarterly, with a faint indication of "fraises" in one quarter, and "crowns" in another; and on the other side a stag, the crest of the Frasers of Lovat; but this quarterly shield appears as early as 1431 (*supra*, p. 97); and an instance of the bearing a crest detached from the shield on a tombstone is given by Mr Cutts ‡ in the case of Gilling of Gilling, in Yorkshire, about 1400.

In 1774 the forfeited estates of Lovat were restored to General Fraser.

Cardonnel published in 1788 "Etchings of Antiquities in Scotland," and gives one of the priory church, with this short description:

"BEAULIEU.

"This priory, commonly called Bewly, is situated upon the river of the same name in Ross-shire, about eleven miles from Inverness, and was founded, according to Fordun, in the year 1230, for monks of the order of Vallis Caulium, by John Bisset, whose charter is confirmed by Pope Gregory III.

"At the dissolution of monasteries, Hugh, Lord Fraser of Lovat,

* The portrait of Duncan Campbell of Glenorchy, who died in 1631, given in the Black Book of Taymouth (Bann. Club), represents him in full armour.
† Proc. Soc. Ant. Scot., vol. ix., p. 28.
‡ Cutts' Sepulchral Slabs, 1849, p. 87, plate 66.

acquired this priory from the last prior, to which family it at present belongs."

The family of Gairloch, who, being descended from Sir Kenneth Mackenzie of Kintail, had continued to use the priory as a burial-place, which Mackenzie of Seaforth, the elder branch, had abandoned for the cathedral at Fortrose, repaired the walls and windows of the north chapel or chapter-house, so as to preserve it from spoliation.

The ruins, however, seem to have been in a disgraceful state in 1815, for in May of that year subscriptions were invited for repairing the breaches in the walls, and particularly for raising and building up the east end of the church, by which idle persons enter and loiter about, to the detriment of the place, and to prevent any access but by the west door. The parties to be consulted were the families of Lovat and Gairloch, the Chisholm, Maclean of Craigscorrie (we may recognise the *Karcurri* of Pope Gregory III., *supra*, p. 14), and the Frasers of Newton, Aigas, and Eskadale.

In August 1844 the following paragraph appeared in the Inverness papers: "The interesting ruins of Beauly Priory are also carefully protected and kept in order, and Lord Lovat, we understand, intends throwing down some unsightly buildings close to the priory, that its ancient and picturesque walls and its noble trees may be seen to more advantage."

In 1845 the rights of those claiming an interest in the ruins were tested by application to the Court of Session. Lord Lovat presented a note to the Court, in which, after setting forth that he was proprietor of the barony of Beauly, and of the heritable office of constabulary and keeper of the palace building and principal messuage of the Priory of Beauly; and that the Priory of Beauly was in a ruinous state, and that he had determined to prevent further dilapidation, and to put the ruins into a state of repair and order, so as to preserve them as long as possible; and that he had addressed circulars to parties, claiming right to interfere with his proposed operations on the plea that they had right to the area of the church as a burying-ground and that certain of their ancestors had been interred there, intimating that he was resolved to prevent interments taking place for the future within the precincts of the priory; he prayed an interdict to restrain the defenders from interfering with his proposed operations, and from intruding into the priory for the purpose of using the same as a burying-ground in future.

The defenders denied Lord Lovat's title to the Priory of Beauly, which they alleged to have passed to the Crown by the Act of Annexation 1587, and they stated that an immemorial usage of sepulture had existed within the priory, the area being covered with tombstones of remote antiquity.

Lord Jeffrey, before whom the case first came, said, " There would seem to be better ground for an interdict at the instance of the respondents, and this is not a shape in which the rights of the noble complainer can be determined. He must proceed by declarator, to which the representatives of the House of Kintail, Gairloch, Chisholm, etc., as well as those charged with the interests of the Crown, must be made parties ;" and, as Lord Ordinary, he refused the interdict.

Lord Lovat afterwards commenced an action of declarator, and reclaimed (appealed) against Lord Jeffrey's order. The Lord Justice-Clerk said, " The right of interment may have had its origin long anterior to Lord Lovat's right," and the Court, on the 19th of December 1845, adhered to the Lord Ordinary's judgment.*

It soon became evident that no case could be made out on the declarator, and ultimately an arrangement, much for the benefit of all parties, was made in the spring of 1847; on the 15th June 1847 the Lords of the Treasury authorised the Commissioners of Woods and Forests to grant a lease to Lord Lovat,† and a lease was accordingly granted, of " all and whole the ruins of the old church and monastery of Beauly, ground within the same and burying-ground adjoining, belonging to her Majesty and her royal successors, as the same are deline-

---

* Lord Lovat v. Alexander Fraser and others, viii., Bell's Sessions Cases.
† Appendix, No. XXXIII.

ated by the red lines on a plan docqueted by the Commissioners and Lord Lovat."

The term is for thirty-one years from Whitsunday 1847. The right of the Crown to restrict and permit interments is reserved. The rent is £1, and Lord Lovat agrees " to maintain and keep the premises in their present state and condition as a venerable monument of ancient times and an object of interest."

APPENDIX.

No. I.

NAME OF BEAULY (p. 15).

In Migne's "Dictionnaire des Abbayes," Paris 1856, eight French monasteries of this name are mentioned: 1. Beaulieu (Diocese de Limoges), Benedictine A.; 2. B. (D. de Langres), Cistercian A.; 3. B. (D. de Troyes), Præmonstratensian A.; 4. B. en Argonne, Benedictine A.; 5. Beaulieu-lez-Duant (Pas de Calais), Augustinian A.; 6. B. près Loches (D. de Tours), Benedictine A.; 7. B.-lez-le-Mans (D. du Mans), Augustinian A.; 8. B.-lez-sur-le-Noble (a Douai, Nord), Augustinian Nunnery. The oldest Beauly is B. en Argonne, seven leagues from Verdun, founded in 642 by St Bodan, who came to France a short time after St Columba. It was called Beaulieu by St Bodan by reason of the great beauty of the situation.

Amongst the Cistercian abbeys founded in the kingdom of Cyprus is mentioned, Beaulieu, Bellus Locus, founded in 1237.

Migne's account of our priory is as follows:

"BEAULIEU.—Bellus Locus (ancien diocèse de Rosse, Ecosse). Abbaye de l'ordre de Citeaux fondée vers l'an 1263. Elle jouissait du titre abbatial, bien qu'elle ne fut cependant qu'un prieuré."

No. II.

LEPERS' HOUSE (p. 24).

This foundation by John Byset is the earliest recorded in Scotland. Some others, besides Maiden Bradley, had been founded earlier in England.

Hugh de Wells, Bishop of Lincoln in 1211, gives, by his will, one hundred marks to be distributed among the leper houses of that bishopric, and three marks to the leper house of Frome Selwood in Somersetshire; three marks to the leper house, without Bath; and three marks to the lepers of Ilchester, in the same county. There were three other leper houses in the county of Somerset alone. One of them, whose endowment now includes a field within the parish of Thorn Faulcon, where this note is written, is first recorded as a leper house in 1236, when King Henry III. grants a protection to the master and brethren of the leper hospital of St Margaret of Taunton, In 1280, 1418, it is similarly styled. In 1472 the indwellers are called "the poor, infirm, and leprous people" of the hospital; in 1544 simply "the poor persons of the spittel house." In 1548 the entry is, "Ther be wthin the same hospital vi poore lazare people." It was saved from forfeiture to Edward VI. by being recognised as an alms-house, which it now is; and, from these notices, it would appear that by 1472 the disease had become less frequent in its ravages, and had ceased in 1540.*

No. III.

CASTLES (p. 40).

The old castles of Lovat, Beaufort, and Erchless have all disappeared; all that remains of the old castle of Urquhart is the ditch. The tower of Beaufort, occupied by Simon, Lord Lovat, is described by Ferguson the astronomer, who visited it, as " a rude tower " (*infra*, p. 302). The present Erchless Castle was erected between 1594 and 1610, and completed by John Chisholm. In his grandson Alexander's time, in 1689, it was (as appears from Mackay's "Memoirs") alternately occupied by the contending troops of James II. and William III.; and whilst Lord Strathnaver's regiment was at Inverness, two companies were lodged in the castles of Urquhart and Erchless. Castle Urquhart is a very prominent object from Loch Ness, and, as Mr G. T. Clark observes (*Builder*, Feb. 17, 1872), combines,

* The Hospital of St Margaret, Taunton. By the Rev. T. Hugo, Somersetshire Archæological Society's Proceedings, 1872.

in a very remarkable degree, natural and artificial defences upon its *enceinte*, and within its area. It has a gatehouse, and is far more extensive than most Highland castles. The keep is an excellent example of the stern rectangular Scottish fortalice of the fifteenth century. It is about 40 feet square, of four stages. "The remains of the castle now standing," says Mr Clark in his exhaustive article, "can scarcely be older than the fifteenth century, and probably it was one of those built about the middle of it, in accordance with the strong recommendation published by James I. on his return from his captivity in England."

No. IV.

LIST OF THE BISHOPS OF MORAY—DE MORAVIA—MORAVIENSIS—FROM A.D. 1115 TO A.D. 1573 (p. 41).

1. GREGORY, "Episcopus de Moravia," "Gregorius Moraviens. epc.," A.D. 1115, and *after* A.D. 1125.
2. WILLIAM I., "Epis. Muraue.," "W. Moruens.," "Will. epis. Moru.," "de Muref," *ante* A.D. 1155, Feb. 27; Papal Legate of Scotland A.D. 1159-1161, from Pope Alex. III.; *ob.* A.D. 1162, Jan. 24.
3. FELIX, Bp. of Moray, *between* A.D. 1162 and A.D. 1171.
4. SYMON I., de Tonei ("de Toeny"), Cistercian monk of Mailros, and Abbot of Cogeshale in Essex, England, to A.D. 1168; *el.* Bp. of Moray A.D. 1171; *cons.* A.D. 1172, Jan. 23, at St Andrews; *ob.* 1184, Sept. 17.
5. ANDREW I., *said to have been* Bp. of Moray *between* A.D. 1184 and A.D. 1186 (but apparently a mistake in Shaw for *Andrew, Bp. of Caithness;* and see *vacant* A.D. 1184-1187).
6. RICHARD, chaplain to King William the Lyon, "clericus Regis," "epis. Moraviensis de Moravia;" *el.* A.D. 1187, March 1; *cons.* 15th of same month at St Andrews; *ob.* A.D. 1203.
7. BRICE de Douglas (Dean of Moray? *ante* A.D. 1200), Prior of Lesmahagu, O.S.B., Tironen.; *suc.* A.D. 1203; "Epis. Moravien. Moravie" at Lateran Gen. Council A.D. 1215-16; *ob.* A.D. 122 , "Bricius epis."
8. ANDREW II., de Moravia, Parson of Duffus; *el.* Bp. of Moray A.D. 1223, *ante* May 12; *cons. ante* April 10, A.D. 1224; *ob.* A.D. 1242, *post* July.
9. SYMON II., Dean of Moray (*ante* A.D. 1232); *suc.* A.D. 1223; *cons.* Bp. of Moray *ante* A.D. 1224; *ob.* A.D. 1251.
10. RALPH, Canon of Lincoln Cathedral, in England (*probably* Ralph de Leicester, treasurer of Lincoln, A.D. 1248; *ob.* March 22, A.D. 1253), "electus est in Episcopum Morafensem in Scotia, *M. Radulphus* ecclesiæ Lincolenensis canonicus," A.D. 1251; *elect.* Bp. of Moray, but *not consecrated.*

APPENDIX. 297

11. ARCHIBALD, Dean of Moray; *cons.* Bp. of Moray A.D. 1253; *ob.* A.D. 1298, Dec. 9.
12. DAVID I., de Moravia, Canon of Moray; *el.* Bp. of Moray A.D. 1299; *conf.* by Pope Boniface VIII. June 30, and *cons.* at Anagni by Card. Bp. of Porto, 28th of that month; *ob.* A.D. 1326, Jan. 9.
13. JOHN I., de Pylmore, Canon of Ross, and Bp.-*elect* of that see (but *unconfirmed*); *el.* Bp. of Moray, but *prov.* by Pope John XXII. A.D. 1326, March 31; *cons.* at Avignon by Card. Bp. of Palestrina, 30th of that month; *ob.* A.D. 1362, Sept. 28.
14. ALEXANDER I., Bur, Archdeacon of Moray; *prov.* to see by Pope Urban V. A.D. 1362, Dec. 23, and *cons.* at Avignon 24th of that month; *ob.* A.D. 1397, May 5.
15. WILLIAM II., de Spynie, Præcentor of Moray and Canon of Caithness; *cons.* Bp. of Moray A.D. 1397, Sept. 16, by Pope Benedict XIII.; *ob.* A.D. 1406, Aug. 2.
16. JOHN II., de Innes, Parson of Duffus, Canon of Moray, and Archdeacon of Caithness; *cons.* Bp. of Moray A.D. 1407, Jan. 23, at Avignon by same Pope; *ob.* A.D. 1414, April 25.
17. HENRY de Lychton; *elect.* Bp. of Moray A.D. 1414, May 18; *cons.* A.D. 1415, March 8, at Valencia, in Spain, by above Anti-Pope; and *trans.* to see of Aberdeen A.D. 1422, April 3.
18. COLUMBA de Dunbar, Dean of Collegiate Church of Dunbar (fd. by his father, George, Earl of March, A.D. 1392), and Dean of Dunkeld; *prov.* to see by Pope Martin V. A.D. 1422, April 3; *ob.* 1435.
19. JOHN II., de Winchester, (English) Chapl. to K. James I., Canon of Dunkeld, and Provost of Collegiate ch. of Lincluden; *el.* Bp. of Moray; *conf.* by Pope Eugene IV. A.D. 1436, April; *cons.* A.D. 1437; *ob.* A.D. 1460 (or 1463?), April 1, having *apparently res.* his see A.D. 1458, May 9, at Cambuskenneth monastery.
20. JAMES I., Stewart, Dean of Moray, Bp. of the see A.D. 1460, *ante* Dec. 12, and *probably* from A.D. 1458-1459? *res.* after May 13, A.D. 1461 (*apparently*); *ob.* A.D. 1466, Aug. 5.
21. DAVID II., Stewart, Parson of Spynie, and Prebendary of Moray; *prov.* to this see by Pope Pius II. A.D. 1462, July 27; *cons. post* June *et ante* Dec. A.D. 1463; *ob.* A.D. 1476, *post* Sept. 5.
22. WILLIAM III., de Tulloch, Bp. of Orkneys, from which *trans.* to see of Moray by Pope Sixtus IV. A.D. 1477, March 31; *ob.* A.D. 1482; *ante* July.
23. ANDREW III., Stewart, Sub-dean of Glasgow, and Provost of Lincluden; *el.* Bp. of Moray *ante* July A.D. 1482; *conf.* and *cons.* at St Andrews A.D. 1483, *post* Jan.; *ob.* A.D. 1501, Sept. 29, *ætat.* 58.
24. ANDREW IV., Foreman, Prior of Pittenweem, O. S. Aug. Can. Reg., Protonotary Apostolic of Pope Alex. VI., and *prov.* by that pontiff to this see A.D. 1501, Nov. 26; *cons. post* Sept. A.D. 1503? Abp. of Bourges, in France, A.D. 1513, Sept. 12; and *trans.* to St Andrews A.D. 1514, Dec. 25.
25. JAMES II., Hepburne, Rector of Dalry and Paitoun, Abbot of Dunfermlyn

(1514-15); el. Bp. of Moray A.D. 1516, ante Oct.; cons. in A.D. 1517; ob. A.D. 1524, ante Nov.

26. ROBERT Schawe, Abbot of Paisley, O. S. B., Cluniac; prov. to this see by Pope Clement VII. A.D. 1525, May 18; cons. ante Jan. 15, 1526; ob. A.D. 1528, ante May 31.

27. ALEXANDER II., Stewart, Dean of Brechin, Abbot of Inchaffray (1514), and of Scone (1518); prov. to this see by Pope Clem. VII. A.D. 1529, Sept. 13; cons. ante July 18, A.D. 1530; ob. ante May 31, A.D. 1538.

28. PATRICK Hepburne, Prior of St Andrews and Abbot of Scone; prov. to this see by Pope Paul III. A.D. 1539, June 14; cons. ante April 16, A.D. 1540; ob. A.D. 1573, June 20.*

No. V.

EXTRACTS FROM RECORDS (pp. 45-47).

The following extracts from, and notes of the records in the Record Office, London, I owe to the kindness of Sir Thomas Hardy:

"*Pat. & Chart.* 27 *Hen. III., p.* 739.—Pro *Johe. Byset.* Rex. Justiciario nro. Hibern. sal. Sciatis quod si *Johannes Byset* ad nos ad partes transm. venire vol. in servit. nostr.; bene volumus quod feodum habet a nobis sicut Jacobus de Savill quondam miles vester idem vobiscum locutus est et potestatem vobis damus daudi illi feodum prædictum. Teste apud Burdegallam xvii die Dec. (1242. Note: Henry III. accession, 28 Oct. 1215)."

"*Pat. & Chart.* 27 *Hen. III., m.* 4.—Pro *Waltero Byset.* Rex comisit *Waltero Byset* manerium de Ludeham cum pertinenciis ad se sustentando in servicio Regis quamdiu R. placuerit. In cujus, &c. Teste Rege apud Burdegal, xxviij die Aug. (1243)."

"*Close Rolls,* 28 *Hen. III.—John Byset. M.* 17. Grant of robes for himself and his three knights. Grant of three does. *M.* 9. Ten casks of the king's wines in Ireland. Justice of Chester to find him a ship for his passage to Ireland as the king's messenger."

"*Close Rolls,* 29 *Hen. III., m.* 1.—The King. The Justiciary of

---

* I have to thank General Stewart Allan for this list. As regards Bishop Brice (No. 7), in 1218 the Pope directs three Scottish abbots to inquire into the complaints of the archdeacon and chancellor of Moray, that this bishop was leading a licentious life, and keeping their rents from them; and in that year, according to Chron. de Mailros (p. 135), he went to Rome to procure absolution.

Ireland is commanded to find a safe passage for *John and Walter Byset* from Anglesey to the king, at Ganock, 7 Oct. (1245)."
"*Close Rolls*, 29 Hen. III., m. 7.—*Byset, Walter*. B. de Sabaudia is commanded to deliver to him two of the king's shields in his custody in Windsor Castle, to go into the king's service in Ireland."
"*Close Rolls*, 30 Hen. III.—Pension given to *Walter Byset*."
"*Chart.* 31 Hen. III., mem. 13.—Sciatis nos dedisse concessisse et hâc cartâ nostrâ confirmasse *Waltero Byset* manium. de Ludeham cum ptinentiis. habend. et tenend. de nobis et hæreds. nostris eidem Waltero et hæredibus suis donec idem Walterus vel hæredes sui recuperaverit terras suas in Scotia quasi volumus, etc. Teste Willielmo Longespe, Rado. Fil. Nicholai, Bertramo de Coyey, Johane de Plessi, Hugo de Vinovar, Polino Peyuer, Roberto de Leegos., Roberto Waleraund, Radfo. de Wormey, Roberto le Norris, et aliis. Datum pen. maner. nostr. apud Clarendon 8 Die Decr. (1246)."
"*Close Rolls*, 31 Hen. III.—*Walter Byset*. 30 oaks in Sherwood Forest."
"*Patent Rolls*, 36 Hen. III., m. 12.—Pro Alano filo. Thom. R. omnibus ti. sal. Sciatis qd. ad instanc. Margar. Regine Scotie fil. nre. pardonamus Alano fil. Thom. Comit. de Athœll de Scoc. transgr. ei impositas intficiendo. quosdam homines *Johis. Biset* in Hibn. in quodam conflictu habito ibidem int. ipsum. Johem. t. pacum. Alan. t. capiendo hostiliter a quibusdam mercatoribus Hib. sex dol. vini t. qudam. partem bladi in obsidione t. expugnacone. cast. de Dunandin. . . . Ita tm. qud. stet recto in cur. nra. si qs. erga eum inde loqui volint. In cujus t. T. me ipso apd. Wudestok xxx die Jan. p. Reg. (1252)."

No. VI.

ENGLISH BYSETS (p. 47).

The grant to the Priory of Thurgarton is confirmed, 14 Hen. II., 1168. William calls himself William Carpenter—*Carpentarius*—not Byset, but calls his father William Byset (Dugdale's Mon., vi. 192). Nash, in his "Worcestershire," ii. 36, says Manassar Byset, whom he calls Manser de Biset, "assumed the name of Biset from a place of that name, near Alveston, in Warwickshire." I can find no mention of such a place. The Irish tradition was that the Bisets were a Greek family, which came in with the Conquest (Reeves' Down and Connor, 388). A Byzantine family named Dassiotes, bore arg. a bend gu. (N. and Q., 4th S., ii. 525). The name is spelt *Buset* (*supra*, p. 75) in 1294. It may have been Βυσσητὸς, from βυσσος, fine linen. There was John Byset in Kent (6 Ed. I., Inq. p. m.). John, husband of one of the Byset heiresses of Maiden Bradley, assumed the name of Byset A.D. 1305 (Hoare's Modern Wiltshire, Mere Hundred, xxi.). William Byset, son and heir of Robert Byset (25 Ed. I., 1302), has lands in England and Scotland (Palgrave, p. 189). This William had been taken prisoner in 1296, and liberated in 1297 on condition of serving the English king in France (Rymer's Fœd., ii. 773).

No. VII.

SCOTTISH BYSETS (p. 48).

Walter Byset founded the Preceptory of the Knights Templars at Culter between 1221 and 1236. See his oath to Herbert, Abbot of Kelso (Reg. de Kalchou, 191), respecting the building he had constructed for the use of the Templars (*Templariorum*), in the territory of the church of Culter (Maryculter). Alexander II. granted them charter of liberty to acquire lands, 12th January 1237 (Reg. Ab., ii. 269). The building included a chapel (Reg. de Kalchou, 182). Walter gave to this preceptory the church of Aboyne (Reg. Ab., ii. 271). The Templars are called "Brothers of the Knighthood of the Temple of Solomon," or, "of the Temple of Jerusalem," in these instruments; so in Dugd. Mon., vi. 817. In 1296, Walter Byset, of the county of Aberdeen, swears fealty to Edward I. (Ragman Rolls). Nisbet, in his "Heraldry" (2d ed., 1802, p. 91), says, Bisset of Lessendrum is chief of the Bissets. Lessendrum is in parish and barony of Drumblate, county Banff. The first Byset of Lessendrum assumed the name in 1364—"Walterus dictus Byseth dominus de

Lessendrum" (Liber Ecc. de Scon., p. 92). In 1355 Walter Byset dominus de Lessyndrum is lieutenant of county Banff (Coll. Aber. and Banff, i. 477). In 1379 Walter Byset of Lessendrum by deed surrenders his whole lands to the legate of Pope Clement VII., to be held by (qu. of) the Holy See (New Stat. Acc., Drumblade). In 1387 it is Patrick Byset de Lessendrum (Reg. Ab., i. 107). In 1403 the superiority of Lessendrum was among the estates partitioned between the Fentons and Chisholms (*supra*, p. 95). In 1652 we have Alexander, heir of Robert Bisset of Lessendrum (Inq. Ret.), and so on to William Bisset of Lessendrum (New Stat. Acc., 1840), and the present Mr Bisset of Lessendrum, the popular master of the Devon and Somerset staghounds—by whose covertside at Bagborough at the Easter Monday meet of the Vale foxhounds, from an odd coincidence, the proof-sheet of *supra*, p. 163 (*n*) was corrected.

No. VIII.

IRISH BYSETS (p. 53).

The Bysets of England were connected with the De Lacys. Henry Byset married the sister of John de Lacy, constable of Chester (Thoresby's Notts, 339). Hugh de Lacy died 1243, and was succeeded in the earldom of Ulster by Walter de Burgh. John de Courcy had given the lands of Ardes or Le Arde, in Ulster, about A.D. 1176, to the alien priory of Stoke Courcy, in Somersetshire; and Hugh de Lacy founded a cell there to Stoke Courcy (Drummond's Noble Families: De Courcy). John Byset the younger's inquisition (*supra*, p. 54) finds that he died seised of, amongst other lands in Ulster, Glenarm, held under Richard de Burgh, the infant heir of Walter. The second family of John Byset, the founder, seems to have got hold of his Irish lands. The Bysets in Ireland, though said by Barbour, in his "Bruce," to have fought against Edward Bruce, in fact sided with him, and Rachrin was forfeited to and granted by Edward II. in 1318 (Patent Rolls, 12 Ed. II.). Dr Reeves says: "From the first John, the family in after-times received the patronymic of MacEoin, and the Four Masters style them MacEoin Bisset, or simply MacEoin

(A.D. 1383, 1387, 1422, 1495, 1512)." Their territory was called the seven lordships of the Glynns of Antrim. The inheritance parted by the marriage of Maria Biset, the daughter and heiress of MacEoin Biset, to Eoin Macangus Macdonnell. Their son and heir was Donald Balloch, who had also his father's patrimony in Scotland and the Hebrides (Reeves' Down and Connor, pp. 325, 388). This is the connection referred to *supra*, p. 277. At Glenarm the Bissets founded a monastery.

No. IX.

CHAPELS (p. 76).

There was a domestic chapel in the House of Innes. In 1490 mention is made of "capella infra locum sive mansionem de Inneys" (Family of Innes, Spalding Club, p. 124). There was a chapel in Cawdor Castle. Generally there was no room, for the castles in the north of Scotland were only towers, not so extensive as the keeps of a Welsh or English castle. What space was there, for instance, in the castle of Beaufort, where Simon, Lord Lovat of 1745, resided, for a chapel? "It was a rude tower, having but four apartments on a floor, and none of these large" (Anderson's Family of Lovat, 157). In a large castle like Castle Urquhart, there was opportunity for including a place for Divine service; accordingly we find there arrangements indicating its existence. "The third floor [of the keep] or fourth stage," says Mr Clark (*Builder*, February 17, 1872), "differs from the rest, in that a small chamber is contained in the south-eastern angle, the door into which is in the south wall, near its east end. This may have been an oratory." * The old chapel of Allangrange (*supra*, p. 82), in the parish of Kilmuir Wester, county Ross, is near the House of Allangrange; and Bishop Forbes, in his journal of 1770, says he was told, when staying at the House, that it was the Bishop of Ross's country seat. It is fifteen feet in width. The east gable remains, with three Early English lancet windows, whose base is four feet from the ground; there is an awmry under-

* Kildrummy, Dunstaffnage, Linlithgow, Rothesay, Tantallon, Borthwick, and Doune Castles had chapels (Muir's Characteristics, pp. 47, 56, 73).

neath the windows. I did not notice a water drain. The good bishop says he went before breakfast to say his prayers in the chapel. Dr Johnson kept his hat off while he was upon any part of the ground where the cathedral of St Andrews had stood (Boswell's Journal, by Carruthers, p. 40).

No. X.

DEL ARD (p. 85).

The entry in 1296 is : " William fitz Steuene de Arde del Counte de Inverness." The Orkney tradition said that Malise, who was Earl of Strathearn, Orkney, and Caithness, 1334 (Lib. Ins. Miss., app. to pref.), had, by a daughter of the Earl of Monteith, a daughter, Matilda, who married Weland de Ard, and had a son, Alexander de Ard (*supra*, p. 95). John de Cheseholme de le Arde is one of the three persons mentioned *supra*, p. 93. In the Chamberlain Accounts for 1342, there is an entry : " Godefridi del Arde t. Isabellæ sponsæ suæ ratione dictæ sponsæ." Without more documents from northern charter chests, the origin and history of this family cannot be traced.

No. XI.

MARRIAGE CONTRACT, 1416* (p. 96).

Jacobus Dei gracia Rex Scotorum Omnibus probis hominibus suis ad quos presentes litere peruenerint clericis et laicis Salutem. Sciatis nos quasdam indenturas factas inter Willelmum de Fenton de eodem ex parte vna et Hugonem Fraser de Lowet ex parte altera super maritagio inter dictum Hugonem et Jonetam de Fenton sororem dicti Willelmi de mandato nostro visas lectas inspectas et diligenter examinatas non rasas non abolitas non cancellatas nec in aliqua sui parte viciatas sed omni prorsus vicio et suspicione carentes ad plenum in-

* Reg. Mag. Sig., iii., No. 95.

tellexisse in hunc modum. This indentur made at the Baky, the third
day of the moneth of Marche, the zher of our Lord a thowsand four
hundreth and xv, betuyx thua nobil lordis and mychty, Villiame
of Fenton, lord of [that] ilk, on the ta part, and Huchon Fraser, lord
of Lowett, on the tother part, proportis and berys wytnes in maner,
forme, and effect efter folowand; that is for to say, that the sayd
Huchon Fraser, lord of the Lowet, God grantand, sal lede in to wyf,
Jonet of Fenton, the syster of the sayd Villiam of Fenton, lord of
that ilk; and in recompensacion and assytht for the sayd mariage
to be made with the sayd Huchon Fraser, the forsayd Villiam of
Fenton, lord of that ilk, haf giffyn and grantit in joynt fethment, and
throw this composicion has confermyt to the sayd Huchon Fraser,
and to Jonet of Fenton, hys syster, and to the langar liffand of thaim
thua, and to the ayris betuyx thaim to be gottyn, thir landis vnder-
wryttyn; that is to say, Ensowchtan Kyrkomyr, Maule and Westyr
Eskdole, lyand in Strathglas, within the barony of the Arde, in name
and assent of xx^{li} markis. Also, the sayd William of Fenton has
grantit to the sayd Huchon and Jonet, in joynt feftment, twa Bown-
tactis in the extent of ten marcis, in maner as is befor wrytyn, of the
landis of Strathglas, vnder this condicion, that quhat tyme that the
landis of Wchterach be recoueryt, the sayd Huchon Fraser and the
sayd Jonet sal resayf tha landis in to joynt feftment in the extent of
x marcis; and gif tha landis of Vchterach be nocht fundyn of the
extent of x marcis be auld extent, the forsayd Villiam of Fenton sal
assytht in conuenable place the vaut of that x marcis, and than the
sayd Huchon and Jonet, and thair ayris, sal frely delyuer vp and gif
to the sayd Villiam of Fenton, or til hys ayris, the sayd landis of
Bowntacte, wythoutyn ony clame of the sayd Huchon, or of Jonet,
or of thair ayris, to be made. Als, it is accordyt betuyx the sayd
partis that the forsayd Huchon sal dow and gif, in name of dowry, to
the forsayd Jonet, xx^{li} lb. in to the lordschip of Golford, lyand wythin
the shirefdome of Narne, and quhair it vaictis of xx^{li} lb. of that land,
he sal assytht and gif hyr dowar of the landis of Dalcors, quhil scho
be fully assytht of xx^{li} lb. Alsua, the forsayd Villiam sal gif chartyr
and possession to the forsayd Huchon and Jonet, and to thair ayris,
as it is forspokyn and falzeand of the ayris betuyx thaim of thar
body lauchfully gottyn. I, Villiam of Fenton, lord of that ilk, wil
that al the forsayd landis, wyth the resort and retour agayne to me,
and to myn ayris. And this thyng lelely to be done and fulfillit, both

the partis hav gyfin thar bodely athe on the haly evangelis. And to the mare sekyrnes, to the part remanand of this indentur wyth the forsayd Huchon, the sele of Villiam of Fenton, lord of that ilk, is to put; and to the part remaynand with the forsayd Villiam of Fenton, lord of that ilk, the sele of Huchon Fraser, lord of the Lowet, is to put. This thing is done the yheir, day, the moneth befor wrytyn. Quas quidem literas donaciones concessiones et condiciones in eisdem contentas in omnibus punctis suis et articulis condicionibus et modis ac circumstanciis suis quibuscunque forma pariter et effectu in omnibus et per omnia approbamus ratificamus et per presentes confirmamus saluis nobis wardis releuiis ac aliis seruiciis de dictis terris debitis et consuetis. In cuius rei testimonium presenti carte nostre magnum sigillum nostrum apponi precipimus testibus reuerendo in Christo patre Johanne Episcopo Glasguense cancellario nostro Johanne Forestarii camerario nostro Valtero de Ogilby thesaurario nostro et Magistro Villelmo de Foulis custode priuati sigilli nostri preposito de Bothwel. Apud Edynburgh xvj die mensis Septembris anno regni nostri vicesimo quinto.

No. XII.

MARRIAGE-CONTRACT — THOMAS DUNBAR, EARL OF MORAY, AND HUGH FRASER OF LOVAT (p. 96).

"At Elgine, the ninth day of the month of August, the yere of our Lord a thousand four hundreth and twenty two yere, betwix ane noble Lord and ane mighty, Thomas of Dunbar, Earle of Murreffe, on the ta part, and ane nobyl man, Hucheon Fraser, Lorde of the Lovet, on the tother part, it is traitit, concordit, and impointit, in form and manner as efter follows, that is to say, that the said Lorde of the Lovet is oblyst, and by this letter oblysis him, that his son and his ayer will name and take to wyff ane dochter of the said Lord the Erle, gotin or to be gotin on Isobell of Innes; and the dochter gotin betwix the said Lord the Erle and the Isobell of Innes, failiand, as God forbid they doe, the said Lord of the Lovet is oblyst that the said his son and his ayer sall marry and tak to wyff ane dochter of the said Lorde the Erle, to be gotin betwix him and his spousit wyff; and this ayer, the son of the said Lord of the

Lovet, failiand, as God forbid he doe, but if he lyf ane dochter ayer or dochters ayirs, the said Lord of the Lovet is oblyste, as before, to give that dochter, his ayer, or his dochters ayirs, to the said Lorde the Erle son, or son to be goten betwix him and his spousit wyff; and thir ayirs, male or female, sons or dochters of the said Lord of the Lovet failiand, as God forbid they doe, the said Lord of the Lovet is oblyst, and by thir letters oblyses him, that his ayirs, whatsoever they be, sall hald and fulfyl the trety, concordance, and impointment, now as before written, to the said his Lord the Erle of Mureff; for the whilk marriage, lelely and truly, to be keepit in form and manners, as is before written, to the said Lord the Erle, bot fraud or gyle, the said Lord the Erle has geffin and grantit to the said Lord of the Lovet, and till his ayers, the baronye of Abertarch, in blench farm, aftir the tenor of his charter perportint in itselfe, and the warde and the relief of umquhile William of Fenton, Lord of the Baiky, and of Alexander of Chisholme, Lord of Kinrossy, pertainand to the said Lord the Erle, within the Ard and Strathglass, in the schirefdome of Inverness, within the Erledome of Murreff, after the tenor of the evidence made to the said Lord of the Lovet thereupon, and fifty marks of the usuall monyth of Scotland, after the tenor of his obligation made thereupon. In witnes of the whilk thing, the sealys of the s^d Lord the Erle, and the s^d Lord of the Lovet, interchangeably are to put, the place, day, moneth, and yhere before written" (Spalding Club Miscell., v. 256).

The *dominium utile* of Abertarff must have belonged to the Frasers before this; they probably derived it from a daughter of Patrick Le Grant, Lord of Stratherrick (Stratharthok) (Forsyth, 21). He and Simon Fresel witness Randolph's grant in 1345 (*supra*, p. 93).

No. XIII.

SIR KENNETH MACKENZIE OF KINTAIL (p. 105).

From an old MS. discovered by Lewis M. Mackenzie of Findon, written by John M'Ra, minister of Dingwall 1704.

Alexander, laird of Kintail, married Anna, M'Dougal of Lorn his daughter, who was mother to Kenneth, his eldest son, heir and successor. He made the match between him and Margaret, daughter to the Earl of Ross. Kenneth was a bold and stout man, impatient

of an affront, and resentive of injuries. The Earl of Ross, living at
Balcony, invited several of his friends to a Christmas feast ; among
the rest invited Mackenzie, his son-in-law, who coming late, and
the earl getting notice he brought not his lady with him, sent word
that others had taken up his apartment, and willed him to take up
his quarters elsewhere * till the next morning. He went straight
home and caused saddle his lady's horse, and desired her keep Christmas with her father, but never see his face again, and so instantly did
repudiate her. The poor lady behoved to give passive obedience,
and went home to her father, who was highly offended, and vowed a
revenge. Kenneth shortly after goes to Lovet's house and sends a
message that he will destroy his country and burn his house unless
Lovet gives him his daughter to wife. Lovet, helpless, is overawed,
and asks his daughter if she is content ; finds her " most willing,"
and " lets her furth to Kenneth."

It seems that Mackenzie knew nothing of M'Donald coming against
him till he was within a day's journey, and then he got together some
six to seven hundred men by the fiery cross. The battle took place
somewhere about Strathpeffer, probably where two upright stones are
at Fodderty Church. Kenneth sent his old father, who was blind,
with two attendants, away to a craig near by, that was called the
Corbie's Craig, during the battle. He then put about two hundred
of his archers in a wood in ambush, and fell on with the rest, so
paltry a force that the Macdonalds laughed at them. A sharpened
bloody conflict ensues, but the Macdonalds get discouraged, and are
at that moment set upon by the ambushed force, and they give way
and flee towards the ford at Moy, where twenty-four Kintail men meet
them, and kill every one that crossed the water. Alexander died, and
Kenneth served heir to him, 2d September 1488. Kenneth, called
Jolair or the Eagle, after this lived peaceably with his neighbours, and
died at Killin. He was knighted by King James IV., and had his
children by Agnes Fraser legitimated by the Pope. Another writer
says, " He dyed the 11 February 1491, as appears by an inscription
on his tomb, which is to be seen in an arch broken out and built on
the east side of the door of St Katherine's Chapel, built by Mary
Bisset (?)." It was February 1492. In September 1491 he is named
as witness, Kinzocht M'Kenzecht of Kintaill.

* Other accounts say at Killichudden (Cullicudden, *supra*, p. 200), a fisher
village nigh by.

No. XIV.

"EXTRA ROMANAM CURIAM" (p. 110).

Curia Romana, or the Roman court, is wherever the Roman Pontiff actually is, whether at Rome or elsewhere. Clement IV. reserved all benefices, and John XXII. all monasteries, held by persons dying within the Curia Romana (Paul, Benefices, ii., p. 171); but in that case the Pope was bound to confer the vacant benefices within a month (Corvini Jus Canonicum, lib. ii., tit. 29). I am indebted for this information to Mgr. Capel.

Later popes, from a variety of grounds, assumed the right to appoint to monasteries when vacant; and they insert the statement of the death occurring without the Roman court (see many instances in Theiner) perhaps to point out that the delay in the appointment, as the right to appoint did not arise from a vacancy *in curia*, was no objection to its validity. The bull "Execrabilis" was against pluralities. The annual value of the priory is stated to fix the amount of the first-fruits or first year's profits which was paid to the Pope.

No. XV.

SANCTUARY OF ARDCHATTAN (p. 150).

The privilege of sanctuary at Hexham extended for a mile round the priory church (Dug. Mon., vi. 180); so at Ripon a mile round the town, marked by crosses, one of which was called the Cross of Athelstan, who gave the privilege; such a sanctuary cross at Armathwaite is depicted (*Gent. Mag.*, 1755). At Glastonbury, by grant of King Edgar, confirmed by Pope John, it extended to the whole hundred of Glaston Twelve hides, containing seven parishes (*ib.*, i. 3). There were Frid-stols at Ripon, Beverley, and York. Spelman (Gloss., *in verbo*) says there were many such chairs in England; but neither are they, nor is the privilege of sanctuary, frequently mentioned among the privileges of English houses in Dugdale. Beaulieu Abbey in England had the privilege; and Margaret of Anjou sought refuge there.

Mr Sutherland reads the inscription—". . . SOMHERLE . . . IOR

DE ARDCHAT . . . QUI OBIT APUD ARDCHATTAN ANNO DOM. 1506."
Ardchattan was annexed to the see of the Isles in 1617 by James VI.,
under the Great Seal, at Blandford in Dorsetshire (Acta Parl. Scot.,
iv. 554).

No. XVI.

FRENCH PRIORIES OF THE ORDER (p. 164).

I have been unable to procure any more accurate information concerning the French priories. They are not mentioned in "Gallia Christiana," which treats of abbeys and conventual priories only; and Migne, although promising future particulars of the order of Val des Choux, does not give any. From his lists of the French MSS., it seems there are none relating to Val des Choux in the public library of Dijon. We must wait the results of the constant investigations made by the antiquarians of France.

No. XVII.

SURNAMES (p. 168).

In the clan system there were no surnames; every one was known by the name of his father, so that Celts have names as long as their pedigree. There were often surnames given to individuals, but they were not at first descendible. The forms of the Church show that there were no surnames when these forms were first established. In the marriage ceremonial, Christian names only are used. The inconvenience of the clan system led, among the Celts in Ireland and the Highlands, to the adoption of the name of the founder of a family, not only by his descendants, but by those who followed him in war, or held property under him in peace; whilst among the Celts in Wales the son took the father's Christian name, with the mark of filiation added. There David's son John was called John Davies, and John's son David was called David Jones; and this was often repeated in successive generations.

Under the feudal system, the lord of a place was styled of that place—in French *de*, and in German *von;* and when the French or German was translated into Latin, these prefixes became DE. It was this surname which first became descendible; and on the entry of the Normans into England and Scotland, hardly any other surname than these territorial ones are borne. Soon, however, the desire to follow the example of their superiors induced men to convert the surname of the father into that of the son, and make it descendible.

The simplest form of surname is the father's name with a mark of affiliation, as Watson in the text. We have in No. II. Gillanders Macysac or *Isaacson*, Augustini or *Austin's*. In No. VII., Macgill and Isaac Macgillanders, perhaps the son of Gillanders Macysac, after the Welsh fashion. In No. XIII. we have Jakson or *Jackson*, Alexandri or *Alexanderson*. Verstegan's "Restitution of Decayed Intelligence" (1634, p. 307), gives nineteen Christian names as the fount of a large number of surnames.

Then the surname was often derived from the country or place where the man came from. In No. II. we have Flandrensis or *Fleming*. That distinction was of no use unless he had migrated.

Also the office held, or trade or occupation, of the man. In No. II. we have Godfrey Arbalaster, the cross-bowman; Henry Cuch, *the Cook;* Yvo Venator, *the Hunter*. In No. VII., Molenctinarius, *the Miller*.

Again from some personal characteristic of body or fortune. The Norman Anglo-French *Le* Graund, or *Le* Graunt, is expressly translated by the Inverness-shire scribe into *dictus* Graunt, and is the origin of *Grant*. Thierry ridicules the condition of the conquerors of Ireland under Strongbow, and says one of the leaders was known as Le Poer, now one of its proudest names.

Fuller, in his "Worthies," ed. 1662, p. 51, points out the changes of surnames from (1.) concealment in time of civil wars, or (2.) for advancement when adopted into an estate. This may explain the change of Sir Christian del Ard into De Forbes, (*supra*, p. 85).

No. XVIII.

VICARS (p. 168).

The term vicar was originally, in ecclesiastical matters, applied to the person who, when a parish had been appropriated to a religious body, actually performed the duties of the parish priest. Sometimes when the religious body was a monastery or cathedral chapter, the

APPENDIX. 311

service was done by a member of the body; more often it was deputed to a chaplain, the tenure of whose office, as well as his stipend, was at the will of the appropriators; and the word vicar, then and about the time of the foundation of our priory, became restricted to mean a minister, who was endowed, and not removable at will. Thus the vicar of Inverness (*supra*, p. 52), was endowed in 1248, and the vicar of Duffus before 1274 (*supra*, p. 58), and the vicar of Conway before that time. The ordination of vicar was a constant subject of papal and episcopal inquisition. In England, in Richard II.'s and Henry IV.'s reigns, the obligation to endow a vicar on the appropriation of a benefice to a religious house was enforced by Act of Parliament.

No. XIX.
NOTE ON LUTHER (p. 181).

"Anno post natum Christum 1513 Leo X^{mus} Pontifex Romanus, nominatus ante Johannes Mediceâ familiâ Cardinalis, Julii 2^{di} Legatus anno superiore ad Ravennam tunc quidem a Gallis captus, sed ex eorum manibus artificiose nonnihil elapsus, circumagente tandem anno, in defuncti Julii 2^{di} locum a Collegio Cardinalium electus, hoc die 3^{tio} nempe Iduum Aprilis qui est XI^{mus} dies Aprilis, Pontifica Thiara exornatus est. Ut scilicet dies, quem prior annus ipsi infaustum obtulerat coronationis suæ celebritate ex atro in candidum verteretur. Anno vero post natum Christum 1521 obijt idem Leo X. Calendis Decembris, sub cujus Pontificatu Martinus Lutheris contra Pontificias Indulgentias, quas in Saxonicis passim locis scurriliter ad modum exaggerabat Johannes Tetzelius Dominicaster primum scripsit, quæ res postea multas et varias de Doctrina Ecclesiastica disputationes, quæ nunc etiam ob oculos quotidie cernimus, excitavit." *

No. XX.
SCOTTISH KALENDAR (p. 184).

The Scottish church and kingdom (*supra*, p. 207), still kept up the rule of commencing the year with the 25th of March, which had

* There are some references to Pope Julius II. not worth printing.

been given up at Rome. The feasts by which, or by reference to which, the earlier documents are dated are not peculiar to Scotland. Nos. IV. and VII. are dated respectively the Thursday and Friday before the feast of the Exaltation of the Holy Cross. No. V., Thursday, within the Octave of the Epiphany. No. XI., by the vicar of Abertarf, on a Sunday, the Sunday before the feast of St Peter *ad Vincula.* No. X. is on Valentine's Day; and Alexander de Chisholm's homage (*supra*, p. 89) is performed on Trinity Sunday. Deeds and charters were often executed on occasions of festivals, as the great men who were the witnesses of the actions to be recorded in them would be present.

No. XXI.

RIVER BEAULY (p. 213).

It must be remarked that the river between Beauly Bridge and Kilmorack church has somewhat altered its course, so that portions of the parish of Kiltarlity here lie on the left bank. The river, from the junction of the Farrar with the Glass, seems, in John Byset's time, to have been called the Farrar. The name Beauly seems, until lately, only to have been given to it up to its junction with the Teanassie Burn. The description of the saw mills at the end of the Dhruim in Forsyth's "Moray" mentions them as being on the Glass.

In the "Index to the Wells Chapter Records," 1876, p. 33, there is a commission of Bishop John, in 1389, to the abbots of Athelney and Muchelney to pronounce sentence of excommunication against any who should catch fish in the Tone river, within the manor of North Curry. Unless at that time this river abounded with salmon, the ecclesiastical thunders were invoked to protect the dace and gudgeon of the Tone, as well as the salmon of the Beauly (*supra*, p. 69).

No. XXII.

FEARN (p. 217).

LIST OF THE ABBOTS OF FEARN—NOVA FURNIA, IN ROSS—PRÆMONSTRATENSIAN CANONS-REGULAR (WHITE) OF ORDER OF ST AUGUSTINE.

1. MALCOLM I., of Galloway, a canon of Whithern—*Candida Casa—nom.* first Abbot, on foundation by Ferquhard, Earl of Ross, *circa* A.D. 1221-22; *died* at "Farne," *c.* A.D. 1236, and after his death "was holdin be his peopill as a *sanct.*"
2. MALCOLM II., of Nig, *suc. c.* A.D. 1236; transferred abbey from "beside Kincardin in Stracharrin" to present site of New Fearn, *c.* A.D. 1238; *died* there before A.D. 1252.
3. MACBETH MACKHERSIN, *suc.* before A.D. 1252, under whom, A.D. 1258, William, Earl of Ross, confirmed his father's donations to abbey, and between A.D. 1261-1264 the convent was finally established there, and rules confirmed by Pope Urban IV.; *died* after A.D. 1274 (erroneously called *Bp. of Ross*, as "Matthæus, or Machabeus," A.D. 1272-74, *vide* Bp. Matthew in *List, supra*, p. 202).
4. COLIN, *suc.* after A.D. 1274, "dompno Colino abbate de Nova Fernia;" witness to charter of William, Earl of Ross, *c.* A.D. 1281; "Sir Colin" *died c.* A.D. 1298.
5. MARTIN (Martein), a canon of Whithern, in Galloway, *nom.* by Maurice, Prior of St Ninian's, *c.* A.D. 1299 (without election by canons of Fearn, who claimed that right); *died c.* A.D. 1311.
6. JOHN I., a canon of same priory, by which *nom.* abbot *c.* A.D. 1311 (though not elected by the canons), and *invested* as abbot against their wishes and protests; *died* A.D. 1320.
7. MARK (son of Sir Mark Ros), a canon of Whitherne, and also not chosen, but *presented* by prior, A.D. 1321; rebuilt abbey A.D. 1338 and following years; *died* and interred there *c.* A.D. 1350.
8. DONALD I., of Peibles, *elected* by the canons (according to their constitutions and Papal decrees), and *confirmed*, after some opposition, by Prior of Whithern, A.D. 1350; *died* there A.D. 1368, July 25.
9. DONALD II., Pupill or Piply ("Donaldus Abbas Novæ Farniæ"), *suc.* his namesake as abbot, A.D. 1368, but whether by free election or presentation from Whithern unknown; under his rule the rebuilding of the abbey church was completed A.D. 1372; and he *died* A.D. 1383.
10. ADAM MONILAW, *suc.* A.D. 1383; *elected* apparently by the canons of Ferne; styled "Abbas de Nova Fernia," A.D. 1398; *died* there A.D. 1407, September 10.
11. THOMAS I., KETHIRNATHIE (Kathirnach or Cattanach), a canon of Whithern; *pres.* by prior (in revival of old claim to nominate the abbot) A.D. 1407, but being rejected by the canons, "he was forced to return from

whence he came," *resigning* abbacy, and it is "uncertain what was his end;" this intruding abbot is also recorded to having been "given to the lusts of the flesh!" (but this is only stated by the conventual chronicler of Fearn.)

12. FINLAY I., MACFAID (or Ferrier), nephew or grandson of Sir William Feriar, vicar of Tayne; *suc. c.* A.D. 1408, "governed for a certain space," and *died* A.D. 1436, October 15.

13. FINLAY II., MACFEAD (Faid or "Fearn"), *suc.* in or before A.D. 1442, ruling as abbot forty-four years (which leaves a *vacancy* between A.D. 1436-1441 unexplained); he built the cloister, and procured an organ, tabernacle, chalices, vestments, and other ornaments from Flanders for his abbey church; a man of piety and great liberality; a favourite of King James III. (but there is some confusion between him and his successor); *died* A.D. 1485 at Fearn, interred in St Michael's aisle there, under a monument, still existing, with effigy and inscription—"Hic jacet Finlaius M'fead abbas de Fern qui obiit anno mccclxxxv;" and on top of ornamented arch over tomb are his armorial bearings (as copied by me A.D. 1840, when much defaced)—*a stag lodged behind a tree, with three stars;* or, heraldically, "az. a stag arg. lodged within a grove of trees, vert, and in chief three stars of the second"—arms of family of *Fearn* of Tarlogie, in Ross-shire (as recorded in Lyon Register and Nisbet's "Heraldry," vol. i., p. 333).

14. JOHN II., FEARN, *suc.* as abbot A.D. 1485, but *died* A.D. 1486, March 17, at Fearn, after a brief rule (these last three abbots appear to have been of the same family—*MacFead*).

15. THOMAS II., MACCULLOCH, *suc.* A.D. 1486-87; he completed the dormitory after A.D. 1488, but being dispossessed of his revenues through forged bulls, produced by his successor, on false representations at Rome, after A.D. 1490, retired to Mid Geanies, near Fearn, where he built a chapel, dedicated to St Bar, but *died* at Fearn A.D. 1516, July 17, being interred in his abbey.

16. ANDREW STEWART, Bp. of Caithness (from Nov. 26 A.D. 1501), and abbot of Kelso (from between A.D. 1506-1511), as also of Fearn *in commendam* (between A.D. 1490-1501, by fraud and usurpation); *suc.* as abbot A.D. 1616; and *died* June 17 A.D. 1517 (*anno consecrationis* 14°), at his palace of Skibo, in Sutherlandshire.

17. PATRICK HAMILTON, *nom.* Commendatory-Abbot of Fearn, A.D. 1517; a boy, and non-resident titular; A.M. of Paris, A.D. 1520, and of St Andrews A.D. 1523; *burnt* "for heresy" at gate of St Salvator's College, in St Andrews, Feb. 29, 1528 (*aged* about twenty-six years, having been ordained priest A.D. 1526).

18. DONALD II., DENOUN (of Dunoon, in Argyleshire), *suc.* as abbot A.D. 1528; *confirmed* by Pope Clement VII. A.D. 1529; a man of good family and learning, as well as a musician; *died* A.D. 1541, Feb. 9 (but in the "Kalendar of Ferne" is recorded: "Obitus bone memorie quondam donaldi denoun abbatis be ferne qui obiit Infra monasterium eiusd. nono die

mensis februa. anno dni. millesimo quad^{mo} quadragesimo Cuius anime ppiciet. deus amen;" unless the year is a mistake—1440 for 1540-41—this might refer to another abbot during the vacancy of 1436-1441, but it appears to be intended for 1540?).

19. ROBERT CAIRNCROSS (Carnecross), Abbot of Holyrood—St Crucis de Edwinesburg (from Nov. 26 A.D. 1528) and Bp. of Ross (from April 14 A.D. 1513), also Abbot of Fearn *in commendam* A.D. 1541 (perhaps 1539-40 by *resignation* of Donald?); wanted to cede this abbey, April 1 A.D. 1545, to *James Carnecors;* and *died* Nov. 30 following, as recorded in "Kalendar of Ferne"—"Obit' bone memorie Reuerendi in Christo pris. et dm. Robti. carncorss epi. Rossen. ac cmediatarii. de ferne qui obiit apd. canonia de Ross ultimo nouebris. ano. dm. mccccxlv°."

— *David Panitar* obtained a grant of temporalities of this abbey in December A.D. 1545 from Crown (as well as Bishopric of Ross, A.D. 1546), but *resigned* Fearn before A.D. 1547.

20. JAMES CARNECORS (Cairncross), Glasguensis clericus, was *conf.* as Commendatory-Abbot of Fearn by Pope Paul III. before A.D. 1547, but *resigned* after A.D. 1550 (though an inscription at entrance of Abbey Church formerly existed, as follows: "Jacobus Cairncors abbas hoc templum finivit anno mdxlv; *suc.* 1545?).

21. NICHOLAS ROSS, Provost of Collegiate Church of Tain (*pres.* A.D. 1549, *res.* 1567); Commendator of Fearn; *suc.* after A.D. 1550; sat in Parliament at Edinburgh in August, A.D. 1560, as "Nichol, Abbot of Ferne;" *resigned* A.D. 1566-7; and *died* at Fearn, Sept. 17, A.D. 1569 ("Nicolas ros comedator. of ferne, provest of tane, decessit the xvii day of September the yeir of god 1569 quhom god assolze"—"Kalendar of Ferne").

22. THOMAS ROSS (of Culnahal), Parson of Alnes (from before A.D. 1560), Provost of Tayne, and also *nom.* Commendatory-Abbot of Fearn, A.D. 1566-67; exiled to Forres A.D. 1569-79; *res.* abbey and provostry A.D. 1584; and died at Tayne, Feb. 14, A.D. 1596; interred in St Michael's aisle at Fearn ("*Obitus* magistri Thome Ros, Abatis Ferne, qui obiit in Tayne 14 die Februarii anno 1595, et sepultur in Ferne"— "*Obitus* Isobelle Kinnard, Sponse ma. thome ros abbatis Ferne apud tane et sepulta in ferne 5 Octobris 1603"—"Kalendar of Ferne").

23. WALTER ROSS (of Morangy), *suc.* as Commendatory-Abbot and Provost of Tayne on his father's resignation, A.D. 1566-7; was last *titular* of Fearn, as the lands were resumed by the Crown A.D. 1587; abbey granted to Patrick Gordon of Letterfourie A.D. 1591; erected into barony of Geanies, in favour of Sir Patrick Murray, by King James VI. A.D. 1598; and *annexed to see of Ross* A.D. 1609 (for Bp. David Lindsay), A.D. 1616 (to Bp. Patrick Lindsay), as confirmed by Act of Parliament, June 28 A.D. 1617; which grants were confirmed to Bp. John Maxwell by King Charles I. A.D. 1633.

The *annual value* of Abbacy, A.D. 1561, was—*money*, £165, 7s. 1¼d.; *bear*, 30 ch. 2 bolls 2 pecks; *oats*, 1 chalder 6 bolls; and in "Liber Taxationum," 400 marks Scots.

AUTHORITIES.—(1.) "The Kalendar of Ferne," MS. fol. at Dunrobin Castle; (2.) "Ane Breve Cronicle of the Earlis of Ross, including notices of the Abbots of Fearn," etc., cr. 4to, Edinb. 1850, pp. 8, 46 (privately printed from MS. at Balnagown Castle, of which an imperfect abridgment was published in "Miscellanea Scotica," 8vo, Glasgow 1820, vol. iii.); (3.) Macfarlane's "Genealogical Collections," MS., Advocates Library, Edinb.; (4.) Lieutenant-General Hutton's MS., *ibid.*, vol. xi.; (5.) "Registrum Episcopatus Moraviensis," 4to, 1637; (6.) "Originales Parochiales Scotiæ," vol. ii., part 2, 4to, 1855; (7.) "Acts of Parliaments of Scotland," fol. i.-v.; (8.) "Liber Cartarum S. Crucis de Edwinesburg," 4to, 1840; (9.) "Liber S. Marie de Calchou," 4to, 1840; (10.) "Liber Domus de Soltre, and Charters of Collegiate Churches of Midlothian," 4to, 1861; (11.) "Epistolæ Regum Scotorum," Edinb. 1724, vol. ii.; (12.) "The Bruces' and the Cumyns' Family Records," 4to, 1870; (13.) "Historical Records of Family of Leslie," 8vo, Edinb. 1869; (14.) Historical Works of Sir James Balfour," Edinb. 1824; (15.) Morton's "Monastic Annals of Teviotdale," Edinb. 1832; (16.) Crawfurd's "Lives of Officers of State in Scotland," fol., Edinb. 1726; (17.) Skene's "Highlanders of Scotland," London 1837; (18.) "Registers of Great and Privy Seals;" and (19.) "Book of Assumptions" (MSS., Register Office, Edinburgh).*

No. XXIII.

CHURCH BELLS OF SCOTLAND (p. 219).

One effect of the Reformation in Scotland was to put an end to "the country's best music," that of peals of bells—"music which, though it falls upon many an unheeding ear, never fails to find some hearts which it exhilarates, and some which it softens." † And so completely was the knowledge of bell-ringing extinguished in Scotland that Scott could write:

> "Though pealed the bells from the holy pile
> With long and measured toll," ‡

as if pealing and tolling bells were the same thing.

This was not so in Scotland in Catholic times; the text tells us of the bell-tower of Beauly, and the bells thereof; and the report sent

---

* I have to thank General Allan for this list also.
† Southey's Book of the Church, ii. 121.
‡ Lord of the Isles, canto iv. 11.

to Rome * on the Abbey church of Arbroath speaks of its excellent tower, containing many bells of the best kind; and on the Abbey church of Kelso, it describes the two towers—the central and western tower—the latter containing many and well-sounding bells. As the use of towers was always for hanging bells, wherever in Scotland we find a pre-Reformation tower, we may be sure there was at one time a ring of bells; and we may confidently assert that the towers of Pluscardine and Ardchattan, and of the cathedral church of Ross, contained suitable peals of bells.

Church bells are first mentioned by Bede, A.D. 680; and the first peal in England was put up by Abbot Tunstal in Croyland Abbey, *ante* 870.†

I know of no ring of mediæval bells now remaining in Scotland save those at Kirkwall Cathedral (*supra*, p. 223). There are four bells—the largest, or tenor, originally given by Bishop Maxwell in 1328, but recast; second bell given by Bishop Maxwell; first, or treble, given by Bishop Maxwell; small bell, without inscription or date, not hung. They are not, and probably never have been, rung by the common processes of wheel or crank, but by a rope applied so as, by a lateral traction, to make the tongue strike the side. The small bell is called the fire-bell, and in the seventeenth century was called the skellat-bell. This is extracted by Mr Ellacombe ‡ from an article in the *Orcadian* for October 1861, by Sir Henry Dryden.

Now compare this with an English county, say Somerset, where the spoliation of its duke, the Lord Protector, who thought one bell enough to summon the people to church, was checked. It had in Camden's time 385 § parishes. It has now among its churches 393, none of which have less than three bells; 43 churches having two bells, and 72 new and old churches with single bells in towers ¶ or bell-cots; altogether, there are 2064 church bells in Somerset (Ellacombe, p. 20).

* Theiner, p. 525.
† Godwin's English Archæological Handbook, 1867, p. 269.
‡ Church Bells of Somersetshire, p. 131.
§ Brit., 1610, p. 240.   ¶ I presume these are new churches.

No. XXIV.

DRESS OF THE MONKS (p. 222).

The difference between the dress of the Valliscaulians and Cistercians is difficult to ascertain. The descriptions (*supra*, pp. 10, 247) are equally applicable to both; they are both called White Monks (*supra*, p. 136), and are said by monkish historians to wear the same dress (*supra*, p. 145). But the text speaks of a difference in the cowls of the two orders, and perhaps it is here the distinction lies. There is a print of a Valliscaulian monk in "Buonanni Ordini Religiosi," part iii., No. 4 (Rome 1710) which would be described as a white cassock with a narrow scapulary.

No. XXV.

CHAPTER OF KIRKWALL (p. 222).

Bishop Robert Reid made a new erection and foundation of the chapter, viz., seven dignities, whereof the first was a provost or dean, to whom, under the bishop, the correction and oversight of the canons, prebendaries, and chaplains was to belong; (2.) An archdeacon, who was to govern the people according to the canon law; (3.) A precentor, who was to rule the singers in the choir in the elevation or depression of their songs; (4.) A chancellor, who was to be learned in both laws, and bound to read in the pontifical law publicly in the chapter to all that ought to be present, and to look to the preserving and mending the books of the choir and register, and to keep the common seal and key of the library; (5.) A treasurer, who was to keep the treasure of the church and sacred vestments, and to have a care of the bread, wine, wax, oil, and lights for the church; (6.) A subdean, who was to supply the place of the provost in his absence; (7.) A sub-chanter, who was bound to play on the organs each Lord's Day and festivals, and to supply the place of the chanter in his absence.

Likewise he erected seven other canons and prebendaries, to wit: (1.) The prebendary of Holy Cross—he was to be a special keeper of holy things under the treasurer, and was to take care of the clock and ringing of the bells at hours appointed, and to take care that the floor of the church was cleanly swept; (2.) The prebendary of St Mary—he was to have a care of the roof and windows of the cathedral, and to have them helped if need were; (3.) The prebendary of St Magnus—he was to be confessor of the households of the bishop, provost, canons, and chaplains, and their servants, in the time of Easter, and to administer the Eucharist to them; the 4th prebendary was to have the chaplaincy of St John the Evangelist in the said cathedral church; the 5th prebendary was to have the chaplaincy of St Lawrence; the 6th was to have the prebend of St Katharine; and the 7th prebendary was to have the prebend of St Duthas.

Besides these, he erected thirteen chaplains: to the first was allotted the chaplaincy of St Peter, and he was to be master of the grammar school; to the second was allotted the chaplaincy of St Augustine, and he was to be master of the singing school; the third was to be *Stallarius*, or the bishop's chorister; the fourth the provost's chorister; fifth, the archdeacon's; sixth, the precentor's; seventh, the chancellor's; eighth, the treasurer's; ninth, the sub-dean's; tenth, the prebendary's of Holy Cross; eleventh, the prebendary's of St Mary; twelfth, the prebendary's of St Katharine; thirteenth, the chaplain's of Holy Cross. To these he added a sacrist, who was to ring the bells, and light the lamps, and carry in water and fire to the church, and go before the processions with a white rod, after the manner of a beadle.

He moreover ordained six boys, who were to be taper-bearers, and to sing the responsories and verses in the choir as they were to be ordered by the chanter (Wallace's "Orkney," pp. 85-87).

There were no ringers of the peal of bells. "This ringing prevails in no country so much as in England, which is called *the ringing island*. It is said that bells were applied to church purposes as early as the sixth century even in the monastic societies of Caledonia" (English Encyclopædia, i. 663).

No. XXVI.

DIARY OF QUEEN MARY'S JOURNEY NORTH, 1562
(p. 234).

A MS., being the Book of the Master of the Household, Sir J. Ogilvie, of Queen Mary, contains the following journey of that queen. The book is in French, and begins the 1st of August 1562, the queen and court being then at Edinburgh:

"The queen remained at Edinburgh from the 1st to the 11th of August; but on the 11th of August she left Edinburgh with a part of her train, and dined at Calder. After dinner, she set out for Lithgow, where she was joined by the rest of her train, and where she supped and slept. On the 12th, the queen and a part of her train dined at Callendar, and slept at Stirling, where she was joined by the rest of her train, who had dined at Lithgow. She continued at Stirling till the 18th of August, when she set out from thence with a part of her train and dined and supped at Kincardine. On the 19th she left Kincardine after dinner, and slept at St Johnston, where she remained till the 21st, when she departed after dinner, and slept at Cowpar in Angus. On the 22d she set out from Cowpar after dinner, and slept at Glammis. On the 23d she left Glammis after dinner, and slept at Guelles [perhaps Edzel]. On the 25th the queen, after dining at Pitarrow, proceeded to Dunotter, where she supped and slept. On the 27th she set out after dinner from Dunotter, and supped and slept at Aberdeen. She remained at Aberdeen till the 1st of September, when she departed after dinner, and slept at Bouquhain. The 2d she left Bouquhain after dinner, and supped and slept at Rothiemay. The 3d she set out after dinner from Rothiemay, and supped and slept at Grange, in Strathisla. On the 4th, after dining at Grange, she set out for Balveny, where she supped and slept. On the 6th, after dining at Balveny, she set out for Elgin, where she supped and slept, and where she remained till the 8th, when she set out after dinner, and supped and slept at Kinloss. On the 10th, after dining at Kinloss, she set out for Tarnway, where she supped and slept. On the 11th, after dining at Mernes, she supped and slept at Inverness; here she remained till the 15th, which she left that day after dinner, and supped and slept at Quittra. On the 16th she departed from Quittra after dinner, and supped and slept at Tarnway. On the 17th, after dining at Tarnway, she went to Spynie, where she supped and slept. On the 19th she departed from Spynie, dined at Cullen, and supped and slept at Craig of Boyne. On the 20th, after dining at Craig of Boyne, she proceeded to Banff, where she supped and slept. She left Banff on the 21st, dined at Turreff, and slept at Gight. She dined at Lessmoir, and supped and slept at Aberdeen on the 22d.

"At Aberdeen the queen remained from the 22d of September till the 5th of November, when she departed after dinner, and proceeded to Dunnoter, where she slept on the 5th. She left Dunnoter after dinner on the 7th, and supped and slept at Crag. On the 9th, after dining at Crag, she proceeded to Boneton, where she slept. On the 10th, after dining at Boneton, she slept at Kinnairde, whence she departed after dinner. On the 11th to Arbroath, where she slept. She left Arbroath after dinner on the 12th, and slept at Dundee. On the 13th she departed from Dundee, dined at Quillespyndy, and slept at St Johnstown, where she continued till the 16th, when she departed after dinner, and slept at Tulliebarne. On the 17th she proceeded after dinner to Drummond, where she slept. On the 18th she departed from Drummond after dinner, and slept at Stirling. On the 21st she left Stirling, and slept at Lithgow, whence she departed after dinner, and slept at Edinburgh.

"On the 28th of December the queen went from Edinburgh to dinner at Haddington, and to sleep at Dunbar. On the 30th she departed from Dunbar after dinner, and slept at Bylle; and on the 31st she dined at Haddington, and slept at Edinburgh."

No. XXVII.

ABERTARFF AND BOLESKINE (pp. 244, 245).

This and the two following Acts of Prorogation of Tacks of Teinds are recorded by Lord Prestonhall, 9th June 1708, under Act 9, 1707; and this Act records that the kirks of Abertarff and Boleskine "are unite in ane conjunct parochine," modifies 520 marks stipend to be paid, 310 out of the "teind sheaves and parsonage teinds of Abertarff, alias Kilquman, by Simon, Lord Fraser of Lovat, notwithstanding the tack thereof of the 13th October 1576, subscribed by Mr John Fraser, prior of Beauly for the time, and by three persons of the chapter thereof," and prorogates the tack, as mentioned in the text. The modification ordains the minister to furnish the elements to the celebration of the communion at the said kirks.

No. XXVIII.

CONVETH AND KILTARLITY (pp. 243-246).

This Act records that these kirks are united "in ane conjunct parochine," and the service appointed to be at Conveth; modifies 520 marks stipend to be paid, 381 marks, 6s. 8d. out of the teinds, parsonage and vicarage, of the said parochine of Conveth, by Simon, Lord Fraser of Lovat, notwithstanding the tack of the teind sheaves thereof, of the 13th October 1576, and notwithstanding the tack of "all and sundry the teind lambs, kids, calves, wool, butter, cheese, lint, hemp, and all small teinds whatsoever of the vicarage and parsonage of Conveth," subscribed by the said prior and three persons of the chapter, the 13th October 1576, and prorogates both tacks. The payment is again stated to be to the minister serving the cure at Conveith, whereunto Kiltarlity is now unite; he was to furnish communion elements.

No. XXIX.

WARDLAW AND FEARNUA (p. 251).

This Act records that the kirks of Wardlaw and Fferneway are unite, the stipend, 520 marks to the minister serving the cure at Wardlaw, 410 marks out of the teinds, parsonage and vicarage, of the said parochine of Wardlaw, by Simon, Lord Fraser of Lovat, that is, 50 marks out of the vicarage and small teinds of the parochine of Wardlaw, and 360 marks out of the parsonage teinds of the said parish, notwithstanding the tacks mentioned in the text, which were prorogated; but the rent of £40 Scots was to be paid to the bishop in addition to the stipend to the minister, which, in the other cases, included the rents payable under the leases.

No. XXX.
THE PRIORY GARDENS (p. 252).

Queen Mary must have thoroughly appreciated the stately gardens of Beauly Priory. In her gardens she delighted to receive and converse with ambassadors and other public men on business, and one of her gardens at Holyrood was the old garden of the abbey. She had gardens at Linlithgow Palace, Stirling Castle, and Perth.*

The Wardlaw MS.,† speaking of Lord Lovat in 1450, says, "This Lord Lovat planted the first orchard in Lovat, having brought with him several spurs of pears and apples from the south, and helped to plant and enlarge the monks' orchard in Beauly."

The "Old Statistical Account of Elgin" says: "A fig-tree was at Pluscarden a few years ago, which annually produced fruit."

No. XXXI.
CONTRACT BETUIX MY LORD HUNTLY AND LORD LOWET, 1570 (p. 264).‡

"At Aberdeine the xxvi day of Julii, the yeir of God M v^c thre scoir ten, it is appointit, agreit, and faithfullie oblist betuix nobill and mychte lordis, George, erlle of Huntlie, lord Gordoun, and Badzenocht, etc., on the one parte, and Heow Lord Lowat on the wthir part, in maner, forme, and effect as efter follows, that is to say, the said erlle binds and oblessis him to assist, fortefie, and maintaine the said Heow Lord Lowat, in all his honest, lauchfull actionis and causis, as he happinis to have ado, and requeris the said erlle tharto, and also sall, at his uttermaist, labour and procure the abbot of Kynloiss to gif and set in fewferme to the saidis Heow and his airis, all and haill the landis and manes of Beowlyne, with the salmond fischeing therof, etc., for the quhilk cause the said lord Lowatt, and for the special luif which he beris to the said erlle, and conserua-

* Chalmers' Queen Mary, vol. i., p. 72.
† *Inverness Courier*, 22d January 1845. Other transcripts of the MS. have "sealed" for "several."
‡ Spalding Club Miscellany, vol. iv., p. 227.

tione of mutual amitie and kyndnes betuix thame in tymis cuming, bindis and oblissis him to concur, assist, and tak pairt with his kyn, frendis, serwandis and assistaris, with the said erll, in quhatsumevir his awn particular actionis and caussis, lelelie and treulie, as he happinis to be requiret tharto, aganis quhatsumevir persone or personis within this realme of Scotland, the authoritie only being exceptt, &c. In werefecatione heirof, baithe the saidis parteis hes subscriuvit the present witht thar handis, day, yeir, and place forsaidis, befor thir witnessis, Adam Gordoun of Auchendoun, William Frasser of Strowy, master Duncan Forbes of Monymusk, and master Donald Frasser, archedein of Ross, witht utheris diuerss.

"GEORGE, erll of Hwntlye.
HEW, lord Fraseir of Louet."

No. XXXII.

SCOTTISH MONASTIC SCHOOLS (p. 279).

There are some observations deserving record on this subject, in a late article in the *Edinburgh Review:* " Previous to the Reformation, the whole educational institutions of Scotland were under the superintendence of the clergy, or more correctly speaking, of the monastic orders. . . . In 1241 . . . the care of the school of Roxburgh had been entrusted to the monks of Kelso, and the 'rector of the schools' was an established officer. . . . The master of the schools of St Andrews appears between 1211 and 1216. At Ayr there was a 'master of the schools in 1234,' who took rank with the deans of Carrick and Cunningham in a commission from the Pope.* In 1256 the statutes of the church of Aberdeen imposed on the chancellor of the chapter the duty of attending to the regimen of the schools, and to seeing that the boys were taught grammar and logic.

"Earlier still, in 1224, there was a similar officer at Abernethy, in our day a country village, and even then probably fallen from its earlier grandeur. The schools of Perth and Stirling were attached to the monastery of Dunfermline, and we read of their existence so early as 1173. These and others were all burgh or grammar schools.

* Innes's Scotch Legal Antiquities, p. 214.

" But there was another and higher class of schools within the walls of the monasteries, chiefly designed, no doubt, for the education of the clergy. To them, however, it would appear that the sons of the nobility were occasionally sent; and in the Chartulary of Kelso an instance occurs in the year 1200, of the grant by a noble woman of a rent to the abbot and monks, on condition that they should board and educate her son with the best boys entrusted to their care. It was in these latter schools, which perished in the wreck and plunder of the Reformation, leaving no substitutes behind them, that the rudiments of the scholastic philosophy were taught, and that such men as John of Dunse must have been prepared for the brilliant careers on which they immediately entered at Oxford, Paris, and Bologna. Nor was this the only direction in which their influence may be traced. Law can scarcely have been taught at the burgh schools, and, as in 1496, the Universities of St Andrews and Glasgow had only been recently founded, it has always seemed probable to us that it was to these monastic schools that the expression 'schules of art and jure,' which occurs in the remarkable statute of James IV. with reference to the education of the sons of barons and freeholders, was intended to apply." *

No. XXXIII.

LEASE BETWEEN THE COMMISSIONERS OF HER MAJESTY'S WOODS, FORESTS, ETC., AND THE RIGHT HONOURABLE THOMAS ALEXANDER, BARON LOVAT, OF THE PRIORY OF BEAULY (p. 292).

It is contracted and agreed upon betwixt the Right Honourable George William Frederick, Earl of Carlisle; Alexander Milne, Esq., and the Honourable Alexander Gore, Commissioners of Her Majesty's Woods, Forests, Land, Revenues, Works, and Buildings, on behalf of her Majesty, her heirs and successors on the one part, and the Right Honourable Thomas Alexander, Baron Lovat of Lovat, in the county of Inverness, on the other part, in manner following, that is to say, the said Commissioners, on behalf foresaid, considering that the said Thomas Alexander, Baron Lovat, has made

* *Edinburgh Review* for April 1876.

application to the said Commissioners for a lease, on the terms and conditions after mentioned, of the Priory of Beauly, in the county of Inverness, which application the said Commissioners have, with consent of the Lords of Her Majesty's Treasury, as signified by their warrant dated the 15th day of June 1847, agreed to grant. Therefore the said Commissioners, on behalf of her Majesty, have set, and in consideration of the tack-duty and other prestations, particularly after specified, hereby set, and in tack and assedation let to the said Thomas Alexander, Baron Lovat, and the heirs succeeding to him in the lands and barony of Lovat, but expressly excluding assignees and sub-tenants without permission specially granted in writing by the said Commissioners or their successors in office, All and Whole the ruins of the old church and monastery of Beauly, ground within the same and burying-ground adjoining, belonging to her Majesty and her royal successors, as the same are delineated by the red lines on a plan docqueted by us, the said Commissioners, and the said Thomas Alexander, Baron Lovat, as relative hereto, and that for all the days, space, and term of thirty-one years, from and after the term of Whitsunday last, 1847, which is hereby declared to have been the term of the said Thomas Alexander Baron Lovat's entry thereto, by virtue of these presents, and from thenceforth to be peaceably possessed and enjoyed by him and his foresaids during the haill space of the said tack, freely, quietly, well, and in peace, without any revocation or impediment whatever. But reserving to her said Majesty and the said Commissioners, and her successors in office, full power to permit or to restrict interments within the said premises as they shall think proper; and, in respect that the floors of the interior of the said ruins are now encumbered with rubbish, and that the said Thomas Alexander, Baron Lovat, is to expend a sum, not exceeding the sum of £20 sterling, in clearing away the same, the said Commissioners bind and oblige themselves and their successors in office to pay to the said Thomas Alexander, Baron Lovat, a sum not exceeding the foresaid sum of £20 sterling, on his producing proper certificates or other evidence of the said clearance being effected; for which causes, and on the other part, the said Thomas Alexander, Baron Lovat, binds and obliges himself and his heirs succeeding to him in the lands and barony of Lovat, to make payment to her Majesty and her successors, or to the said Commissioners and their successors, or to any keeper, collector, or receiver, or other person or persons, whom the said Commissioners may from time to time authorise to receive the same, the sum of £1 sterling yearly, in name of rent or tack-duty, payable the said tack-duty at the term of Whitsunday yearly, beginning the first term's payment thereof at the term of Whitsunday next for the year immediately preceding, and the next term's payment thereof, at the term of Whitsunday thereafter for the year following, and so forth yearly thereafter during the currency of this tack, with a fifth part more of each term's payment of liquidate penalty in case of failure, and the legal annual rent of the said yearly payments from the time the same became due during the not payment thereof. And the said Thomas Alexander, Baron Lovat, also hereby binds and obliges himself, his heirs and successors, that he and his foresaids shall and will, from time to time, and at all times during the said term hereby granted, use his and their best endeavours to preserve and keep the said ruins and grounds from spoil and injury, and shall keep and preserve in good repair the walls at present erected on the outside of the said red lines, which walls are the property of the said Baron Lovat, and shall not, for want of care and due attention, permit the said ruins to fall into greater dilapidation and decay than must naturally occur from the effect of time and the increasing antiquity of the buildings, and shall not, nor will convert or use the said premises or any part thereof into or for a residence or dwelling-house, or barn, stable or outhouse, of any kind or description, but maintain and keep the same in their present state and condition, as a venerable monument of ancient times, and an object of interest, and shall not, nor will permit or suffer any alteration to be made thereon, or any additional building or erection, to be made or set up on any part of the said premises; and that it shall be lawful for the said Commissioners of her Majesty's Woods, Forests, Land, Revenues, Works, and Buildings for the time being, or such other person or persons as they shall appoint, at seasonable and convenient times in the day, yearly or oftener during the said term hereby granted, to enter into and upon, and to view and inspect the said ruins and premises hereby let, and to take a map or maps of the same, if they shall think fit, and to give notice in writing to or for the said Thomas Alexander, Baron Lovat, his heirs, executors, and successors, of any neglect or want of care of the said ruins, fences, trees, or premises, which may be found on any such view; and the said Thomas Alexander, Baron Lovat, hereby binds and obliges himself and his foresaids to amend and make good all such damage as shall have been caused by such neglect or want of care, within three months after notice thereof, given or left as aforesaid, and at the end of his possession, by virtue of these presents, to leave, surrender, and yield up the said whole premises in as good a state of preservation as the same now are (decay from time and damages by storm or tempest excepted), unto the Queen's Majesty, her heirs and successors, or to the Commissioners for the time being of her Majesty's Woods, Forests, Land, Revenues, Works, and Buildings, or to such person or persons as the Queen's Majesty, her heirs and successors, or the said Commissioners for the time being, shall authorise and appoint to receive the same; and further, the said Thomas Alexander, Baron Lovat, binds and obliges himself and his foresaids, on each day of the week, or on such days in every week, and at such hours in the day, and subject to such restrictions and regulations as the said Commissioners for the time being of her Majesty's Woods, Forests, Land, Revenues, Works, and Buildings, shall from time to time prescribe or approve of, or deem fitting for the preservation of the said ruins and premises, and the prevention of injury and disorder thereon, permit and suffer all and every persons and person whomsoever, upon request made to him or them for that purpose, to enter and remain upon the said site and premises, and view the said ruins, and make drawings or sketches of the same, or any part thereof; and the said Thomas Alexander, Baron Lovat, binds and obliges himself and his foresaids to flit and remove himself, his servants, goods and gear, furth and from the possession of the said ruins at the expiry of this tack, and to leave the same void and redd, to the effect the said Commissioners and their successors in office, or others on behalf of her Majesty and her royal successors, may enter thereto immediately, and peaceably possess the same in all time thereafter, and that without any previous warning or process of removing to be used against him or them to that effect. And lastly, both parties bind, etc. In witness whereof, etc.*

* The area of the church is given as 31 poles 25 roods. Captain White states the length of nave and choir to be 138 feet by 21 in breadth, inside walls. The Ordnance Survey measurement is followed in the ground plan, *supra*, p. 280. Mr Muir says, "in length as to breadth Beauly is nearly six and a quarter times;" apparently the largest proportional length in Scotland.

PRIORS OF BEAULY.

A.D.			
1222.	GIACOMO BATTISTA,	. .	Wardlaw MS.
	DUVALLUS MATHESON,	. .	,,
1279.	——, Prior of Beauly,	. .	Reg. Moray, 140.
1289.	——, ,,	. .	Acta Parl. Marg. Reg.
1341.	ROBERT, ,,	. .	Balnagown Charters, O.P.S., ii. 2, 509.
1356.	,, ,,	. .	,, ,,
1357.	,, ,,	. .	,, ,,
1362.	SYMON, ,,	. .	Coll. Ab. and Banff, ii. 384.
1371.	ALEXANDER FRISALE,	.	Kalendar of Fearn, *supra*, p. 90.
1372.	SIR MAURICE ,,	. .	Balnagown Charters, O.P.S., ii. 2, 509.
1440.	THOMAS FRASER,	. . .	Wardlaw MS.
1479.	Brother of SIR KENNETH MAC-KENZIE of Kintail,	. .	*Supra*, p. 105.
1480.	SIR JOHN FYNLA,	. .	*Supra*, No. XIII.
1497.	HUGH FREZEL,	. .	*Supra*, No. XV.
1498.	DOUGAL RORIESON, .	. .	*Supra*, No. XV.
1514.	,,	. .	*Supra*, No. XXI.
1525.	NICHOLAUS, .	. .	Lovat Charters, Findon MSS.
1529.	MASTER JAMES HASWELL,	.	Reg. Sec. Sig., L. viii., fol. 59.
1530.	ROBERT REID,	. .	*Supra*, p. 218.
1553.	WALTER REID,*	. .	*Supra*, p. 226.
1573.	JOHN FRASER, .	. .	*Supra*, p. 275.

John Fraser was the last clerical Prior of Beauly. We find mention of Adam Cumming, Commendator of Beauly in 1613, as being represented by his wife, Elizabeth Home, Prioress of St Bothans, in granting a lease of some of the possessions of that priory (Scots Acts, v. 135; N. Stat. Acc., Berwickshire, 105). The commendatorship expectant upon his decease seems to have been given to the Hays by James VI.; for we have a letter of provision under the Great Seal of the Priory of Beaulieu in Ross-shire, on 10th May 1607, in favour of Sir James Hay of Kingask (Douglas' Peerage, Earl of Kinnoul, citing L. Mag. Sig., lxiv., No. 4). There is an entry in the Scots Acts, dated 1612 (vol. iv., p. 522): "Ratification to the Lord Hay of Sala of his erection of Beaulie." But there must be some mistake here, for Sir James Hay's son was not created Lord Hay of Sauley, county York, till 29th June 1615. He was ultimately Earl of Carlisle, and after spending £400,000 worth of royal grants, on his death in 1636, "left," says Clarendon, "not a house nor acre of land to be remembered by." Beauly fell back again, doubtless, to the Crown, so as to enable Charles I. to annex it to the bishopric of Ross in 1639.

* Forsyth mistook Ferrarius' expression "Abbot Walter," and made Walter Hetton Abbot of Kinloss. Mr Walcot makes him Prior of Beauly, but Walter Hetton was only the Precentor of Kinloss, and not at all connected with Beauly.

INDEX.

A.

ABERTARFF, parish of, 240-246, 306, 321, 322.
Alexander I., 258.
  II., 17-19, 28, 36, 124-127, 148, 149.
  III., 6.
  III., Pope, 296.
  IV., Pope, Bull of, 191.
  VI., Pope, Bull of, 106-110, 113-120, 297.
Allangrange, chapel of, 302, 303.
Annexation, Act of, 278.
Ardchattan, Priory of, 146-156, 248, 283, 308, 309.
  seal of, 170.
  Priors of, 149, 152-154, 156, 181.
Ardnagrask, lands of, 274.
Argyle, David, Bishop of, 152, 156.
  Robert, Bishop of, 152.
Armour, 290.
Athole, David de Hastings, Earl of, 45.
  John, Earl of, 264, 265, 273.
  Patrick, Earl of, murder of, 43-45.
  Thomas de Galloway, Earl of, 24, 299.

B.

BALIOL, John, 54.
Battista, Giacomo, Prior of Beauly, 329.
Bar, Alexander, Bishop of Moray, 132.
Beaufort Castle, 40, 76, 211, 295.
  chapel of, 76.
Beaulieu, Abbey of, Hampshire, 15.
Beauly, charter-roll of, 260, 262.
  extension of priory church, 281, 282.
  fairs at, 259.
  form of prior's oath, 111, 112.
  origin of name, 7, 294.
  Priors of—Nicholas, 329; Robert, 329; Simon, 329.
  pronunciation of name, 15.
  revenues of priory, 235-238, 247, 248, 257-260, 271, 272.

Beauly—*continued*.
  salmon-fishings of, 29, 87, 88, 165, 212, 213, 237, 253, 265, 266, 270, 271, 288.
  seal of, 170.
  tack of lands, 254-256, 265-268, 272, 291-293, 325-328.
Bells in Scottish churches, 316, 317.
Benale, John, Prior of Urquhart, 136.
Benedict XIII., Pope, 297.
Bifort, Llewellyn, Bishop of Ross, 202.
Bigod, Roger, 6.
Boleskine, parish of, 242, 244, 245, 321, 322.
Boscho, Alexander de, 85.
  Andrew de, 54, 63, 64, 67.
  Elizabeth de, or Byset, 67.
  John de, 67.
  Joneta de, 67.
  Mariota de, 67, 95.
Bourdeaux, John Byset in, 45.
Boyd, Robert, Lord, 276.
Boys, William de, Prior of Pluscardine, 138.
Bruges, trade of, to Beauly, 165.
Bullock, John, Bishop of Ross, 195, 198, 203.
  arms of, 195.
Bulls, Papal, of Alexander IV., 190, 191.
  Alexander VI., 106-109, 113-119.
  Gregory IX., 14.
  Gregory XI., 91.
  Innocent III., 8-11.
  Julius II., 177-181.
Bursaries, Church, 241.
Buy, Sorley, Lord of the Route, 277.
Byset, origin of name, 300.
  arms of, 34.
Bysets (or M'Eoins), the, of Antrim, 53, 301, 302.
Bysets, the, in *England*—
  Alfreda, 47.
  Ausold, 20.
  Christiana, 36.

Bysets—*continued.*
　Ernulph, 20.
　Henry, 17, 20.
　John, 20, 45, 300.
　Manassar, 20, 299, 301.
　Margaret, 20, 45.
　Walter, of Lowdham, 46, 47.
　William, of East Bridgeford, 20, 299, 300.
Bysets, the, in *Ireland*—
　Henry, 301.
　John, 46, 298, 299, 301.
　Maria, 302.
　Walter, 298, 299.
Bysets, the, in *Scotland*—
　Agatha, 53, 54.
　Alexander, 301.
　Anselm, 24.
　Cecilia, 54, 64, 68, 69, 73-76.
　Elizabeth, 54, 64, 75.
　John, of the Aird and Lovat, 7, 14, 16-19, 21, 23-26, 28, 37, 40, 43, 47, 48, 52, 53, 54.
　John, the younger, 4.
　Mary, 55.
　Muriel, 54, 64. *See* De Graham.
　Patrick, 288, 301.
　Peter, 24.
　Robert, of Upsetlington, 25, 36, 53, 300, 301.
　Thomas, 48.
　Walter, of Aboyne, 19, 25, 35, 36, 43-48, 300.
　Walter, of Lessendrum, 300, 301.
　William, 24-26, 33-36, 44, 48, 301.

C.

Cairncross, James, Abbot of Fearn, 315.
　Robert, Abbot of Fearn, 315.
　Robert, Bishop of Ross, 199, 203, 223, 230.
Calendar, Scottish, 311, 312.
Cameron, Ewen, of Lochiel, 230.
Campbell, Duncan, of Glenorchy, 290.
　Janet, 230, 250, 274, 277.
　Sir John, of Cawdor, 230, 251, 265.
Cardonnel's "Etchings of Antiquities in Scotland," 290, 291.
Carrick, Nelo de, 67.
Cassilis, Earl of (A.D. 1558), 227.
Cattanach, Thomas, Abbot of Fearn, 315.
Chapels, domestic, in Scotland, 302, 303.
Charters, forged, 29, 31.
　the, of Lovat, 11-13.
Charters of Alexander II., 125.
　Andrew, Bishop of Moray, 38, 39, 128, 129.
　Andrew de Boscho, 63, 64.

Charters of—*continued.*
　Cecilia Byset, 74.
　David de Innerlunan, 60, 61.
　Henry de Totyngham, 56, 57.
　John de Urchard, 87.
　Laurence, the knight, 49.
　Patrick de Grahame, 78, 79.
　William Byset, 33-37.
　William de Fenton, 83, 84.
Chartreuse, the Grande, 1.
Chisholm, Alexander de (1368), 88, 96, 98, 306.
　Alexander, of Comer, 251, 295.
　Alexander W., M.P., 269.
　John, of Comer, 230, 295.
　Robert de, 90, 93, 132, 133.
　the, 291.
　Thomas de, 90, 92, 93, 96.
　Weland, 176, 184.
Chrystal, Thomas, Abbot of Kinloss, 217, 247.
Cistercians, 59, 145.
Clanranald, Ranald. *See* Ranald Galla.
Clement IV., Pope, 308.
　VII., Pope, 205, 207, 298, 301 314.
Clerk, Alexander, 254, 257.
　John, 254, 257.
Cockburn, Henry, Bishop of Ross, 203.
　Robert, 203, 206, 214.
Collace, Margaret, of Balnamoon, 232.
Comer, parish of, 238-240, 242.
Contract between Lords Huntly and Lovat, 323, 324.
Contract of marriage, Fraser and De Fenton, 303-306.
Conveth, collation of, 101-103.
　presentations to, 104, 105, 167, 168.
　lands of, 23, 269, 270, 322.
　revenues of, 238, 241-243.
Corbet, Sir Archibald, 81.
　Sir Hugh, 81.
Corfe Castle, 84.
Cordiner's "Antiquities," 288, 289.
Council, fourth Lateran, 4.
　fifth Lateran, 214.
Courtois, Jacques, 143, 159, 162, 164.
　letter of, 157-159, 161, 162.
Craigscorrie, Maclean of, 291.
Cromarty, first Earl of, 29, 30, 216, 263.
Culdees, the, 5, 186.
Culter, preceptory of Knights Templars at, 300.
Cumin, Walter, Earl of Menteith, 127.
Cumming, Adam, Commendator of Beauly, 329.
　Alexander, of Altyre, 221, 248.
Curia Romana, 308.

D.

DALCORSE (Dalcross), lands of, 304.
Darius, Sylvester, Papal Nuncio, 205, 210, 214.
Darnley, Lord, 252.
David I., 186, 187.
Deans, Christian, 42.
De Burgh, Hubert, 46.
  Hugh, 6.
  Richard, 301.
  Walter, Earl of Ulster, 301.
De Courcy, John, 301.
De Lacy, Hugh, Earl of Ulster, 301.
  John, Constable of Chester, 301.
De Toesny, Simon, Bishop of Moray, 296.
Del Ard, barony of, 304.
  Alexander, 94, 95.
  Christian, 77, 84, 85.
  Donald, 77.
  Godfrey, 303.
  Harold, 77.
  Isabella, 303.
  John, 79, 97, 303.
  Margaret, 90, 94.
  Weland, 303.
  William, 84, 303.
Denoon, Donald, Abbot of Fearn, 214, 216, 217, 314.
Diary of Queen Mary's northern journey, 320, 321.
Dominicans, the, 5, 6.
Donald Bane, 18.
Douglas, Archibald of, 127, 132.
  Brice, Bishop of Moray, 22, 24, 34, 41, 129, 296, 298.
  Henry, 98, 173, 175, 211.
  Mariota, 98.
  Sir James, 98, 175.
Dow, Donald, vicar of Wardlaw, 250.
  James, vicar of Abertarff, 244, 245.
Dunballoch, lands and parish of, 23.
Dunbar, Alexander, Dean of Moray, 232.
  Captain Dunbar, 11.
  Columba de, Bishop of Moray, 297.
  John de, Earl of Moray, 133.
  Patrick, Earl of, 45, 127.
  Thomas, Earl of Moray, 96, 305, 306.
Durward, Allan, *ostiarius*, 6.

E.

EDINBURGH, University of, founded by Prior R. Reid, 228.
Elder, Adam, 221, 226, 227.
Elgin, cathedral chapter of, 41.
Elphinstone, William, Bishop of Ross, 203.
Erchless, castle and lands of, 23, 295.

"Estimate of Scottish Nobility," 264.
Eugene IV., Pope, 297.

F.

FEARN, Abbots of — Colin, Donald, John, Macbeth, Malcolm, Martin, 313; Finlay, 314.
  lands of, 23, 322.
Fearnua, parish of, 26, 240, 250.
Fenton, Cecilia de. *See* Byset, Cecilia.
  Janet de, 96, 98, 173, 284, 303, 304.
  John de, 72.
  Margaret de, 98, 172.
  Walter de, 98, 172, 269.
  William de, of Baky, 239, 303, 304, 305, 306.
  William de, of Beaufort, 54, 68, 69, 72, 83, 84, 96.
Ferrarius, historian of Kinloss, 218-222.
Fleming, Bartholomew, the, 34.
Finlay, Sir John, Prior of Beauly, 329.
Forbes, Duncan, 12, 260, 324.
  John de, 85.
  John, of Pitsligo, 50.
  Margaret de, 86.
  Sir Christian de, 85.
  William of Kinaldie, 50.
Forman, Adam, 119, 121, 123.
  Andrew, Bishop of Moray, 168-170, 297.
Forne, salmon fishings of, 29.
Foulis, Lord, 278.
  William de, 305.
Fraser, Agnes, 307.
  Alexander, of Lovat, 12, 93, 219, 230, 231, 250.
  Amelia, 12, 21.
  Donald, Archdeacon of Ross, 324.
  General, 290.
  Hon. Archibald, of Lovat, 13.
  Hugh, of Fraserdale, 12.
  of Foyers, 255.
  of Guisachan, 251.
  of Lovat, 12, 89, 92, 95-99, 174, 205-208, 211, 214, 223, 224, 241, 242, 251, 253, 259, 263-265, 272-277, 282, 284, 286, 287, 289, 291-293, 295, 303, 305, 323, 324.
  James, of Foyers, 225.
  John, Bishop of Ross, 193, 196, 199, 203.
  John, minister of Conveth, 275.
  John, Prior of Beauly, 243, 329.
  Mr, of Abertarff, 16.
  Robert, 210, 211.
  Simon, of Lovat, 12, 243, 244, 247, 250, 276, 277, 279, 280, 286, 289, 302, 321, 322.

INDEX.

Fraser—*continued*.
  Sir Alexander, of Doors, 279, 284.
  Thomas, of Lovat, 56, 97, 98, 174, 175, 184, 206, 208, 210, 211, 215, 326.
  Thomas, of Strichen, 244, 276, 278-280.
  Thomas, Prior of Beauly, 329.
  William, of Struy, 251, 324.
Frasers, annals of the, 13.
  the, of Aigas, 291.
  the, of Eskadale, 291.
  the, of Lovat, arms of, 97; crest of, 290.
  the, of Newton, 291.
Fresel, Hugh, 110, 164, 329.
  Robert, Dean of Ross, 183.
  Simon, 93, 306.
Frisale, Sir Maurice, Prior of Beauly, 329.
Frisel, Alexander, Prior of Beauly, 90, 329.

G.

GALLOWAY, Alan de, 47, 290.
Gardens of Priory, 221, 252, 323.
Gilchrist, Earl of Angus, 62.
Gillanders, 33, 310.
Gillebride, Earl of Angus, 62.
Gillechrist à Rosse, 17.
  Macgilliduffi, 61, 62, 268.
Giraldus Cambrensis, 3.
Glasgow, John, Bishop of, 305.
Glenarm, lands of, 301, 302.
Glenmoriston, Grants of, 224.
Golford, lands of, 304.
Gordon, Adam, of Auchindean, 324.
  Alexander, 234.
  George, Earl of Huntly, 323, 324.
  Janet, 175.
  Patrick, of Letterfourie, 315.
Gorrie, family of, 94.
Graham, Margaret de, 89.
  Matilda, 303.
  Muriel de, or Byset, 55.
  Sir David de, 54, 67, 68, 71.
  Sir Patrick de, 68, 71, 72, 75, 76, 78-80.
  arms of, 68 (*n*.).
Grants, origin of the, 53.
  Gregory le, 55.
  John and Andrew le, 80.
  John, of Freuchy, 184, 219, 221, 248.
  Patrick le, 80, 306.
  Robert le, 53, 55.
  Rodolph, 80.
  Sir Laurence le, 53.
  William le, 47.
Gregory IX., Pope, 14, 15, 189, 190.
  XI., Pope, 91.
Guthrie, John, Bishop of Ross, 203.

H.

HAAG, Andrew, Prior of Pluscardine, 137.
Halyburton, George, of Gask, 211.
  James, of Erchless and Gask, 175, 211.
  John, of the Aird, 99, 175.
  of Pitcur, 211.
  Walter, 98.
Hamilton, Patrick, Abbot of Fearn, 314.
Hastie, Thomas, Subprior of Beauly, 223.
Haswell, James, Prior of Beauly, 329.
Hay, James, Bishop of Ross, 199, 203, 209, 215.
  of Sauley, Earl of Carlisle, 329.
  Sir James, of Kingask, 329.
  Thomas, Bishop of Ross, 203.
Hepburne, James, Bishop of Moray, 297, 298.
  Patrick, Bishop of Moray, 298.
Hetton, Walter, Precentor of Kinloss, 329.
Home, Elizabeth, Prioress of St Bothans, 329.

I.

INNERLUNAN, David de, 60.
Innes, chapel of, 302.
  John de, Bishop of Moray, 297.
Innocent III., Pope, 1, 4, 8-11.
Inverness, vicar of, 52.
Islands, peninsulas called, 51.

J.

JAMES II., 173.
  IV., 122, 123.
John XXII., Pope, 308.
Julius II., Pope, 177-181, 214.

K.

KELSO, Herbert, Abbot of, 300.
Kilcoy, lease of, 67.
Kilmorack, church of, 213, 214, 249
  fishings of, 213.
Kilravock, Rose of, 214, 234, 264.
Kiltarlity, church of, 23-27, 36, 212, 245, 322.
  fishings of, 170.
Kingillie, 211.
Kinlochy, battle of, 224, 225.
Kinloss, Abbey of, 200.
  Abbots of, 201, 205, 217, 226, 247.
  Book of, 13.
  revenues of, 247-249.
Kirkhill, parish of, 23, 322.
Kirkwall, chapter of, 318, 319.

L.

Langside, battle of, 253.
Lascelles, Alan de, 81.
Lauder, Sir Robert, of the Bass, 133.
Lennox, Earl of, Regent, 274.
Leo X., Pope, 311.
Leper houses in Scotland, 294, 295.
Leslie, Alexander, Earl of Ross, 198, 199.
    George, Earl of Rothes, 198.
    Walter de, 195-197.
Lesley, John, Bishop of Ross, 188, 192, 203, 204.
Lessendrum, Bissets of, 95, 300.
Lindsay, Alexander, Earl of Crawford, 173.
    David, of Lethnot, 98, 173.
    Sir David, of Edzell, 174, 175.
    Patrick, Bishop of Ross, 193.
    Walter, of Beaufort, 173.
Lochslyn, castle of, 216.
Lords of the Isles—
    Alexander, 93, 94.
    Angus, 94.
    Donald, 122, 123, 184.
    Godfrey, 94.
    John, 94, 122.
    Reginald, 197.
    Somerled, 6, 147, 148.
Lorn, Dougal of, 6, 7, 148.
    Duncan Macdougal of, 147, 148.
    Ewen of, 149.
    John of, 150.
Lovat, Master of (1554), 224, 225, 276.
    Castle, 295.
Low, Bishop, 168.
Lowdham, manor of, 46, 298, 299.
Luther, Martin, 311.
Lychton, Henry de, Bishop of Moray, 297.

M.

MacConnell, M'Angus, 277.
MacCulloch, Thomas, Abbot of Fearn, 314.
Macdonald, Donald, 277.
Macdonnell, Donald, 302.
    John Angus, 302.
Macdougal, Anna, of Lorn, 306.
Macdougals, the, Priors of Ardchattan, 152-154, 156, 181.
MacEoins (or Bysets), the, of the Glynns, 301, 302.
Macfarlane, Gillespie, 6.
    John, 30.
    Walter, his MSS., 11, 12, 30.
Macintagart, Sir Ferchard, 187.
Mackenzie, Alexander, of Fraserdale, 12.

Mackenzie—*continued.*
    Alexander of Kintail, 105, 306.
    Catherine, 279.
    Colin, of Kintail, 273, 278, 285.
    John, of Kintail, 230.
    Lewis, of Findon, 306.
    Prior of Beauly, 105, 285.
    Roderick, of Kintail, 230.
    Sir George, of Rosehaugh, 263.
        of Tarbat, 29, 30, 262, 263.
    Sir Kenneth, of Kintail, 105, 211, 251, 290, 291, 306, 307.
    the, of Gairloch, 291.
Macranald, Alexander, of Glengarry, 184.
Maiden Bradley, Bissets of, 20, 300.
Maitland, Richard, of Thirlstane, 35.
Malvoisin, William, Bishop of St Andrews, 3-6, 127.
Mar, Earl of, Regent, 275.
Margaret Atheling, Queen of Scotland, 186.
Martin V., Pope, 297.
Master, title of, 58.
Matheson, Duvallus, Prior of Beauly, 329.
Maxwell, John, Bishop of Ross, 315, 317.
    Robert, Bishop of Orkney, 223.
M'Culloch, Angus, 251.
    Marion, 251.
Monilaw, Adam, Abbot of Fearn, 313.
Monro, George, of Tarrell, 251.
Montealto, William de, 30, 61.
Monteith, Earl of, 302.
Moravia, Alexander de, 92.
    Andrew de, 61, 191.
    John de, 130.
    Malcolm de, 130.
Moray, Alexander, Bishop of, 296.
    Andrew de, Bishop of, 25, 27, 34, 38, 104, 128, 129, 168, 296.
    Archibald, Bishop of, 28, 69, 72, 296.
    David de, Bishop of, 297.
    Felix, Bishop of, 296.
    Gregory, Bishop of, 296.
    Ralph, Bishop of, 296.
    Richard, Bishop of, 296.
    Simon, Bishop of, 241, 296.
    William, Bishop of, 296.
Moreville, Hugh de, 169.
Morton, Earl of, Regent, 192, 242, 275.
M'Ra, Rev. John, 306.
Murray, Sir Patrick, 315.

N.

Narne, David, of Sandfurde, 173.
Nottyngham. *See* Tottyngham.

INDEX. 335

O.
OGILVY, Alexander, 173.
John, 174, 175.
Marjory, 172.
Patrick, 172, 174, 175.
Walter de, 98, 172, 175, 305.
Orkney, Robert Maxwell, Bishop of, 223.
Robert Reid, Bishop of. *See* Robert Reid.

P.
PANTER, David, Bishop of Ross, 203;
Abbot of Fearn, 315.
Parliament, Scottish, Lords of, 37.
Paul III., Pope, 298, 315.
Pennant, account of Beauly, 288.
Person, John, instructor of novices, 218.
Pilmore, John, Bishop of Moray, 297.
Pius II., Pope, 297.
Pluscardine, Priory of, 123, 124, 248, 287.
    Charter of Priory, 125-127.
    Priors of—
        Alexander, 134.
        John, 137.
        Robert, 123, 138, 256.
        Symon, 130.
        Thomas, 133.
        William, 57, 58.
    seal of, 170.
Presentations to church of Conveth, 104, 167, 168.
Pylche, Alexander, 85.
    William, 85.

Q.
QUERITINUS (Curitan), founder of Rosmarkyn, 185, 186, 250.
Quinci, Roger de, 127.

R.
RAEBURN, Sir Andrew, Prior of Urquhart, 136.
Ranald Galla, 224, 225.
Randolph, John, Earl of Moray, 93, 183, 306.
    Thomas, Earl of Moray, 96, 129.
Rathlin (or Rachrin), isle of, 46, 301.
Record Office, extracts of, 298, 299.
Reformation, the, in Scotland, 231-233.
Register, the, of Moray, 2.
Reid, Katherine, 232.
    Robert, Abbot of Kinloss, Bishop of Orkney, etc., 205, 210, 214-223, 225-232, 248, 318, 319, 329.
    Walter, Prior of Beauly, 226, 227, 231, 232, 234, 237, 241, 242, 252, 256, 265, 271, 272.

Rheindoun, lands of, 274, 287.
Roll, Baginont's, 66.
Rolls, Ragman, 84.
Roricson, Dougal, Prior of Beauly, 110, 120-123, 182, 329.
Rose, Hugh, of Kilravock, 67, 95, 105.
    Thomas, of Geddes, 29, 30.
    William de, 95.
Ross, Bishops of (Catholic), 187-204.
    Alexander, 202.
    David, 203.
    Gregory, 202.
    Griffin, 202.
    Henry, 203.
    James, 203.
    John, 203.
    Macbeth, 187, 201.
    Matthew, 202.
    Reginald, 202.
    Robert, 24, 27, 199, 202, 203.
    Roger, 202.
    Simeon, 187, 202.
    Thomas, 80, 184, 203.
    William, 203.
Ross, Bishops of (Episcopal)—
    James, 287.
    Patrick Lindsay, 193.
Ross Cathedral, church of, 191-196, 198, 199.
    diocese and chapter of, 199-201.
    Stockford of, 258.
Ross, Earl of, 306.
    Euphemia, Countess of, 92, 195-198.
    arms of, 197, 198.
    Farquhar, Earl of, 24, 187, 313.
    Hugh, Earl of, 50, 84, 89.
    Hugh, of Philorth, 50.
    Janet, 225, 230.
    Joanna de, 50.
    John, of Balnagowan, 192, 248.
    Margaret, 306.
    William, Earl of, 30, 50, 66, 91, 131, 195, 197, 313.
Rothes, Earl of (1558), 227.
Ruthven, William, Lord, 192.

S.
SANCTUARY, right of, 308.
Savill, Sir James de, 46, 295.
Schools, Scottish monastic, 324, 325.
Seaforth, M'Kenzie of, 291.
Schanwell, Elizabeth, 212.
Robert, 217, 218.
Shaw, Robert, Bishop of Moray, 298.
Sinclair, Henry, Bishop of Ross, 192, 203.
Sixtus IV., Pope, 297.
Spottiswoode, John, 31.

Spynie, Lord, 244.
   William de, Bishop of Moray, 297.
Stewart, Alexander, Bishop of Moray, 298.
   Alexander (the Wolf of Badenoch), Earl of Buchan, 92, 196, 197.
   Andrew, Abbot of Fearn, 314.
   Andrew, Bishop of Moray, 297.
   David, Bishop of Moray, 297.
   James, Bishop of Moray, 297.
   Sir David, of Rosyth, 98.
St Ninians, Maurice, Prior of, 313.
Strathbolgy, David de, 24.
Strathglass, bees of, 26.
   lands of, 304.
Strathnaver, lands of, 295.
Strivelyn (Stirling), Alexander de, 67.
   John de, 95.
   Peter de, 95.
Stuart, Elizabeth, 273.
   Henry, Lord Darnley, 252.
   James, Earl of Moray, 232, 233, 251, 253, 264.
   Mary, Queen of Scots, 7, 225, 226, 227, 233, 234, 251, 252.
   William, Bishop of Aberdeen, 218.
Surnames, origin of, 309, 310.
Sutherland, William, Earl of, 61, 131.

T.

Tarlogie, Fearns of, 314.
Tarradale, parish of, 268, 269.
Thirlestane, Thomas of, 6, 34, 35, 241.
Thornfaulcon, 221, 295.
Tithes, law of, 243.
Tomson, William, a travelling priest, 160, 164.
Tottyngham, Henry de, 56-59.
Tulloch, Thomas, Bishop of Ross, 198, 203.
   William, Bishop of Moray, 297.
   Bain of, 251, 274.
Tunstal, Abbot of Croyland, 317.

U.

Urban IV., Pope, 130.
Urchard, John de, Vicar of Abertarff, 87, 88.
Urquhart, Adam, 30.
   Agnes, 29.
   Castle, 224, 295, 296, 302.
   Priors of, 136.
   Priory of, 135.
   Thomas, Bishop of Ross, 184, 203.

V.

Val des Choux, Monastery of, 142-146.
   Gallowitz, Prior of, 145, 146.
Valliscaulians, order of, 2, 6, 8, 111, 112.
   priories of, in France, 309.
   dress of, 318.
Viard, 2, 143, 144.
Vicar, office of, 310, 311.
Vitri, Cardinal Jacques de, 8.

W.

Walters, Donald, 104, 169.
Wardlaw MS., the, 16, 20, 21, 269.
   parish of, 249, 250, 322.
Waus, David, 274.
   John, of Lochslyn, 209, 215, 216.
   Magnus, 209, 210, 215, 216.
   Robert, 209, 215.
Wells, cathedral chapter of, 42.
   Hugh de, Bishop of Lincoln, 295.
Whisky, 260.
William the Lion, 3, 4, 18, 21, 52.
Winchester, John de, Bishop of Moray, 297.
Wiscard, William, 54.
Wodman, John, Bishop of Ross, 203.
Woods of Farley and Urchany, 269.
Wyse, John, Prior of Pluscardine, 131.

www.ingramcontent.com/pod-product-compliance
Lightning Source LLC
Chambersburg PA
CBHW030309240426
43673CB00040B/1110